PASTORAL THEOLOGY

OTHER BOOKS BY THOMAS C. ODEN

Radical Obedience

The Community of Celebration

Kerygma and Counseling

Contemporary Theology and Psychotherapy

The Promise of Barth

The Structure of Awareness

Beyond Revolution

The Intensive Group Experience

After Therapy What?

Game Free

TAG: The Transactional Awareness Game

Should Treatment Be Terminated?

The Parables of Kierkegaard (editor)

Agenda for Theology

Guilt Free

Pastoral Theology

ESSENTIALS OF MINISTRY

Thomas C. Oden

HarperSanFrancisco

A Division of HarperCollinsPublishers

To the congregations
Edrita and I were privileged to serve
when I was a young pastor:

Ninnekah and Whitebead, Oklahoma (1951–54)
Dallas, Texas (1954–55)
Prairie Hill, Oklahoma (1956)
Lexington, Oklahoma (1958)
Waukomis and Carrier, Oklahoma (1962–64)

with gratitude and affection

Biblical quotations, unless otherwise noted, are from the *New English Bible,* © The Delegates of the Oxford University Press and the Syndics of the Cambridge University Press, 1961, 1972. Reprinted by permission.

Designer: Jim Mennick

Library of Congress Cataloging in Publication Data

Oden, Thomas C.
    PASTORAL THEOLOGY.

    Bibliography: p. 321
    Includes indexes.
    1. Pastoral theology.   I.   Title.
BV4011.O33   1982   253   82-47753
ISBN 0-06-066353-7

95 96 97 HAD 20 19 18 17

Contents

Preface

This book is written for all those who have ever considered entering the ministry; for those who, for any reason at all, want to know more about what clergy do and why; for "second career" persons who have pursued some other vocation but now are considering ministry; for those who are currently studying for ordained ministry; and for those who, having been in ministry for some time, now want to review their own life work in the light of a systematic reflection on the pastoral gifts and tasks.

This book does not assume traditional Christian belief in the reader, but it tries to express accurately what the Christian ministry believes about its own empowerment. It is written for those who are frankly skeptical about ministry's claims and want either to dismiss them or to hear them stated more convincingly. It is also for those who are thoroughly committed to ministry yet want to see its biblical and ethical grounding developed more clearly.

Although this book focuses on the work of clergy, there are many nonclergy who sense the crucial importance of pastoral work for society and wonder how it could better serve the commonweal. Others are feeling a sense of hunger or pathos about ministry today, wondering where the prevailing winds are blowing us, and yearning for a ministry whose direction is more carefully charted by Scripture and historical Christian experience. Still others do not have any preconceived idea or interpretation of ministry, yet would like to see one carefully hammered out. These are among the persons for whom this book was written.

My method is simple: I have tried to set forth what is most commonly said in the central Christian tradition about ministry. I have tried to distill the best ideas of the two millennia of ecumenical Christian thinking concerning what pastors are and do. My purpose is to develop an internally consistent grasp of classical Christian thinking about the pastor and to provide a minimal curricular foundation for that knowledge of the pastoral office requisite to the practice of ministry. Thus, for a person preparing for ordination, this book hopes to review key issues leading to ordination—hence the subtitle: *Essentials of Ministry*.

Regrettably, the deliberate study of the pastoral office and its functions (traditionally called pastoral theology) has been neglected in our time. In reclaiming the classical pastoral tradition, our entire effort pivots around the quiet but steady assumption that obligations in ministry are best understood as responses to God's unmerited love and are supported by many layers of active divine grace. Tasks of ministry are funded by gifts of ministry.

The Bibliography is necessarily extensive, due to the fact that it must cover both historical and contemporary sources. I have, therefore, chosen to be sparing in making references, and have tried to resist the temptation to double the size of this effort by including a running commentary on these references, in order that this book not be diverted inordinately toward the genre of a bibliographical essay. However worthy such a project, it does not correspond with the practical demands of this present task.

At the end of each chapter I have provided a brief documentary excursus indicating major chapter references and further readings suggested. The full reference for any of these items may be found in the Bibliography. Interspersed throughout the text are crucial classical references. Although these references do not claim to account exhaustively for all pertinent voices of the tradition, they nonetheless provide a useful guide to pivotal references, and reveal significant varieties of views within the central tradition. I have preferred primary biblical and patristic sources to secondary sources. For the scholarly pastor, this Bibliography may be one of the most functional and practically useful aspects of this work. I hope it will prompt further inquiry into long-neglected texts. It will also enable the lay reader to identify quickly the date and sequencing of the major sources.

In order to serve the reader's practical interests, references in the text are condensed to the sparest form. Each reference contains either a date or an abbreviation. Abbreviations are listed just before the Bibliography. A date will signal a particular work by that author that is more fully noted in the Bibliography (with multiple dates arranged chronologically). When the date of death is noted, it indicates that the author's whole corpus of writings is pertinent. Page references will be provided when needed in the annotations included in the text.

Among persons to whom I am particularly indebted for teaching me of the pastoral office and modeling its gifts wisely are my former pastors Finis Crutchfield, John Russell, James Ault, William Holmes, and Harry G. Ryan; my current pastor, James Tiller; W. E. M. Brogan, who first challenged me to consider ministry; friends in ministry Dean Lanning, William I. Smith, Jr., and Jackson M. Smith; persons in ministry in my own family, especially my sister Sarah and her husband, James E.

Hampson, an Episcopal priest, Amy Oden, Marilyn and William B. Oden, and Eugene Moore and family; several former colleagues, especially Albert C. Outler and James E. Kirby; and longtime partners in dialogue like Don Browning, David Switzer, and Frank Lake. Among colleagues at Drew Theological School who have read and offered valued critical service in review of the manuscript are Thomas and Mary-Lynn Ogletree, Stanley Menking, Janet Fishburn, Edward Leroy Long, Nelson Thayer, Kenneth Rowe, William Stroker, Kalyan Dey, Harold Brack, Virginia Samuel Cetuk, and William Presnell. For invaluable technical assistance with the manuscript I am indebted to Scott McDonald, Peter Oliva, David Czar, and Daniel Davies. Valued partners in dialogue offering insightful Third World perspectives on theology and ministry include Livingstone Buama of Ghana and Young Ho Chun of Korea.

Introduction:
What Is Pastoral Theology?

Strike the shepherd,
and the sheep will be scattered.
Zech. 13:7

Pastoral theology is that branch of Christian theology that deals with the office and functions of the pastor. It is theology because it treats of the consequences of God's self-disclosure in history. It is pastoral because it deals with those consequences as they pertain to the roles, tasks, duties, and work of the pastor.

Pastoral theology is a special form of practical theology because it focuses on the practice of ministry, with particular attention to the systematic definition of the pastoral office and its function. Pastoral theology is also a form of systematic theology, because it attempts a systematic, consistent reflection on the offices and gifts of ministry, and their integral relationship with the tasks of ministry.

Pastoral theology is distinguishable, yet inseparable, from exegesis, historical and systematic theology, ethics, liturgics, and psychology of religion. Even though it interweaves insights from all these disciplines into its understanding of the practice of ministry, it deserves to be viewed as a distinctive discipline (Gregory, *ACW*, vol. 11, pp. 45–89; Vinet, 1853, pp. 1 ff.; Hoppin, 1884, pp. 1–23).

As theology, pastoral theology is attentive to that knowledge of God witnessed to in Scripture, mediated through tradition, reflected upon by systematic reasoning, and embodied in personal and social experience (Outler, 1957, pp. 105 ff.; *BD*, pp. 78–85). It seeks to give clear definition to the tasks of ministry and enable its improved practice. Because it is a pastoral discipline, pastoral theology seeks to join the theoretical with the practical. It is *theoretical* insofar as it seeks to develop a consistent theory of ministry, accountable to Scripture and tradition experientially sound and internally self-consistent. Yet it is not merely a theoretical statement or objective description of what occurs in ministry. It is also a *practical* discipline, for it is concerned with implementing concrete pastoral tasks rather than merely defining them. Its proximate goal is an improved theory of ministry. Its longer ranged goal is the improved practice of ministry.

In recent decades, pastoral theology has suffered from neglect of sustained theoretical reflection and from isolation from companion theological disciplines. To achieve a wise perspective, pastoral theology must not be artificially detached from homiletics, liturgics, or catechetics, as if these disciplines could go their own way without interacting with one another. Pastoral theology wishes to gather the kernels of their varied insights into a single, unified account of the pastoral office, without limiting the range of these disciplines or challenging their discrete validity. If preaching, worship, and teaching are all functions intrinsic to the very idea of Christian ministry, they must be of primary interest to pastoral theology.

Suppose someone is called pastor yet never preaches or breaks bread or teaches Christianity. The question eventually must arise how that person can be a pastor without doing what pastors do. This is already a perplexity for some who call themselves pastoral counselors yet engage in few other acts of ministry than fee-basis secularized psychotherapy. They continue to appeal to the office of pastor for their professional identity and fees, yet without a well-defined conception of the pastoral office; some may trade off the exceptional trust that people have in the office of pastor, yet with minimal interest in the ministry of word and sacrament. Others, who in concentrating on developing special skills to serve human need have moved narrowly into special ministries, now may find themselves carrying out these duties with an uneasy conscience or uncentered spirit. I hope this study will serve them in their developing attempts at centering and in the recovery of pastoral identity.

Pastoral theology is dependent upon and intrinsically connected with each of the disciplines of the wider theological curriculum. As theology, pastoral theology wishes to bring exegetical and historical materials to bear on the theory and practice of ministry. Pastoral theology is as deeply indebted to historical theology and ecclesiastical history as to systematic theology or social ethics. If homiletics, liturgics, pastoral counseling, and Christian education are discrete and valued departments in a theological school, each of which has its own integrity as a discipline, pastoral theology differs from them respectfully in one way: it seeks to serve them by unifying them with a single theory of pastoral ministry that leads to an improved integral practice of ministry (Baxter, 1656, pp. 111 ff.; Bridges, 1847, pp. 31 ff.; Hoppin, 1884, pp. 3–6). Therefore, it deals inevitably with proclamation, sacrament and order,

Christian education, and pastoral counseling, not in full detail, but in the relation of each to the overarching theory of ministry presupposed by all.

Some might say that it is beyond the competence of a book or an instructor or a school to teach pastoral theology, that it must be learned through experience. There is indeed much to be said for that view, but it cannot be absolutely argued. It is not that practice cannot be taught. Practice must be practiced. Yet the practice of ministry can better be engendered by solid reflection on its theological and biblical grounding. More strongly put: It is dangerous to the health of the church for ministry to be practiced without good foundation in Scripture and tradition, reason and experience.

One distinct feature of this discussion is that it is addressed not to theological students alone as a primary audience (although it is designed for possible use in classes). It is also addressed to the working pastor. Many persons who have been already many years engaged in ministry have never had the opportunity to read (or even see!) a systematic pastoral theology. Few have been attempted in this century. Hiltner's *Preface* is exactly that. Martin Thornton's *Pastoral Theology* is a superb collection of miscellaneous essays on sacramental theology and pastoral themes, but it makes no claim of covering the broad range of the standard pastoral theologies of the preceding century (Sailer, Nitzsch, Cannon, Shedd, Kidder). Recent works by Oates, Brister, Browning, Thornton, Southard, Stein, Stollberg, and Switzer are admirable in their attempts to treat various discrete themes of pastoral theology, yet none of them has attempted to write a systematic pastoral theology that covers the basic range of their distinguished predecessors like Vinet or Hoppin.

Pastoral theology as a unifying discipline was flourishing a century ago and remained robust until the beginning of this century, yet it has largely faded into such hazy memory that none of its best representatives is still in print. We hope to hammer out a rudimentary pastoral theology half as good as any of a dozen that were available a century ago.

I

BECOMING A MINISTER

1. The Discovery of Pastoral Identity

Movies and television show us faded stereotypes of the dissipated pastoral office, often either a deceptive, money-grabbing, cornball fundamentalist bigot in a white suit or a hip, chic superliberal frantic to accommodate to pop culture. The media minister is often portrayed marrying couples parachuting out of planes or smoking grass to the hushed beat of tom-toms or reciting a mantra on a nude beach. This hungry anxiety to accommodate to modernity is a major clue to the loss of clarity about ministry in our time. Another stereotype is of a benign cipher, nice but incompetent. None of these reveals much about the actual pastors we meet and know.

A Centered Ministry

All the varied activities of the pastor have a single center: life in Christ. Pastoral theology seeks to point to that center in credible contemporary language and to see every single function in relation to that center. The center is Christ's own ministry for and through us, embodied in distortable ways through our language, through the work of our hands, and quietly through our bodily presence.

A major part of the task ahead is to sharpen anew the needed distinction between clergy and laity, while at the same time respecting a continued stress on the general ministry of the laity—but not so as to deny or accidentally misplace the ministry of the clergy. This will be a recurring theme rehearsed in almost every chapter ahead.

We are searching for a unifying, centered view of ministry. Regrettably, the disciplines serving the modern pastoral office have become segmented into wandering, at times prodigal, subspecializations. Although we have produced an abundance of literature on pastoral counseling, the question remains as to what is "pastoral" (*distinctively* pastoral) about much so-called pastoral counseling. Sermons abound, and sermonic aids superabound, but few operate out of an integrated conception of the pastoral office that melds liturgical, catechetical, counseling, and equipping ministries. Having borrowed heavily from pragmatic management procedures while forgetting much of their traditional rootage, church administration has become an orphan discipline vaguely wondering about its true parentage. The loss of centered identity in ministry is mirrored in the excessive drive toward specialization of the disciplines intended to serve and unify ministry. This is why the need has arisen for a renewal of the discipline of pastoral theology, which has always viewed its task precisely as the search for this unity.

This loss of pastoral identity breaks in upon us in amusing ways. Pastors are asked to bless football games, but never ice hockey, and no one knows why. Ministers visit newcomers, but sometimes wonder how they differ from town "boosters." Clergy have ministries to scout troops, fire departments, peace initiatives, and veterans' groups, and often pray in a given week for intensely conflicting causes. Matrimony remains a Christian doctrine, the guardianship of which is directly accountable to the pastoral teaching office, yet in some weddings, what the photographer does seems far more central and essential than what the minister does.

The most astonishing example of this confusion of pastoral identity is in modern pastoral counseling, in which extensive professionalization has been attempted under the confusing rubric of pastor. The shingle of the therapist has been borrowed and put up, often with radical loss of anything resembling historical pastoral identity. The resulting irony is an attempt at a new profession that names itself by a name ("pastoral" counselor) whose meaning has been curiously forgotten. Later I will show how pastoral counseling stands ready to be reincorporated into a richer historic pastoral identity. But much pastoral counseling as popularly conceived today has little awareness of classical models of the care of souls. It is time for pastors to repudiate flatly much that recently flies under the name of "pastoral counselor." So preoccupied has "liberated" pastoral counseling been with obtaining credentials acceptable to the hospital team or the psychological accreditation board that it has systematically forgotten what every pastor in the seventeenth century knew quite obviously: that pastoral counsel expresses and embodies a clear pastoral identity based on ordination which stands deliberately and self-consciously under Christ's commission, melding integrally with the work of pastor as teacher, liturgist, and helper of the sick and poor.

For those who may be confused by fee-basis pastoral counseling (offering pastoral empathy only on the basis of a contracted direct fee), the classical pastoral tradition roundly opposed the idea that fees can be properly accepted as a direct money exchange for a specific pastoral service (*Apostolic Constitutions, ANF,* vol. 7, pp. 433 ff.; Council of Chalcedon, 451, *NPNF* 2nd, vol. 14, pp. 269 ff.). There is a simple theological reason for this: acts of ministry are not directly contingent on money. Rather, church support for ministry is premised on an entirely different basis: freely bestowed gifts from concerned laity to care for the troubled as Christ has cared for us in our troubles. Ministry does not offer a bedside prayer for a fee, as bedside medical services are offered.

Ordinary working pastors have a clear right and strong historical precedent actively to reclaim the term pastoral counselor for their daily work and not let it be borrowed or loaned or drained away to secularized, hedonically oriented fee-basis "pastoral psychotherapists" who may or may not be committed to the ministry of word and sacrament. Tentmaking ministries are commended, but while they are making tents or money they should take care in using the term *pastoral.* Whether sewing and marketing tents or psychotherapeutic services, the making of a living or entrepreneurial interests should not be accidentally confused with the practice of ministry itself as proclamation of the word, celebration of the sacraments, and equipping of the laity. If services are directly contingent upon fees, they are best not confused with the church's ministry, whether of counsel, sacrament, or preaching, which is properly offered openly to all without strings or monthly billings.

Our purpose is to assist in the salvaging and mending of the ailing pastoral office in an era in which it has been badly shaken and bruised. This can only be achieved the hard way, by working carefully through the deep, symbolic factors that hold pastoral identity together.

Doubtless a major cause of "burnout" in ministry is the blurring of pastoral identity, or the confusion concerning what ministry is. The neglected remedy is solid rerooting in classical pastoral wisdom, which has carefully held together Christ's ministry and ours, God's gift and the church's task, grace and responsiveness. Many complications of burnout in ministry could have been prudently avoided by building a better biblical foundation, one that rings with the wisdom of twenty centuries of experience in ministry.

For students preparing for ministry, this book is something like aerobic exercise in preparation for a long run. The best way to battle through the pastoral identity crisis is to think thoroughly about the pastoral office in one's earlier periods of study for ministry. But there are always opportunities, often through continuing education, to reformulate pastoral identity after a significant midcareer period of questioning.

Why Now?

How does this effort differ from available literature on pastoral care and practical theology? Every author has some obligation to show why a book is not the same thing read twice before. Without artificially claiming absolute distinctiveness, here is my account sheet:

An Inclusive Vision of Ministry

No full-ranging pastoral theology has yet been attempted that includes as one of its normative premises the assumption that women are fully and irreversibly involved in the ordained ministry. While respecting more conservative opinion, we will argue for sexual inclusiveness in Christian ministry, that both men and women may be called to sacred ministry. We have heard far more discussion about the relevance of women's issues to the doctrine of God, language about God, and social ethics than to ecclesiology or pastoral ministry. Although much has been written on the changing roles of women in society and on the ordination of women, we have not yet seen a systematic presentation of the practice of ministry that takes seriously into account the full power and presence of women in ordained ministry as a working assumption. We will take the ordination of women as a key normative presupposition of pastoral theology, and develop some of its consequences for a wide range of questions on the office and practice of ministry.

As one who has a strong conviction concerning the promise of women in ministry and who feels deeply that it is God's own intention that women preach the word and celebrate the sacraments and fulfill all the offices of ordained ministry, I am grateful for the gifted women in my own seminary classes who are preparing for ordained ministry. Their talents, insights, and aspirations have convinced me that the theory and practice of ministry needs to be systematically reconceived in a way that takes into fuller account the reception of the gifts of ministry by women.

We are privileged witnesses in our time to an exciting period in the history of Christ's ministry, in which God's Spirit is pouring out remarkable gifts upon women who will positively influence the quality of the Christian life and the shape of the church to come. The Spirit has always made these gifts available to women, but now the church is finally becoming more open to both the Spirit and the gifts. If this continues, it will profoundly affect every aspect of the study of pastoral theology. Yet, to date no integral, inclusivist pastoral theology has been written. We are hoping to take some modest steps in that direction.

Two brief notes on language in this connection: First, I have tried to eliminate sexual inequities from my language. Except in cases where style or syntax would be confused, I have preferred words like *person*, *they*, or *humanity* to *man*, *he*, or *mankind*. At times I have inserted brackets in quotations to indicate amendments that convey more inclusive intent. Second, taking special note of the maternally nurturing images associated with the third person of the Holy Trinity in its classical, orthodox, ecumenical formulation, I will speak of the Holy Spirit in the feminine, as "she," since the neutered *pneuma,* and even more, the feminine Hebrew *ruah,* allow this as justifiably as the more familiar "he." Since the Holy Spirit is divinely personal, and not an "it," I urge ordinands to refer to the Holy Spirit in the personal mode of "he" or "she," rather than the impersonal "it." Although the use of the feminine is not, strictly speaking, a well-worn, linguistically orthodox path, I believe it to be in spirit and intention orthodox and inwardly consistent with Christ's gospel.

The Search for Pastoral Roots

Some will wonder why I have preferred premodern to modern sources. Some may suspect that I "quit reading twenty years ago." My intent is much more radical, in the sense of "root-oriented," for I am trying hard to catch up with the fourth century. After having been enamored as a theologian with a long parade of novelties that promised the moon and delivered green cheese, I now avoid the pretences of creativity. So I have deliberately sought out earlier pastoral writers, especially when they speak more sensibly than modern ones. Somewhat hardheadedly, I have intentionally avoided quoting modern sources if a better statement of the idea appears in the classical pastoral tradition.

Each chapter has been written in the same way: I deliberately have tried to constrain my own opinion and look intently and responsively toward the central consensual tradition. I have sought to state without embellishment the core of that ancient ecumenical consensus on the office, gifts, and practice of ministry. This is the single most important thing I have learned about theological method in the last decade: take the risk of listening attentively and obediently to the wisdom of the tradition. It makes far better theology than I could ever invent on my own. I will spare the reader any grand proposals for reshaping ministry that come fancifully spun out of my imagination. My intent is undisguised. I am hoping to offer a classically grounded systematic pastoral theology that is not insufferably dull. I seek simply to bring the available wisdoms of the pastoral tradition into clear, sharp contemporary expression, pertinent to the practice of ministry today. That is why I intentionally quote very few modern writers and stress more heavily the most consensual patristic sources, weighing most heavily the eight "great doctors of the church": Athanasius, Basil, Gregory of Nazianzus and John Chrysostom from the East and Ambrose, Jerome, Augustine, and Gregory the Great from the West.

It is in this spirit that I hope this work will be as unoriginal as possible. This is the first time I have attempted to write an entire text with an

absolutely clear commitment to unoriginality. I do not want to convey
the pretence that I am inventing anew or "radically reformulating" the
discipline of pastoral theology. Contemporary preaching, liturgics, and
pastoral care are strewn with the wreckage of such fantasies. What we
most need to know today in pastoral practice is not derived from looking anxiously for some new quick fix from modernity, but more from
listening anew to centuries of tested pastoral experience.

If this effort should go wildly amiss and accidentally be thought to
engender a new doctrine or Christian teaching, it would miss its mark
like a bazooka inadvertently shot in precisely the wrong direction.

Reversing the Antinomian Momentum

The tradition has used the term *antinomianism* (from "against law,"
or "lawlessness") to speak of that undernourished view of God's grace
that views the gospel as if it implied no moral response or ethical constraint or norms of redemptive behavior. Antinomianism is the weird,
wild, impulsive, unpredictable sleeping partner of much contemporary
pastoral care. It mistakes the gospel for license, freedom for unchecked
self-actualization, and health for native vitalism. The classical pastoral
tradition has struggled mightily against "cheap grace" solutions and
premature reassurances in a way that will be reflected on almost every
page that follows.

Keep in mind that antinomianism is our own doing. We cannot con-
veniently claim to be victims of some external, evil, socially alienating
force. We have welcomed it, confusing it with genuine Christian liberty.
Its modern forms are sexual permissiveness, egocentric romanticism,
and a vague taste for anarchy. If its strength and appetite were less, we
would bother less about it. But antinomian hopes have been set loose
like Mediterranean fruit flies upon both church and ministry by misguided exegetes and well-meaning but unwise theologians (to whom the
popular media are insatiably attracted). Now, full circle, they have
brought us to an "improved theology" that assumes that God loves us
without judgment, that grace opposes obligation, that "oughts" are
dehumanizing if not sick, and that the gospel always makes the law
questionable. History is now requiring of us that we unlearn much that
we have prematurely learned about aborted "Christian freedom." This
freewheeling grace-without-law theology infects many ancillary problems of pastoral practice.

A weakened theology has taught collusive pastoral practice to misplace its identity in a song with four verses: (a) there is no really significant distinction between ordained ministry and general lay ministries;
(b) sacraments are not the living presence of Christ, but symbolic culturally derived paradigms of the general notion of redemptive sacrifice;
(c) the resurrection did not in any real sense happen, and its eventful-
ness cannot be central to faith; and (d) interlaced with these seductive

assumptions, the innocent-looking, haloed face of antinomianism: God's unconditional love demands nothing of us, no moral response, no behavioral change, no exemplary life, no "works of the law."

As if having watched too much television, we have become dazed and addled with an oversimplified gospel that most laypersons easily recognize as innocuous-looking pabulum with highly toxic side effects: God loves me no matter what. Nothing is required by this merciful God. Don't worry about any response to God in order to feel completely OK with yourself and God. Feelings of guilt are considered neurotic. God turns out to be a naive zilch who permissively turns his eyes away when we sin. How strangely different from the Holy One of Amos, Isaiah, and Jesus.

The central tradition of pastoral care prior to this century would have frankly called this talk nonsense. But we suffer fools gladly with a bored smile. How often we are obliged to cherish it as if it were "obviously good" theology. So when we are engaged in pastoral counseling, we withhold all ethical judgments, aping ineffective psychotherapies. When we preach, we avoid any hint of morally evaluative ("preachy") demeanor and risk no admonition, disavowing the prophetic office. We offer the sacraments as if this were a morally irrelevant act. The classical pastoral tradition requires us to challenge these assumptions.

The Atrophied Discipline

With such pressing needs it is all the more surprising that no systematic, scripturally grounded pastoral theology has been written for an English-speaking ecumenical audience since Washington Gladden's *The Christian Pastor* (1898). I respectfully challenge readers who may think otherwise to produce one. I do not ignore the fact that several fine contemporary writers have attended well to many discrete, specific issues in pastoral theology. Wayne Oates, Howard Clinebell, Seward Hiltner, Don Browning, Martin Thornton, C. W. Brister, David Switzer, Frank Lake, and Joachim Scharfenberg, and many others have produced a vast literature in pastoral counseling and other aspects of the practice of minstry. It is not all wasteland. Although I have deliberately avoided heavy dependence upon modern writers in this book (unlike my earlier studies of Rudolf Bultmann, Carl Rogers, Karl Barth, Eric Berne, Paul Tillich, Teilhard de Chardin, and others), I do not want that to signal any loss of interest or respect for companion attempts that indeed do seek to correlate their modern pastoral efforts with the classical pastoral tradition. Among these Frank Lake's (1966) is most exemplary, but regrettably little read. In some cases these recent efforts (especially by Oates, Browning, and Thornton) are serious and substantive. But what we do not have in our time is what was so widely available one hundred years ago: a cohesive, systematic discipline of pastoral theology that integrates these otherwise disparate pastoral functions into a single theory of ministry. To attempt such a broad-ranging, yet unified, systematic statement is the task at hand.

Students enter lean and hungry into my course on "Pastoral Theology." Naturally I have scoured *Books in Print* for current resources, and failing to turn up an adequate textbook, I have tried search services and rare book sources. No available textbook of the genre "Pastoral Theology" even come close to adequacy. Instead we find books with special cases to plead or denominational identities to uphold, pieces of the puzzle treated as if they were the whole. Regrettably, the best pastoral theologies remain the nineteenth-century works long out of print (Vinet, Hoppin, Shedd, Köstlin, Fairbairn, Sailer, Kidder). The closest recent contenders are Hiltner, Oates, and Thornton. However laudable, such efforts are incomplete attempts at a comprehensive pastoral theology. Despite some solid strengths, the serious attempts at pastoral theology by evangelical scholars such as Frank Segler (Southern Baptist), Armin W. Schuetze and Irwin J. Habeck (Wisconsin Lutherans), and Jay E. Adams (Orthodox Presbyterian) have not proven to be fully adequate and are prone to miss large segments of the broader ecumenical church, especially its Catholic and liberal segments, that we seek to address.

Can an Ecumenically Centrist Pastoral Theology Be Developed?

This pastoral theology seeks to be ecumenically centrist. A big piece of my motivation is to try to absorb and work seriously with a wide variety of confessional and denominational viewpoints on ministry. I have tried to listen carefully to the creatively radical offshoots of the central Protestant tradition (Mennonite, Quaker, and others), and especially, as a Protestant, tried to deal seriously with the Roman Catholic tradition on ministry, and the traditions of Eastern Orthodoxy. I have sought reasonably to bring all these voices into a centrist, historically sensitive integration, with special attention to historical consensus.

I have applied where possible the fifth century Vincentian canon, preferring to affirm that which has been believed "everywhere, always, and by all" (Vincent of Lerins: *"quod ubique, quod semper, quod ab omnibus creditum est"*). Vincent maintained that the final ground of truth is in Scripture, yet by this threefold test of universality, antiquity, and consent, the minister can better distinguish between true and false traditions.

The intent is not lukewarmly ecumenical in the usual liberal Protestant sense that excludes or diminishes the patristic, medieval, and counter-Reformation views. Rather, my intent is classically ecumenical, with primary attention to the Christian ecumenical consensus of the first five centuries. I wish to try to develop a mediating position on ministry that reasonably could be recognized as acceptable, on the whole if not in every snippet, by liberal and conservative Protestants and Roman Catholics—admittedly a large order, but I think not as impossible as it might at first sound. This is an irenic effort that will not satisfy numerous particularist interests but nonetheless remains my sincere aim.

I come from a culturally accommodative, centrist American Protestant tradition that itself is deeply indebted to Anglican centrism, which in turn is richly steeped in patristic and medieval theological models that correlate companionably with many Roman and Eastern Orthodox pastoral sensitivities. I come by catholicity honestly, if Wesley's sermon "The Catholic Spirit" be a guide. My own pastoral experience has ranged from two United Church of Christ parishes, to several United Methodist parishes, plus ten years teaching in a Disciples of Christ seminary, and over another decade in a United Methodist Seminary—a fair amount of ecumenical exposure to the liberal and free church tradition. To this I add a long-term interest in the Roman tradition, beginning dramatically with my experience as a visitor to some of the ground-breaking sessions of Vatican II, and a growing fascination with patristic, medieval, and counter-Reformation thought. This is the experiential basis upon which I now seek to develop a centrist view of ministry that my free church friends and my Roman Catholic confidants might both happily affirm without feeling that the office and gifts of ministry I am describing are completely out of touch with their own traditions.

Method in Pastoral Theology

What are the sources from which reasonable guidance can be derived for the work of the pastor? By what method shall pastoral theology proceed?

Since pastoral theology is theology, it proceeds by the same method as any well-formed theology, utilizing a well-known quadrilateral of sources for understanding God's self-disclosure in history: Scripture, tradition, reason, and experience.

Scripture provides the primary basis for understanding the pastoral office and its functions. We will treat Scripture as the church's book, rather than as the exclusive turf of the historian or social theorist. Pastoral wisdom has lived out of key *locus classicus* texts that have enjoyed a rich history of interpretation long before the advent of modern historical research. We are free to learn from and use that research without being handcuffed by some of its reductionist assumptions.

Pastoral theology lives out of Scripture. When the pastoral tradition has quoted Scripture, it has viewed it as an authoritative text for shaping both its understanding and its practice of ministry. We do not put Scripture under our examination, according to criteria alien to it, in order to understand ministry. Rather, Scripture examines our prior understandings of ministry. It puts them to the test.

When understood in this way as *canon* (a measurement of appropriate teaching) long agreed upon by ecumenical consensus, the texts of

Scripture become something more than an object for our optional perusal or incidental historical investigation. They are the Word of God, addressed to us for our healing, instruction, and benefit.

Tradition at bottom is the history of exegesis. It implies an ongoing process of trying to understand the address of Scripture in various historical settings. Pastoral ministry has been activated in extremely varied political climates, historical situations, and sociocultural environments. It is not without historical experience. We do well to listen carefully to the richly varied voices, harmonies, and dialects of that experience. Otherwise we easily become entrapped in the narrowed, biased, often demeaning assumptions of our own limited modern cultural consciousness. A crippling deficit of modern pastoral care has been its intense resistance to premodern pastoral writers. Many modern pastoral writers have looked cynically, disdainfully, and even ignorantly on these historical achievements. In this we fully share the narrow pride of our own modern cultural ethos.

The application of reason as a criterion for pastoral reflection implies an effort to think constructively, rigorously, and consistently; to argue cogently; and to reflect systematically on the cohesive ordering of pastoral wisdom. What is needed is not a long list of detached aphorisms, but a gathering, organizing, and systematic development of a sustained, internally consistent pastoral reflection, so the working pastor does not have to go through the hazards of trial and error experimentation at the expense of dazed parishioners in order to catch up with the wisdoms of the past.

Personal and social experience forms the fourth branch of the quadrilateral of theological method for pastoral theology. This includes factoring into our conception of ministry not only our own existential experience and personal story, but also the experience of others we know who have been engaged in ministry. The best pastoral insight is derived from lived experience of ministry.

Accordingly, pastoral theology seeks to be critically aware of its own cultural situation, its political context, it ever-changing surrounding ethos. Since the gospel addresses us in a particular here-and-now situation, rather than as a timeless abstraction, it is impossible properly to conceive of ministry apart from studied awareness of its current context. This does not imply an uncritical acceptance of surrounding cultural assumptions, but rather a serious listening to emerging contemporaneity. We do not wish to foster any conception of a method of pastoral theology that would forget its present cultural context or neglect realistic political analysis or fail to address modernity, even though pastoral theology must have the courage at times to struggle against the skewed assumptions of modernity.

The apostolic ministry has been through many cultural crises and historical ordeals. We can draw from those experiences to avoid mistaken judgments and despair that could harm the body of Christ. We begin from the assumption that the vast social experience of historical Christianity is still useful and reliable and not to be despised. Yet it needs urgently to be correlated with contemporary language, symbol systems, and social realities.

Why Ministry?

It is no small effort to which we set ourselves. The task about which we are seeking to think integrally is none other than learning properly to shepherd the body of Christ. One would expect physicians or attorneys to have grasped an integral theory of their task, some overarching conception of their official duty, before beginning their practice. But in ministry, in the last decades, some have thought it acceptable to proceed without any such general conception or overarching vision. Yet the importance of the office of pastor still quietly pleads with us to think with extraordinary care about the better and worse ways in which that office might be conceived and practiced.

Compared with other tasks, what vocation is more laden with potentiality for good and for error? Both for helping and for hurting? What other vocation is professionally entrusted with the witness to God's own self-disclosure and the task of awakening appropriate responses to it? What other sphere of action has in mind such an auspicious aspiration as that of witnessing to God's intention to save humankind from sin and thereby to engender spiritual happiness, and to pray and work for the sanctification of human life to the glory of God? It is precisely because of the momentousness of the task that we do ourselves injury by not having thought deeply about the nature of pastoral ministry (Chrysostom, *NPNF* 1st, vol. 9, pp. 33 ff.).

It seems strange and awesome that such auspicious tasks are committed to ordinary human beings with a short lifespan, with limited knowledge of the cosmos, and with the same temptations to pride and twisted desire to which everyone else is subject. Human beings, not angels, are the ones called to ministry. Not all, only some. The church fathers marveled at this fact.

How odd that it is apparently not God's purpose to minister day by day to the world by direct revelation. Rather, the surprising fact is that God has chosen to minister to humanity through a scandalously visible community, the church, and to minister to the church through human agency, by calling ordinary, vulnerable, pride-prone persons into the ministry of word and sacrament. However vulnerable ministry may be to wretched distortions and abuses, curiously enough it seems to be God's own idea (Gregory Nazianzus, *NPNF* 2nd, vol. 7, pp. 208 ff.).

Is ministry necessary to God's design? The proper answer hinges on a finely made classical theological distinction between absolute and contingent necessity. If God is the only necessary being, then we can easily admit that ministry is not necessary absolutely to God, as if God could not really get along without us. But nothing is absolutely necessary in this sense, according to classical Christian teaching, except God. But if God should will creation, then creation is contingently necessary, namely, contingent upon God's willing it. If God wills to call into being the church (to participate in God's plan to save fallen creation) and to provide an ordered means for its guidance, we can then say that ministry is contingently necessary, that is, contingent upon God's offering and providing it. But keep in mind that what God wills toward persons with free agency is always subject to rejection and distortion by free agents. The whole problem of sin is precisely this: the willed abuse of a good creation. Yet God apparently wills to keep trying to penetrate our sin, to call us back to the original divine intention for us.

Ministry is, therefore, classically thought to be necessary to God's purpose in ordering the church for the salvation of humankind (Calvin, 1559, 4. 1). Yet to say that ministry is necessary for the church is itself subject to the potential abuse of forgetting that ministry exists to serve the church.

A Personal Word

Finally, a personal word to the reader concerning the curious individual pilgrimage that has brought me to this study. Every author who writes a book having written others previously hopes that the reader will build on some understanding of those previous writings. Yet each book must stand on its own for readers who have not met that author before. This study flows out of and depends upon the research and argument of my previous works, yet hopes to be understandable without constant reference to them. Some indication may nonetheless be useful to the reader concerning how the author himself sees this relation, in order that the reader may return to those previous points along the author's path to see the roots exposed or to inspect the foundation upon which this structure is built.

In this case, four themes of previous works stand quietly but powerfully in the background as particularly relevant to this study: (a) the critique of psychotherapy, especially the crucial importance of the "outcome studies" of the effectiveness of psychotherapy that present challenging evidence against the prevailing assumption that typical modern psychotherapies are generally effective (these I have treated in *After Therapy What?* pp. 174 ff.; "A Populist's View of Psychotherapeutic Deprofessionalization," *Journal of Humanistic Psychology*, 14:2 [1974], pp. 3–18; and *Game Free*, chap. 3); (b) the critique of modernity, along with neo-orthodoxy and fundamentalism (in *Agenda for Theology*, chaps. 1 and 2), accompanied by the celebration of a newly emergent postmodern orthodoxy; (c) the continuing critique of antinomianism (first in *Radical Obedience*, but more fully developed in *Guilt Free*) and the positive hope for the recovery of the classical dialectic between gospel and law, grace and obedience; and (d) a critique of the antihistorical bias of the modern pastoral counseling tradition ("Recovering Lost Identity," *JPC,* 34:1 [1980], pp. 4 ff.), linked with a call for the rediscovery and republication of the great texts of the classical tradition of pastoral care, from Chrysostom and Gregory to Herbert and Baxter.

These four themes represent major turning points in my own intellectual pilgrimage during the last decade as I have sought to bring psychology and theology into a more realistic dialogue. Prior to these pivotal decisions of the last decade, however, I was at work trying to bring psychotherapy into an effective accommodation with contemporary theology. Some readers, upon reading what follows, may draw the conclusion that I have not taken modern psychotherapy seriously enough. Partly in self-defense, I want these readers to know that in previous works I have offered detailed treatments, on the whole affirmative, of (a) Carl Rogers and client-centered therapy (in *Kerygma and Counseling*); (b) Seward Hiltner, Paul Tillich, Rudolf Bultmann, and others (in *Contemporary Theology and Psychotherapy* and *Radical Obedience*); (c) the existential psychologists, from Kierkegaard and Binswanger to May, Boss, Caruso, and Frankl (in *The Structure of Awareness*); (d) experimental encounter groups, T-groups, and growth groups (in *The Intensive Group Experience*); (e) Eric Berne and the transactional analysts (in *Game Free*), and (f) behavior therapy and the behaviorist tradition of study of interpersonal relations (in *TAG: The Transactional Awareness Game*).

I am not hinting that it is necessary for the reader to go back and unpack those arguments, but I would hope that serious critics at least would know about them, and recognize where my footprints have been, rather than prematurely supposing that I had never been there. Even with these caveats, I remain braced for the *non sequitur* that he who quotes premodern writers has therefore failed to deal with modern writers.

The immediate task ahead is to clarify how one becomes a minister. What is meant by a "call" or vocation to sacred ministry, and what steps lead to ordination?

REFERENCES AND FURTHER READING

Principle classical works on pastoral theology include: Ignatius of Antioch (d. 107), Cyprian (d. 253), Gregory Nazianzus (d. 389), Nemesius (c. 390), Gregory of Nyssa (d. 394), John Chrysostom (d. 407), Augustine (*ACW*, vol. 9), Leo the Great (d. 461), Gregory the Great (*ACW*, vol. 11), Rabanus Maurus (d. 856), Thomas Aquinas (*ST*, vol. 2, pp. 2143 ff., 2629 ff.), Wyclif (d. 1384), Luther (*LW*, vol. 40), Bucer (1538), Herbert (1652), Taylor (d. 1667), Baxter (1656), and Burnet (1692).

Various efforts at a rudimentary pastoral theology in the sixteenth and seventeenth centuries include Sarcerius (1562), Wegmann (1577), Porta (1582), Binsfeld (1599), Barclay (1678), and Owen (d. 1683). By the eighteenth century, pastoral theology became a recognized field among theological disciplines, as evidenced by Borromeo (1701), Seidel (1729), Baumgarten (1752), von Mosheim (1763), Plitt (1766), Töllner (1767), Jacobi (1774), Ostervald (1781), Sailer (1788). Gerard (1799), and Rivers (1799).

Building on the strength of these efforts, the nineteenth century became the period of greatest activity in pastoral theology, as represented by the work of Schenkl (1802), Gollowitz (1803), Graeffe (1803), Reichenberger (1805), Schlegel (1811), Kaiser (1816), Sailer* (1817), Powondra (1818), *Medicina Clerica* (1821), Boroth (1823), Bridges* (1829), Harms* (1830 ff., cf. Schulz, 1934), Schleiermacher* (d. 1834), Gougel (1834), Pond (1847), Loehe* (1851 ff.), Vinet* (1853), Cannon* (1853), Blunt (1856), Palmer (1863), Shedd (1867), Walther (1869), Kidder* (1871), Vilmar (1872), Blaikie (1873), Kübel (1874), Fairbairn (1875), Schweizer (1875), Murphy (1877), Bedell (1880), Hoppin* (1884), Hogue (1886), Renninger (1895), Köstlin* (1895), and Gladden* (1898).

This was followed by relatively few integral efforts at systematic pastoral theology in the twentieth century, among which are the German writers Krauss (1904), Fichtner (1931), Asmussen (1937), and Pfliegler (1966); and English and American writers Wilson (1903), Cunningham (1908), Dewar and Hudson (1932), Balmforth et al. (1937), Davis (1938), Hiltner* (1958), Segler (1960), Schuetze and Habeck (1974), and Newbigin (1977). To these must be added several collections of essays on pastoral theology by Underhill (1927), M. Thornton* (1958 and 1961), and Oglesby* (1969); and the new genre of writings on the theology of pastoral care by Tillich (1946), Roberts (1950), Outler (1954), Hulme (1956), Thurneysen (1962), E. Thornton (1964), Browning (1966), Hielema (1975), Cobb (1977), Narramore and Carter (1979), and Lake (1980); none of which attempts to cover the same broad range as the pastoral theologies of the nineteenth century that are asterisked above.

Readers who might wish to explore the history of care of souls are referred to T. Harnack (1878), Cutten (1911), Brett (1912–21), Watkins (1920), Kirk (1946), McNeill* (1934 and 1951), Kemp (1947), Niebuhr and Williams (1956), Schuster (1964), Kelsey (1963), Bouyer (1963, 1968, 1974), Pompey (1968), E. Thornton (1969), and Leech* (1979). A number of editors have sought in various periods to collect key pastoral writings or primary documents in pastoral care; among these are *The Clergyman's Instructor* (1708), Brown (1826), Moorman (1958), and Clebsch and Jaekle (1964). Other documentary collections more broadly based, but that also provide primary documentation for classical pastoral care, are Gee and Hardy (1896), *The Apostolic Fathers* (1909), Kidd (1911), Ayer (1913), Schaff (1931, 6th ed.), Schroeder (1937), Quasten (1950 ff.), Bettenson (*DCC*, 1956), Denzinger (1957), Leith (*CC*, 1973), and the multivolume collections listed in Abbreviations.

For discussions of the method of pastoral theology, readers are referred to Schleiermacher (1810, 1966 ed.), Hagenbach (1846–47), Rogers (1912), Arnold (1949, 1964), Rahner (1960), Delahaye (1964), Waltermann (1966), Hiltner (1958), and Rau (1970).

---

* Asterisks indicate the most important contributions.

Practical theology is a field distinguishable from, but overlapping with, pastoral theology. Major writers who defined and contributed to its tasks are Schleiermacher (1850, vol. 13), Marheineke (1837), Nitzsch (1847 ff), Moll (1853), Ebrard (1854), Ehrenfeuchter (1859), W. Otto (1866), von Zezschwitz (1876), Harnack (1877–78), van Oosterzee (1878), Krauss (1890–93), Weedner (1891), Achelis (1898, 2nd ed.), Schenck (1903), Niebergall (1918–19), Fendt (1938–39), *Baker's Dictionary of Practical Theology* (1957), Haendler (1957), Trillhaas (1964), Offele (1966), and Grimes (1977).

2. The Call to Ministry

Suppose a person is considering ministry, and thinks a call to ministry might have been received, but is unsure. Is such a call intrinsically untestable? Or is it possible to examine the evidence of God's address to the heart in a call to ministry? Classical pastoral wisdom has thought it to be testable, and dangerous if unexamined.

Inward Call: A Self-examination

Anyone can ask him- or herself whether the awareness of being called to ministry is persistent or occasional. If it is occasional, do not proceed hastily, but continue to listen for stronger and recurring signals. If it is persistent, be attentive to it, with caution and self-critical realism.

Are there obvious blockages or irreversible encumbrances? Is there severe physical incapacity or bodily limitation?

Be honest in asking yourself: Is my intellectual ability up to it? Can I write complete sentences? Think critically? Spell *sacrament?* Speak intelligibly? Identify a leap in logic? No one can answer these questions for another. They must be answered candidly. After all, if it is God who is calling, it is God who is listening.

The simplest questions one asks oneself inwardly are often the toughest: Have I learned to pray? Have the means of grace (worship, sacraments, Scripture) begun to be deeply ingrained in my lifestyle? If unsure, one had best let those seeds grow, and ask this question about call to ministry later.

It has occasionally happened that a person feels an urgent call to ministry, yet has had little sustained experience in a worshiping community. Do not act too quickly on such a momentous first impression. Let an initial impression grow quietly in a community of prayer until it becomes a sustained conviction.

Ask: How much am I willing to give up in order to serve the poor, the alienated, the sick? How deeply have I probed my own willingness to offer my very life sacrificially, if need be? Isn't the willingness to bear the cross and die to the world which is requisite for true discipleship also requisite of ministry (Polycarp, *ANF*, vol. 1; Chrysostom, *NPNF* 1st, vol. 9, chap. 4)?

How deep is my empathic capacity to feel another's hurts? Has *agape* begun to grow? If evidence of these gifts is very meager, it is less likely that the inward call is being confirmed (Ambrose, *NPNF* 2nd, vol. 10, book I; Gregory, *ACW*, pp. 33 ff.).

Am I competent to lead a community of faith? Can I learn to communicate the Christian message with persuasiveness and integrity? Am I cultivating the spiritual disciplines? Am I a person in whom the community of faith can place full trust? Am I capable of becoming a competent interpreter of Scripture? Am I willing to be instructed by the wisdom of the Christian tradition? Can I reason consistently about faith sufficiently to present the Christian message sensibly to intelligent contemporary people? Can I in good conscience be accountable to the authority of my church body, abide by the demands it places upon its ordained ministry, and be faithful to the vows of ordination? I then can ask to what extent the gifts of ministry have been tested out in public teaching and service so as to be well-received by the believing community (Ambrose, *NPNF* 2nd, vol. 10, pp. 463 f.).

Questions like these echo through centuries of tradition and conscientious personal struggle. They continue to be hints and glimpses of the deeper kind of self-examination that must be attempted in the inmost heart of the potential minister, standing alone and accountable before God.

Having first engaged in such an inward self-examination, I must then consult with others concerning their perception of my potential gifts for ministry. In informal, but candid, ways, I will submit my preliminary internal conviction of a call to ministry to the searching judgment of others in whom I trust. If I am strongly resistant to this sort of inward soul-searching, should I launch out on the risky business of guiding the soul-search of others? If unwilling to hear the critical judgment of others, should I pursue a lifelong task of making critical judgments? It may be better to say, "Give the inward call time to grow before making a premature, tentative, or ill-advised commitment to ministry." After all, according to its traditional conception, ordination is for life, not a London semester or a summer work camp.

If preliminary signals should prove positive on most of these questions, then I may advisedly inquire whether this felt inward call can receive a more deliberate outward confirmation by the church. The focus then shifts from my internal sense of calling to others' deliberate assessment of my abilities and promise, judged by rigorous criteria. Can an outward call from the church validate my preliminary sense of inward calling?

The Outward Call

The call to ministry requires not only a private, inward, intuitive feeling that one is called by God to ministry; if we had only that, we would invite the abuses of self-assertive, subjective, individualistic self-righteousness. To avoid these abuses, it also requires the affirmation of the visible, believing community. It is the church that outwardly confers the office of ministry. It is not conferred by a private person or by the state or by the ordinand alone, but by the church, and not merely the local church but the whole church on behalf of the apostolic tradition (Cyprian, *ANF*, vol. 5, p. 370; Augustine, *NPNF* 1st, vol. 4, pp. 519 ff.).

The purpose of the outward or external call to ministry is to examine and confirm the preliminary intuition of an inward call by deliberately testing and assessing the candidate's potential for service to the body of Christ. The agent by which the external call is made is the visible church—that means fallible, ordinary people in the living body of Christ—through duly authorized pre-ordination procedures.

Ordination committees are not made up of angels but of human beings, limited in knowledge, shaped by social presuppositions, and influenced by historically changing values, just as is the ordinand. The church's outward call comes in regional accents, enmeshed in history—through human voices, mimeographed papers, and votes of committees.

These fallible people are specifically asked not to "ordain suddenly" (1 Tim. 5:22). Hasty, reckless ordinations are prohibited both by specific biblical injunction and tradition (cf. First Council of Nicaea, 325, *NPNF* 2nd, vol. 14, p. 10). It is assumed in the apostolic tradition that there is somehow vested in the church's ministry the power of making good judgments under the guidance of the Spirit on new candidates for ministry. In due time a proper discernment will emerge. The church prays and, at times, agonizes over these judgments, hoping that the best will emerge. Sometimes the church is disappointed. Sometimes these ordination committees act irresponsibly. But the hope and faith of the church is that they will act with wise discernment. It sometimes takes longer than the candidate wishes. This may be a time of increased anxiety for candidates. It can also be a time of spiritual growth as one deliberately re-examines one's call.

If the answer has to be no, it should not be defensively received or harshly given, or overly righteous or accompanied by too much self-confidence. Those who hear an outward no to their inwardly felt call should not forget how difficult these decisions are for others to make. The energies of those who are better fitted for the general ministry of the church than the ordained ministry should be compassionately redirected. Sparks may fly, and sincere opinions may clash, but the faithful are asked on the whole to trust the process (Council of Neocaesarea, 315, *NPNF* 2nd, vol. 14, pp. 79 ff.). Without it there would be even greater madness.

It is to the ordered ministry itself that the injunction was given to "watch lest wolves enter into the fold" to harm the flock (Acts 20:29). The candidate may feel that playful puppies are being taken for wolves. On the other hand it may be that the ordaining body has forgotten altogether what wolves look like. In selecting new candidates for ministry, examining clergy do well to have a keen eye for the long-range welfare of the people of God, a good ear for both talent and palaver, and wide tolerance for intergenerational differences.

In order to exercise fairly this abusable power that has been bestowed upon pastoral leadership since New Testament times, there must be an approved procedure, an orderly apparatus, an agency, a committee of due process, through which candidacy can be appropriately evaluated and qualified candidates publicly affirmed (Council of Ancyra, 314, *NPNF* 2nd, vol. 14, passim). All this is scandalously necessary to a church that exists not in heaven but in ordinary history attempting to respond to God's revelation. If the church were already sanctified or made up of angels only or exempt from visible history, all this would be much simpler.

This "power" outwardly to call ministers and reject those unqualified is not an absolute power. It cannot arrogate to itself unambiguous, inevitable divine inspiration. It can only pray for the guidance of the Spirit. At best the power of ordaining bodies is a self-restrained, duly authorized, compassionately exercised power. It is not a power that can properly be exercised apart from devout prayer for the mind of Christ and awareness of our human limitations. It is a "power" that assumes personal sensitivity and wisdom, without which it loses its legitimate authority. Its very task is to set apart the best available persons for ministry for the true and faithful teaching of faith and the nurture of the Christian community (Council of Neocaesarea, *NPNF* 2nd, vol. 14, p. 84). It sounds simple, but it is simple only in theory. In practice heads knock, influence is exerted, occasional cries of anguish may be heard, and many questions will be answered only years later.

Criteria

Here are some of the criteria that have been traditionally applied to the outward call and that may help both candidate and examining body sort things out.

- By tradition the candidate should have reached canonical age, which for presbyters was fixed by the Council of Neocaeserea in 314 as thirty years (*NPNF* 2nd, vol. 14, p. 84), later reduced in the Roman tradition to twenty-five, and in some traditions to twenty-one. Modern practice has tended to circumvent this criterion by requiring educational experience. But child evangelists would probably have been either smiled at or frowned upon by the ancient church councils.

- Having wrestled with their own inward sense of calling, candidates should be presently convinced that the ordained ministry is the best way to fulfill their response to God.
- The candidate should have personal gifts for ministry. These include a realistic self-awareness, the ability to work patiently with others, love, compassion, and respect for other people.
- The candidate should be in good health. The candidate should be reasonably free of disabling defects that would disproportionally encumber ministry.
- The candidate's good character should be affirmed by those who know the candidate best.
- The candidate should have a capacity to preach and teach Christian doctrine in good conscience, accountable to Scripture and tradition. (Councils of Ephesus, 431, and Trullo, 692, *NPNF* 2nd, vol. 14, pp. 218 ff., 374 ff.).

The purpose of all this is to safeguard the Christian community from inept leadership, misinformed teachers, or bad pastors whose misjudgments or malpractice could harm the flock. If the examination is entered into with an open mind, the approved ordinand should come out of the process with a clear sense that his or her calling has been fully endorsed by the community. That is no small matter, larger at least than a rubber stamp. From this there can ensue a sense of support, affirmation and validated calling. From then on one may rely not merely on one's private, subjective, intuitive sense that one is called, but on the more objective fact that the whole community is saying yes to one's ministry and sending one out on its behalf.

Impediments

The prevailing assumption is that God would not call a person into ministry who was not fit for it, who by health, physical abilities, psychological soundness, or capacity for communication could not possibly carry out effectively the proper duties of the office. A candidate who has some gifts of ministry yet remains severely incapacitated in one of these ways does well to engage in a probing self-examination before presenting her- or himself to the ordaining board.

The question may come down to a tough proportional judgment: To what degree does this defect or impediment constitute a sufficient probable encumbrance or burden on present or future congregations or on the judicatory that it might outweigh other gifts? Or do the other gifts clearly outweigh the deficit so that grace will work through this individual even more powerfully?

Both candidate and examining committee do well to search for equitable wisdom in such an assessment, with all parties having the larger interest of the laity as their primary concern rather than personal self-actualization or some alleged inherent right to vocational self-expression (Seven Ecumenical Councils, *NPNF* 2nd, vol. 14, pp. 23 f., 46 ff. 429 f.). Ordination is not an absolute or natural "right" that just anyone can arbitrarily claim (Ambrose, *NPNF* 2nd, vol. 10, pp. 1 ff., 67 ff.).

Another equity to be assessed is the balance between intellectual and practical interests, since ministry requires both in good proportion. Suppose an intelligent candidate comes before the examiners with a confessed predominant interest in the theoretical study of religion, but minimal interest in practical pastoral duties? An examining committee would be justified to ask the candidate to work toward developing a balance among these interests and the skills necessary to accomplish them with effectiveness.

On the other hand, suppose another has many practical gifts for church administration and pastoral visitation, but has not thought through even the most elementary issues of Christian teaching about God, Christ, salvation, sacrament, social ethics, or eschatology? Suppose the candidate displays a vast boredom toward such issues. Such a person should be required to explore these concerns before being endorsed for ordination. Ministry intrinsically requires a reasonably high level of intellectual ability in order for the pastor to probe the complex reflective issues with which believers struggle. No simple formula of casuistry will be found. Both candidate and ordination committee must search for a wise, proportional assessment (Calvin, *Inst.* 4.3; Hoppin, 1884, 82 ff.).

The Role of Doubt in Faith as a Problem of Ordination

Should profound doubts about the faith be a part of an examination for ordination?

Suppose a candidate, having studied theology, comes before the committee with wrenching unresolved issues concerning the truth of the Christian faith. Let us assume that this person's interpersonal skills, gifts of communication, and leadership capacities are all adequate. It should be acknowledged that virtually every thoughtful Christian at times has doubts about aspects of Christian teaching. That should not be considered shocking or unusual. Both the person and the committee need to assess whether such doubts are ancillary, creative, and being constructively developed. Or are such doubts fundamentally addressed to the center of faith, persistent, tending toward blatant heresies, and potentially destructive to the community of faith? For the ordinand, the question is one of conscience: Can the faith be affirmed? For the church body the question is: Will the faith be affirmed?

If critical skills are to be developed, room must be given for a reasonable amount of debate, doubt, theoretical questioning, and creative hypothesizing. The committee has good reason to probe seriously, however, if there appears to be a fundamental absence of faith or persisent inability to believe. Then it may be that the person is not prepared to teach and preach the gospel with the kind of conviction that the Christian community deserves and should not be encouraged to pursue ministry—or perhaps should be encouraged to search further until more deeply rooted in good conscience and in the apostolic tradition.

Special Providence

Can or should alleged special inspiration be examined? How far is it possible or desirable for an ecclesial examining body to seek to assess alleged providential events or personal revelations that may have influenced a candidate's conception of ministry or calling? Such special "leadings" need to be sensitively explored with reserved good judgment. God works providentially in many different ways (Pastor of Hermas, *ANF*, vol. 2, pp. 14 ff.; Constitutions of the Holy Apostles, *ANF*, vol. 7, p. 420). It is not wise to apply a single flat rule or narrow definition to the ways God the Spirit can make her call effective. Paul was called in a way that was different from Matthew, and Matthew, from Phoebe. There may be no special, dramatic revelation at all, only the gentle, gradual guiding of the Spirit (Clement of Alexandria, *ANF* vol. 2, p. 312).

It may be intuitively important to the candidate to assess where doors are opening or closing in the pursuit of ministry, how a peak experience, a bereavement, university admissions, a serious accident, or a broken love affair may have seemed to signal something personally significant so as to impinge upon the interpretation of the possible call to ministry. In what sense do such events suggest a providential direction to that person's vocational choice? Even though their interpretations of calling may vary widely, most who feel strongly called to ministry have experienced some sense of providential direction or leading. Some are more dramatic, like combat experiences or aesthetic peak experiences or responses to massive social injustice, and have pointed the individual toward an acute sense of mission or clear-cut ministry. Other people may experience a quieter "hedging" of the way, in which certain options seem to be silently blocked off and other doors quietly wedged opened. These developments may take years to unfold. There is no single normative way to approach the assessment of providential calling. It is not for us to limit the ways in which God the Spirit can or cannot work, with or without our permission. Some may simply interpret the absence of negative signals or obstacles as a positive indication of inward calling.

Central to all of these assessments, however, is the correspondence between internal and external call. For the internal call is a result of the continued drawing or eliciting power of the Holy Spirit, which in time brings an individual closer to the church's outward call to ministry. The external call is an act of the Christian community that by due process confirms that inward call. No one can fulfill the difficult role of pastor adequately who has not been called and commissioned by Christ and the Church. This is why the correspondence between inner and outer call is so crucial for both the candidate and the church to establish from the outset with reasonable clarity.

There may be times when an individual may ask for too much infallibility in assessing a call or may excessively desire absolute clarity or unequivocal affirmation from all persons prior to pursuing ordained ministry. Such unanimity and absolute certitude is seldom found in history. Such persons are asked to trust the good judgment of the fallible people of the ordaining body while praying earnestly for the Spirit's guidance.

Having conscientiously gone through the rigors of this examination process, in which the inward call has been confirmed by the outward call, there is no further reason for the candidate to dwell moodily upon the validity of his or her calling. It is time to say with Isaiah (6:9): "Here am I, send me." With all this behind, the candidate is free to respond with an unencumbered commitment of the individual will to the divine will, and to come to be set apart for ministry in the sacred vows of ordination.

REFERENCES AND FURTHER READING

For various classical approaches to the doctrine of vocation to ministry, see Pastor of Hermas (ANF, vol. 2, pp. 14 ff.), Clement of Alexandria (ANF, vol. 2), Apostolic Constitutions (ANF, vol. 7; pp. 420 ff.), Ambrose (NPNF 2nd, vol. 10, pp. 67 ff., 463 f.), Seven Ecumenical Councils (NPNF 2nd, vol. 14), John Chrysostom (NPNF 1st, vol. 9, 33 ff.), Gregory the Great (ACW, p. 41 ff.), Thomas Aquinas (d. 1274, ST, vol. 3, p. 2685 f.), Luther (LW, vol. 40), Calvin (1559, 4.3), Herbert (d. 1633), Brett (1712), Mather (1728), Dodwell (1672), Baxter (PW, vol. 5, pp. 107 ff.), Bownas (1767), Hueffel (1843), Kidder (1871, pp. 74–124), Fairbairn (1875, pp. 61–73), Hoppin (1884, pp. 82–93), Gladden (1899, pp. 66–82). Major twentieth-century writers on call to ministry include Dykes (1909, pp. 31–36), Jowett (1912, pp. 9 ff.), Webb (1922), Beebe (1923, pp. 245 ff.), Guffin (1951), Barraclough (1955), Southard (1957), Segler (1960), Schwermann (1960), McDonnell (1970), Schuetze and Habeck (1974).

Pastoral Office vs Pastoral Role

3. The Meaning of Ordination

All Christians are called to discipleship, and therefore to share in Christ's ministry in a general sense. But only a few are called to ordained ministry. Why not all? What is the difference?

The General Ministry of the Laity

Ministry in the Christian community is a participation in the ministry of Christ. It is the ministry of the Father through the Son by the Spirit. It is a ministry offered to the whole church as gift and task. Baptism, confirmation, and responsible church membership are visible signs of acceptance of this ministry.

All believers are called to witness to the gospel, visit the sick, serve the needy, and assist in the building up of the community. This general ministry is committed to every Christian (Matt. 5:16, 28:18–20).

Yet there are persons within the ministry of the baptized who are called of God and set apart by the whole church for the specific tasks of an ordered ministry. Ordained ministry is different from the general ministry of the laity in that one is duly called, prepared, examined, ordained, and authorized to a representative ministry on behalf of the whole people (*laos*) of God.

Is this true?

Here we stumble upon a major dilemma of recent pastoral theology: the need wholeheartedly to affirm the general ministry of the laity without implicitly diminishing the validity of ordination. Throughout the various chapters of this discussion, we will again and again affirm the general ministry of the laity in various arenas often thought to be the special preserve of ordination: in lay visitation, lay witness, lay theological education, lay services to the sick and poor. Yet our basic task is to show how a well-equipped general ministry of the laity stands in constant need of an equipping, ordained ministry (Eph. 4:11–14). Thus our next question.

Why Ordination?

Essential to ordination are the reception of the gift (*charisma*) of ministry and the rite through which that gift is received. The rite has two key moments: the laying on of hands and the church's intercessory prayer. Ordination combines an internal grace with an external act in which the inner reality is the reception of the divine gift and the external event is the laying on of hands with prayer.

Ordination is done only once and (barring special circumstances that would invalidate the original act) not repeated (*Seven Ecumenical Councils*, NPNF 2nd, vol. 14, pp. 40, 268, 376, 464, 598), just as baptism is not repeated, since it has reference to a lifelong covenant relationship. It enacts a solemn covenant not to be entered into lightly. It "sets apart" the person for ministry by a formal rite of induction on behalf of the worldwide, intergenerational apostolic tradition.

Who is entrusted with the power to ordain? Although there are different viewpoints in the modern Christian tradition as to whether bishops, presbyters, or *laos* ordains, or some combination of them, there remains consensus at these points:

- Ordination is enacted on behalf of the whole church. Even in free church congregational traditions in which the local church ordains, it does so not just on behalf of the local church but on behalf of the historical, ecumenical church. Just as one is baptized not into the local church alone but the whole church, so one is ordained not merely by synod, denomination, diocese, or conference, but on behalf of the apostolic tradition set apart by and for the whole church.
- Ordination is enacted only after a due process of examination so that no one will lay hands on another quickly (*NPNF* 2nd, vol. 14, pp. 10 f., 126, 514 ff.).
- Whoever undertakes ordination stands accountable to and responsible for the apostolic tradition that they are thereby entrusted to guard (Chalcedon, *NPNF* 2nd, vol. 14, pp. 243 ff.).
- Ordination to ministry publicly authorizes and commissions the candidate to the ministry of word, sacrament and order, and prays for the empowerment of that ministry.

What Does the Imposition of Hands Imply?

The laying on of hands has been symbolically employed from ancient times publicly, formally, and openly to commission persons to office, as well as to grant blessings, offer gifts and sacrifices, and heal. The Hebraic tradition employed this demonstrative act on many auspicious occasions (Gen. 38:14, Deut. 34:9, Lev. 24). Levites were set apart for their office by the rite of laying on of hands (Num. 27:18–23).

Moses commissioned Joshua by laying on of hands (Deut. 34:9); scribes and rabbis received the same commission. It is understandable that this tradition should be continued by Jesus and the apostles as a means of authenticating their choice of those to maintain the apostolic tradition and to affirm its kinship with the religious leadership of ancient Israel.

The twelve were called and sent forth to ministry by Jesus himself, as it was remembered in Mark 3:13–19 and Luke 6:12–16, 10:1–16. We are thinking out of the New Testament as the church's book, Spirit-shaped, canonized by ecumenical consensus as a revered recollection of salvation events. This makes it more than a document under our control, for our analysis, as an object of our historical investigation. When the pastoral tradition has quoted Scripture, it has viewed it as a canonical text that has been understood over many centuries to authorize and instruct ministry. We do not examine Scripture purely as a historical inquiry; rather, Scripture examines us.

The calling of the twelve was remembered as a solemn occasion for which Jesus prayed all night before making his selection (Luke 6:12,13). From there on we can see a continuous flow of events in several stages:

the twelve were called and commissioned by Jesus;
the seventy were sent out by the Lord's command to proclaim the kingdom;
when Jesus' earthly ministry ended, the church gathered to celebrate the resurrected Lord, to secure continuity between Jesus' ministry and the apostolic ministry, and to receive the gifts of the Spirit (Acts 2); and
the twelve commissioned others by ordination to continue the apostolic ministry intergenerationally until the end of time.

Ordination thus developed out of the Jewish concept of commissioning to office. It was transmitted by Jesus, received by the Twelve, then the seventy, and soon passed on to the larger apostolic and ecumenical tradition. This continuity between Jesus and our current ministry has for almost two thousand years been symbolized by this ancient rite of authorizing and legitimizing leadership—the laying on of hands with prayer.

Key New Testament references to ordination are Acts 6:1–6, where the first seven were ordained to the diaconate, and Acts 13:1, where Barnabas and Saul were set apart: "After further fasting and prayer, they laid their hands on them and let them go" (v. 3). They were thought to be sent out on their way by the Holy Spirit (v. 2). Both accounts (Acts 6 and 13) specifically mention the twofold center of the act of ordination: (1) laying on of hands with (2) intercessory prayer.

Are Gifts of Ministry Received?

The Pastoral Epistles contain several passages rich in implications for ordination. Timothy is counseled to "not neglect the spiritual endowment you possess, which was given you under the guidance of prophecy, through the laying on of hands of the elders as a body" (1 Tim. 4:14). This text suggests that:

- a charisma was bestowed by the Spirit through elders;
- this internal gift was received by means of the rite of laying on of hands;
- the bestowal of this gift was guided by the Spirit; and
- the charisma of ministry should be carefully nurtured and not neglected.

Later, the same writer pointedly returns to the same theme: "That is why I now remind you to stir into flame the gift of God which is within you through the laying on of my hands" (2 Tim. 1:6). The implication is that the gift of ministry is itself a grace to be re-awakened in current awareness. Once given, it is to be recurrently kindled. The flame that originally was started or at least confirmed in ordination through the laying on of hands must be carefully tended and fanned anew by the recipient. The flame is the gift of the Spirit.

Is ordination indelible? Time may reveal that alleged gifts do not build up the church. A call that once appeared firm may later seem dubious. Is ordination an unretractable covenant for both parties? Traditionally, ordination has been considered a lifelong, indelible covenant (*Seven Ecumenical Councils, NPNF* 2nd, vol. 14, pp. 116 ff., 464, 598), analogous to baptism for the general ministry. Like the baptized, however, it is possible for the duly ordained to neglect, reject, or re-interpret the gift of ministry. Thus, in most church bodies, procedures exist by which ordained ministers can elect to follow other paths than full-time ministry of word, sacrament, and order. In these cases, ordination is not, strictly speaking, withdrawn or withheld, but rather it is inactive or quiescent and could by due process be later re-activated.

Is Ordination Necessary?

Most Protestant views of ordination do not focus on the physical event of ordination itself. Ordination as an *opus operatum*—the notion that the rite is something that of itself by the simple doing of it infuses supernatural power directly by the laying on of hands—has been resisted. Rather it is viewed as a gift of the Spirit necessary for the well-being and good order of ministry.

Reformed theology has sometimes argued that since Timothy was ordained by presbyters or elders, not bishops, and since Titus was sent as an evangelist to teach in Crete where there was no settled episcopate, there is no necessary literal, historical succession of bishops presupposed in ordination. The notion emerged quickly and remained persistently, however, that ordination is a conveyance of spiritual power (*dunamis*) that the apostles received from Christ himself and passed on to his successors by Christ's own command and design. Since the ordaining clergy were by definition thought to be successors of the apostles, it was expected that they would earnestly pray for the Spirit to convey the gifts presupposed in ministry (Jerome, *NPNF* 2nd, vol. 6, pp. 16 ff.). This is why the declaration "*Accipe Spiritum Sanctum*" ("Receive the Holy Spirit!") was incorporated centrally into the early medieval services of ordination. Cyprian (*ANF*, vol. 5, pp. 305 ff., 340 ff.) powerfully developed the theme (1 Tim. 4:14) that ordination conveyed an extraordinary gift or charisma of ministry. But neither in its earlier or its later phases was it understood in a simplistic, reductionist way as if the manual contact with the bishop were the main event or the direct medium through which the gift is mechanically transmitted; this is a modern reductionist caricature of patristic views of ordination.

The effective inner meaning of ordination is the earnest intercession of the church, invoking the Spirit to empower and bless this ministry. This internal side is manifested externally by a visible event: the imposition of hands. The intercession asks God for a continuing endowment of these gifts and for the abiding presence of the Holy Spirit (Cyprian, *ANF*, vol. 5, pp. 483 ff., 491 ff.). This is not to deny that persons must make their own disciplined effort in stirring up these gifts, once given. But once the imposition of hands has occurred with sincere prayer of the church by its duly authorized ministry, the ordinand has good reason to rely upon that intercession, to credit it, to be re-assured by its authenticity, and to recollect happily that his or her work is commissioned, not just by oneself through private inspiration, but rather by the whole historical church, by due process, in the expectation of fruitful outcome (Chrysostom, *NPNF* 1st, vol. 13, pp. 509 ff.).

The Unity and Continuity of Christ's Ministry

One of the earliest distinctions that arose in Christian ministry was that between the missionary who went abroad to preach and the local pastor who stayed behind to nurture the flocks already begun. This correlated to some degree with the distinction between the more mobile apostles and prophets and the relatively less mobile bishops, presbyters, and deacons who were serving settled flocks. After the earliest generations of apostles and prophets had died, it increasingly fell to this second group of more settled ministers to develop the core of the traditional threefold doctrine of ministry (to be more fully discussed in the next chapter):

- deacons, or serving ministries;
- elders, or guiding ministries;
- bishops, or overseeing ministries which, though much challenged, remains widely affirmed in historical ecumenism (Irenaeus, *ANF*

vol 1, pp. 415 ff., 497 ff.; Cyprian, *ANF*, vol. 5, pp. 581 ff.; *Apostolic Constitution, ANF*, vol. 7, pp. 482 ff.).

Though disputed, some concept of threefold orders remains a centrist position. Within the variety of tasks of ministry, the unity remains. For it is Christ's one ministry that unites our varied ministries, in various times, places, and languages (Chrysostom, *NPNF* 1st, vol. 14, pp. 278 ff.).

By medieval times the Roman tradition had developed a more complex conception of grades of ministry. In addition to the bishop, three major orders (priest, deacon, and subdeacon) were distinguished from minor orders (acolytes, exorcists, readers, and doorkeepers). Most medieval scholastics considered the major orders sacramental (cf. Thomas Aquinas, *ST*, vol. 3, pp. 2680–92 on seven orders). Protestantism rejected the view that ordination was properly speaking a sacrament yet nonetheless continued to view ordination under various analogies as necessary for public ministry.

Most traditions, with few exceptions, have held that orders are conferred by the whole church through duly elected bishops or presbyters (elders) on behalf of the whole church, acting as successors to the apostles. Some free church traditions have viewed the congregation as the agent of ordination. Through whatever sequence of continuity it is thought to be channeled, however, most Christian doctrines of ordination view the rite as standing in some sort of historical or symbolic sequence of apostolic leadership (Hippolytus, *ANF*, vol. 5, pp. 10 f.). The traditions continue to debate whether the continuity is historical or symbolic. The purpose in either case is to assure the faithful of the continuity of God's church and to seek to guarantee the authenticity of its witness to the Word.

There remains some evidence that ordination was at times conferred by clerics other than bishops. According to Jerome, the bishop of Alexandria was consecrated by the presbyters of the city. According to Hippolytus, some martyrs were regarded as having received the equivalent of ordination. The earliest texts of rites of ordination are to be found in Hippolytus in the early third century and the *Apostolic Constitutions* in the late fourth century.

What does the public rite of ordination confer? A classical Protestant answer from Chemnitz (1593, p. 36) is fivefold: (1) ordination is a public testimony by which the call of God is openly declared to be approved by the church; (2) through ordination the ministry is committed formally to the ordinand; (3) through the ordinand's solemn vow, the one who has been called "becomes obligated to the church in the sight of God to render the faithfulness in the ministry that the Lord requires"; (4) through ordination "the church is reminded that it is to recognize that this pastor has divine authority to teach"; and (5) in ordination the whole church earnestly prays to "commit to God" the ministry of one who is called, expecting that God will accompany this ministry.

Is the ordinand's family involved? In traditions that emphasize celibacy as a precondition of priesthood, this question is circumvented on the assumption that the freedom from family responsibilities is joyfully affirmed in order to fulfill Christ's ministry (Council of Trullo, 692, *NPNF* 2nd, vol. 14, pp. 359 ff.). In the Protestant traditions, where celibacy has been largely replaced by married clergy, ordinands not only commit themselves but also, in some real sense, their present or future family to ministry. The underlying assumption is not an autonomous individualism which would assume that what I do with my life is my own business. Rather it is a more social and organic view of human existence that views the marriage covenanters and their offspring as bound together inextricably in covenant co-responsibility. Clergy persons may choose to be single, and thus follow Paul in his appeal to unmarried clergy (1 Cor. 7:26–35). But if they elect to marry, also within the bounds of Pauline theology, they will do so with a joint sense of responsibility to both family and ministry that are deeply affected by the decision. No one who experiences a preliminary sense of call to ministry can justly withhold this awareness from a marriage partner or intended spouse. It deserves to be treated as a mutual decision in full awareness of its consequences.

The Ordination Charge

The traditional charge given to ordinands in the rite of ordination is found in 2 Tim. 4:1–2: "I give you this charge: Preach the Word; be prepared in season and out of season; correct, rebuke and encourage—with great patience and careful instruction" (*NIV*).

A comparative review of ordination services of various traditions will show many similarities and a wide consensus about what is occurring. Usually the ordination service calls the ordinand to "make full proof of thy ministry" (2 Tim. 4:5, KJV; cf. NEB: "Do all the duties of your calling") in the following ways:

- to study "to show yourself worthy of God's approval, as a labourer who need not be ashamed" (2 Tim. 2:15),
- "rightly dividing the word of truth" (2:15, KJV),
- to be an example to believers "in speech and behaviour, in love, fidelity, and purity" (1 Tim. 4:12),
- to be "ready for any honourable form of work" (Titus 3:1),
- to be able to communicate Christian teaching in a "tolerant and gentle" yet disciplined way (2 Tim. 2:23 f.).

There is some evidence of an attempt very early in the pastoral tradition to develop something like a primitive theological education in a rudimentary sense. Timothy was deliberately instructed: "You heard my teaching in the presence of many witnesses; put that teaching into the charge of [persons] you can trust, such ... as will be competent to teach others" (2 Tim. 2:1,2). The principle: Those who are "taught of God" should be able to teach others. Timothy was entrusted to select persons for ministry who had talent to offer instruction, not simply to catechize local believers or teach the rudiments. This is why we are not amiss to suggest speculatively that some progenitor of a theological school may have been already modestly or analogously present in the context of the Pastoral Epistles. Jesus, Paul, and all the apostles were without exception concerned to provide careful instruction for deliberately chosen persons so as to improve their capacity to receive the Word entrusted to them and pass it on without undue distortion. The Fourth Gospel, Irenaeus, and Hippolytus all continued this evident concern to maintain accurately the apostolic teaching. Thus, it was out of the original vitality of the earliest Christian tradition that the doctrine and practice of ordination emerged, intrinsically connected with theological education of a prototypical sort, as an expression of the overarching concern for continuity with the living Christ. This is why ordination is as important today as it was in the context of Acts, chapters 6 and 13.

REFERENCES AND FURTHER READING

Early rites of ordination are found in Hippolytus (ca. 215), the Liturgy of Saint Serapion (d. after 360), and *Apostolic Constitutions* (*ANF*, vol. 7, pp. 430 ff., 482 ff., 491 ff.). Classical texts on ordination include Clement of Alexandria (*ANF*, vol. 2, pp. 453 f., 504 ff., 535 f.), Irenaeus (*ANF*, vol. 1, pp. 415 ff.), Cyprian (*ANF*, vol. 5, pp. 305 ff., 483 ff., 581 ff.), Chrysostom (before 392, *On Priesthood*, *NPNF* 1st, vol. 9), Gregory of Nyssa (d. 394, *NPNF* 2nd, vol. 5), Jerome (*NPNF* 2nd, vol. 6), Thomas Aquinas (*ST*, vol. 3, pp. 2681 ff.), Luther (*LW*, vol. 40), Calvin (1559, 4.3, 4.4), Chemnitz (1593, pp. 35 ff.), Taylor (*TPW*, vol. 2, p. 118), and Mather (1728).

For more recent discussions of ordination see Gore (1888), Hort (1897), Moberly 1899), Neill (1947), Manson (1958), Kirk (1946), Lohse (1951), Erhardt (1954), Bruns (1963). For various views of the imposition of hands, see Hooker (1594–1618), Smith (1913), Easton (1922–23), Shepherd (1962), Parrett (1968–69), Galtier (1972), and Ferguson (1975). For discussion of the general ministry of the laity, as distinguished from ordained ministry, see Krimm (1953), Manson (1956), Kraemer (1958), Wingren (1958), Congar (1959), Eastwood (1960), Newbigin (1960), Minear (1960). On preparation for ministry see Vinet (1853), Cannon (1853), Kidder (1871), Hoppin (1884), LaPlace (1975), Niebuhr et al. (1957), and Feilding (1966).

Although this study of the church's ministry cannot fully discuss the doctrine of the church and many ancillary ecclesiological problems, it nonetheless presupposes fuller treatments of the church. We need not provide here a full bibliography of discussions of the church, but among the better recent ones we note the following as being especially useful as propaedeutic to the discussion of ministry: Mascall (1946), Davies (1954), Nygren (1956), Torrance (1956), Abba (1957), Welch (1958), Newbigin (1960), Minear (1960), Rahner (1963b, 1964a), Küng (1968), Pannenberg (1971a), Schillebeeckx (1973), Lee (1974), Dulles (1974), and Moltmann (1975, 1977). My two previous books on ecclesiological issues (*The Community of Celebration*, 1963, and *Beyond Revolution,* 1970) will also reveal many concerns that may be viewed as general background to the consideration of these issues of ministry.

4. Women in the Pastoral Office

From Philippians 4:2–3 we have clear evidence that women were involved in positions of leadership in the church. Paul, who was trying to settle a conflict between Euodia and Syntyche, writes affectionately of "these women, who shared my struggles in the cause of the gospel . . . whose names are in the roll of the living." Paul was gladly affirming the privilege of laboring side by side with these women for the gospel. They vitally shared his mission and struggle. There is no warrant to assume in the passage that there was any subordinate relationship, nothing except the full equality of men and women working together in the ministry of the gospel.

Similarly in Romans 16:1–16, where Paul is commending a number of Christians to the church at Rome, he lists several women mentioned alongside men as "fellow workers" in Christ. They are as follows:

- "Phoebe, a fellow-Christian who holds office in the congregation at Cenchreae" (v. 1). Phoebe "has herself been a good friend to many, including myself." His Roman readers were urged unambiguously to "stand by her in any business in which she may need your help" (v. 2).
- "Prisca and Aquila, my fellow-workers in Christ Jesus. They risked their necks to save my life, and not I alone but all the gentile congregations are grateful to them. Greet also the congregation at their house" (vv. 3–5).
- "Mary, who toiled hard for you" (v. 6).
- "Tryphaena and Tryphosa, who toil in the Lord's service, and dear Persis who has toiled in his service so long" (v. 12).

It is astonishing that in Paul's deliberate account of the fellow workers whom he commends and relies upon most, so many of them are women. It is striking that women apparently had such important roles in the mission already at this exceptionally early state of the transmission of the apostolic tradition to the Roman world, especially when seen in the light of the cultural assumptions about the assumed roles and place of women.

Ephesians 5:21–33 hinges significantly on this crucial christological image: the symbol of the head (*kephale*). The analogy is that the husband is the head of the wife in the same way that Christ is the head of the church. But what sort of headship does Christ have over the Church? It is a headship that implies suffering for others and redemptive love. Essential to this mode of headship is self-sacrificial, radical self-giving. This passage is not talking about a coercive, authoritarian type of headship or superordination. If that were the sort of headship meant, the passage would not have proceeded so consistently from its central premise: "Be subject to one another out of reverence for Christ" (v. 21). Rather, the kind of headship indicated is that of the self-giving, righteous, redemptive *kephale*, Christ the head of the church.

It is precisely by that analogy and none other that man is called to be the self-sacrificial and serving "head" of the family. The analogy is not suggestive of oppression but of service. That point is further reinforced in the next phrase where the analogy takes this amazing turn: "Husbands, love your wives, as Christ also loved the church and gave himself up for it, to consecrate it, cleansing it by water and the word" (Eph. 5:25). On the basis of this pivotal analogy we conclude that the concept of subjection or *hupotassatai* does not refer specifically to an intrinsic super- and subordination of power but to self-giving service strictly seen according to the analogy of Christ's own self giving to us.

The Issue

We have been attempting to ground the office of pastor consistently in historical Christian pastoral wisdom. That makes this present turn of argument all the more challenging. For we now turn our attention squarely to deal with this exceptionally controversial subject, one that many will perceive as lacking the kind of historical consensus to which we have previously appealed. The issue, however, is as unavoidable as it is important: It is the potentially divisive yet promising issue of women in holy orders, and in general, the gifts of women for ministry. What is less traditionally Protestant or Catholic, one might argue, than women in the office of pastor, liturgist, preacher, and church administrator? How can we now appeal in the way we have previously appealed to the rule of Vincent of Lerins that a doctrine is best judged as ecumenically trustworthy when it has been believed "everywhere, always, and by all"? Even more poignantly, how can we affirm the scriptural canon, as we wish to do in all critical moments of a pastoral theology, and at the same time speak in good conscience of women being called and ordained to ministry?

In probing this question I want to appeal immediately to a brilliant

principle of theology found in the writings of Cardinal John Henry
Newman, namely, that there is a depositum of faith given in the Christ
event that is the same always, yesterday, today and forever, and yet we
see historical development that bestows ever-new meaning on this complex depositum. There are many laborious developments in the history
of the Christian tradition that, in effect, have awaited a slowly unfolding historical process in order for their hidden meaning to be fully
revealed. That is not a denial of cohesiveness in the tradition, but rather
a joyful beholding of the tradition unfolding with previously un-
received meanings. The ideas of equal dignity of persons before God
under law, representative democracy, and human rights, which are implicit in key threads of Scripture and tradition, nonetheless had to await
tedious historical development before their deeper original intention
was properly understood. Our own contemporary period is far from
finished in its grasp of the implications of God's good news (Newman,
1845, chap. 5; 1864, pp. 15 ff.).

On the basis of this principle, we will argue that both women and
men may be called to representative ministry, and that this view is deeply embedded in Christ's own intention for the church and in major
strands of the primitive Christian tradition, even though it has had to
await a dubiously meandering stream of historical development before
it could to some degree become realized in living Christian community.

We do well to confess early that far too much of the Christian tradition has been unrepresentatively male dominated in priesthood and has
failed to recognize adequately God's call to women in ministry. Women
have always been more ready to serve than the church allowed. What
they lacked was the opportunity. But historical conditions make it
now more possible to fulfill the deeper intention of the historical tradition.

Right or Rite?

Why not view the issue of women in ministry simply as a civil right,
analogous to other employment, to which equal access is rightly due? It
is an important assumption of religious liberty that ordination is not a
civil right, that is, it is not under government authority, but rather, is a
solemn rite of the believing community. Ordination exists only by divine calling and by the outward affirmation of the believing community. So the question of whether women should be or are capable of
being ordained to ministry requires a theological, not merely a legal,
answer or investigation. It is not merely a question of civil law, it is a
question of sound theological, exegetical, and historical reflection.
Christian civil libertarians are rightly resistant to those who would
superficially view the question of ordination essentially as a matter for
government surveillance, judicial dispute, or legislative whim. No government can ordain. Only the church can properly call, examine, and

ordain persons to ministry. This is all the more reason that it be done justly, fairly, and in good order.

Catholic and Protestant traditionalists against women's orders have rightly expressed their concern for continuity in tradition, fitting liturgical representation, and faithful exegesis. But it is now on all three of these grounds that we wish to offer plausible reasons for the ordination of women. Despite sturdy efforts at retrenchment, the theological arguments are piling high on the side of the ordination of women, from Scripture, tradition, reason, and experience.

The clearest theological beginning point is the penetrating analogy between baptism and ordination. For in baptism, all members of the body of Christ, neither one sex nor the other exclusively, are called and committed to the general ministry. By analogy, if all the baptized are to be properly represented in a representative ministry, it is fitting that neither one sex nor the other be arbitrarily excluded from the ordained ministry of word, sacrament, and care.

Rather than treat the historical church with disgust and impatience, we do better to think empathetically with the struggling church through the slowly developing choices that it has faced in different stages of its historical development. We have something to learn from the church's wide experience. The historical church has faced conflicts, sufferings, and limitations that we have never dreamed of. It is far too cheap for moderns to assume that we obviously could have done much better or acted more justly, within the specific historical encumberances, political impediments, and constricted social traditions that prevailed during the times of Paul, Jerome, Thomas Aquinas, or Calvin.

Our modern chauvinism easily tempts us to imagine that we would not have perpetrated or allowed these injustices to occur. But an assessment of the responses of our own modern church to current social inequities is hardly reassuring.

In the past the church has vigorously sought to affirm and lend deeper meaning to the ordinary struggles and labors of women, particularly those of mothering and family nurture. In much traditional pastoral reasoning (reflecting common societal assumptions to which few exceptions can be found), these valuable tasks precluded participation in priesthood. Most premodern cultures have seemed, according to their own moral lights, to have had valid reasons for so strongly affirming these tasks of nurture of the family that they have by implication denied both ordination and priestly activity to women, as was common in much of the ancient world.

However, in our culture, which is an unfinished product of a great struggle for equal justice and equal dignity of all people, it simply is unacceptable to assume that women by virtue of their sex are incapable of being empowered by God the Spirit to preach the word, administer the sacraments, and provide pastoral care for the flock.

Rather than viewing the question of ordination of women strictly as a question of revising unchangeable dogma, we do better to think of this question as a matter of evolving and debatable theological interpretation amid the changing shapes of human cultures. Properly framed, the question assumes the church's ability and responsibility to listen ever afresh to the divine address through Scripture and tradition amid changing historical circumstances. Rather than viewing this as a question of fundamental theological backtracking, we do better to see the current church as now belatedly trying to catch up with the deeper unfulfilled intention of Christ (Mark 14:3–9, Luke 8:3–11, Rom. 16:1–15, Gal. 3:28). We are now at a point of historical development in the Christian community where it is at last possible to see more deeply and insightfully into the nature of representative ministry than has been possible under previous ambiguous historical conditions. Now we can clearly grasp that which was hidden yet implicit in the earliest Christian tradition and Scripture.

If a minister is to be a representative of Christ in the midst of the church and representative of the people before God in prayer, then it seems far more reasonable that both men and women be included in that representative function. For both male and female contribute inseparably to the wholeness of the human family.

Key Biblical Passages Rethought

In asking whether a woman can be a pastor, we intend to focus primarily on biblical and theological reasoning, rather than sociological or psychological or political arguments, which receive full treatment in other bodies of literature. We are not asking whether women may be shown empirically to be psychologically fit to do the work of ministry, nor are we asking a question of political timing about when congregations will have a more open mind and be ready to welcome women into traditional pastoral roles. However important, these questions should not prematurely eclipse the prior theological question: Based on Scripture, tradition, reason, and experience, can we properly conclude that women are called into ministry as truly as men?

The first major task is to think openly about the problematic passages of Scripture that often are alleged to constitute an unanswerable argument against the ordination of women. Here are the key problematic texts that make our case challenging:

- In 1 Cor. 11:2–12, Paul objected to women praying or prophesying bareheaded, and argued that men should exercise the same headship toward the family that Christ exercised toward the church. Yet Paul acknowledged that "in Christ's fellowship woman is as essential to man as man to woman" (1 Cor. 11:11).
- Later, in 1 Corinthians 14:33–35, Paul appealed to the Torah in

enjoining women not to speak publicly to the congregation without authorization.

- Again, in Ephesians 5:21–33, everything hinges on the illuminating analogy between Christ's sacrificial self-giving love for the church and the husband's love for the wife. The notion of "headship" is decisively illuminated by Christ's own self-giving mode of headship. "Be subject to one another out of reverence for Christ. Wives, be subject to your husbands as to the Lord; for the man is the head of the woman, just as Christ also is the head of the church. Christ is, indeed, the Saviour of the body; but just as the church is subject to Christ, so must women be to their husbands in everything. Husbands, love your wives, as Christ also loved the church and gave himself up for it, to consecrate it, cleansing it by water and word, so that he might present the church to himself all glorious, with no stain or wrinkle or anything of the sort, but holy and without blemish. In the same way men also are bound to love their wives, as they love their own bodies. In loving his wife a man loves himself. For no one ever hated his own body: on the contrary, he provides and cares for it; and that is how Christ treats the church, because it is his body, of which we are living parts. Thus it is that (in the words of Scripture) 'a man shall leave his father and mother and shall be joined to his wife, and the two shall become one flesh.' It is a great truth that is hidden here. I for my part refer it to Christ and to the church, but it applies also individually: each of you must love his wife as his very self; and woman must see to it that she pays her husband all respect."
- Similarly, in Colossians 3:18–19, married men and married women are reciprocally enjoined to the high responsibility of building a marriage. Wives are called to be responsive to their husbands and husbands to love their wives and not be harsh with them. But this is stated in such a way that it could lead to an interpretation of women as subordinate.
- The last of these problematic texts combines many of the above themes, and adds the "saved through motherhood" theme, namely, in 1 Timothy 2:9–15, where women are enjoined to be learners, to listen, and not to "domineer over man," which hinged on a traditional rabbinic interpretation of Genesis 1 and 2, that from the outset of human history women have led men into sin, and yet they "will be saved through motherhood—if only women continue in faith, love, and holiness, with a sober mind."

These are the major texts most often quoted to defend a male-only ministry. Other Pauline texts (such as Gal. 3:28) that reflect an amazingly equalitarian view of men and women in Christ are not heard through these volleys. Although the opposite case (that ministry is inclusive) is made more challenging by the above texts, the theological discussion is far from over. The other side of the case has not yet received a full hearing. Even though this exclusivist evidence may appear weighty indeed, we believe the case for women in ministry can and should be made primarily on exegetical grounds. We are in fact currently in the middle of a wide-ranging discussion in New Testament studies as to whether Paul at a deeper level was an advocate of the equality of women (see Robin Scroggs, who argues that the apostle Paul was "the only consistent spokesman for the liberation and equality of women in the New Testament," *JAAR*, 40, 1972, p. 283).

In 1 Corinthians 11:4–5, for example, it seems probable that Paul was assuming that women will be in fact praying and prophesying, that they will be speaking on important matters in the public context of the church, and that the only question being debated was whether their heads should be veiled or not ("a woman . . . brings shame on her head if she prays or prophesies bare-headed," v. 5).

It should be kept in mind that the early Christian communities were struggling valiantly against charges of sedition, moral irresponsibility, social corruption, and being a revolutionary danger. The social assumptions about women in the first-century context took for granted that faithful women would use discrete judgment in their public appearance. That, for instance, meant that they would be covered with a veil if they went outside their home. That was not a matter of faith, but rather of a prudent choice not to upset unnecessarily the prevailing social customs about the proper public behavior of women.

Neither Paul nor the New Testament church invented that custom. Rather, it was a part of the context to which they were trying to address the gospel. It might be considered somewhat analogous to another question of cultural assumptions that was more fully treated in the New Testament, namely, whether eating certain food consecrated to heathen deities was permissible and whether that was related to faith in Christ. Paul's answer: "Certainly food will not bring us into God's presence: if we do not eat we are none the worse, and if we eat we are none the better. But be careful that this liberty of yours does not become a pitfall for the weak" (1 Cor. 8:8–9).

What is astonishing is not the familiar ancient practice of women wearing a veil. Rather, it is the fact that within such a culture there would be Christian women who would take strong initiatives in the early church, exercise significant leadership, and be long remembered for their courage in ministry.

In the light of these prevailing cultural assumptions, it is no small point that women were baptized equally with men. For that in itself sharply distinguished the Christian rite of initiation from the Jewish rite of circumcision, which was for males only. This new eschatological community of the resurrection took an enormous political risk by encouraging the primary involvement of women in the community in a way that was virtually without parallel in the ancient Near Eastern context. No serious exegete can simply extract Paul out of that context and assume that he was speaking as if in an already equalitarian society. That was not the case.

The idea that husband and wife are before God equal in distinguishable functions is developed in Ephesians 5. Husband and wife are one with each other in the same way that Christ and the church are one body and united with each other. That is hardly a customary statement of social super- or subordination, inequality, oppression, or inferiority. Rather, it is precisely and only in the differentiation of the sexes that a complementarity between equal but different persons can lead to mutual fulfillment.

Since Paul himself, in 1 Corinthians 11:7-9, appealed directly to Genesis 1 and 2, it is appropriate that we review those passages. For in Gen. 1:27 it is very clear that it is not just male, but male and female, that are created in the image of God. "So God created man in his own image; in the image of God He created him, male and female He created them" (Gen. 1:27). To view woman as the "glory of man" is hardly to demean her, or to detract from the central Yahwist affirmation that both men and women are made in the image of God.

The issue is further clarified by looking more closely at the Hebrew word that is often translated "helper," or "help." For Eve was created, it is said, as Adam's helper (*ezer*). But *ezer* does not imply the low status or demeaning role that is often attached to the English word *helper*. For in Psalm 33:20, the same word *ezer* ("helper") is used to describe God as our helper. Elsewhere the Psalmist wrote: "Blessed is he whose help [*ezer*] is the God of Jacob" (Ps. 146:5). This is the same word that was used to speak of Eve. *Helper* does not in this case suggest an inferior order of dignity, or subordinate status, but a relation of mutuality and complementarity.

The quality of this complementarity is most accurately stated in 1 Corinthians, chapter 11: In communion with Christ, "woman is as essential to man as man to woman. If woman was made out of man, it is through woman that man now comes to be" (v. 12). The heart of the issue is whether men are more necessary to women than women are to men. According to Paul, they are equally necessary to each other, and God is equally necessary for both. If, in the case of one man, woman was made out of man, it should also be remembered, notes Paul, that all other men radically depend upon woman for their very being, their very coming to be. Here we have a powerful image of sexual complementarity that has a great potential impact upon understanding the office of ministry, ironically found right at the heart of one of the passages most often quoted to show sexual subordination. How, we ask, can the office of ministry be a fully representative office in the church unless it represents that complementarity of humanity through both male and female ministers?

This is why the deeper stratum of Pauline thought is far better expressed in Gal. 3:28 where Paul had been talking about the law as a kind of tutor or custodian to train and instruct and guard us until Christ comes, through whom we are justified by faith. Now through faith, he says, you all are "baptized in the union with him" (Gal. 3:27). He immediately reflects on the implications of this union for the tragic aspect of human social divisions, including that between men and women. "You have all put on Christ as a garment. There is no such thing as Jew and Greek, slave and freeman, male and female; for you are all one person in Christ Jesus" (v. 28). For those who belong to Christ live in a new creation that transcends the categories of oppression, self-justification, boasting, unjust subordination, and dominance of one person over another. These are cultural-historical antipathies that were thought by Paul to be outmoded by the love of God in Jesus Christ.

The Marian Analogy

Some have argued against women's ordination on the grounds that Mary is the unchanging pattern of the general ministry of women. The analogy is that Mary as mother is the model for the general ministry of women, whereas Jesus and the apostles, all being male, are models for ordained ministry. Yet how awkward and forced is that analogy. Strictly read, it leaves women without children in an untenable position. Furthermore, it is disproportionately applicable to the general ministry of women. For there is no comparable analogy proposed for the general (lay) ministry of men.

This otherwise disarming analogy seems to be true in what it affirms and false in what it denies. For Mary, indeed, is properly a key model not only for the general ministry of women, but of men as well. She has been celebrated for almost twenty centuries as the epitome of eschatological hope, prayer, and faithfulness. Furthermore, she is celebrated as an incomparably good mother. Good motherly care is of such great importance to human well-being and future happiness that one might even be inclined to rejoice with the writer of 1 Timothy 2:11–15 that women are especially gifted through the bearing of children—men can not bear children, a fact that has moral and religious significance, so much so that it seemed plausible to conclude that it is through the quality of a woman's faith and hope and holiness and modesty in the bearing of children that special gifts of the Spirit are being given and received. So crucial is this task that the salvation of the person to whom it is committed cannot be viewed as separable from it (v. 15). All this can be proportionally affirmed without disproportionally denying that women are capable of serving holy orders.

If one hastily presses the argument in the direction that childbearing is the one and only essential ministry of women, which is far more than our text suggests, then it is all the more difficult to square with other texts of the New Testament on ministry. For never is childbearing even mentioned among the various lists of spiritual gifts, either in Ephesians or Corinthians. One would assume that if childbearing in itself were of such importance in the order of salvation, it would at least have received some mention somewhere among the lists of charismata.

Given the socio-economic assumptions about women in the first century, however, is it not reasonable to expect that faithful, baptized women, fully participating in the body of Christ should think of their tasks of childbearing and child nurture to be central to their general ministry and their participation in the mission of Christ? That needs to be affirmed without denying that women can share in sacred ministry.

The Scandal of Particularity

Some argue that women cannot be ministers because Christ himself was male. That is a fact, but what it signifies is the scandal of God's coming to us personally in a particular time and place. For if God is to come into history as an individual human being, it must be either in the form of a man or a woman—for it is not possible for a single human being to be both.

Given the cultural setting in which God chose, oddly enough, to come into history as a child of a poor family, set amid the hopes and historical expectations of a particular people, the Incarnate Lord had to be either male or female. There is no third way to be a human being. It was admittedly a distinctly patriarchal history into which the saving deed of God appeared. Then, it was widely assumed that the hoped-for messiah would be male. It would have been an even more incredible surprise than Christmas already is if God had come to the Jews as a woman. That is hardly beyond the competence of God, and indeed it is a significant meditation in speculative theology to reflect on the consequences of a female incarnation. Males in ministry should not too quickly dismiss such questions.

The central scandal of Christian revelation is that the holy God chose to become known personally in a particular time and place (Kierkegaard, 1850, 79 ff.), through an individual human being who lived out of a particular history, the people of Israel in the period of Caesar Augustus. In line with the expectations of Israel, the promised one appeared through the male line of Jesse, consistent with prophetic hopes. We can not thereby conclude that there is an absolute necessity that God's self-disclosure must, therefore, have been in the male line. Rather that it occurred through the male line is a remembered event of salvation history, another scandal of particularity, which Christians the world over celebrate at Christmastide.

We have no warrant to conclude that God is male. Even though male images are frequently used in Scripture to speak of God, female images are also used (as in Isa. 49:15 and 66:11–13). Luke 15:8–10 likens the redemptive God to a woman who sweeps the house looking for a lost coin, and when she finds it she calls her neighbors together to rejoice. In one of his moments of highest pathos, Jesus used a feminine image of God as he addressed the city of Jerusalem: "The city that murders the prophets and stones the messengers sent to her! How often have I longed to gather your children, as a hen gathers her brood under her wings" (Luke 13:34–35). But that does not mean that God is female. Rather it means that personalistic, anthropomorphic language is happily employed to talk about the personal love of God, the care and anger of God, the frustration and empathy of God who transcends all human emotions. If we did not have such personalistic imagery, Scripture would be the worse for it because it would narrow its speech to objectifying, descriptive, impersonal language (Augustine, *LCC*, vol. 6, pp. 73 ff.).

Indeed, Jesus was male and not female. But he was also Jewish and not gentile, born in Palestine and not Norway. He is also of Davidic descent and not of some other family descent. All of these dimensions of Jesus' identity are connected with his role in the fulfillment of the messianic promises of God to Israel (Athanasius, *LCC,* vol. 3, pp. 87 ff.). Similarly, when Jesus gathered together his twelve disciples as an analogy to the tribes of Israel, if the analogy was to be consistent and credible to Jewish hearers, the symbolic twelve would most likely be Jewish free men. Given the prevailing cultural assumptions, it would have been far more difficult for twelve women to have understandably symbolized the unity of Israel.

There remains no compelling theological reason why women should be viewed as incapable of ministerial orders. Rather, there is every reason to believe that the deeper intention of the gospel is to bring men and women into a full relationship of mutuality, complementarity, covenant love, and self-sacrificial giving that is not well represented by the super- and subordination motifs. Our English translations of words like *headship* and *helper* have given us the impression that super- and subordination are normative in the earliest Christian tradition, an error long due for correction.

Article thirty-four among the Anglican Articles of Religion wisely reminds us that we should not confuse matters of faith with time-conditioned, culturally-determined matters of social custom: "It is not necessary that traditions and ceremonies be in all places one, or utterly alike; for at all times they have been divers, and may be changed according to the diversity of countries, towns, and . . . manners."

The exclusion of women from orders is not to be found in any of the early Christian confessions. It is not an article of the Apostles'

Creed, it is not mentioned in the Nicene Creed, and it was never asserted as *regula fide.*

Women may be equipped physiologically and psychically to do some
tasks of ministry better than men. With a different hormonal structure
that elicits differently nuanced patterns of responsiveness, women may
be more natively gifted in empathy. It may be that some of the nurturing responses implied in the pastoral metaphor may come more easily
for women, whose culturally conditioned chemistry promotes deep and
sustained caring. This is all the more probably the case in the context of
parishioners faced with miscarriage, childbirth, mastectomy, hysterecto-
my, and menopause, where men may have less access to the felt dynamics of feminine psychology. We say "may" in each of the above
statements, hoping that further experience and research will yield more
reliable conclusions in these areas.

Full participation in the sacramental life by both women and men
will better symbolize to the worshiping church the full humanity that
Christ intends for us all. Clergy leadership will come from a larger pool
of competent people. The shepherding image is a parenting image, just
as applicable to women as men, and perhaps even more so. In the human past, women have cared for flocks just as often and well as men.
Women who have been socialized and acculturated to cooperate and
nurture rather than to compete and dominate will profoundly affect
the future of Christian ministry. Little will be taken away from ministry
except its barriers.

God the Spirit is working in our time particularly to call women into
significant ordained ministries, gifted ministries that will affect the life
and the ethos of the church in many positive ways in the years to come.

REFERENCES AND FURTHER READING

For various views of the role of women and the issues of women's ordination, see Tertullian (d. ca. 220), Cyprian (d. 253), Athanasius (*LCC*, vol. 3, pp.
87 ff.), Augustine (*LCC*, vol. 6, pp. 73 ff.), Jerome (d. 420), *Apostolic Constitutions*
(*ANF*, vol. 7, pp. 429–432), Calvin (*Commentaries*, vol. 20, pp. 350 ff.), Hooker
(1594–1618), Teresa of Avila (d. 1582), Newman (1845, chap. 5; 1864, pp. 15
ff.), Palmer (1846), Willard (1889), Gibson (1911), Turner (1919), Leenhardt
(1948), Thrall (1954), Rengstorf (1954), Bliss (1954), Kierkegaard (1844b), Ryrie (1958), Bailey (1959), Brunner (1960), Kähler (1960, 1962), Danielou
(1961), Leipoldt (1962), World Council of Churches (1964, 1966), Hodgson
(1966), Stendhal (1966), *Women and Ordained Ministry* (1966), *Women and Holy
Orders* (1966), Lampe (1967a), Beckwith (1969), Boucher (1969), Lewis (1971),
Thomas (1971–72), Scroggs (1972), Myers (1972), Bruce and Duffield (1972),
Daly (1973), Hewitt and Hiatt (1973), Mascall (1973), Trible (1973), Reuther,
ed. (1974), Feuillet (1974–75), Jewitt (1975), Walker (1975), Wilson (1975), Trible (1976), Scroggs (1976), Graham (1976), Wyngaards (1977), Montefiori
(1978), Oepke (*TDNT*), Rowe (1980), and Jewett (1980).

II

THE PASTORAL OFFICE

5. Shepherding as Pivotal Analogy

The Christian minister has been called by many names and viewed under widely varied analogies. Each of the following titles reveals implicit expectations that the community of faith has toward ministry:

- *Parson* emphasizes the notion of the minister as embodying the person ("parson") or soul of the community before God in prayer.
- *Elder* points to the dimension of maturity and experience in the guidance of the church. Often carrying the connotation of "teaching elder" or "ruling elder."
- A *curate* is one who has a "cure" ("care of souls," or *cura animarum,* in a parish), a curacy.
- *Preacher* is a characteristically American usage that stresses the publicly declared Word and evangelical witness as a central function of the pastoral office.
- *Priest* places sacramental acts at the center of ministry, stressing the mediation of divine grace through appointed means and the representation of the people before God in intercessory prayer.
- *Minister* suggests that service is crucial to all other aspects of the work of clergy.
- *Evangelist* stresses the itinerant ministry of proclamation of the Word.
- *Clergy* (root word: *clerk*) emphasizes the clerkly skills and learning that were and are still expected of ministers. A cleric, in medieval times, was one educated in church law and prepared to officiate in pastoral services. In medieval usage, to have "benefit of the clerical office" meant to have benefit of education.
- *Reverend* or *the Reverend* (from *reverendus,* "worthy of being revered") is an epithet of respect applied to clergy since the fifteenth

century, preferably used with the definite article—"the Reverend" —and often prefixed to the name in correspondence.
- *Chaplain* (from *chapel*) is a minister who conducts services in a chapel of a public institution, and is often used to refer to military, hospital, or various institutional ministries.

Persons in ministry should not be surprised to be addressed by any one of these designations. They express common expectations of ministry. Each reveals different dimensions of the central, unifying biblical image of ministry: pastor (Gregory, *ACW*, vol. 11, pp. 22 ff.). This is why we call our subject matter pastoral theology rather than clerical theology or priestly theology or preaching theology. For "pastoral theology" best summarizes and encompasses all other functions and expectations.

Our purpose now is to define the basic idea of the pastor, relying heavily upon bibilical images and themes to inform a systematic definition of this pivotal concept. It is not likely that we will be able to rethink the nature of pastoral identity and show its correlation with pastoral activities (a central goal of this book) unless we have first suitably defined the concept of pastor.

What Is a Pastor?

Christian ministry is energized by the pivotal conviction that Christ himself ordained and established the pastoral office for the edification and guidance of the church. Christ intended that our current ministries continue to embody his own ministry to the world. Christ promised that his own presence would sustain and nourish the church and remain with it to the end of time (Matt. 20:28; Augustine, *NPNF* 1st, vol. 3, pp. 347 ff., 369 ff.).

If we are to form a clear conception of Christian ministry, we do not first turn inward and begin in a highly individualistic way to ask how we feel about it this moment, as if that would make all the difference. For we may feel differently tomorrow. Nor do we turn to public opinion polls to obtain a proper definition of ministry. Rather, we ask how Christ's own ministry may enliven, empower, and sanctify our own acts of ministry (Clement of Rome, *ANF*, vol. 1, pp. 16 ff. Origen, *ANF*, vol. 4, pp. 595 f.). If we independently attempted to define ministry apart from Christ's ministry, we would be like thirsty leaves cut off from the branch (John 15:1–5). "If the blind lead the blind, both shall fall into the ditch" (Matt. 15:14).

"The pastor," concisely defined, is a member of the body of Christ who is called by God and the church and set apart by ordination representatively to proclaim the Word, to administer the sacraments, and to guide and nurture the Christian community toward full response to God's self-disclosure (cf. Gregory, *ACW*, vol. 11, pp. 25 ff., Calvin, *Inst.*, 3.20, 4.3, 4.9).

The pastoral office is thereby technically distinguished from those aspects of the Levitical priesthood that involved animal sacrifices and ceremonial laws no longer required in Christian ministry (*Apostolic Constitutions, ANF*, vol. 7, p. 409; Calvin *Inst.*, 4.14). The pastor is also distinguished from a candidate (or postulant, licentiate, or probationary member) who has not yet been invested with the office of pastor. Even the external view of the sociological observer can see that ordination is the rite that distinguishes pastors from others (Chemnitz, 1593, pp. 36 f.). Following ordination, the office of pastor is solemnly entrusted to the individual who has been called and examined.

Is Shepherding a Fit Analogy for Contemporary Society?

Are modern writers correct to suspect (along with A. Harnack, 1896; R. Bultmann, 1941; C. Wise, 1951; and others) that "modern man" is estranged from the meaning of such premodern images as shepherding and can hardly understand their force? This view may have sold short the capacity of the modern imagination. For modern secularized persons have retained a deep hunger for natural, rural, pastoral images. This is evident from our continued fascination with ecological and pastoral themes such as the wilderness, natural foods, endangered species, and organic gardening.

Rather then prematurely rule out pastoral images as meaningless to modern consciousness, we do better to listen carefully to them so as to ask how they resonate vitally with contemporary human aspirations. Listen intently to the contemporaneity of the shepherding analogy in John 10:1–18:

- The intimacy of the shepherd's knowledge of the flock. He holds them in his arms.
- The way the shepherd calls each one by its own name.
- The shepherd does not, like the thief or robber, climb in the pen by some unusual means, but enters properly by the gate, being fully authorized to do so.
- The flock listen to the shepherd's voice. They distinguish it from all other voices.
- The shepherd leads them out of the protected area into pastures known to be most fitting—feeding them, leading them "out and back in."
- The shepherd characteristically is "out ahead" of them, not only guiding them, but looking out, by way of anticipation, for their welfare.
- Trusting the shepherd, the sheep are wary of an unproven stranger who might try to lead them abruptly away from the one they have learned to trust, through a history of fidelity.
- Jesus is recalled as the incomparably good shepherd who is willing to lay down his life for the sheep.

- The good shepherd is contrasted with the hireling or temporary worker who, having little at stake, may be prone to run away when danger approaches.
- All members of the flock of which Jesus is the shepherd are one, united by listening to his voice.

Who is to say that ordinary modern people cannot grasp such powerful, moving, straightforward images? It is demeaning to modern people to suggest that these words are beyond their grasp. Furthermore, these images apply to women as well as men. We are well served by a central image of ministry that is nurturant, life-enabling, and noncombative except in extreme emergency, when the sheep are endangered. Modern stereotypes that portray shepherds always as males fail to grasp the fact that in primitive pastoral societies, women as often as men were active in caring for valued animals, the source of wealth in nomadic families.

This is the vocation of the pastor: to know the parish territory, its dangers, its green meadows, its steep precipices, its seasons and possibilities. The pastor leads the flock to spring water and safe vegetation. The flock recognize their own good through the shepherd's voice. They do not see it in their interest to follow strangers. They know their own shepherd will not mislead them. The shepherd is able to anticipate their needs in advance and is willing to deal with each one individually.

This is no incidental, take-it-or-leave-it image for ministry. Consistently it remains the overarching analogy under which all descriptions and functions of ministry tend to be embraced: the good pastor, whose vigilant caring is an expression of Christ's own eternal caring. Other important images of ministry, such as teacher, overseer, liturgist, elder, or priest, became infused with special significance by analogy to good shepherding.

Pastor is our central paradigm. It is one that does not limit or demean, but enhances, centers, and extends the meaning of other ancillary images. The Greek word for shepherd is *poimēn*. This is why pastoral theology is sometimes technically called poimenics, or the systematic study of the office and functions of the *poimēn*-pastor-shepherd.

Picture the shepherd patiently moving ahead, but not too far ahead, of the sheep—calming and at times entertaining them with music, gently guiding them to green pastures beside still waters. The figure of shepherd was so widely imprinted on the minds of the people of biblical times that it needed no elaboration. Anyone knew the difference between a good shepherd and one who was untrustworthy, one who might abandon the sheep when they were endangered or miss out on the best pastures (Gregory Nazianzus, *NPNF* 2nd, vol. 7, pp. 255 ff.). The good shepherd gently leads those that are with young, carrying lambs in his bosom (Isa. 40:11), combining vigilance and courage with tenderness and trust. This pivotal analogy decisively informs the unique notion of authority in Christian ministry.

The Paradox of Pastoral Authority: Leadership as Service

The shepherd is not without authority, but it is of a special sort. The shepherd's authority is based on competence grounded in mutuality, yet this authority requires accurate empathy to be properly empowered. Pastoral authority is not primarily a coercive authority, such as that of a judge or a policeman, but rather an authority based on covenant fidelity, caring, mutuality, and the expectation of empathic understanding (Gregory, *ACW*, vol. 11, Part 2).

This conception of authority has a christological base in the minds of Christian believers. From where else did Christianity learn this unusual view of authority? It is precisely from the servant messiah that we learn of the paradoxical unity of dignity and service. It is from the true God, true man, who though he was rich became poor for our sakes (2 Cor. 8:9), "who, though he was in the form of God, did not count equality with God a thing to be grasped but emptied himself, taking the form of a servant, being born in the likeness of men. And being found in human form, he humbled himself and became obedient unto death, even death on a cross" (Phil. 2:6–8, RSV). The pattern of authority is that of the incarnate Lord, who expressed in a single, unified ministry the holiness of God amid the alienations of the world, the incomparable power of God that was surprisingly made known in an unparalleled way amid crucifixion and resurrection.

Wherever Christians speak of authority or dignity of ministry or headship of the shepherd, these are not properly understood as coercive modes of power, but persuasive, participative modes of benevolent, empathic guidance. This is an extraordinarily complex, subtle, and highly nuanced conception of authority, but it is intimately familiar to those who love Christ and listen for his voice. The proper authority of ministry is not an external, manipulative, alien power that distances itself from those "under" it, but rather a legitimized and happily received influence that wishes only good for its recipient, a leadership that boldly guides but only on the basis of a deeply empathic sense of what the flock yearns for and needs. The analogy of shepherd was not promiscuously or thoughtlessly chosen by Jesus as the centerpiece of ministry, but wells up from the heart of God's own ministry to the world.

The pastoral office implies a clearly definable distinction between the laity (general ministry) and clergy (ordained ministry). The difference is based not on supposed moral superiority or political expediency, but upon the inward call of God to representative service, outwardly confirmed by the whole church in ordination. Laity and clergy are alike in faith, hope, and love. They are equally justified, and both stand in need of the sanctifying power of the Spirit. The difference between clergy and laity cannot be adequately accounted for in the language of superior and subordinate. Rather, it awaits the sensitive application of intimate interpersonal analogies like those of shepherding, nurturing, and empathic caring that intrinsically respect the latent potentialities of the recipient.

Any time ministerial leadership or authority is asserted as a bald, coercive power over against the will of the recipient, it has already become alienated from the interpersonal analogies that show evidence of its deeper participation in the body of Christ. This is why external political authority differs from Christ's noncoercive authority and the inward authority of Christ's ministry (Augustine, *NPNF* 1st, vol. 2, pp. 284 ff.). For the legitimate authority of the pastor is by definition interwoven with the serving role (Clement of Rome, *ANF* vol. 1, pp. 16 ff.).

What is the Christ-shaped center of this correlation? Embedded squarely in the very word-root of ministry is the undergirding idea of service (*diakonia*). No well-conceived view of the pastoral office can ever set aside or leave behind this basic diaconal pattern: serving God through service to the neighbor. Diakonia is an essential layer of every theory, grade, or proper definition of ministry. Every *presbuteros* ("elder," "priest," "presbyter") is the first of all and unremittingly *diakonos* ("servant," "deacon"). In becoming presbuteros one does not ever cease being deacon. The diaconate is not transcended but extended and embodied in so-called higher offices like elder or bishop. The service of liturgy remains a serving role. The minister as steward of God's mysteries transmutes the idea of temporal accountability. The visiting of the sick and needy is a service that meets Christ concretely through the needy neighbor. Leadership itself is thought to be a service that enables others to use their gifts more effectively for the church and the world.

There is no office of ministry that can properly abandon the role of diakonia. Despite good intentions, some secularized equalitarian thinking has prematurely viewed the image of servant as demeaning, treating serving as if it were by definition degrading. Yet no image is more central to describing the pastor than that of serving. This vocation is uniquely determined by the redemptive self-giving of the Servant-Messiah, who said: "I am among you as one who serves" (Luke 22:27, RSV). Preaching itself is intrinsically an exposition of the serving role, for "it is not ourselves that we proclaim; we proclaim Jesus Christ as Lord, and ourselves as your servants, for Jesus' sake" (2 Cor. 4:5).

Reductionism and Triumphalism: Twin Errors, Modern and Ancient

There are two distorted directions in which the pastoral task may become misunderstood: modern reductionism and archaic triumphalism. Both misplace the paradoxical core definition of ministry as pastoral service.

Reductionism, the characteristically modern misjudgment about ministry, attempts to reduce the essence of ministry to a human social function or the philosophical insight or to moral teaching or to psychological counseling or to political change advocacy. These views diminish the pastoral office by failing to see its distinctive self-understanding, its divine commission, its Spirit-led calling, its dependence upon revelation, and its accountability to apostolic faith. The tension is lost between the divine calling and the life of the world by viewing divine calling as being socially determined and dissecting it as a quantifiable object. Reductionism dilutes the ministry of the incarnation to its fleshly side by reducing it to quirks of parenting or social determination.

Indeed there remains something valuable even about this truncated view of ministry, however imbalanced. For it is true that the good pastor functions as philosophical guide and psychological counselor and social change agent and moral mentor at various times. Historically and in the present, such guidance has been sought from pastors by many persons who hunger for the wisdom of historical Christian experience. But when these are disconnected from their historical identity and tradition and from the history of revelation and the capacity of God to address the heart, they easily become too cheaply accommodative to the present culture and lose the finely balanced judgment that the tradition has called wisdom.

Admittedly, the pastor is friend to many, even as Jesus was friend to many, expressing through ordinary human relationships the extraordinary love of God. But reductionism makes the mistake of seeing this friendship purely by analogy to human friendship, rather than through the lens of the divine-human friendship. The reductionism that sees ministry only as objectifiable sociological or psychological phenomena is not wrong, it only needs to be placed in a larger context and evaluated in terms of a more basic norm. When the divine and human sides are held together, ministry can be seen more wholly as human response to divine gift, a beautiful amalgam of graced nature and naturally embodied grace.

Triumphalism, the opposite distortion of ministry, is a habit more characteristic of premodern consciousness. It loses track of the human, finite side of ministry in the interest of inordinately stressing its divine origin and eternal purpose. It is more prone to allow ministry to be elevated to a privileged caste or an exclusive sacerdotal order. Instead of being set apart for representative service, ministry may become separated from the people as something over against them, alien to their here-and-now world and hence perceived as irrelevant. The tension is lost between the holy calling and the ordinary spheres it is called to serve.

This distortion misplaces human friendship in ministry in the interest of disproportionately asserting the divine companionship. It dilutes the ministry of the incarnation by ignoring the finite, temporal instruments of the divine will. This is the point at which classical Protestantism complained about medieval, sacerdotal conceptions of ministry, wherein priesthood had itself become trapped in the subtle or overt management of power and prestige, amid its well-intended attempt to mediate between God and people. Ironically, Protestantism itself later fell into the same trap in different guise (Troeltsch, 1931, vol. 2).

There remains something legitimate even about the triumphalist, sacerdotal view of an elevated priesthood, in that it rightly stresses the priority of the divine commission, recalling that ministry is a divinely instituted office for the feeding of the vulnerable body of Christ in a hazardous world, that the holy should never be mistaken for the temporal, and that the church is not reducible to the world. However legitimate these emphases may be, the triumphalist excess has tempted priesthood to become inwardly turned toward its own self-importance and thus separated from the *laos* as if it were intrinsically superior, to the neglect of engaged service in the life of the world.

In both of these misconceptions of pastoral authority there is a distortion of the essential idea of ministry: holy calling amid the life of the world (Gregory, *ACW,* vol. 11, p. 62).

How Is Pastoral Authority Consistent with Pastoral Servanthood?

The valid aspects of these two competing sets of images for ministry are fittingly combined under the incarnational analogy. For there is a perennial tension between these two sets of terms:

episkopos	*diakonos*
overseer	steward
headship	sonship
presbuteros	*doulos*
elder	servant

It is unique to Christian ministry that these two sets of terms be held in constantly interfacing tension, as if they belonged together under a unifying, sense-making analogy. The sense, of course, is made by seeing them in relation to the incarnation. The holy God enters our sphere as servant. The high God becomes lowly (Kierkegaard, 1850). God the Father shares our sordid history as God the Son, becoming flesh, sharing our suffering, even unto death. Similarly, our ministry gratefully received its holy calling not for itself but for redemptive engagement in the life of the world.

The excessive reduction of minister to friend, social promoter, philosophical guide, or political activist links hand in glove with the familiar Ebionite christological heresy that affirms Christ as *vere homo* but not *vere deus*. The Christology that misses the holiness of Christ will also misplace the holiness of Christ's ministry.

On the other hand, a one-sided Christology that so stresses Christ's divinity that his humanity is misplaced, will probably be unconsciously linked with an ecclesiology that sees only the oversight, the dignity, the authority of the pastoral office and misses the servant task. The triumphalist excess is intrinsically akin to the Docetic heresy, which never has felt comfortable with the scandalous idea that God became flesh, or "dwelt among us" in person.

These two mistaken exaggerations about ministry are corrected by the apostolic teaching that Jesus is truly God and truly human (Council of Chalcedon, *NPNF* 2nd, vol. 14, pp. 262–265). Ecclesiology follows Christology. "Among you whoever wants to be great must be your servant [*diakonos*], and whoever wants to be first must be the willing slave [*doulos*] of all. Like the Son of Man, he did not come to be served [*dikonēthēnia*], but to serve [*diakonēsai*], and to give up his life as a ransom for many" (Matt. 20:26).

The perennial problem of the theory and practice of pastoral authority is to keep these two tendencies in proper tension, as did Paul, who did not hesitate to assert the authority of his pastoral office under the bold analogy of ambassadorship, yet gently mixed this with diaconal images of servanthood, reconciliation, *kenōsis*, and hospitality to strangers. In this way ministry is both sent and called, both commissioned by Christ himself and called to visit prisons and clothe the naked. It is both an ambassadorship from God and a service to humanity. If not held in the closest integration, the whole idea of the pastoral office easily becomes twisted toward either reductionism or triumphalism through misconceiving its inner determination through Christ.

The Natural Foundation of the Pastoral Office

Pastor is hardly an important term for religious leadership in Judaism, Islam, Buddhism, and other major world religions. It does not even appear as a topic in the *Jewish Encyclopedia* or the *Encyclopedia of Islam,* and it is difficult to find any mention of it in most standard reference works of the great non-Christian religious traditions. Although it has richly symbolic Jewish roots, its core definition has been principally hammered out in Christian experience.

Nonetheless, there are many analogies borrowed from nature, general anthropology, and the history of religion that have fed into Christian understanding of the pastor. These overlapping analogies appear in many religious traditions. Thus, before proceeding further into biblical teachings and instructions on the pastoral office, it is appropriate to ask to what extent the Christian pastoral office is a response to natural or societal impulses, energies, or needs found generally throughout human social experience, rather than the outcome specifically of a community of faith grounded in historical revelation.

The Christian life is a response to God's self-disclosure in history, rather than to naturalistic impulses. But, according to Jewish and Christian Scripture, that does not rule out the ways in which God may use physical hungers, natural or instinctual drives, or social processes as means through which to make the divine will known. Grace works through nature to fulfill the divine purpose. This is an elementary point of most early Christian theologians. Augustine, Thomas Aquinas, and Calvin all taught that there is a natural capacity in the human mind and spirit (however distorted by sin) to hunger for and desire anticipatively to receive God's revelation.

It would not then be unreasonable to hypothesize that this elemental hunger for God engenders religious communities. It is in fact extremely rare in human history to find a society in which the need to pray does not manifest itself socially and institutionally. When politically suppressed, this hunger often emerges with all the more determination.

Search the most varied historical situations for human social institutions that have a claim to universality. Tradition-bearing religious leadership appears to be among the most general. Why not, given the importance of this social function? Like totems, tribal identities, language, and the ordering of sexuality, it appears that communities of prayer with deliberately chosen religious leadership are deeply expressive of hungers intrinsic to human experience. So commonly is this found that one is tempted to conclude that wherever there are human beings one is likely to find religious institutions with traditioned leadership that provides spiritual counsel, shamanistic insight, healing, prophetic witness, or priestly intercession, or some combination of these.

Human passions create social processes. The deeper the passion, the more inevitable the social process. Just as the passion for food, shelter, and services creates economies, or the passion for order and relative justice creates governments, so there appears to be some deep, underlying divinely elicited passion that continues to create communities of prayer and the social apparatus to guide them spiritually. So even if the history of revelation were to be set aside temporarily, so as to view humanity abstractly without it, there remains a general human need for religious shepherding and guidance toward moral self-understanding. This is the natural basis of the office of pastor that reductive naturalism may tend to exaggerate as sole cause.

The human need for spiritual guidance has not diminished in the modern so-called secularized period, despite much premature speculation to the contrary. The priestly role is as alive today in Marxist Poland or high-tech Japan or rapidly changing central Africa as at any time in history. To know our modern selves accurately is to know that we too need to be meaningfully shepherded into God's presence or, at least, moral clarity. That requires a well-instructed, trustworthy guide and system of guidance. Our deepening modern awareness of our moral inadequacies only intensifies our need for surer guidance through the hazards of modernity. The increase of objectively accessible data and scientific knowledge and technological know-how also increases the chances for moral mismanagement. Those who expected the pastoral function to be quietly phased out by technology have not grasped the inner moral meaning of the microchip, which packs both the potential threats and the potential promises of technology into tiny circuitry.

Inevitably, the passion for spiritual direction finds ways of recognizing itself and organizing itself, and it eventually seeks to routinize itself in canonical structures of guidance (such as scriptures and moral maxims); in due course it requires selected leaders chosen through deliberate procedures for the good of the community. This is not unique to Christianity. If historical experience be our guide, communities of prayer perennially engender social processes in which the office and duties of religious leadership become publicly exercised (Levi-Strauss, 1968, 167 ff.). Persons are carefully chosen by due process to fill roles rather than chosen haphazardly on the basis of unexamined charismatic immediacy. This social regularity does not rule out charisma, but wishes to bring native gifts of religious leadership into some more reliable, socially functional framework of expectations (Weber, 1958, pp. 245–253). Consequently, it is hoped that communities who look to that leadership will be better protected from the abuses of charlatans or manipulators who might exploit these powerful passions for their own individual interests. That is the social function of routinization and ordering of charismatic gifts.

Shepherding is thus not just an archaic image. It is as much needed amid the concrete canyons of modern urban centers as it is in the rural scenes in which its intriguing images were spawned (Berger and Neuhaus, 1976).

Christian Ministry Begins with Christ's Ministry

Christian ministry is not fully understandable merely as a sociological function based on the group's need for leadership. Nor is it reducible to a psychological function based on the unresolved inner need to care for others, as if that were a complete explanation. Rather, Christian ministry from the outset has been conceived as a continuation of Christ's own ministry. Christ is head of the church. The church celebrates Christ's capacity to discern what was subsequently to be needed for the continuation of his ministry (Clement of Rome, ANF, vol. 1, p. 16; Gregory, ACW, vol. 11, pp. 26 ff.).

From the earthly ministry of Jesus of Nazareth, we learn the rudiments of Christian ministry. Jesus' vision and practice of ministry is significant for all Christian vision and practice of ministry. If ministry cannot be clearly established as the continuation of Jesus' own intention and practice, we lose its central theological premise.

By both teaching and example, Jesus left the church a highly suggestive, if not explicitly developed, conception of ministry. He himself personally addressed and called individuals into discipleship, patiently taught and nurtured them toward apostolicity despite their resistances and misconceptions, and then sent them out with the promise of his continuing presence. This sequence entered into later doctrinal formulations of the sequence leading to ministry that spoke systematically of Christ's calling, Christ's preparation, and Christ's commissioning of an ordered ministry.

- Jesus called the apostolate.

No one became one of the original disciples without first hearing Jesus' call and freely consenting to follow. Repeatedly, the synoptic gospels stress the simple, direct picture of call and response. "Jesus was walking by the Sea of Galilee when he saw two brothers, Simon called Peter and his brother Andrew, casting a net into the lake; for they were fishermen. Jesus said to them, 'Come with me, and I will make you fishers of men.' And at once they left their nets and followed him" (Matt. 4:18–20). Ministry today still begins with attentiveness to the calling of God—first to discipleship, and only on that basis to a set-apart ministry.

- Jesus prepared the apostolate.

The call should not be exaggerated as the central feature of ministry, however, for it is only the first step of a long journey. Jesus did not call without detailed follow-up. The call is followed by careful instruction, personal guidance, interpersonal dialogue, and the gradual clarification of the divine purpose.

When scholastic theology came to distinguish between calling, preparation, and commission as stages of entry into ministry, it was rehearsing a pattern implicit in Jesus' own design and practice. Before sending out his apostles to proclaim the governance of God, Jesus lived closely with them, walked and talked with them, interpreted holy history and universal history to them. He himself served as example of all that he taught. His words were accompanied by remarkable deeds, healings of chronic illnesses, and the aura of finality. Jesus was not merely a theoretical instructor of pastoral practice, but one who himself embodied the pastoral touch. Only after due preparation did he send his laborers to the harvest, and then only with clear awareness that his own incomparable power would accompany them.

- Jesus commissioned the apostolate.

This sending forth emerged in several stages: first by sending the original twelve, then seventy, then many more. Their message: in Jesus' ministry, God's governance is made known. The mission began with the "lost sheep of the house of Israel" (Matt. 10:6), and would reach toward "all nations" (Luke 24:47) to the "ends of the earth" (Acts 13:47).

In this commissioning, the Fourth Gospel placed great stress on the intrinsic relation of Jesus' ministry to ours, as if Christ were the vine and we the branches (John 13). We live in Christ. Without him we are lifeless. If I imagine for a moment that I am a leaf on the tip of a high branch, I may immediately grasp how completely my life depends upon connectedness with the hidden roots that tap deep water. Apart from this relationship, we are like fallen leaves. But if we, by analogy, participate organically in the body of Christ, the root, branch, and leaf together "bear fruit in plenty" (John 15:8). Our "joy is made complete" in this fellowship with Christ, awakened by his joy in us (John 15:11).

In this, his farewell discourse, Jesus was deliberately preparing his disciples for the time when he would be with them not in body, but in Spirit. He carefully appointed persons to continue his ministry, asking them to trust that he himself would be present with them through the Spirit. Pointedly he reminded them of how they got there: "You did not choose me, I chose you. I appointed you to go and bear fruit" (John 15:16). So in calling, guiding, and appointing them, Christ promised that God's own eternal Spirit would guide then into all truth and show them things to come after the crucifixion and resurrection.

There is a poignant phrase in John 16:12 that shows deep pastoral sensitivity, when Jesus chooses not to reveal more to his disciples than they could bear. "There is still much that I could say to you, but the burden would be too great for you now." Thus from Jesus we receive a general maxim of pastoral care, that what we say in pastoral guidance has something to do with the capacity of the person to receive it in that context. You will not try to say everything you think or feel or speculate, but limit your speech to that which is "hearable."

Incarnation and Apostolicity

Jesus prayed: "As thou hast sent me into the world, I have sent them into the world" (John 17:18). A moving analogy here begins to unfold between incarnation and apostolicity, between God's engagement in the world in Christ and our engagement in the world as ambassadors for Christ. As Christ is sent by the Father into the alienated world, so are his ministers sent into the darkened world by the Son. Listen to the analogy echo: For their sake I now consecrate myself, that they too may be consecrated by the truth" (v. 19). As Jesus is stranger in the world, so will the apostles be strangers. Jesus then prays "that they may all be one" as he is one, and "that the world may believe" (v. 21). There is a stunning congruity in all this. The apostolic mission is sent from God into the world and is therefore not finally explainable in terms of the world's criteria, yet it is sent in service to the real world to proclaim the healing word, that the world may believe and be saved (Chrysostom, *NPNE* 1st, vol. 14, pp. 296–306).

The ascension narrative powerfully shows the inner connection between Jesus' ministry and ours. In the last climactic sentences of Luke's Gospel it is said that Jesus "opened their minds to understand the scriptures. 'This,' he said, 'is what is written: that the Messiah is to suffer death and to rise from the dead on the third day, and that in his name repentance bringing the forgiveness of sins is to be proclaimed to all nations. Begin from Jerusalem; it is you who are witnesses to it all. And mark this: I am sending upon you my Father's promised gift; so stay here in this city until you are armed with the power from above' " (Luke 24:45–49). There Luke ends. Acts begins. One part of the drama is over, another begins.

Jesus was everywhere remembered as one who left his disciples, after the resurrection appearances, with an unmistakably clear commission. Christian ministry still serves under that commission (Augustine, *NPNF* 1st, vol. 7, p. 42). The closing sentences of Matthew's Gospel state the authorization to ministry unequivocally: "Full authority in heaven and on earth has been committed to me. Go forth therefore and make all nations my disciples; baptize . . . everywhere in the name of the Father and the Son and the Holy Spirit, and teach them to observe all that I have commanded you. And be assured, I am with you always, to the end of time" (Matt. 28:18–20).

We may debate the details of how these oral traditions were transmitted, who remembered what, when, and why—all legitimate questions for historical research. But the church's memory is clear that Jesus' ministry necessarily elicits and funds a continuing apostolic ministry (Clement of Rome, *ANF*, vol. 1, pp. 16–20). The divine command to preach, baptize, and teach in Christ's name relying upon his presence is the ground floor of pastoral theology and the practice of ministry. Take away the Lord's command, and the living presence to which it witnesses, and we have little upon which to build any significant idea of Christian ministry.

REFERENCES AND FURTHER READING

Classical texts defining the pastoral office include Clement of Rome (*ANF*, vol. 1, pp. 16 ff.), Ignatius (d. ca. 107), Hermas (fl. 140), Tertullian (d. ca. 220), Origen (*ANF*, vol. 4, pp. 595 ff.), Cyprian (d. 253), *Apostolic Constitutions* (*ANF*, vol. 7), *Seven Ecumenical Councils* (*NPNF* 2nd, vol. 14), Basil (d. 379), Gregory Nazianzus (d. 389), Gregory of Nyssa (d. 394), John Chrysostom (before 392), Augustine (d. 430), John Cassian (d. 435), Gregory the Great (d. 604), Thomas Aquinas (*ST* vol. 3, pp. 2563 ff.), Luther (*LW*, vol. 40), Zwingli (d. 1531, 1905 ed., vol. 3, pp. 1 ff.), Calvin (1559, 4.3, 4.9), Chemnitz (1593, pp. 36 ff.). The office and duties of the pastor were the subject of active study in the seventeenth century, notably by Herbert (1652), Taylor (d. 1667), Baxter (d. 1691), Burnet (1692), Patrick (1692), Sprat (1695). Works on the pastoral office by Gibson (1717), Mather (d. 1728), Roques (1741), Hort (1742), Mieg (1747), Bengel (d. 1752), and J. Smith (1798) were followed by many nineteenth-century pastoral writers: Haas (1812), Köster (1827), Hoffman (1829), Alexander (1834), Haas (1834), Macher (1838), Barrett (1839), Meade (1849), Kierkegaard (1850), Oxendem (1857), R. Smith, (1859), Tying (1874), How (1883), Achelis (1889), Jensen (1895), and Upham (1898).

This century's studies of the pastoral office include McClure (1904), Inskip (1905), Quayle (1910), Beebe (1923), Adams (1932), Burgon (1883), Owens (1935), Pleune (1943), Blackwood (1945), Wise (1951), Sommerlath (1951), Münter (1955), Schillebeeckx (1969), Brandon (1972), Nouwen (1972), Berger and Neuhaus (1976), Wagner (1976), and Newbigin (1977).

Studies of the shepherding analogy and its biblical roots may be found in Jefferson (1912), Temple, (1939–40), Kempfe (1942), Quasten (1948), Thompson (1955), Robinson (1955), Hiltner (1959), Birdsall (1960), Eichrodt (1961 ed.), Schmidt (1964), Tooley (1964), Bultmann (1952), Derrett (1973), Bauer (*EBT*, vol. 3 pp. 444 ff.), and Jeremias (*TNDT*, vol. 6, 485 ff.).

Monographs on the work of the Christian minister and the purposes of ministry include Dodwell (1672), Hartmann (1678), Sailer (1788), Wayland (1863), Hoppin (1869), Vilmar (1870), Watson (1898), Lindsay (1902), Hardeland (1907), Pattison (1907), Dykes (1909), Robertson (1911), C. R. Brown (1927), W. A. Brown (1937), Griffith-Thomas (n.d.), Oman (1936), Calkins (1941), Dakin (1944), Jenkins (1947), Neill (1947), Spann (1949), Sherrill (1949), Manson (1956), H. R. Niebuhr et al. (1956), Rodenmayer (1958), Bromiley (1960), Meyer (1963), Anderson (1979), and Lefroy (1981). For further reading on the natural analogies to the pastoral office see Van der Leeuw (1963), Levi-Strauss (1968), Wescott (1969), and Eliade (1977 ed).

Among many discussions of Jesus' view of ministry and Jesus as pastoral pattern, we note especially John Chrysostom (*NPNF* 1st, vol. 9, pp. 33 ff.), Gregory the Great (*ACW*, vol. 11), Luther (*LW*, vol. 40), A. B. Bruce (1871), Beck (1885), Kittell (1917), Manson (1931), Dodd (1936), Calkins (1942), H. R. Niebuhr (1951), Bultmann (1952), Johnston (1959–60), Schweizer (1960), Betz (1967), Pannenberg (1968), and Jeremias (1971b).

6. The Offices and Gifts of Ministry

How did the concept of pastor take firmer shape in the period following Jesus' earthly ministry? How was the office understood and shaped in response to emergent needs and crises of the primitive Christian community? How did the New Testament writers remember and interpret the available preceding oral tradition? What does the church's book, canonized Scripture, have to say about the offices and gifts of ministry?

Our purpose here is not an historical account of the development of these offices, such as that provided by R. Bultmann, J. Weiss, E. Lohse, W. Schmithals, E. Schweizer, L. Goppelt, T. W. Manson, K. H. Rengstorf, or H. D. Betz. We will focus our attention on the church's earliest written memories of its tradition, rather than on debates as to how that tradition emerged developmentally. We will give particular attention to the Pauline tradition, Luke-Acts, and the General and Pastoral Epistles.

One way to reveal the priorities implicit in the mind of the remembering church is to consider the peculiar order of the earliest events reported in Acts. We ask which of the following events occurred first, or had priority in time:

- The Spirit was poured out upon the church on the Day of Pentecost.
- Three thousand were converted by the preaching of Peter.
- Matthias was selected to continue the apostolic ministry abandoned by Judas.

The answer is revealing. Somewhat surprisingly, the last item of this auspicious list occurred first. Any other answer may have underestimated the unparalleled importance to the early church of the office of ministry, instituted to maintain the continuity of Jesus' ministry. According to Luke, the first public act of the apostles following Jesus' ascension was the apostolic commissioning of Matthias (Acts 1:15–26). Peter's first speech to the newly born ecclesia (even prior to the gifts of Pentecost) focused intently on the maintenance of the apostolic tradition through the office of ministry (*diakonia*, Acts 1:25).

The Tradition of the Choosing of Matthias

The immediate issue was who would take the place of Judas among the twelve. They had just returned from Olivet to the upper room with the eleven remaining apostles, along with "a group of women"—note carefully the continuing presence and importance of women in the company that selected Matthias in the first ordination of the postresurrection church!

Peter stood up before the assembly of about one hundred and twenty. He spoke with wrenching pathos about the apostasy of Judas who, having been chosen as one of the twelve, tragically fell away and gravely abused this trust. Peter thought that Judas' place should be filled immediately by someone who had been in their company "all the while we had the Lord Jesus with us, coming and going, from John's ministry of baptism until the day when he was taken up from us—one of those must now join us as a witness to his resurrection" (Acts 1:21–22). Two names were put forward: Joseph and Matthias. The church then earnestly interceded for divine guidance for a proper replacement: "Thou, Lord, who knowest the hearts of all . . . declare which of these two thou hast chosen to receive this office of ministry and apostleship which Judas abandoned" (vv. 24,25). Even at this point, ministry was already being clearly conceived as a definable office, intergenerationally transmitted, functionally distinguishable from (though not morally superior to), the *laos,* and gratefully received by the interceding church. After this prayer and whatever deliberation may have accompanied it, they chose according to the providence-receptive custom of taking lots to discern the divine will, and Matthias was immediately "assigned a place among the twelve" (v. 26). The premise of lot-casting (as foreshadowed by 1 Sam. 14:41) was that God had already chosen his servant, and that the community, rather than autonomously choosing, was simply trying to discern the divine choice.

This company of men and women apparently considerd it Christ's own will and design that a visible ministry be provided so as to maintain intergenerational continuity with Christ's ministry after his resurrection. Ironically, it became the first order of business in the postresurrection church (cf. Calvin, *Inst.,* 4.3.13 ff.). *Replace Judas*

THE OFFICES OF MINISTRY

It is difficult to achieve an ecumenical consensus as broad as one might wish on such a divisive issue as the offices of ministry. But we will try to follow the most central part of the stream of ecumenical tradition in viewing the offices of ministry as a threefold order of *diakonos, presbuteros,* and *episkopos.*

Diakonos

The rudiments of the office of *diakonos* may hark back as early as Jesus' Galilean ministry, when Luke says of Jesus that he was "journeying from town to town and village to village, proclaiming the good news of the kingdom of God. With him were the twelve and a number of women who had been set free from evil spirits and infirmities: Mary, known as Mary of Magdala, from whom seven devils had come out, Joanna, the wife of Chuza a steward of Herod's, Susanna, and many others. The women provided for them out of their own resources" (Luke 8:1–3).

Anyone who easily denies women a place in orders of ministry does well to think carefully about the implications of this crucial text. For here it becomes evident that quite early in Jesus' own ministry a group of women followed him faithfully at some risk. They were particularly concerned with supplying funds and material resources for his ministry. Specifically they "ministered unto him of their substance" (KJV) or "out of their possessions" (*ek tōn huparchontōn,* v. 3). The self-giving stewardship of these women may be the model for the subsequent apostolic pattern for "holding everything in common," selling "their property and possessions" to "make a general distribution as the need of each required" (Acts 2:45). Luke 8:1–3 is an amazing reference, sometimes neglected in the heated discussions on women in ministry. For it is arguable that the subsequently male-dominated office of deacon emerged by analogy with the work of these women who were inconspicuously caring for the temporal and physical needs of the twelve during Jesus' earthly ministry!

Some may imagine that the elder's orders are prior to deacon's orders, and that the diaconate is therefore dependent for its existence and interpretation upon "higher orders" of ministry. Not so. Chronologically the office of deacon predates that of elder and bishop. The sequence of events leading to the creation of the office is carefully reported in Acts 2–6.

The newborn church was meeting "constantly to hear the apostles teach, and to share the common life, to break bread, and to pray" (Acts 2:42). The primitive apostolic ministry focused on these four essential elements:

teaching (*didachē*)
fellowship (*koinōnia*)
breaking of bread (*te klasei tou artou*)
and prayers (*proseuchais*)

On this steady basis "day by day the Lord added to their number" (v. 47). But soon there were so many believers that it became necessary that other persons than the original twelve be selected and ordained to serve them.

In a short time it was decided that seven deacons, "full of the Spirit and of wisdom" (Acts 6:3), would be ordained to the task of serving the company associated with the apostles. How were the seven ordained? Luke says only that they were "presented to the apostles, who prayed and laid their hands on them" (v. 6).

The immediate shape of their original diaconal task was plain and practical: nothing more august or impressive than serving tables in order that the apostles could better devote themselves "to prayer and to the ministry of the "Word" (Acts 6:4). With this now more carefully ordered division of labor, "the Word of God now spread more and more widely; the number of disciples in Jerusalem went on increasing rapidly, and very many of the priests adhered to the Faith" (Acts 6:7).

We do well not to project simplistically on the original diaconal texts all the functions and dignities that have slowly attached themselves to the office of deacon by historical accretion. The same is true of other orders of ministry that in their origin usually had a more slender definition than they came in time to have. Granting this, it is still true that the Greek terms given to these three pastoral offices (*diakonos, presbuteros, episkopos*) carry root meanings and vivid images the energy of which still persists (cf. Ignatius, *ANF*, vol. 1, pp. 66 ff.; *Apostolic Constitutions, ANF*, vol. 7, pp. 479 ff.; *Cannon*, 1853; *Principles of Church Union*, 1966). These terms indicate less a fully normative definition of orders than a spirit or direction. This is profoundly so in the case of *diakonia*, which in Latin became *ministerium* ("empathic, personal service"). These terms were used to translate the Hebrew verb *shārath*, "serve."

The Pauline tradition offered this description of diakonos in Ephesians 3:7–9: "Such is the gospel of which I was made a minister [diakonos], by God's gift, bestowed unmerited on me in the working of his power. To me, who am less than the least of all God's people, he has granted of his grace the privilege of proclaiming to the Gentiles the good news of the unfathomable riches of Christ, and of bringing to light how this hidden purpose was to be put into effect." The pattern of the diaconate remained Jesus himself who "came not to be ministered unto, but to minister" (*diakonēsai*, Mark 10:45, KJV).

It is significant for the issue of women's ordination that the same root word for deacon also applies to women in ministry, as in Romans 16:1, where Paul commends to the Roman church Phoebe, a minister (*diakonōn*) of the church in Cenchreae (NEB: "who holds office in the congregation at Cenchreae"). The context of 1 Tim. 3:11 leaves room also for the interpretation that *gunaikas* is referring not just to women

in general or wives, but to women in ministry, "women of high principle
. . . sober and trustworthy in every way."

Presbuteros

Shortly after the ordination of the seven deacons (Acts 6:7), there
were subsequent ordinations of "elders in every church" (*kat' ekklēsian
presbuterous*, Acts 14:23—NEB: "They also appointed elders for them in
each congregation, and with prayer and fasting committed them to the
Lord"). Later, in Titus 1:5–6, the notion of elders "in each town" re-
appears: "My intention in leaving you behind in Crete was that you
should set in order what was left over, and in particular should institute
elders in each town. In doing so, observe the tests I prescribed" (cf.
Clement of Alexandria, *ANF*, vol. 2, pp. 504 ff., 523 ff.; Chrysostom,
NPNF 1st, vol. 9, pp. 45 ff.). From this follows an apparently deliberate
list of four preliminary qualifications for the office of elder:

- unimpeachable character (which makes it difficult to argue that the
  eldership has no exemplary aspects)
- sexual fidelity in marriage (from the beginning, sexual lifestyle was
  thought to impinge significantly upon ordination, and celibacy was
  not normatively assumed)
- being a good parent, "having faithful children" (if one is a parent,
  wouldn't the quality of one's parenting mirror the promise of high-
  quality caring for Christ's flock, and ability to teach and nurture an
  intergenerational community of faith and witness? [cf. Tertullian,
  ANF, vol. 3, p. 46; *Apostolic Constitutions*, *ANF*, vol. 7, p. 410;
  Chalcedon, *NPNF* 2nd, vol. 14, pp. xiv, 278 f.])
- "under no imputation of loose living" (for what elder has the right
  to risk discrediting Christian ministry there and elsewhere?)

What did these elders do? There is considerable evidence that they
exercised general pastoral guidance of a congregation: preaching,
teaching, breaking bread, and witnessing to the resurrection (cf. Clement of Rome, *ANF*, vol. 1, p. 17; Polycarp, *ANF*, vol. 1, p. 34; Ignatius,
ANF, p. 172). The Greek term we are translating "elder" is *presbuteros*. It
is variously translated as "priest," "elder," "ruler," "presbyter," or "presiding officer." It is the Greek way of referring to the presiding officer
of the Jewish synagogue, whose functions easily became transmuted
and transferred to the presiding officer or elder of the local Christian
congregation. Synagogues were governed by a council headed by a ruler, or ruling elder. The pattern of polity in the early Christian communities quite naturally followed this rabbinical model. The *zāqēn* ("elder")
of the synagogue doubtless functioned much like the *presbuteros* of the
Christian *ekklēsia* (*DNTT*, vol. 1, pp. 193 ff.).

Presbuteros was curiously shortened into the English word "priest"—
confusingly so, because "priest" also renders *hiereus*, just as priesthood

renders *heirateuma* (in Latin, *sacerdos* and *sacerdotium*), which typically did not refer to a Christian minister in the New Testament, but rather mainly to Jewish priests and the Levitical priesthood (as in Matt. 8:4, Luke 1:5,8, Luke 17:14).

In the letter to the Hebrews, Jesus Christ is viewed as the culmination of the high priesthood, as one who reconciles God and humanity, fulfilling that which had been foreshadowed by previous Jewish conceptions of sacrifice. Jesus is viewed paradoxically both as high priest and "the Lamb slain from the foundation of the world" (John 17 and Rev. 13). Through baptism the whole church shares in his priesthood. This is the core notion underlying the idea of the "priesthood of all believers," which does not refer to the priesthood of each separate believer in an individualistic sense, but of the whole church taken together as the body united in Christ. Through him we have "access to the Father in the one Spirit" (Eph. 2:18).

When the elders acted together as a body, they were called the *presbuterion* (1 Tim. 4:14). On at least one occasion Paul is said to have presided over such a presbytery (Acts 20:17 ff.). Paul had sent out a call from Miletus to gather the elders of the church in the region of Ephesus. There he sketched a poignant picture of the tasks of the ministry. He was keenly aware that his ministry was risk-laden and that he might not see them again. He then deliberately reviewed the sort of work in which he had been engaged from the time he "first set foot in the province." His key recollections could serve as a skeletal outline of a pastoral theology: personal encounter, proclamation, teaching, visitation, and the willingness to suffer for faith:

- He had held nothing back from the people that was for their good.
- He had preached, calling for repentance and faith.
- He had taught in public.
- He had visited in their homes.
- He had endured toils and trials uncomplainingly.

These remain a penetrating summary of key acts of the eldership.

Paul continued by reporting that he was on his way to Jerusalem under the constraint of the Spirit. He then left the other elders with this memorable pastoral charge, based on the same shepherding pattern that had been predominant in Jesus' teaching: "Guard yourselves and all the flock over which the Holy Spirit has made you overseers (*episkopous*). Be shepherds (*poimainein*) of the Church of God" (Acts 20:28, NIV). This Lukan recollection of Paul demonstrates the intricate integration of these several images of ministry: presbuteros is poimēn is episkopos. The same office is also counselor, for Paul next reminded them of how "for three years, night and day, I never ceased to counsel (*nouthetōn*) each of you, and how I wept over you" (v. 31). One gets the impression from this moving scene that Paul's ministry at Ephesus was one of deep empathic pastoral involvement.

After Paul had finished speaking, he prayed with them and there were "loud cries of sorrow from them all, as they folded Paul in their arms and kissed him. What distressed them most was his saying that they would never see his face again" (vv. 36,37). The picture is one of a deeply enmeshed, engaged ministry of mutual caring, witness, and shared life together. It gives us a moving glimpse of the role of the minister by one who was primarily influential as a model in defining that role.

Another model is seen in 1 Pet. 5:1 ff., where the author is appealing "to the elders of your community, as a fellow-elder and witness of Christ's sufferings, and also a partaker in the splendour that is to be revealed." Note the careful balance of freedom, liberality, and mutuality in this charge to the elders: "Tend the flock of God whose shepherd you are, and do it, not under compulsion, but of your own free will, as God would have it; not for gain but out of sheer devotion; not tyrannizing over those who are allotted to your care, but setting an example to the flock" (1 Pet. 5:2,3). Both Acts 20 and 1 Pet. 5 suggest the close interweaving of eldership with pastoral caring. The images associated with *presbuteros* cannot be artificially separated from those associated with the caring shepherd (*poimēn*).

The twofold moral ground upon which congregations were urged to "obey the shepherd" (i.e., be responsive to the pastor's guidance), was subsequently stated in Heb. 13:17–18: (a) the evidence of the pastor's empathy, for they have time and again shown themselves to be "tireless in their concern for you"; and (b) the assumption that pastors themselves must be finally accountable before God (v. 17).

The image of pastor as watchman, or protective, vigilant all-night guard, was already well developed by the Hebrew prophets. Radical accountability to God was the central feature of this analogy, as dramatically stated by Ezekiel: "The word of the Lord came to me: . . . I have made you a watchman for the Israelites . . . it may be that a righteous man turns away and does wrong . . . I will hold you answerable for his death" (Ezek. 3:16–21). Such injunctions for prophetic accountability have often been transferred by analogy to the Christian office of elder.

Listen to the analogy: The watchman over a city is responsible for the whole city, not just one street of it. If the watchman sleeps through an attack, the whole resultant damage is his responsibility. This was the covenantal analogy later applied repeatedly to the pastor, who was charged with nothing less than caring for the souls of an analogous small city, the *ekklēsia*. If the congregation falls prey to seductive teaching or forgetfulness, whose responsibility can it be but that of the presbuteros, the guiding elder?

Given such profound responsibility, who is able to take on such a heavy burden? Paul himself felt its awesome weight, yet celebrated that such a task could be undertaken, and would be divinely supported by grace. "I came before you weak, nervous and shaking with fear," Paul wrote to the Corinthians (1 Cor. 2:3). He was keenly aware of the narrow boundaries of his own finitude, his bodily limitations, and the clouded horizons of his own knowledge and will, but he also knew that God's strength is made perfect through our weaknesses.

Episkopos

"Bishop" translates *episkopos,* which is derived from the family of Greek words referring to guardianship, oversight, inspection—accountably looking after a complex process in a comprehensive sense. *Episkopos* implies vigilance far more than hierarchy. The term is applied to Christ himself as "the Shepherd and Guardian [*episkopon*] of your souls" (1 Pet. 2:25).

We have two parallel lists of qualifications for the episcopal office, both of which stress nine points in slightly different language. The *episkopos* is expected to be:

1 Timothy 3:1–7	Titus 1:7–9
above reproach, blameless with good reputation	unimpeachable character among the non-Christian public, so as not to expose the community to scandal
sexual fidelity to spouse and good parent who wins responsiveness from children	devout and self controlled
sober, not a brawler, avoiding quarrels	sober, no brawler
a forebearing disposition, temperate	not overbearing or short-tempered
courteous, hospitable	hospitable
no lover of money	no money-grubber
of highest principles	right-minded, just
apt to teach	able to move hearers with wholesome teaching
not a new convert	able to confute objectors, adhering to true doctrine

Since the effectiveness of the church's mission hinges significantly on the episcopal office, a great deal is expected of it, both in guaranteeing the authenticity of the contemporary witness to apostolic faith, and in overseeing the spiritual, moral, and temporal development of the churches (Justin Martyr, *ANF*, vol. 1, pp. 188 ff.; Cyprian, *ANF*, vol. 5, pp. 281 ff.).

More than any other office of Christian ministry, *episkopos* is concerned with public defense of the Christian community against distortions of its message or challenges from the surrounding world. This is why central emphasis is placed upon unimpeachable character and the ability to state the teaching of the church to those who have not been catechized by it or who might be prone to misunderstand it (*Seven Ecumenical Councils*, *NPNF* 2nd vol. 14, pp. 77 ff., 104 ff.; 374 f.).

There is some evidence that *presbuteros* and *episkopos* (elder and bishop) were at times used virtually interchangably (Acts 20:28, Titus 1:5–10). Yet there are other texts where a clear distinction is made between these two offices, as when the qualifications for presbuteros (Titus 1:6) are spelled out in a way different from episkopos (Titus 1:7).

Keep in mind that all three pastoral offices carry on the same work of the ministry of Christ, even though with these somewhat different emphases, in a reasonable division of labor:

- *diakonos* being relatively more focused on temporal needs and the serving role
- *presbuteros* centering more specifically on the pastoral instruction, guidance, and leadership of local congregations, and
- *episkopos* relatively more concerned with the oversight and public defense of the flock, often on an area-wide basis

This familiar threefold conception of offices of ministry remains subject to much debate. Presbyterians place the episcopal function in the collegium of elders (Calvin, *Inst.*, 4.3–5; cf. Jerome, *LCF*, p. 189). The congregationally governed traditions resist episcopal theories and exegesis. Some free church traditions view deacons and elders as lay offices. But current ecumenical discussions on ministry continue to point toward some sort of imaginative re-appropriation or re-interpretation of the three orders or offices of ministry as a likely centrist position that may come to serve the ecumenical church as well in the future as it has in the past. We have yet to see how the modern ecumenical consensus may take more detailed shape and learn to maintain itself intergenerationally.

Having discussed the principle offices or orders of Christian ministry, we now turn to the gifts that empower these orders. God, the Spirit, gives many gifts to the church to enable it to fulfill its mission. Classical discussions of ministry are not content with merely describing the orders by which the work of ministry is structured. They also discuss the widely varied charismata through which ministry is enabled.

THE GIFTS OF MINISTRY

The Lists of Charismata

Twice in the Pauline tradition there appears a deliberate list of the gifts (charismata) of the Spirit to the church. Though slightly different, both lists are carefully put in sequence in a way that gives the impression that their general order was a widely understood, oft-repeated part of the oral tradition prior to Paul. Here are the lists, side by side:

1 Corinthians 12:28	Ephesians 4:11
Within our community God has appointed	These were his gifts:
in the first place apostles	some to be apostles
in the second place prophets	some prophets
	some evangelists
	some pastors and
thirdly teachers	teachers
then miracle-workers	
then gifts of healing	
the ability to help others	
those who can get others to work together [administrators]	
those with the gift of ecstatic utterance	
	to equip God's people for work in his service, to the building up of the body of Christ

Two caveats are needed as we interpret this sequence of gifts of ministry, relying principally on the version in the twelfth chapter of First Corinthians:

First, it is proper to consider these not just as gifts of ministry but gifts to the church. However, on behalf of the whole church, these specific gifts are given by the Spirit to individuals for the good of the community. The set-apart ministry seeks to elicit these gifts for the good of all and celebrates their reception on behalf of all.

There are many passages in the New Testament on gifts of the Spirit. Some could as easily refer generally to the laity as to a set-apart ministry (as in 1 Cor. 1:7 and 7:7, or 1 Peter 4:7–11, or 1 Cor. 12:5–11, where wise speech, discernment, and ecstatic utterance could refer to *laos* as well as *poimēn*). But in others, such as Romans 12:6–8, the gifts appear to be intended less for laity than for various forms of called, prepared, and appointed leadership: prophecy (*prophēteia*), ministry (*diakonia*), teaching (*didaskalia*), exhortation (*paraklesis*), and governance (*proistēmi*). Some passages, however, speak very deliberately about the gifts of an ordered ministry "for the equipping of God's people" (Eph. 4:12), or for those whom "God has appointed" or set in place in the church ("*kai hous men etheto o theos en tē ekklēsia,*" 1 Cor. 12:28). Note that 1 Tim. 4:14 and 2 Tim. 4:10 also are clearly intended for an ordered ministry. These are the passages we will explore in this section.

Second, it is not implied that the ministerial office itself is divided up or abruptly segmented into prophets, teachers, or evangelists, so that one disconnected part of ministry would teach, while another unrelated segment would exercise the gift of healing, and so one. Rather, all of these gifts work together for the good of the body. No single member fully possesses all of these gifts, yet all benefit from each of them. Each individual participates in the one body that possesses all of these gifts. "One [person], through the Spirit, has the gift of wise speech, while another, by the power of the same Spirit, can put the deepest knowledge into words. Another, by the same Spirit, is granted faith; another, by the one Spirit, gifts of healing, and another miraculous powers; another has the gift of prophecy, and another ability to distinguish true spirits from false; yet another has the gift of ecstatic utterance of different kinds, and another the ability to interpret it. But all these gifts are the work of one and the same Spirit, distributing them separately to each individual at will" (1 Cor. 12:8–11), for the good of the whole.

Paul argued that gifts differ "according to the grace given to us" (Rom. 12:6), and are intended for the benefit of the whole Christian community (1 Cor. 12:7). None gives grounds for individual "boasting." If one is missing a particular gift, there is no reason to despair over it. For the Spirit is nurturing that gift somewhere else in the community, a cause for celebration.

These gifts are diverse and specific. Hospitality (*philoxenia*) is a charisma (1 Pet. 4:7–11; cf. 1 Tim. 3:2) in the simple sense that some are more gifted at welcoming strangers. Public speaking (*lalia*) is a gift (1 Pet. 4:11). Even the self-control that makes possible sexual chastity in the celibate state is described by Paul as a charisma (1 Cor. 7:1–7). Yet, however diverse, taken together they express the complex, multifaceted unity of the body of Christ.

Apostolos: The Gift of the Apostolate

The first gift of ministry, logically and chronologically, is *apostolos*. Apostolos has the primary meaning of a fully prepared and authorized messenger sent forth as an ambassador or legate with a clear commission to deliver a particular message. Jesus called the core group of original disciples *apostolous* (Luke 6:13), and deliberately commissioned them to act in his name (Luke 24:46–48).

The twelve were distinctive because:

- Jesus called and commissioned them
- They were eyewitnesses to his ministry and especially his resurrection
- The emergent church depended upon them for accurate reporting and inspired interpretation of the originative events of faith

Not only was Matthias viewed as an apostle under the special circumstances reported in Acts 1, but also Paul was regarded as *kletos apostolos*, a "called apostle" (1 Cor. 1:1), since he had been "entrusted with the Gospel for Gentiles as surely as Peter had been entrusted with the Gospel for Jews. For God whose action made Peter an apostle to the Jews, also made me an apostle to the Gentiles" (Gal. 2:7,8). Even though "born out of due time" (1 Cor. 15:8), Paul was nonetheless an apostle by special calling and, in a unique way, an "eyewitness."

There were others also who were referred to as apostles yet not among the twelve: Barnabas (Acts 14:4), Andronicus and Junia (Rom. 16:7), and James the brother of Jesus (Gal. 1:9). So it appears that many who were not among the twelve who symbolically reconstituted the twelve tribes of Israel into a "new Israel," were nonetheless acknowledged as "apostles" because they had seen the Lord and witnessed the originative events of faith. Among these were some five hundred (1 Cor. 15) who had seen him in his resurrection appearances. But in its primary sense, the term *apostle* was reserved for the twelve and Paul (Schmithals, 1969, pp. 231 ff.).

The church was "built upon the foundation laid by the apostles and prophets, and Christ Jesus himself is the foundation-stone" (Eph. 2:20). It was through the apostles that the authentic memory and interpretation of the saving events were recalled, proclaimed, and made part of the tradition through time. This is why apostolos is a pivotal gift of ministry on which subsequent ministries remain always dependent.

Is there a continuous line of descent from the apostles to the present through episcopal succession? How important is such an uninterrupted succession? Much of the free church tradition has quarreled with literal, visible, historical claims to uninterrupted succession with no irregularities through an absolutely definable linear order of bishops. Nonetheless, even the strongest objectors to historical succession would still talk about some kind of unbroken symbolic descent from the apostles. Only a few would try to leap nineteen centuries in one giant Protestant long jump to claim apostolic warrant without any concern about (or perhaps even with repudiation of) all intervening links. But even in such extreme cases, some indirect appeal to apostolicity remains. Some view of succession is needed to solve the problem left by the death of the original apostles. The word of the eyewitnesses cannot transmit itself intergenerationally without a continuing ministry in the apostolic tradition. Even views of the apostolate that reject unbroken historic succession nevertheless seek to establish the symbolic point that the work of ministry today is essentially the same as in the days of the apostles, so that the apostolic teaching remains applicable to Christian ministry today, judiciously appropriated in the contemporary setting (Irenaeus, *ANF*, vol. 1, pp. 415 ff.; Hippolytus, *ANF*, vol. 5, p. 10; Cyprian, *ANF*, vol. 5, p. 305).

Ministry today is free to look to both Jesus and the apostles as criteria for assessing itself. We stand in dialogue both with Jesus the pioneer and pattern of good shepherding and with the apostles who were first to discover and work through the implications of Jesus' ministry in their practice of ministry. We continue to be edified by both Jesus and by the first respondents to his call, as well as subsequent respondents who stand in the same line of recollection and celebration.

Prophetēs: The Gift of Prophecy

In New Testament lists of charismata, the gift that is usually assigned a place second only to that of the apostle is that of the prophet (*prophetēs*), an extraordinary ministry of special inspiration, of discernment of the meaning of events already revealed or, in some cases, yet to be revealed (Origen, *AF*, vol. 4, pp. 612–20; Augustine, *NPNF* 1st, vol. 2, pp. 337 ff.; Clementine Homilies, *ANF*, vol. 8, pp. 181 ff., 241).

That God the Spirit continues to illuminate particular Christian ministries in special ways is clear from the lives of Saint Polycarp, Saint Anthony, Saint Francis, John Bunyan, and Pascal. The Spirit's special prophetic leading did not cease with Amos, Jesus, the daughters of Philip (Acts 21:9), Martin Luther or Martin Luther King. To these and others yet to come, the Spirit has given an extraordinary measure of spiritual insight to grasp the divine leading for others.

The prophetic Christian ministry, however, does not propose itself as a completely new source of truth. Rather, at best it is fresh discernment of the truth already revealed in the history of Israel and Christ. "Just as the Old Testament prophet stood in a subordinate relation to Moses, who provided the doctrinal norm of sound teaching, so the New Testament prophet stood towards the apostles, and was bound to submit all to the test of that which they declared as the word of God. It is in this sense that the apostle urged the Church of his day, and would urge us also, to desire earnestly to prophesy: not to desire the notoriety of doctrinal innovators, but to contend earnestly for the truth once for all delivered to the saints" (J. A. Motyer in *NBD*, p. 1045).

The same point is appropriately made concerning all the charismata (gifts of the Spirit): miracles, healing, discernment, glossolalia. These gifts do not transcend or nullify the apostolic witness, but rather they illuminate and extend it, and manifest it more meaningfully in the present. They are not to be sought or honored independently of apostolic faith. This is precisely where Christian spirituality clashes with many secularized claims of paranormal gifts.

Euaggelistēs: The Gift of Proclamation

We are well advised not to separate too sharply the work of pastor and evangelist (*euaggelistēs*), a designation given to Philip, one of the seven (Acts 21:8), and to Timothy, who as a pastor was at the same time exhorted to continue "the work of evangelist" (2 Tim. 4:5). Although all Christians had responsibility to proclaim the good news, it appears that some had extraordinary gifts to do so with unusual effectiveness. They were thought to have received a distinct gift of the Spirit. Subsequently, in ordinary pastoral practice it has been assumed that all pastors are already evangelists, or at least that they would pray for that gift. This will be further developed in Chapter 9.

Dunameis: The Gift of Miracle

The power of working miracles (*dunameis,* "mighty works," "extraordinary acts of power") was regarded throughout the New Testament not as evidence of any inherent power in individuals, but rather of the presence of the divine power working through finite means. Here Christian ministry parts company with manipulative dilettantes of paranormal phenomena who want to achieve the power to autonomously "work miracles." For the miracles that occur in the apostolic ministry are done in the name of and by the power of Christ, in continuity with his teaching and Spirit. As Christ's own miracles pointed beyond themselves to attest the coming governance of God, so did God's mighty acts with the apostles attest the living presence of Christ (Irenaeus, *ANF,* vol. 1, p. 409; Lactantius, *ANF,* vol. 7, p. 127). They are not an end in themselves.

The gift of *dunameis* is never given for sheer exhibition, nor is it an isolated revelation of the divine power, as if separable from the history of revelation. Rather, this gift points beyond itself to remarkable occurrences that edify the revelation already given, so that these events make even clearer the apostolic witness.

Whether the gift of miracles was confined to the apostolic period or whether it extends into contemporary ministry has been widely debated. Those who say the former are usually trying to protect ministry from fanaticism. Those who argue for the latter are trying to avoid putting arbitrary limits on the power of the Spirit to act in the present. (These arguments are fairly summarized in John Wesley's *Earnest Appeal to Men of Reason and Religion.*)

Since the gift of miracles is potentially subject to considerable abuse (as are all the gifts—teaching, healing, helping), it is in the church's interest to scrutinize carefully any claims of miraculous power made on Christ's behalf. Not all paranormal events are miraculous. Some simply do not fall within our available scientific paradigms. We are made wary by a sad history of abuse of alleged miracles by unscrupulous persons who have derived profit from false claims. It is not wise to focus on miracle as the self-authenticating centerpiece of Christian ministry or to allow the ministry to become predominately defined by this gift, as if ministry had the right to "require" God to perform miracles on demand. Such a tendency was specifically rejected by Jesus.

Iama: The Gift of Healing

There can be no doubt that healing (*iama,* 1 Cor. 12:30) was a part of the larger apostolic ministry in Paul's view. When Jesus commissioned the twelve, he charged them to heal (*therapeuein*) every disease. Similarly the seventy were commissioned to heal (*therapeute*) the sick (Luke 10:9). The cures of many bodily ailments that took place during Jesus' own ministry and the disciples' ministry were thought to be signs of the coming kingdom (Luke 9:2,11; Acts 10:38), fulfilling Old Testament prophecy. Jesus rejected a narrower legalistic view that every sickness was the direct result of a particular sin (John 9:2 ff.), yet without denying the mystery of the intermeshing of sin and sickness. Healing is often mentioned as an apostolic gift (in addition to 1 Cor. 12, note the use of *therapeuō* in Matt. 10:18 and Mark 6:13 and of *iaomai* in Luke 9:2 and Acts 2:43; cf. Oden, 1966, chap. 5). The relation of apostolic healing to healing in ministry today is still under considerable debate. We will discuss these difficult issues more thoroughly in the chapter on pastoral care of the sick.

Ministry today, as earlier, cannot ignore the body-spirit interface. The deep inner relation between bodily disease and spiritual malaise remains a perennial concern of pastoral wisdom. Every pastor is called not only to palliate bodily discomfort so as to improve the possibilities for spiritual growth, but also to seek to mend souls in such a way that it has bodily effect.

Glossolalia: The Gift of Ecstatic Utterance

Another remarkable gift of the Spirit is glossolalia (from *glossa,* "tongue"), speaking in tongues, or gifts of ecstatic utterance. Some in the Pentecostal tradition would argue that glossolalia is an ever-present, constant mark or normative gift of ministry without which the church would not truly and appropriately exist. In contrast, others in the Christian tradition would seek to rule out glossolalia altogether. The mainstream flows between these two viewpoints. From the Day of Pentecost to present-day Protestant and Catholic charismatics, many witness to having received this gift. Yet seldom in history has it been regarded as normative or unambiguously definitive for the Christian life.

The two principle passages that guide our understanding of the reception of this gift are Acts, chapter 2, and First Corinthians, chapters 12 through 14. In Acts, chapter 2, referring to the Day of Pentecost, the gathered church was "filled with the Holy Spirit and began to talk in other tongues, as the Spirit gave them power of utterance" (v. 4) as a fulfillment of prophecy in Joel 2:28–32: "I will pour out my Spirit upon all flesh, and your sons and your daughters shall prophesy, and your young men shall see visions, and your old men shall dream dreams" (RSV).

The more crucial passage for ministry is First Corinthians, chapters 12 through 14. Paul, in seeking to heal the divisions and problems present in the church at Corinth, speaks of the variety of gifts engendered by the one Spirit. In both lists of charismata (1 Cor. 12:8–11 for the laity and 1 Cor. 12:28–31 for those whom "God has appointed"), there appears the gift of ecstatic utterance. It does not seem to be an incidental inclusion. In time it became the source of troublesome vexation for Paul, and some difference of interpretation in the church. This is why Paul carefully linked the gift of ecstatic utterance with another gift, namely, "the ability to interpret it" (v. 11).

First Corinthians, chapter 13, then sets this gift within its proper context, the agape of God. Even if one had the ability to "speak in tongues of men or of angels," without divine love, it is as hollow as "a sounding gong or a clanging cymbal" (13:1). The tongues of ecstacy will cease, but love does not (13:8–13). Although the language of ecstasy may be good for oneself, Paul argues, it is prophetic teaching in clear language that "builds up the Christian community" (14:4). So the person who "falls into ecstatic utterance should pray for the ability to interpret" (14:13). Paul concludes with an acknowledgment that he himself had experienced this gift, but that it needs to be seen within the context of instruction, enlightenment, and language that is intelligible: "Thank God, I am more gifted in ecstatic utterance than any of you, but in the congregation I would rather speak five intelligible words, for the benefit of others as well as myself, than thousands of words in the language of ecstacy" (1 Cor. 14:18–19).

For further discussion of this important and complex subject, see Irenaeus (*ANF*, vol. 1, pp. 430, 531), Tertullian (*ANF*, vol. 3, pp. 188, 477), Eusebius (*NPNF* 1st, vol. 1, pp. 231 f.), Gregory Nazianzus (*NPNF* 2nd, vol. 7, pp. 318 ff.), Thomas Aquinas (*ST*, vol. 2, pp. 1919 ff.), and, more recently, the works of Walter J. Hollenweger, Morton Kelsey, Killian McDonnell, and Krister Stendahl.

Didaskalia: The Gift of Teaching

To feed the flock spiritually, the pastor is necessarily an educator (*didaskolos*, "teacher"). Since chapter 10 is devoted to the task of the pastor as teaching elder, we will not detail this gift here, except to say that teaching has consistently been regarded as an intrinsic part of ministry from its beginnings, with Jesus teaching the apostles and the apostles teaching the remembering church and providing for an ordered ministry through which the authenticity of this teaching might be maintained and developed.

Oikonomia: **The Gift of Administration**

Another image applied by Scripture to the gifts of Christian ministry is that of steward (*oikonomos,* from which we get our word *economics*), one who is entrusted with the task of conserving and dispensing resources justly. The steward is manager, guardian, "one who is over a house." Although all Christians are in a general sense stewards, pastors are called to stewardship of a special sort, as "stewards of the mysteries of God" ("*oikonomous mustēriōn theou,*" 1 Cor. 4:1), to whom the sublime mystery of God's self-disclosure has been entrusted. The pastor is also the steward of the resources of the community and charged with the administration of the work and mission of the church. When Paul tries to compare this responsibility with other forms of human responsibility he finally concludes that it is incommensurable (vv. 2–5). No human court can quite grasp this responsibility. It can only be judged by God eschatologically (v. 5). Since we will devote an entire chapter to equipping the laity for ministry, we will leave the detailed examination of these issues until later.

Having briefly reviewed the orders that manifest ministry and the gifts that empower it, we now return to the prior question

Why Ministry?

Why did Christ institute the office of ministry? Why not leave all these tasks to the laity? The persistent assumption of classical Christian thinking is that (a) duly ordered Christian ministries exist by God's own intention and design. Christ's ministry has awakened our ministeries, extending itself in time through human hands and speech; (b) Jesus himself called and commissioned the apostolic tradition and engendered a historic ministry accountable to it; (c) Jesus himself intended to provide a means by which not only his teaching but also his living presence should continue to be vibrantly alive in subsequent generations; and (d) the laity share Christ's general ministry, but on their behalf some in particular "God has appointed" (1 Cor. 12:28) or ordered to the work of apostles, prophets, evangelists, pastors, and teachers (Eph. 4:11) to better equip the laos for their service in the world.

It might seem an embarrassment to the divine omnipotence that God would condescend to call, prepare, and ordain poor, finite human beings, inadequate persons of limited vision and skewed knowledge, born in a particular time and social system with limited moral sensitivities, to continue Christ's own ministry. We speak of plain persons such as Saul of Tarsus, Priscilla, Barnabas, James, Phoebe, and Stephen. Ordained ministry is living proof that God's grace works through considerable human imperfections. Apostolicity boldly implies that ordinary persons are sent into the world to witness to the extraordinary—the resurrection and its meaning. These apostles were common laborers at nets whom Jesus called to be fishers of persons.

REFERENCES AND FURTHER READING

For various discussions of the orders and offices of ministry, see Clement of Rome (*ANF*, vol. 1, p. 17), Polycarp (*ANF*, vol. 1), Ignatius (d. 107), Irenaeus (*ANF*, vol. 1), Justin Martyr (*ANF*, vol. 5., pp. 281 ff.), Clement of Alexandria (*ANF*, vol. 2, pp. 504 ff., 523 ff.), Tertullian (*ANF*, vol. 3), Cyprian (*ANF*, vol. 5), Hippolytus (*ANF*, vol. 5), *Apostolic Constitutions* (*ANF*, vol. 7), Origen (d. 254), *Clementine Homilies* (*ANF*, vol. 8), John Chrysostom (*NPNF* 1st, vol. 9, pp. 33 ff.), Gregory Nazianzus (*NPNF* 2nd, vol. 7, pp. 318 ff.), Jerome (*LCF*, p. 189, Augustine (d. 430), Thomas Aquinas (*ST*, vol. 3, pp. 2682 ff.), Luther (d. 1546), Calvin (1559, 4.3), Bucer (d. 1551), Cranmer (d. 1556), Simons (d. 1561), Council of Trent (1545–1563), Laud (d. 1645), Turretin (1688–90), T. Wilson (1708), Wesley (*WJW*, vol. 7), Pelliccia (1833 ed.), Harnack (1862), Bruce (1871), Paludan-Mueller (1874), Latham (1891), Knodt (1894), Zimmerman (1930), Rahner (1975). For more recent specific discussions of the *diakonos*, *presbuteros*, and/or *episkopos*, see Miller (1832), Goulooze (1937), Barnikol (1941), Schnackenburg (1949), Payne (1952), Krimm (1953), Conzelmann (1960), Telfer (1962), Nolan (1968), and Beyer.

For a variety of viewpoints of the gifts of ministry see Chrysostom (393), Schweizer (1961), Kelsey (1964), Stagg et al. (1967), and Conzelmann (1975). On the apostolate, apostolic authority and its development, see Eusebius (d. ca 340), Thomas Aquinas (*ST*, vol. 2, pp. 2226 ff., 2424 ff.), Calvin (1559), Baur (1852), V. Taylor (1933), Dodd (1936), Lietzmann (1937), Käsemann (1942), Kirk (1946), Munck (1950), Ehrhardt (1953), Cullmann (1953), Lohse (1953), Marxsen (1958), Altaner (1960), Lawson (1961), Rahner (1964b and 1966), H. Chadwick (1967), Bultmann (1968), Dix (1945), Hengel (1968), Schmithals (1969), Rengstorf (1969), Goppelt (1977), C. K. Barrett (1972), Pannenberg (1970–73), and Newbigin (1977). For discussions of the relation of history and tradition, see Childs (1962), W. D. Davies (1962), Rahner and Ratzinger (1964), Bruce and Rupp, eds. (1968), and Pannenberg (1970–73).

III

WHAT CLERGY DO
AND WHY

Birth
Baptism
Confirmation
Marriage
Death

These priestly occaisions define the pastor

7. The Pastor of the Worshiping Community

The Five Days

There are five incomparable days in the believer's life. The day one is born, when life is given. The day one is baptized, and enters anticipatively into the community of faith. The day one is confirmed, when one chooses to re-affirm one's baptism, and enter by choice deliberately into the community of faith and enjoy its holy communion. The day one may choose to enter into a lifelong covenant of fidelity in love. The day one dies, when life is received back into God's hands.

What do those five days have in common? Who is invited to share them all? They are incomparable, pivotal moments in life. Besides the family, what persons or professionals are welcomed into the intimate circle of significant participants in all of those days? Only the clergy.

Would you wish to have a vocation in which you would be invited to participate in those five days and offer them a significant interpretation? If you answer yes, then your calling has a priestly bent. For these days bring dramatically into focus what Christian ministry is all about. In priestly service, we are being commissioned and ordained to point to the gracious presence of God on each of these unforgettable occasions, as well as many others.

Precisely what is the work of clergy? If asked by an efficiency expert to identify every twist and turn of a week's work, carefully timed, few weeks would look alike. Compared to most modern occupations, the activities are amazingly varied. In all these diverse acts, however, whether visiting a postoperative surgical patient, studying exegesis, attending a mayor's committee for fair housing, or leading a litany, the pastor is a priest to the people. That means: offering the love of God to the world, and offering before God the prayers of the people.

Pastoral theology seeks to bring these varied actions into cohesive interpretation. Without a proper energizing center of identity, these tasks may become so diffuse and hazy that they feel impossibly fragmented, so much so as to end in demoralization. It is hard for the center to hold when so many claims tend to pull pastoral identity apart.

One of the strongest forces in pastoral identity is the public role of leader of the worshiping community. However diverse their other social roles, pastors are publicly identified most often as leaders of worship. Wherever they go, people characteristically think of them in relation to this distinctive public task and context. Thus, even if one's central interests may lie elsewhere, one is well advised to understand this expectation clearly and carefully examine one's own attitudes toward it.

WHAT IS PRIESTHOOD?

The Distinction Between Prophet and Priest

The Christian ministry of word and sacrament unites and transmutes two venerable offices of the older Hebraic tradition: prophet and priest. This is the crucial difference between them:

- The prophet spoke for God to the people.
- The priest spoke for the people to God.

Christian ministry does not pretentiously presume to speak for God each time the pastor addresses the people. But it does wish to open up through Scripture the lively address of God. That is its prophetic task (cf. Clement of Alexandria, *ANF,* vol. 2, p. 194; Origen, *ANF,* vol. 4, pp. 613–20). But it also wishes to pray pastorally for the whole church, interceding on behalf of the whole world. This is the priestly side of the work of clergy (Origen, *ANF,* vol. 4, pp. 488, Calvin, *Inst.,* 4.19). If either side of ministry is grossly imbalanced, the lack will be felt eventually by the people.

At first glance the prophetic ministry of the word seems to have closer affinity to the Protestant tradition, and the priestly ministry of the sacraments might appear to be closer to the Catholic tradition. Better understood, both viewpoints are powerfully present in the pastoral ministry of both traditions, and each needs to complement its own gifts and resources with the other. As there was complementarity between Moses and Aaron in the formative period of Hebrew religion, so later did prophets like Amos and Isaiah make the pathways for the priestly tradition that Ezra, Nehemiah, and others diligently maintained. Similarly in the New Testament, the elements of proclamation and maintenance of tradition are complementary, as in First Corinthians chapter 15 (cf. Calvin, *Inst.,* 2.3.12; 3.25.3 ff.). It is the bold intention of Christianity to combine the ministry of word and sacrament, the prophetic and priestly ministries, into a single ordained public office in which one person serves both the priestly office of conducting public worship and the prophetic office of providing religious insight, instruction, exegesis, and proclamation of the word (Calvin, *Inst.*, 4.3 ff.).

At times we may emphasize one more than the other. One may teach without receiving Holy Communion, or worship without a homily. But how lacking is the Eucharist without the lively preaching of the word. And how diminished is the preached word without the liturgically enacted Word. The complementarity and inner connection of these two functions urgently needs to be pastorally grasped, else there may be a loss of center in ministry, a constant drag toward identity diffusion, burnout, and disillusionment.

Modern Protestants often react defensively to long-gone priestly stereotypes that prevailed in the sixteenth century, when medieval abuses required vigorous opposition. These stereotypes still remain stubbornly in our minds four centuries later. Protestant ministers sometimes get edgy and apologetic when thinking about themselves as priests. Yet Protestants need to learn to better integrate the priestly functions into their ministry, just as Catholics are already learning much from Protestant traditions about proclamation, charisma, and freedom. It is time for all to work toward the recovery of a unified doctrine of ministry that integrates the priestly prayer for humanity with the prophetic witness to God's word (Chrysostom, *LCF*, p. 174).

The Distinction Between Priest and People

Priesthood is arguably as old as human culture. For good or ill, it is found in some form in virtually every human society. Even in modern culture, which thinks of itself as having been secularized out of priestly hocus-pocus, we still find Ersatz priests in good supply, making blessings, offering invocations, marrying and burying, and trying to coax meanings out of potential absurdities.

The work of ministry is poorly understood when it is thought of exclusively under only one of the following rubrics: empathic listener, pithy preacher, whiz administrator, brilliant teacher. The good pastor undertakes each of these tasks at certain times, but through all of them he is seeking to fulfill the heart of the priestly office: interpreting humanity to God, holding up the human condition before God in prayer. The priest speaks a human, all too human, word to God, prays empathically *with* and representatively *for* the here-and-now community amid all its confusions and self-assertiveness, humbly beseeching divine hearing and interceding for the visible community.

The Protestant tradition has rightly spoken of the whole people of God as a priesthood, following Hebrews, chapter 6, but the priesthood of all believers has never meant the priesthood of each independent individual believer, but rather of the whole community, gathered and unified in Christ, the high priest, who ironically is also the sacrificial lamb slain on our behalf. Some might be tempted to conclude that all believers are therefore able to hear confession and provide pastoral care and preach the word fittingly, and (why not?—so this line of reasoning goes) all believers would equally serve Holy Communion, leaving little need for a set-apart ministry. Indeed there is some truth in the view that the laos, the whole people of God, can within bounds hear confession and pray and address the Christian brother or sister with God's forgiveness. Yet centuries of experience show that the laity best pray under the guidance of the apostolic tradition mediated by a prepared and informed ministry. Laypersons best "confess their sins to one another" when that dialogue is being guided by the Holy Spirit in the faith once for all delivered to the saints. The community has need to hear the word proclaimed authentically, not mistakenly, and in a trustworthy, not half-informed, fashion; to receive the sacraments fittingly, not in idiosyncratic ways (Hippolytus, *ANF*, vol. 5, pp. 9 ff.; *Apostolic Constitutions, ANF*, vol. 7, pp. 429 f.; Luther, *SWML*, vol. 4, pp. 90 ff.).

That is why Christ gave order to ministry. That is why not everyone is authorized by the whole church to act representatively on its behalf to offer the Eucharist, to lead the community in pastoral prayer, to preach and counsel. Jesus and the apostles anticipated our religious needs by providing the laos with an ordered ministry of word, sacrament, and care. This requires committed and informed persons who have studied that tradition in more than a slapdash way as a serious lifelong pursuit and intentional vocational commitment and who have been set aside both by their inner sense of calling and by the outward action of the church.

There remains a line as thin as a hair, but as hard as a diamond, between ordained ministry and the faithful layperson. For in ordination spiritual gifts are recognized and the gifted are commissioned to preach and celebrate the sacraments and to act in the name of the whole church and with the authority of the apostolic tradition. Through ordination a sacramental office is conferred on the ordained that is not so conferred on all baptized Christians (Eusebius, *NPNF* 2nd, vol. 1, p. 211). It is not merely through the personality of the minister, but by reason of the office, that the pastor becomes an effective symbol of the grace of God acting through the church (Hooker, pp. 1594 ff.; Calkins, 1941; Holmes, 1971).

This assumes that the church is not just a voluntary band of enthusiasts who are gathered to navel-gaze or increase their psychic powers or redistribute political power (for none of those defines the Christian community per se). Rather, the Christian community exists because God calls it into being for the extension and embodiment of Christ's ministry. If God has determined to reveal himself in history, that requires a historical community, a living body of Christ, a community to receive sacramental grace so as to be empowered in the performance of its mission to the world.

This is why the problem of ministry is essentially a christological issue. If you begin with a theology that assumes that the divine reality is made known in history, that requires some kind of historical community to receive, recollect, attest to, and pass on that revelation. This in turn requires an ordained ministry to offer those sacramental gifts through which divine mercy is imparted and sustained. It does not imply that grace is impossible through other channels, but that grace is indeed channeled through these appointed means of grace (Thomas Aquinas, *ST*, vol. 1, 1123 ff.; Wesley, *WJW*, vol. 7, pp. 363 ff., vol. 8, pp. 322 ff.). All this requires some sort of Christian version of priesthood.

Timely Prayer

According to most Protestant interpretations of priesthood, the minister is no longer an offerer of sacrifice to God according to the Levitical pattern, because that has already adequately occurred in Jesus Christ. So what remains for the Christian minister to do in the priestly office? The Christian minister representatively intercedes on behalf of the faithful community before God in prayer as a timely, public, verbal, hearable act. To illustrate:

In the pew sits an elderly woman who has lost her son, yet who does not fully understand that loss and cannot articulate its depth. It is not that God needs her prayer in order to hear her, but rather that she needs to hear better articulated what she already feels in her heart. But if she, more than God, needs the ministry of prayer, it is also clear that God invites it and responds to it. Ministry seeks to offer language for the prayer in her heart.

Next to her sits a young man with gutter-low self-esteem, who has felt dozens of opportunities slip by, who now feels an unspecific anxiety about his ability to cope with any daily task. He comes to the service of Christian worship unconsciously needing to interpret himself before God but hardly knowing how to take the first step. He needs someone to help him enter into the presence of God. The pastor as representative liturgist leads the community in prayer, and in doing so enables and facilitates their own praying. Pastoral prayer does not eclipse or diminish the prayers of the laity, but rather, hopes to engender them and breathe into them new life.

Behind him is a young woman who is struggling with real guilt tinged with elements of hidden neurotic guilt. She knows that she has been cold and cruel to one about whom she deeply cares. She is aware of her inadequacy, but needs someone to interpret it in the presence of God, to offer prayer for forgiveness in a personally significant way so as to relieve and transform the real guilt, and help her under-

As if pastor is the only one.

stand the neurotic guilt. She comes to the gathered church to hear that prayer spoken, even though she could not have told you that in advance.

In the back row is a person who has slipped in late, feeling a bit awkward, who did not even know until the service began that he needed someone to interpret for him, as if standing before God, a recent moment of intense joy and aesthetic fulfillment. He discovers to his amazement that he needed a worshiping community with a representative ministry to place his deep joy in the context of a larger sense of the joy of God over creation.

This is what ministry does: says these things openly, offers these prayers fittingly, gives praise for the community heartily, offers God's forgiveness to the contrite—calling all to a lively response to the power of grace (Gregory, *ACW*, p. 70). To receive this priestly service is in large part why people come to church.

Priestly ministry seeks to give language, form, symbol, and expression to these otherwise unspoken human experiences, by offering them symbolic interpretation in a community of prayer. By analogy, only because Christ knew what was in human hearts was he prepared to be priest to humanity. By empathetically sharing in our human condition, entering our fleshly sphere of suffering, even unto death, Christ came to know who we are, so as to interpret us before God. Pastorally this suggests a deep analogy between God's incarnate love and the care of souls.

The Christian ministry follows this incarnational pattern of Christ in entering into the depths of human experience, seeking to understand it, not be self-deceptive about it—to penetrate its masks, not ignoring its limits or evil dimensions. In the service of worship we hold all this human amalgam up before the Lord. This beholding-interceding activity occurs not just on Sunday, but throughout the hourly encounters of each week. Only the minister who has visited, who knows the people, who is in touch with their hurts, hopes, and possibilities, can on Sunday morning pray believably for the whole people. The pastor who has been immersed in the lives of the people daily is then ready to carry these needs, aspirations, and longings before God in prayer and before the gathered community by means of homily.

The Chief, But Not Sole, Liturgist

As liturgical leader of the congregation the pastor is responsible for organizing, interpreting, and presiding over the whole arena of worship, usually in consultation with laity through a church commission on worship. The chief liturgist not only must be thoroughly prepared for worship, but also is charged with helping others prepare to participate so as to bring the worshiping community together in an appropriate act of adoration, confession, affirmation, and dedication. On theological as well as aesthetic grounds, last minute preparations and hurried plans should be avoided.

Pastoral theology wishes to reflect biblically, systematically, historically, and practically about the nature of public worship for which ministry is responsible. The purpose of worship, according the Luther, is that "our Lord himself may speak to us through his holy word, and that we in turn may speak to him through our prayers and hymns"—a concise summary of the two speaking partners in the dialogue we call Christian worship: God's address to us in Scripture, and our address to God in prayer (Luther, *SWML,* vol. 2, pp. 371 ff., vol. 3, pp. 387 ff.).

Like other good dialogues, this one is so intermeshed and interactive that it is difficult to distinguish completely between its two partners. When mother and child communicate, the phases of the communication are subtly intermixed and confluent. One cannot say, now the mother is speaking, and now she ceases and the child begins. Rather, both occur simultaneously. So in Christian worship, the attempts at divine-human communication are not superficially disjointed into parts but flow as a whole, interactive exchange. If you separate them, you no longer have a dialogue. So in Christian worship, one cannot strictly separate God's speech in word and sacrament from human speech through prayer and hymns, even though they can be conceptually distinguished.

In these liturgical acts, the minister is *proestōs,* "presiding officer," the one who unites the congregation as one voice in adoration, affirmation, and dedication to God. The congregation needs a single voice representatively to combine the hearts of all those present in awe, praise, and confession. The congregation expects that this representative person will be, by inner calling and its outward confirmation, one who is responsible for fitting prayer, purified by discipline.

Yet this does not imply that the minister accomplishes the task alone. Rather, the task is to enable the whole community to express in song, prayer, and word, the varied gifts of the Spirit to the whole people of God. "When you meet for worship, each of you contributes a hymn, some instruction, a revelation, an ecstatic utterance, or the interpretation of such an utterance, all of these must aim at one thing: to build up the Church" (1 Cor. 14:26). The chief liturgist is not sole liturgist but the duly appointed person seeking to elicit and enable the prayers of the whole laos and to give expression to the many gifts of the community.

"Who shall ascend unto the hill of the Lord? Or who shall stand in his holy place? He that hath clean hands and a pure heart; who hath not lifted up his soul unto vanity, nor sworn deceitfully" (Ps. 24:4). This does not imply that the priestly representative must be sanctified to the least toenail or morally unapproachable. It does mean that the congregation expects that the chief liturgist shall have come to the task with

disciplined preparation, with a contrite heart, good intent, and single-
ness of mind.

Nor does this priestly tradition suggest a role so set apart from ordinary life that it remains irrelevant to the daily struggles of the people.
Hebrews 13:11–16 clarifies the politically relevant sense in which Jesus
is our high priest and we share his priesthood. In the previous Jewish
tradition of priesthood, it recalls, there was the sacrifice of animals
"whose blood is brought as a sin-offering by the high priest in the sanctuary," and whose bodies were ritually "burnt outside the camp" (v. 11),
so Jesus was brought as a sin-offering for the whole world. He suffered
outside the camp, as one alienated, in the sense that his crucifixion
occurred outside the gate of Jerusalem, and in doing so symbolically
reached out for all alienated persons through his suffering. Similarly
Christian worship implies that we too go "outside the gate" as he did,
risking worldly securities, "bearing the stigma that he bore. For here we
have no permanent home, but we are seekers after the city which is to
come" (v. 14).

What then is worship, with this New Testament priestly image in
mind? "Through Jesus, then, let us continually offer up to God the
sacrifice of praise, that is, the tribute of lips which acknowledge his
name, and never forget to show kindness and to share what you have
with others; for such are the sacrifices which God approves" (vv. 15,16).
We are to recall God's good deed and reveal God's kindness through
our modest acts of kindness. The sacrifice of which God approves is
that we share in Jesus' sacrifice, imitate Christ, bear the stigma he bore,
show mercy, proclaim his word. This is how Christ has transmuted the
ancient tradition of priestly sacrifice into Christian worship (Irenaeus,
ANF, vol. 1, pp. 432 ff., 574 ff.; cf. Calvin, *Inst.*, 4.18.17, *Commentaries*,
vol. 22, pp. 348 ff.).

Leitourgos

Leitourgos ("minister," "priestly servant") referred to a person who
discharges a representative official function on behalf of others and,
more particularly, a priestly or sacrificial service, (*leitourgia*) at the altar
of God. This term was borrowed from the surrounding culture by the
early Christian community and applied to speak of those who represent
the whole congregation in Christian worship and, more particularly, in
the celebration of the Eucharist. Any public divine service, but especially Holy Communion, became referred to as liturgy. The word also
became used for written texts that embody such services, such as the
Liturgy of Saint John Chrysostom. Later the subject of liturgics became
that branch of theology that studies these liturgies.

In the Christian tradition many liturgies have emerged in a succession of historical developments. We find within Roman Catholicism the
Gallican, the Ambrosian, and others; those of Basil and Chrysostom in

the east; and in the Protestant tradition other families of liturgies developed, several Lutheran, several Reformed, and many within the English tradition alone. There is not one absolutely correct form of liturgy for all cultural settings and all times. But that some form be intergenerationally transmitted was always thought to be of utmost importance. Our contemporary visions of liturgy do well to stand under their instruction. They display astonishing basic consensus despite obvious variables.

The element of antiquity, the sense that our acts of worship stand in the ancient apostolic tradition, is an essential dimension of Christian liturgy. Even when efforts are made to reform long-standing liturgies, such efforts generally appeal to earlier traditions. This is good evidence of the principle of antiquity that is ordinarily assumed even in efforts at reform. There are doubtless many ways to recollect the apostolic tradition, but any worship that arrogantly disavows this claim would be obviously suspect. Vinet correctly observed that the liturgy "should not therefore be retouched by the church, except at long intervals and with great care" (1853, p. 185). This excellent maxim leaves room for occasional, but not frivolous, liturgical experimentation. At times, as in the last quarter century, the need for liturgical renewal has been widely felt and the search for its center has been deep and thoroughgoing. The individual minister should abstain from making arbitrary changes on his own individual authority, on the assumption that one person is more creative this weekend than centuries of time-tested pastoral tradition. The minister today remains morally accountable to a historical series of liturgies that lend suggestive voice, order, and symbolic power to contemporary celebration.

Modern secularists who might wander into a service of Christian worship will sense instantly that they are in touch with an intergenerational, historically rooted community. Some who are already harshly prejudiced against any echoes of premodern consciousness may feel offended or dismiss liturgical language as dated. Even the best efforts of consensual liturgical renewal in our time may to such persons seem impossibly antiquated. But pastoral leadership today need not cave in too quickly to such "modern chauvinism" (Oden, 1979, chaps. 1–3).

Liturgical renewal rightly continues to look for language to better express the ancient tradition. Preaching must bring premodern symbols and meanings into fresh language, connecting with contemporary feelings and sensibilities. But the essential language of the historical Christian liturgy remains deeply anchored in premodern symbol systems and assumptions. It has something valuable to bring from past wisdoms—the apostolic tradition refracted through many different historical lenses.

The liturgy provides a concise summary of the whole of Christian faith and experience. Eucharist is not a flat, sketchy, skeletal abridgment of Christian faith but the center of living faith bodily communicated in an act—a concise glimpse, like a strikingly accurate portrait.

The liturgist holds up, like a mirror to contemporaneity, the historical memory of the *sanctorum communio,* its psalms, hymns, long-recollected prayers, and above all the address of Scripture. No well-instructed liturgist would presumptuously assume that Christian worship can be invented on a blank slate as if the tradition never existed, or solely as an original expression of a creative group process. For we speak to and for a community that is heir of the prophets, apostles, and martyrs, the grace-laden heritage of centuries of costly confessing faith.

Axioms of Liturgical Leadership

In order fittingly to lead the worshiping community, we do well to keep in mind several axioms of liturgical leadership:

- It is God whom we worship. We gather not to worship ourselves, our desperate struggles for God, our hungers for God, or our immediate feelings for God, but nothing less than God alone, who awakens our thirst for his presence and who stands at the beginning and end of our struggles, hungers, and feelings. We worship not a political ideal, not a local community, not a family, not an economic system, but God the giver of all of these possibilities. Worship that does not address God, listen to God, speak to God, is not Christian worship.

- Worship requires some outward order to be accountable to its inner reality. No garden exists without order; without it the land merely spawns weeds. Christian worship from its earlest beginnings has been ordered, for example, around a regular day of the week. The Jewish sabbath became transmuted into a celebration of the resurrection. Christians hallow time not only through the regular Sunday service, but throughout the year in a meaningful sequence of seasonal celebrations. In this way the presence of God is recalled in a way more fitting than if done purely on the basis of immediacy, feeling flow, and spontaneity. The order itself is not God, but God is worshiped through the ordering of time.

- The experienced liturgist comes especially to appreciate those recurrent signposts and familiar pathways that remind the community of its historical experience and continuity through time. As the psalmists have sung, we now sing. Where the prophets, apostles, and martyrs have walked, we now walk. Gradually there is engendered a rich sense of placement in time that has a reference point transcending time. One sees one's current activity as illumined by that placement in time (Augustine, *NPNF* 1st, vol. 2, pp. 180 ff.; Cullman, 1953). Eucharist is something that the communicant has done before and tasted many times anew. Part of the liturgist's task is to look for ways in which those pathways and signposts can still function meaningfully to address modern consciousness. The pastor does well to resist exaggerated forms of faddism and hunger for novelty which so plague modern religious aspirations. But on the other side, the pastor does well to make good use of the wisest and best efforts at liturgical renewal that have been consensually formed on the basis of careful scriptural and historical study.

- Even within the context of an orderly, recurrent memory, every discrete service of worship itself should be a new act of adoration, like the dew of each morning. Worship will freely use the ancient patterns to evoke the fresh, new contemporary insight. That is a dialectic in which the good liturgist delights. The service gains spontaneity not by divesting itself of historical awareness, but by bringing historical awareness into lively expression in the present. It transcends form with spirit. According to classical Christian psychology, it is the soul alone that prays, confesses, and adores. Since the soul is alive, it wishes to live anew, in each new moment. We do a disservice to Christian liturgy by assuming that it is merely a form or that it is "mere talk." It is a living event. The language and form are the body or outer shell in which the living event, the contemporary celebration of the risen Christ, is re-enacted and renewed.

- Christian worship requires community. Imagining a strictly community-less worship is like imaging an absolutely wordless prayer. There is a dialectic in the service of worship between individual and corporate prayer, in which the liturgist serves both the person's solitary consciousness of God and the community's need for a unified voice. These are not as antagonistic as sometimes portrayed. Good liturgy assumes that these dimensions are complementary, and are to be united in a corporate act of celebration. Public worship wishes to serve the worshiping person. Either within or apart from the congregation, we can shut the door and pray to the Father who is in secret (Matt. 6:6). But the solitary consciousness needs the regular reinforcement of a community that will challenge, correct, and complete it (Acts 2:42). The pastor as chief liturgist is assigned the happy task of feeding, nurturing, and developing the environment for both corporate and individual worship.

The greatest theological treatises on prayer do not give us a choice between private and public prayer. They view private prayer as preparatory to and an accompaniment of the public liturgy, and common prayer as re-funding the daily life of prayer of the scattered people of God. When you find the question bifurcated as private versus public prayer, it is usually misstated.

- <u>Christian worship of God cannot do without silence, but neither can it do without words.</u> We may admire Quaker and Trappist concerns for receptive silence in worship. The central tradition is grateful for them but has not viewed them as normative or fully adequate to the social nature of human beings and to the verbal capacities of the human imagination. Admittedly, the worship of God transcends and breaks to pieces our frail language. No human language captures the reality of God. Worship is transcended, by definition, by the One to whom we speak in worship.

  Christian worshipers need the discipline of silence, the meditative prayer and quiet centering. But that does not deny the need at other times for language. The Lord's Supper is an embodied word that language cannot finally capture, but it uses language nonetheless. It is a concentrated word-event. We are touched by the water. We eat the bread. It is more than words, yet not without words. Liturgical events seek to bring into a concentrated, harmonious enactment the central recollections and understandings of Christian faith.

- Only music is capable of expressing much that occurs in worship. The profound relation of worship and music, though beyond the range of this discussion, remains a point of meditative reflection for the serious liturgist. <u>It is a regular weekly practical issue and challenge to the pastor to bring worship and music into proper integration. It cannot be turned over</u> to someone else.

Pastor's job

  There is a profound analogy between worship and music that reminds the modern reader of bicameral brain theory. The right side of the brain is unanalytical. It does not dissect, count, or sort data, as does the left side, but rather, intuitively integrates them. Music is "heard" through the right side of the brain. So in liturgy we have an integrative function. Similarly, as music addresses not just a part of us, but the soul through the ear, according to early Christian psychologies, it differs from objective data gathering that may or may not address the soul, the whole centered person. So worship wishes to address the center of our being and reach from there to the circumference.

  The ministry of music is important for the worshiping community. In early Christianity there is recurrent reference to the community singing God's praises (cf. Clement of Alexandria, *ANF*, vol. 2, pp. 248 f.; Cyprian, *ANF*, vol. 5, p. 280; *Teaching of the Apostles*, *ANF*, vol. 8, p. 669). Colossians 3:16 invites, "Sing thankfully in your hearts to God, with psalms and hymns and spiritual songs." "Let the Holy Spirit fill you: speak to one another in psalms, hymns, and songs; sing and make music in your hearts to the Lord" (Eph. 5:19).

The Improvement of Pastoral Prayer

In pastoral prayer the liturgist offers pastoral direction not only corporately for the gathered community, but also for the prayer life of individuals in the community.

Philip Doddridge offered these helpful guidelines to the pastor concerning pastoral prayer: "Avoid the extremes of too mean and too pompous a style. Do not reduce prayer to familiarities and chatter." Aim at nothing but the "pouring out of the soul to God in the most genuine language." Your purpose is not to "pray as nobody ever prayed before." Let prayer be informed by Scripture and Christian memory. Converse much with your own heart; get acquainted with the state of your own soul. Remember it is the peculiar office of the Spirit of God to help us in prayer. Seek "a unity of design . . . and let one petition be connected with another by natural, but never laboured transition." Let the "prayer be agreeable to the sermon," but do not turn it into "a preaching prayer" (*LP*, pp. 71 ff.).

One of the ways we most often offend against decency in public prayer is by incoherent, wandering speech that bears no evidence of coming from either the mind or the heart. We overload public prayer with the "vain repetitions" against which Jesus warned (Matt. 6:7).

Some may smile at the "prayer lists" of pietists but in a deeper sense it is a commendable habit of ministry to keep some record or mental note—or at least a ready recollection—of persons that are subjects of intercessory concern during a given week, both for private and public worship. Some specific names of persons who are sick, traveling, or facing special risk or contingency may be held up before God in worship. Most pastoral intercessions will be quite private, and remain unknown to the congregation.

The Dilemmas of Prayer

The well-prepared pastor should be ready to deal with the most familiar questions about prayer. Sometimes they are casually, sometimes deeply, asked. Here are six of them: (1) Is prayer merely a form of self-deception? When we pray do we really just talk to ourselves? (2) Isn't prayer for those bottoming out in Skid Rows and in foxholes? How is it also for the strong? (3) If God is omniscient, is it necessary for us to state what we want or need? Doesn't God know our needs already? (4) Has scientific learning outmoded prayer? Does prayer contradict natural law? (5) Is prayer inequitable? Is it asking a special favor of God, perhaps unjustly, for private advantage? (6) Do written prayers limit the Spirit? No pastor will serve long without hearing such questions.

These questions require that the pastor engage in serious theological reflection before entering the scene of crisis or doubt. If unprepared theologically, the pastor may easily fall into senseless contradictions or sentimentalities. A thorough answer will hinge upon the pastor having worked carefully through the problems of theodicy discussed in Chapter 15. Here, in brief form, are some kernels of insight from the pastoral tradition in response to these perennial questions:

- Far from being self-deceptive, we may be helped by the Spirit to cut through the layers of self-deception to genuine disclosure and candid self-appraisal (Augustine, *NPNF* 1st, vol. 1, pp. 57 ff.; *Apostolic Constitutions, ANF,* vol. 7, pp. 467 ff.). We can pray also for an end of self-deception. Since true prayer is honesty before God, it resists self-deception.

- Isn't it a different prayer the shipwrecked pray than those safely in port? The difference is the circumstance, not the listening of God. Prayers are varied because circumstances are varied. Because time and experience change, prayer changes, yet it remains addressed to the One who transcends and encompasses all change (Augustine, *NPNF* 1st, vol. 1, pp. 166 ff.; Kierkegaard, 1849b, 101 ff.; 1851–52, p. 228).

- Jews and Christians have believed that far from making prayer unnecessary, divine omniscience makes prayer all the more necessary and significant. The pastoral tradition has always acknowledged that God knows our needs before we speak them, but that is no reason to leave them unspoken, if God freely welcomes dialogue. We speak our prayers on God's own cordial entreaty (Ignatius, *ANF,* vol. 1, p. 65; Cyprian, *ANF,* vol. 5, pp. 286 ff.).

- The suggestion that empirical science outmodes prayer seems to forget that empirical science itself is limited and changing in its scientific paradigms and conceptions of knowing the truth. As Thomas Kuhn has shown, these paradigms from time to time undergo radical historical revisions. Most recently, paranormal psychology studies have profoundly challenged many assumed scientific absolutes (Kelsey, 1963, pp. 307 ff.; Moss, 1974). That is why they are regarded as "para" ("beyond"): they go beyond the assumption of curent science. Meanwhile, an overwhelming majority of persons living in secularized high-technology society continue to believe that God exists and answers prayer.

- As for the question of unjustness in making requests of God, it should be remembered that the most fundamental form of prayer in the pastoral tradition is Jesus' prayer in Gethsemane: "Nevertheless not my will, but thine be done" (Luke 22:42, KJV; cf. Calvin, *Inst.,* 2.16.12). It is the sure pattern of all Christ-like prayer. What faith asks of God must not simply be a sheer assertion of human will but a yielding to God's will. The crass instrumental use of God is hardly an adequate conception of prayer. One cannot wisely dismiss prayer on the basis of a grossly inadequate conception of it.

- It is a fanatical notion that we interfere with the Holy Spirit if we make any preparation for prayer. The theological deficit in that assumption is that the Holy Spirit would not have us reason or use foresight or imagination or fit language (Wesley, *Appeals*, 1975 ed., pp. 51 ff.). It assumes incorrectly that the only part of us that the Spirit wishes to work through is emotive impulsivity and spontaneous feeling-flow. It assumes incorrectly that the Holy Spirit does not also work through discipline, reason, reflection, and organization.

The Triune God and the Modes of Prayer

The liturgist needs a firm grasp of the ways in which the acts of prayer correlate with the heart of Christian doctrine, namely, the Christian teaching about the triune God. Nothing is more uniquely a mark of the Christian understanding of God than the notion that the one God is Creator, the Father whose Son Jesus came to us with redemption and forgiveness as incarnate Lord, crucified and risen, and out of the Father and the Son proceeds the Holy Spirit who evokes, guides, comforts, challenges, and empowers the community of celebration (Cyril of Jerusalem, *LCC*, vol. 4, pp. 168 ff.). The triune God, who is incomparably One in these three persons, is similarly present in unifying diverse acts of prayer (Tertullian, *ANF*, vol. 3, pp. 597 ff.).

The public worship that the pastor leads must itself be clearly understood by the pastor. There are three phases or clusters of motifs that recur—usually in sequence—that need to be clearly grasped by the liturgical leader.

- awe/invocation/adoration/thanksgiving—the opening sequence of acts
- confession/repentance/supplication/affirmation of faith/witness— the central sequence of acts of worship
- grateful responsiveness/dedication/oblation/commitment to the Christian life—the concluding sequence of acts of common prayer

These three liturgical acts do not just haphazardly appear, but constitute a meaningful order that makes up a wholesome and well-ordered act of worship. The service proceeds from a sense of awe fitting to God's holiness and mystery, toward thanksgiving and praise, which itself tends toward radical self-examination in which we become aware of our sin and guilt and in repentance bring ourselves before the divine mercy. Then true repentance becomes the proper basis upon which the contrite person can hear the good news of God's forgiveness, so as to be able conscientiously to utter the affirmation of faith that rehearses the story of God's self-giving in Jesus Christ. Our response in offertory and benediction is to offer ourselves as God has offered himself to us.

This, in summary form, is what happens in Christian worship. This threefold sequence of worship is implicitly triune (Augustine, *LCC*, vol. 8, pp. 38 ff.; cf. Oden, 1963, pp. 127 ff., 1972, pp. 103–111). The oft-discussed distinction between "types of prayer" correlates with the triune doctrine of God.

This sequence is important for the practice of ministry because the minister as chief liturgist is called upon to understand and at times clarify the inner meaning structure and theological rationale of worship. Our thesis: prayer is an oft-enacted sequence of approaches and responses to God that correspond to the reality of God as Father, Son, and Spirit.

This formulation helps us work through a common discontent that is experienced in discussing the distinguishable modes or types of prayer, namely, that we tend to bifurcate and disunite prayer in our attempts at analytical definition. We tend to separate what is inseparable: the act of prayer is separated from the Holy One to whom prayer responds. Consequently the psychology of prayer is disjoined from the triune God to whom prayer is addressed. Meanwhile, awe is considered separable from confession, or confession from commitment. Prayer can be better understood in terms of a threefold pattern that resonates throughout classical pastoral reasoning about the triune God, in which unity is affirmed amid distinguishable acts (Ambrose, *NPNF* 2nd, vol. 10, pp. 201–205, 92 ff.). Accordingly, there are three fundamentally interrelated modes of prayer.

Prayer to God the Father

In prayer we meet God first in the consciousness of awe, a due sense of reverence for God as unsearchable mystery, incomparable goodness, and insurmountable power. The holy God evokes in us a sense of reverence that remains "the beginning of wisdom" (Ps. 111:10). We know ourselves to be radically dependent upon this mysterious and transcendent reality. That is the opening mood of prayer in the Jewish and the Christian traditions. Adoration only ascribes to God the glory that is God's due. It says to God, "You are so different from all else in our experience that we can only sit in amazement. We ask for nothing but simply to worship You."

It is this adored reality that we call upon and beseech to be present with us in our worship. We collect together and present ourselves before God. We invoke God's name, inviting God to make his living presence known and felt among us. The moving language of the Anglican collect for Holy Communion concisely grasps this approach: "Almighty God, unto whom all hearts be open, all desires known, and from whom no secrets are hid; cleanse the thoughts of our hearts by the inspiration of thy Holy Spirit, that we may perfectly love thee, and worthily magnify thy holy Name; through Christ our Lord. Amen" (*BCP*, 1662, p. 173).

We offer our praise and thanksgiving to the Creator God not only for the goods of creation but also for their source in the insurmountable divine goodness. Thanksgiving in due course is addressed to God the creator, God the redeemer, and God the sanctifier (Father, Son, Spirit; beginner, mediator, fulfiller). We begin by thanking the creator for our lives, continue by thanking the redeemer for our salvation, and conclude by thanking God the Spirit for the ongoing work of sanctification, even until the end of time (Augustine, *NPNF* 1st, vol. 3, pp. 250 ff.).

Prayer to God the Son

We have taken the good creation and with our free will abused it, seeking lesser goods, exalting limited values as if they were absolutes, falling away from the greatest good so as to find ourselves ever more deeply enmeshed in adoring limited goods. The result is social, historical, political, and personal sin that is primordially engendered, intergenerationally mediated, and unawarely received. In confession, we hold up before God precisely this alienated human condition. We know that we have strayed like lost sheep, followed too much the devices and desires of our own hearts, and left undone those things that we ought to have done, and that there is no health in us (*BCP*, 1662, pp. 42 f.). We petition earnestly for God's mercy and forgiveness.

The Christian service of worship remembers the good news of Jesus Christ, and in its light, we pray for the pardon made known through the Son. The Affirmation of Faith, that God the Father has met us through his Son Jesus Christ, includes Scripture reading, creed and sermon, and the hearing the word read, confessed, and exposited. The written word is spoken aloud from the law, prophets, psalms, and apostles. The creed is a condensed statement of the rule of faith in the triune God implicit in the baptismal formula. The homily then seeks to make clear to the contemporary believer that God the Father has come to us in his Son Jesus Christ to offer us newness of life, forgiveness, freedom, and love (Ambrose, *NPNF* 2nd, vol. 10, pp. 203 ff.).

Prayer to God the Spirit

This then calls for another turn in the sequence of prayer. Having received the gospel, the prayers of the faithful are addressed to God the Spirit, who wills to complete the work begun in the Father and dramatically revealed in the Son, so as to finish the work of redemption that was needed because of the fallenness of creation. The prayer for sanctification essentially exists as a response to the gospel, asking for guidance of the Spirit to enable us to respond fittingly.

Here we pray in the mode of petition. We ask God to purify our
hearts and to bless our human efforts. Petition may take the form of
asking for illumination, hoping for God's presence to be with us as we
listen to Scripture so that we may discern its meaning clearly. We pray
that God the Spirit may work effectually in our hearts. Petition may
come not only in the form of supplication (petition for oneself) but also
of intercession (petition for others). We intercede on behalf of those
imprisoned, sick, lonely, alienated, and not for individuals only but for
collective distortions in both the church and society. We especially intercede for those who are radically vulnerable: the poor, those in dire
need, the dying, the bereaved. Their suffering is viewed and beheld in
direct relation to God's own suffering for us. Bidding prayers may intercede for someone or something in particular: for God's grace to be
poured upon a marriage or on a new life coming into being or for
comfort amid loss.

All of this leads to the prayer of oblation or dedication, when we
offer ourselves to God in response to God's offering of himself to us.
The benediction symbolizes the return into the world with God's
strength and blessing to embody his love to the world as it has been
embodied to us in Christ.

This then reveals an implicit trinitarian design embedded in common prayer. It is called common because, as distinguished from private
prayer, it occurs in community, in common with other believers. The
minister who does not understand this order may be confusing the congregation. Its inner structure is best grasped in relation to the center of
ancient ecumenical orthodoxy: God is one, Father, Son, and Holy
Spirit. If the service jumps awkwardly backward from pardon to the
concern for penitence, or from oblation to awe, the triune sequence has
lost its unity and become confused, and the faithful believer senses
something amiss. If the liturgist fixates on one part of that sequence to
the neglect of the other aspects, the inner logic of the service becomes
distorted. Christian worship proceeds from awe through pardon to
dedication, and from God the Father through the Son to the inspiration
of the Spirit. This pattern of prayer correlates with the creator who
gives us life, the redeemer who brings us back to the original purpose
of life when fallen, and the Spirit who sanctifies and completes what is
offered and given in Christ.

The End Time Drama

In Christian worship we have essentially an end time drama. In
every service we celebrate the apostolic faith in God as original ground
of being, confessing our fallen history and remembering God's saving
action and the hope of fitting consummation. An interpretation of universal history is packed into each well-conceived worship service: The
good creation, fallen into sin, is redeemed by the Son and brought into

effective expression and fulfillment through the power of the Holy Spirit.

Watching worship unfold is something like watching the development of an embryo, in that the embryo gradually recapitulates a whole massive evolutionary history, in which previous achievements are included in each subsequent stage. So it is similarly that in worship, each step is not artificially separable from that which precedes it, but embraces, includes, and fulfills each previous phase. In this way the whole process recapitulates the meaning of history, focusing on God's encounter with his creation, loving it amid its fallenness, and guiding it to a recovery and fulfillment of God's original purpose.

Thus Christian worship implicitly rehearses the order of salvation (*ordo salutis*), which is the familar sequence of themes found in systematic theology. This sequence moves from the reality of God, through creation, the fall, providence, sin, Christology, atonement, justification, redemption, and salvation, and then finally to sanctification, pneumatology, ecclesiology and eschatology. Throughout there is a continuing dialogue in which God speaks to humanity through creation, conscience, history, and revelation, while persons respond to God in praise, affirmation, and dedication. God addresses humanity in Christ's redemption; faith responds in trust. God addresses the gathered community through Scripture and its exposition; the gathered community responds with prayer and praise. God the Spirit addresses us in a call to discipleship, and we respond in self-offering. All of this is epitomized in the Eucharist, where God's convenant love addresses us in and through the body and blood of Christ.

Within this drama there is a steady building of emotive energy, from a quiet and holy, but awesome, beginning, through a tragic set of complications, to an astonishing resolution with a powerful, moving, hopeful conclusion. From invocation to benediction, there is a principle of ascension, like movement up a spiral staircase, from awe, which moves to praise, then to confession, joy, and finally to self-giving in response to God's gift to us (cf. Shepherd, 1950; Abba, 1957).

All of this occurs weekly in the sanctuary in the divine service. It seeks to provide a unified interpretation of history. It is comprehensive. It unites our hearts before God. It has an intrinsic order. It is an embodied action.

REFERENCES AND FURTHER READING

Among classical texts that treat of the pastor as liturgist, see Ignatius (*ANF*, vol. 1, 65), Irenaeus (*ANF*, vol. 1, pp. 432 ff.), Justin Martyr (*LCC*, vol. 1, pp. 282 ff.), Clement of Alexandria (*ANF*, vol. 4, pp. 613 ff.), Tertullian (*ANF*, vol. 3, pp. 597 ff.), Origen (*ANF*, vol. 4, pp. 613 ff.), Hippolytus (*ANF*, vol. 5, pp. 9 ff.), Cyprian (*ANF*, vol. 5, 447 ff.), Early Liturgies (*ANF*, vol. 3, pp. 529 ff.),

Apostolic Constitutions (*ANF*, vol. 7, pp. 429 ff.), Minucius Felix (*ANF*, vol. 4), Eusebius (*NPNF* 2nd, vol. 1), Chrysostom (*LCF*, pp. 174 ff.), Ambrose (*NPNF* 2nd, vol. 10, pp. 92 ff., 201 ff.), Cyril of Jerusalem (*LCC*, vol 4, pp. 168 ff.), Benedict (d. 550), Thomas Aquinas (*ST*, vol. 2, pp. 1539 ff.), Luther (*LW*, vol. 40; *SWML*, vol. 4, pp. 387 ff.), Calvin (1559, 1.11, 4.10), Hooker (*ATP*, pp. 345 ff., 369, 407 ff.), and Kierkegaard (1849b, 1851–52). More recent discussions on Christian worship include L. Thornton (1941), Scott (1927), Calkins (1941), Dix (1945), Jones (1954), Abba (1957), and Strathmann and Meyer (1964 ff.).

For various discussions of priestly ministry see John of Damascus (*NPNF* 2nd, vol. 9, 81 ff.), Tarnow (1623), Spener (1677), Wesley (*WJV*, vol. 7, pp. 363 ff.), H. Thompson (1832), Moberly (1899), Duchesne (1919), Weiss (1954), Torrance (1955), Abba (1957), Manson (1958), Best (1960), Hubbard (*NBO*, pp. 1028 ff.), Eastwood (1960), Schillebeeckx (1969), and Holmes (1982).

For various descriptions or interpretations of the work of clergy, including the task of leadership in the worshiping community, see Pond (1844), Spurgeon (1946 ed.), Tilden (1899), Schaller (1913), Erdman (1924), A. Palmer (1937), J. Fichter (1961), and Glasse (1968).

Among the service books and liturgies consulted were the Common Service Book (1930), the Book of Offices (1936), The Book of Common Order (1940), The Book of Common Worship (1946), The Book of Worship for Church and Home (1944, 1964), Shepherd (1950), The Book of Common Worship (1963), The Book of Common Prayer (1559, 1662, 1928, 1979), as well as various contemporary efforts at liturgical renewal. Other resources concerning the pastoral direction of the life of prayer include Evagrius Ponticus (d. 399), Augustine (*LCC*, vol. 7), Gregory the Great (*ACW*, vol. 11, pp. 105 ff.), Thomas Aquinas (*ST*, vol. 2, pp. 1538 ff.), Valdés (*LCC*, vol. 25, pp. 353 ff.), Calvin (1559, 3.20), Preston (1635), Wollebius (*RD*, pp. 203 ff.), Voetius (*RD*, pp. 265 ff.), Paley (1830 ed.), Otto (1925), Cullmann (1953), Cross (1960), Danielou (1967), Rowley (1967), Howe (1974), and Segler (1960, 191 ff.).

8. The Ministry of Baptism and Eucharist

Pastoral theology asks what clergy do and why. Having discussed liturgical leadership in general, we now tighten the focus to speak more specifically of its most condensed, summary acts: baptism and Holy Communion. In the mainstream Christian traditions, ordination bestows upon the ordinand the solemn obligation and distinctive privilege of providing the faithful community with the proclaimed word in preaching and the enacted word in sacraments.

This sacramental ministry is not a subsidiary, optional, or incidental duty, but central to Christ's essential purpose in ministry (Thomas Aquinas, *ST*, vol. 3., pp. 2382 ff. Calvin, *Inst.*, 4.16 ff.). It behooves the pastor to think carefully about the biblical and theological grounding of the simple acts of baptizing and breaking bread.

THE EMBODIED WORD

The pre-Christian Greek tradition used the word *mustērion* to point to a secret or riddle to which the answer had not yet been found, yet was in the process of being gradually disclosed. The Latin writers later translated *mustērion* as *sacramentum,* from *sacrare,* "to set apart," "to consecrate for holy use." Our English word *sacrament* still powerfully reflects connotations of mystery and of being set apart, with the implication that ministry is by analogy set apart precisely to offer the holy sacrament.

The idea of mystery (from *mueō,* "to instruct in sacred things"), was never meant to suggest incomprehensibility or absurdity, but rather the teaching of spiritual meaning that was as yet not fully revealed for all to see, yet anticipatively revealed, at least in its basic direction, for those who have eyes to see. In the New Testament *mustērion* refers to the divine plan of salvation hidden in past ages, but now brought to light in Jesus Christ (Eph. 1:2). The mystery was not that God was wholly un- revealed, but that his holy will had now at long last become manifest, that his governance was already present in the community of faith, and that the banquet of the end time was in anticipation already being set with bread and wine as lively indications of God's own real presence (Chrysostom, *NPNF* 1st, vol. 12, pp. 139 ff. 148 ff., 163 ff.; cf. Chem- nitz, 1593, pp. 39 ff.).

The Bath and the Meal

What do pastors need to know about the sacrament that they alone are commissioned and privileged to offer? A familiar definition states: "Sacraments ordained of Christ are not only badges or tokens of Chris- tian . . . profession, but rather they are certain sure witnesses, and effec- tual signs of grace, and of God's good will toward us, by which he doth work invisibly in us, and doth not only quicken, but also strengthen and confirm our faith in him" (*CC*, pp. 274, cf. pp. 357 ff.).

Through these visible re-enactments, God's grace is awakening and empowering our participation in the life of Christ. We are born in Christ in baptism, and through Holy Communion we are nurtured, sustained, and, it is hoped, eventually sanctified (made mature in holy living) in Christ. The ministry that misunderstands these decisive sacra- mental acts or relegates them to a secondary position does a grim dis- service to the Christian community.

One of the first things a minister is required to understand about ordination is that it is intrinsically connected with assumptions about what it means to be commissioned by the community to baptize and serve the Supper. Lay persons in most traditions are not authorized to administer the sacraments except at times when they will assist ordained ministers. This is an office that by tradition and for good order has been reserved for those duly authorized and prepared to offer it, and which in large part defines their ordination. The ordained are those who have been called inwardly by God to ministry and whose inward call has been outwardly affirmed by the visible church precisely to pro- vide the community with this enacted word in an appropriate way, fit- ting to Scripture and tradition (Cyril of Jerusalem, *NPNF* 2nd, vol. 7, pp. 130 ff.; Calvin, *Inst.*, 4.4; *Conclusions of Berne*, 1528, *CC*, p. 150).

The sacraments presuppose that God has met us in history and that this meeting calls us to regular recollection and re-enactment in order to experience God's real presence in our midst. The grace of God is offered to us in and through these sacraments in a way that we cannot grasp by our own moral efforts. Protestants revolted against what they perceived to be superstitions of medieval penance and sacramentalism (Luther, *SWML*, vol. 1, pp. 43 ff., 355 ff; Calvin, *Inst.*, 4.14.14). Yet never do the Protestant confessions lose sight of the basic idea that grace is being offered and, by faith, communicated to the believer in baptism and Holy Communion by Christ's own ordinance. They are means of grace (Hooker et al. in *ATP* pp. 407 ff.; Calvin, *Inst.*, 4.1 ff.; Wesley, *WJW*, vol. 7).

Water, bread, and wine express promises, not that we make to God but that God makes to us, to which we may respond in obedient faith. They are signs of God's mercy to us and of God's immediate presence in our midst. We are cleansed through water and fed through bread. We are brought into the community by baptism and sustained in the community by communion (Cyril of Jerusalem, *LCF*, pp. 42 ff.; *Thirty-nine Articles, CC*, pp. 274 f.).

There is something refreshingly simple about the sacraments Jesus instituted; they are hardly more impressive than a bath and a meal. Life in Christ begins with a cleansing bath of repentance and pardon; it continues with nurturing food and drink. Christian worship takes these ordinary elements of life and consecrates them to divine service (*lei-tourgia*). It is this simplicity, far more than complex doctrinal formulation, that has sustained Christian belief over many centuries of cultural change (Augustine, *NPNF* 1st, vol. 4, pp. 411 ff.).

These lowly, earthly things—bread, wine, and water—are freely used by God to convey that which is highest: divine mercy, covenant faithfulness, and suffering love, all of which are necessary for our salvation. No high learning or auspicious display is required. Rather, we have simple acts adapted to our capacity to receive the truth. It may be that we will not always understand the Scriptures or exegete them properly or grasp all of their historical antecedents and influences, but when we sit down to the Lord's table, God has adapted his living Word to our capacity to receive it. The mighty and the learned sit down at the same table with the plain and the poor on equal footing in the presence of the living Christ. There is an awesome equalitarian strain implicit in the mystery of Christ's presence in the sacraments.

Though distinguishable, word and sacrament are inseparably intertwined. The word spoken in preaching is visibly enacted as sign and seal of the preached word. Together in regular antiphonal order they echo harmoniously.

Faith assumes the priority of grace to faith. It is not that we begin with faith and search for grace in the sacraments, but rather that grace searches for us, seeks to call forth our faith in God through the ministry of sacraments. What happens in Holy Communion is not to be assessed essentially in terms of what happens to me emotionally on a given day, how bored or inspired I feel, but rather by scriptural and traditional criteria: Is Christ freely and truly present through the means of grace he ordained?

A major deficiency of pietistic views of sacrament is the tendency to hinge the efficacy or meaning of sacramental acts too absolutely on our emotional responses to them, so that the Almighty God is reduced to being present to us only when we feel good about it. The corrective is clearly set forth in Eph. 2:8: "By grace ye are saved through faith; and that not of yourselves; it is the gift of God" (KJV).

Broken bread bespeaks the brokenness of Christ for us. Jesus did not ask us to contemplate bread or wine or water, but rather to embody the divine word through simple acts: break, drink, pour. He did not say *look* at this in remembrance of me, but *do* this in remembrance of me. The focus is not upon the water itself, but upon the act of cleansing the unclean, not upon bread as such but upon feeding the spiritually hungry. Only by corporate activity, not individual introspection or contemplation, does the sacrament become means of grace (Augustine, *NPNF* 1st, vol. 4, pp. 615 ff.).

Circumcision, Baptism, Passover, and Eucharist: Signs of Covenant

In order to grasp clearly the significance of the sacraments, it is necessary that we carefully review two pairs of analogous biblical rites or celebrations in which the inner and outer aspects of the covenant of grace are rehearsed:

circumcision	baptism
Passover	Eucharist

All four ideas have a similar structure, which we will now clarify. Each has the character of a sign, but none is reducible to "mere signs."

The children of Abraham were instructed to keep covenant between God and themselves and their descendents by circumcision. "It shall be the sign of the covenant between us" (Gen. 17:11). In the Jewish tradition circumcision visibly expresses the sign of God's promise. The newborn are brought into the community by means of this sign. In the Passover, similarly, it was said that "the blood will be a sign on the houses in which you are: when I see the blood I will pass over you" (Exod. 12:13).

Note the subtle way in which these Hebraic rites were transmuted, according to the New Testament, by faith in Christ's righteousness: "We say, 'Abraham's faith was counted as righteousness'; in what circumstances was it so counted? Was he circumcised at the time, or not?" Paul almost playfully made this deft point. "He was not yet circumcised, but uncircumcised; and he later received the symbolic rite of circumcision as the hall-mark of the righteousness which faith had given him when he was still uncircumcised" (Rom 4:9–11). For Paul, circumcision was a symbolic rite that was for Jews a hallmark (or "seal," KJV) of the righteousness of faith, a sign of God's promise that points beyond itself (Ambrose, *LCF*, pp. 184 ff.; Augustine, *LCF*, p. 245, *NPNF* 1st, vol. 2, pp. 523 ff.).

Signing and sealing are legal images. If a document is properly signed and sealed, whoever conveys or receives that document knows that the communicator has written his own signature on it and sealed it properly in order that all may be assured of its authenticity. Similarly, in the breaking of bread the message sent and the grace communicated is God's own incomparable grace in Christ, sealed and signed by God himself (*Early Liturgies, ANF,* vol. 7, pp. 537 ff.).

Suppose you received a banknote for ten thousand dollars, and it had on it the signature of an esteemed banker. You would not then focus inordinate attention on the signature, but upon what the signature empowers: negotiable wealth. Only one exception should be noted: If there is some reason to suspect that the banknote was not properly signed, then you must guarantee its authenticity, make sure it is the banker's actual signature, in order that you may properly receive the money. Ordinarily, in the sacraments no extravagant attention needs to be paid to the signature itself, the bread and water as such, but rather to that reality toward which they point, the grace communicated through them. The visible outward signs are God's own way of validating or sealing or signing his promise of his coming again and again in Christ through the sacraments (Tertullian, *ANF,* vol. 3, pp. 672 ff.; Hooker, *ATP,* pp. 407 ff.; Bridges, 1847 ed.).

Why are these sacraments so important? The pastor will be asked that question at inconvenient times. It needs a well-thought-out answer. Minimally these acts are not to be viewed as "commandments of men" (Matt. 15:9) or socially determined conventions or psychologically derived routines, but as God's own intention through Christ's direct institution (Augustine, *NPNF* 1st, vol. 5, pp. 28 ff.). If sacrament is of human institution and not God's own means of grace, then we in ministry need make no fuss about it. But let us suppose that our pastoral reflection on the sacraments takes into account the ancient church's most elementary teaching about them, that they are appointed by God the Son himself for our benefit as signs of his covenant.

The signature analogy is decisive: We are talking about God's own verified signature—verified by Christ's own suffering and the communion of saints (*Seven Ecumenical Councils, NPNF* 2nd, vol. 14, pp. XIV 39, 108 f., 597 ff., 610 f.). If a forger has sent the banknote, then we need to find out about it. Yet the fact that one has chosen to be ordained suggests an implicit affirmation that this promise is not counterfeit, but God's own self-communication.

The Gifts of God for the People of God

No one but God can finally speak almightily. No one but a forgiving God can divinely forgive. If the sacraments are essentially social inventions or customs that are explained exhaustively through naturalistic reductionist models, then the benefits they confer must be human, not divine, benefits. The word they express cannot be God's own word, but human words. That is precisely what distinguishes believers from nonbelievers. That is why it is a central premise of the ministry of the sacraments that they are of divine institution (Calvin, *Inst.*, 4.18; Chemnitz, 1593, p. 109). They are not, in the mainstream tradition, merely symbolic "badges of distinction" to help us sort out the difference between the visible church and the world, although indeed it is a secondary sociological result of the sacraments that they do tell us something about that difference. But that is not their essential definition.

According to Scripture, all of these rites and celebrations (circumcision, Passover, baptism, and the Supper) are offered on God's own invitation. The scriptural accounts of their institution in each case go out of their way to underscore the divine initiative:

- "God said to Abraham, 'For your part, you must keep my covenant, you and your descendants . . . circumcise yourselves' " (Gen 17:9–11).
- "Thus will I execute judgment, I the Lord . . . as for you, the blood will be a sign" (Exod. 12:13). The "I" speaking is Yahweh. In the tenth day of the month they were to take a lamb without defect, ritually slaughter it, and put blood on the doorframes of their houses. In the memory of Israel, this was not initiated by the priesthood or the people, but directly by Yahweh (cf. Exod. 12:1, 2 Chron. 35:6).
- "Jesus . . . said: 'Full authority in heaven and on earth has been committed to me . . . baptize [persons] everywhere' " (Matt. 28:18, 19).
- Where did Paul get the tradition of the Lord's Supper? He states clearly: "The tradition which I handed on to you came to me from the Lord himself: that the Lord Jesus, on the night of his arrest, took bread" (1 Cor. 11:23,24).

The moment that pastoral reasoning grants the decisive point that sacraments are of human invention, and thus subject fully to this or that naturalistic explanation, then what else remains to be said theologically? It then becomes merely a case for psychological, sociological, or historical definition of causes. No plausible sacramental doctrine can be retrieved from that point on. For one has already decided overgenerously to give away the single point most crucial, according to classical reasoning about the sacraments.

It could be argued that the Christian community could easily do without the visible sign as long as it already has the inner word, grace, and this preached word. Classical pastoral reasoning answers this by pointing to the proportionality of our capacity for reasoning about God. Since God's mercy is infinite, there is far more of it than we are able to assimilate. But sacramental acts appeal not just to our ears, but to sight, touch, and taste. Faith comes indeed through the hearing of the word, but it is strengthened by the Supper that is savored and incorporated bodily (Augustine, *LCF*, pp. 246–48). Our bodies literally are fed by the body of Christ. This is a more powerful vehicle of learning and immediate address than language simply addressed to the ear.

But in Scripture there are many visible signs of divine mercy. The rainbow, the cloud, Gideon's fleece, the sun standing still—all might be cited as visible signs of God's mercy. Why aren't they sacraments? They are temporary signs circumstantially given, not permanently instituted by God's command, as are circumcision and Passover for Jews and baptism and Communion for Christians. These rites differ from ordinary dispensations of grace like rain and sun. They are permanent, recurrent celebrations, so that in any place or time you would find Christians, you would find them breaking bread and baptizing as visible signs of Christ's presence, just as in any place or time you encounter the Jewish faith you will find circumcision and the celebration of Passover.

But however much we may deem it necessary that these signs be visible, just as you would want to be able to actually see the signature on your ten-thousand-dollar note instead of having it written in invisible ink, nonetheless the important thing is not the signature itself, but what it signifies, enables, and empowers, namely, the redemptive grace of God in resurrection and atonement.

What is communicated through this embodied word? The living Christ present in these acts, who promises to share participatively in them:

- "Is not the cup of thanksgiving for which we give thanks a participation in the blood of Christ" (1 Cor. 10:16, NIV).
- "As Christians you are unleavened Passover bread; for indeed our Passover has begun; the sacrifice is offered—Christ himself. So we who observe the festival must not use the old leaven" (1 Cor. 5:7,8).

In addition to baptism and Communion, five other rites are viewed as sacraments in the Roman tradition: confirmation, penance, ordination, matrimony, and last rites. Protestant analogues and counterparts of all these will be discussed in due time as dimensions of an ecumenical pastoral theology, although not under the rubric of sacraments. Confirmation stands in profound correlation with the sacrament of baptism, while penance, matrimony, and last rites stand in close connection with the ministry of Eucharist. Ordination authorizes not only the fit administration of baptism and the Supper, but many other pastoral acts consequent from them.

The seven Catholic rites and the many functions of Protestant pastoral care need to be studied in a synchronic way for mutually beneficial analogies. The structure, sequence, and deeper intention of the medieval doctrine of the seven sacraments was stated classically by the Council of Florence (1438–45), which itself was a concise summary based on Thomas Aquinas and earlier medieval theologians:

> The first five have been ordained for the spiritual perfection of every individual in himself, the last two for the government and increase of the whole Church. Through baptism we are spiritually reborn; through confirmation we grow in grace and are strengthened in faith. Having been regenerated and strengthened, we are sustained by the divine food of the eucharist. But if we become sick in soul through sin, we are healed spiritually through penance, and healed spiritually as well as physically, in proportion as it benefits the soul, through extreme unction. Through orders the Church is governed and grows spiritually, while through marriage it grows physically.... There are three of the sacraments, baptism, confirmation, and orders, which imprint on the soul an indelible character, i.e., a kind of spiritual seal distinct from the others. They are not, therefore, to be received more than once by the same individual. The rest, however, do not imprint a character and may be performed more than once. (Denzinger, pp. 253–54.)

From a contemporary ecumenical viewpoint, we may ask similarly how the ministry of sacraments embraces and includes other acts of ministry:

- Within the sphere of the ministry of baptism, we may grasp the inner dynamic of the ministry of confirmation (or reaffirmation of the grace of baptism) and the ministry of evangelism (or restoration of the lapsed) as well as the process of reception of church members.
- Under the ministry of the Eucharist we may grasp and consider the pastor's general leadership in Christian worship, as well as the tasks of counseling persons in repentance, confession, offering of God's pardon, and care of the sick and dying.

The service of baptism is the rite of initiation into the community. The service of the Lord's Supper is the means of nurturing the community in strength and health. So by developing these two foci we are already speaking implicitly of a wide-ranging process of entry into the community, as well as the nurturing of persons in faith through many acts of pastoral care, and of equipping the laity for their ministry in the world.

Keep in mind that this definition of Christian ministry already involves a community, *koinonia*, a circle of faith. It is not to be thought of simply as a ministry to individuals. It is from the outset a spiritual ministry to a community, and to individuals through a community.

THE MINISTRY OF BAPTISM

The scriptural authority for the ministry of baptism is grounded in the great commission, Matt. 28:19: Make disciples of all nations, baptizing them in the name of the triune God (Augustine, *NPNF* 1st, vol. 4, pp. 495 ff.). Discipleship and baptism are thus intrinsically connected. To make disciples we baptize and teach.

From the running footprints of the early church in Acts, it appears that the earliest pastors and teachers took this command quite seriously (Acts 2:38,41, 8:12 ff., 9:18, 10:47 f.). There is constant reference to repentance and baptism, as if they were viewed together as the preconditioning event of entry into the community (Tertullian, *ANF*, vol. 3, pp. 661 ff.; Gregory of Nyssa, *LCF*, pp. 158–62). Baptism visibly signaled the believer's dying to an old way and being born into a new way, a symbolic participation in the death and resurrection of Christ (Romans 6; cf. Cyril of Jerusalem, *NPNF* 2nd, vol. 7, pp. 14 ff.). Baptism is not a rite that emerged slowly over a long period of tedious development, but rather, it appears to be substantially present from the beginning of Jesus' ministry as a sign of the meaning of that ministry—primordially in the baptism of John as a sign of repentance, and then, after Jesus' resurrection, as a participation in Christ's death and resurrection.

Believer's Baptism and the Children of Believers: The Complementarity of Two Traditions

During the last half of the first century, when much of the New Testament was being written out of available oral traditions, there were fewer children of believers than there were later. The gospel was first preached principally to adults who made public confession by means of the act of baptism as a bodily demonstration of their penitent response and faithful participation in the death and resurrection of Jesus. From these early precedents, the church has continued to baptize adult converts. But what then becomes of children of believers? Should they be baptized?

Two complementary streams of interpretation have emerged, both of which can find some evidence in the New Testament texts, which remain inconclusive and debatable. We will argue that the two traditions of believer's baptism and infant baptism are intrinsically complementary early traditions, each of which needs the other to achieve theological completeness.

The infant baptism tradition has pointed more clearly to the priority of grace to faith (Cyprian, *ANF*, vol. 5, pp. 353 f.; Augustine, *NPNF* 1st, vol. 4, pp. 461 ff.). The believer's baptism tradition has pointed more conspicuously to the importance of the believer's response to grace (*CC*, pp. 334 ff.). Both of these points need to be held together in tension in a well-conceived doctrine of baptism.

If the tradition of infant baptism is completed by a seriously pursued confirmation in which persons who come of age clearly choose to confirm or reaffirm their baptism, it defuses much of the resistance that the tradition of believer's baptism has given to the idea of infant baptism (mainly, that the faith of the baptized is overlooked).

The worldwide tradition of believer's baptism emphasizes baptism only of confessing believers who share self-consciously in the grace of Christ's death and resurrection. "By baptism we were buried with him, and lay dead, in order that, as Christ was raised from the dead in the splendour of the Father, so also we might set our feet upon the new path of life" (Rom. 6:4). This view emphasizes responsible, free adult decision. It avoids the awkwardness of assuming that the individual infant is capable of a response to faith, which presupposes volition, intelligence, and accountability.

The tradition of infant baptism, on the other hand, stresses the divine initiative prior to our human response, arguing that prevenient grace goes before our faith (Thomas Aquinas, *ST*, vol. 1, pp. 1114 ff., vol. 2, pp. 2382 f.). All this is symbolized precisely by the fact that the child is unable to have faith by her- or himself; the child's parents, as Luther argued (*WML*, vol. 6, pp. 197 ff.), are seeking to have faith on behalf of the child until the age of accountability. We subsequently learn to love God only because God first loved us (1 John 4:10). This tradition remembers that it was little children who came to Jesus and were blessed and embraced by him (Mark 10:13–16) and of whom he would say, "for such is the kingdom of Heaven." The case is sometimes argued that children already have a primordial trust that the adult believer has to some degree lost and may be trying to rediscover.

It is said in Acts 16:5 that when Lydia opened her heart in response to Paul's message, "she and the members of her household were baptized." Paul wrote in 1 Cor 1:16, "I also baptized the household of Stephanus," (cf. also 1 Cor. 16:15). One could reasonably argue that children could have been baptized as part of these households, since there is no reason to assume that the household had no children.

Baptizō can mean "dip," "immerse," "bathe," or "wash," depending on its context. In the case of Luke 9:38, when Jesus had been invited to eat with the Pharisee, it was noticed that Jesus did not wash (*baptizō*) before the meal, so it appears that *baptizō* can be used for other modes than immersion, since only the washing of hands was referred to, not the whole body. Yet Mark's version of the baptism of Jesus by John clearly seems to imply immersion, for "he came up out of the water" (Mark 1:10).

On whichever side of these debates one perceives the greater truth, what seems less debatable is that baptism stands by analogy in continuity with the rite of circumcision as an initiatory rite of entry into community, which defines the membership of the community of faith. As Jews enter the covenant community through circumcision, Christians enter the covenant community through baptism.

One major difference remains, however, between circumcision and baptism. Circumcision is for males only. It is a point of no small importance that Christians joyfully baptized females and males from the very outset. That Christian baptism is from the outset sexually inclusive must have some connection with the early Christian preaching that in Christ "there is no such thing as . . . male and female, for you are all one person in Christ Jesus" (Gal. 3:28). Many women quickly entered into the stream of the Christian community and made pivotal contributions to it.

There is a comic dimension in the analogy between circumcision and visible community. If you are going to have a palpable sign from God that divine grace is visibly present in the community of celebration, you have to have something that can be seen. Oddly enough, the prevailing symbol for this overt participation in the people of God, according to the Abrahamitic covenant, is precisely circumcision. God apparently wishes to create a sign that is visible to the whole world, yet it is visible only when nude—a neglected premise for a stand-up comedy routine.

Although circumcision was not required for gentile Christians, the idea of circumcision remained but was reinterpreted in hellenizing Christianity. Circumcision became transformed into the idea of contrition, circumcision of the heart or true penitence (Origen, *ANF*, vol. 4, pp. 370 ff.; Wesley, *WJW*, vol. 5, pp. 202 ff.). "The True Jew is not [one] who is such in externals . . . [but] who is such inwardly and the true circumcision is of the heart" (Rom. 2:29; cf. Tertullian, *ANF*, vol. 3, pp. 153 f., 458, 564). Such persons are "directed not by written precepts but by the Spirit" (v. 29). Circumcision of the heart therefore becomes a transmuted sign of entry into, and the beginning of participation in, the Christian community, that is, by repentance (*Epistle of Barnabas, ANF*, vol. 1, pp. 142 f.; Wesley, *WJW*, vol. 6).

Paul himself candidly asked: What value has circumcision? His answer is revealing: "Great in every way. In the first place, the Jews were entrusted with the oracles of God. What if some of them were unfaithful? Will their faithlessness cancel the faithfulness of God? Certainly not! God must be true though every [one] living were a liar" (Rom. 3:1–3). God's promise stands prior to our response in both circumcision and baptism. Suppose the people who are circumcised default on their side of the promise, and do not follow the divine command and promise? Does their disbelief annul the grace of God? Of course not. Similarly in baptism, it may occur that people do not live up to their baptism, but God is not averse to making his promise to us and continuing to do so even when we refuse it. God is patient, infinitely so (Exod. 34:6; Ps. 86:15, 103:8; 1 Pet. 3:20). Certainly we are being called to live in radical responsiveness to God's promise, but our failure does not annul God's promise (Augustine, *LCF*, pp. 204 ff.).

It is hardly adequate to regard the ministry of baptism essentially as a dedication service in which parents on their own initiative bring their children to offer them to God for moral improvement. What happens in baptism has less to do with the parents promising moral effort than with God promising grace to support their moral effort (J. Taylor, *ATP*, pp. 428 ff., 451).

Just as the Jewish child did not wait until the years of discretion to enter into the promise of the covenant community, so the child of the believer, in the pedo-baptist majority of Christian traditions, does not wait until the years of discretion to enter the faithful community. Just as the Jewish child was born already into a Jewish inheritance, so the Christian child, before consciousness or awareness, enters by grace into a community that promises responsively to care and nurture and teach the heart to obey God's command and receive God's promise. As circumcision was promised not only to contemporary believers but to all their descendents, similarly, in the Christian life baptism promises God's active grace for present and future generations (Justin Martyr, *ANF*, vol. 1, 202 ff.; Cyril of Jerusalem, *NPNF* 2nd, vol. 7, pp. 29 ff.).

Yet without faith and obedience, circumcision becomes uncircumcision (Rom. 2:25). Insofar as circumcision suggests works righteousness, it must be resisted (Gal. 5:2 ff.), yet its transmuted meaning as "Christ's way of circumcision" (Col. 2:11) is retained in baptism. "For in baptism you were buried with him, in baptism you were also raised to life" (Col. 2:12).

So it seems wise in the ministry of baptism to avoid both the extreme notion of moral dedication by the parents of the child and the opposite extreme of miraculous, supernatural regeneration that would tend to ignore human will, moral training, discipline, education, and decision (the voluntary side that believer's baptism has correctly emphasized). These two sides need to be held closely together: the prevenient grace of God and the voluntary response of faith.

In the time of John the Baptist, baptism was a shocking symbolic act. Most pious Jews whom John addressed already understood themselves to be unambiguously included in the elect covenant community. But John called for the baptism of repentance in a way that implied that one could not view circumcision in itself as completed evidence of participation in the elect community which John thought to be fallen and alienated. It was no small thing for the Jew to be baptized. It meant that he was no longer to boast about his self-evident participation in the people of Abraham, but rather was to repent and bring forth the fruits of repentance. Thus, when the adult faithful were called to cleanse themselves ritually in the baptism of repentance, this was a radical act in first-century Judaism for those who had taken for granted their belonging to the covenant community. This same dramatic penitential act was profoundly transmuted in Christian worship and sacramental life into an event that enacts our participation in Christ's death and resurrection.

Baptism as a Pastoral Act

The act of baptism belongs in the context of the worshiping community (Augustine, *NPNF* 1st, vol. 4, pp. 503 f.). It is not ordinarily enacted privately except in cases of extreme necessity.

In some traditions, attention is given to the name of the child, as a way of symbolically suggesting identity within the community of faith. Traditionally the names of saints have been used. This act of naming personally places the child in the Christian family by offering him or her a "given name" in this community. Since the child has a family name and a Christian name, the rite of naming of children combines both nature and spirit, both family and divine promise, both human generation and divine grace. In this way the Christian person is offered identity, in an anticipative sense, within this community, this family of God (Luther, *WML*, vol. 6, pp. 197 ff.).

One is baptized by water (immersion or effusion) in the name of the Father, Son, and Holy Spirit (Basil of Caesarea, *LCF*, p. 87). This ancient baptismal formula, which brings persons into the community in the name of the triune God, was fixed long before the details of trinitarian doctrine emerged. It set the tone and frame of reference for all later trinitarian teaching. Like the Nicene Creed that followed it, it was considered a way of summing up faith. Most subsequent credal affirmations were organized in three articles around the three persons of the baptismal formula (cf. Ambrose, *NPNF* 2nd, vol. 10, pp. 205 f., 299; Luther, *WLS*, vol. 1, p. 48).

It is a distinct part of the ministry of baptism to keep accurate records, to inscribe on a permanent parish book of record the names of baptized persons, and to present families with certificates of baptism. Teaching confirmation classes should be regarded as an intrinsic part of one's ministry of baptism (Cyril of Jerusalem, *NPNF* 2nd, vol. 7, pp. 6 ff.). Infant baptism without confirmation is like prevenient grace without obedience, or justification without steps toward sanctification. We will consider further the ministry of confirmation, or re-affirmation of baptismal vows, in Chapter 10.

THE MINISTRY OF THE EUCHARIST

The ministry of the Eucharist includes more than officiating at the Lord's Supper, although that is clearly at its heart. For just as baptism marks the beginning of participation in the body of Christ, so is the Lord's Supper the sacrament of continuing life in Christ, seeking to nurture further seasonal growth.

When the pastor thinks properly about the ministry of Holy Communion, it will include all aspects of nurture and soul-care in the community of faith in the living Christ. Although the ministry of Holy

Communion has its center in the altar-table, its circumference is very broad, and includes many acts of pastoral care, like confession, empathic listening to and guidance of parishioners in their struggle with sin, the ministry of penance that looks realistically toward concrete acts of reparation for wrongs done, and all representative pastoral acts proclaiming and expressing the forgiveness of God. Other pastoral interactions concerned with the building up of community, visiting the sick and dying, hearing confession, and offering pardon, are best seen as refracted through the lens of the ministry of the Eucharist (Calvin, *Inst.*, 4.17 ff.; J. Taylor, *ATP*, pp. 495, 520, 615; Balmforth et al., 1937, pp. 97 ff.).

The Pastor at the Lord's Table

Every Christian pastor is enlisted on behalf of the apostolic tradition to break bread fittingly for the community. This is not an incidental addendum to the ministry, for one does not get closer to the heart of Christ's ministry than when one is offering the broken bread and poured wine. It should never be viewed as an occasional exercise preliminary to "the real thing that worship is all about," however that might be conceived.

The New Testament authority for the Lord's Supper is boldly stated in Paul's letter to Corinth: "For the tradition which I handed on to you came to me from the Lord himself: that the Lord Jesus, on the night of his arrest, took bread and after giving thanks to God, broke it and said: 'This is my body, which is for you; do this as a memorial of me.' In the same way, he took the cup after supper, and said: 'This cup is the new covenant sealed by my blood. Whenever you drink it, do this as a memorial of me.' For every time you eat this bread and drink the cup, you proclaim the death of the Lord, until he comes" (1 Cor. 11:23–26; cf. Ambrose, *NPNF* 2nd, vol. 10, pp. 278 ff.). Paul clearly assumed that this act of sharing in Christ's brokenness was instituted by Jesus himself, that it is central to the apostolic tradition, and that it in fact defines the essence of that tradition. For it is precisely a "handing down" (*paradosis*, 2 Thess. 2:15) to the church from Jesus himself.

Matthew 26, Mark 14, and Luke 22 similarly relate the accounts of Jesus' own institution of the Lord's Supper before his crucifixion. Since that upper room celebration, Christians the world over have gathered to celebrate Communion with Christ in virtually all the world's languages, times, and places—for almost two millennia. Wherever Christ is present to his church, he is remembered by the breaking of bread (*Seven Ecumenical Councils, NPNF* 2nd, vol. 14, pp. 38 ff., 401 ff.; Hilary of Potiers, *LCF*, pp. 57 ff.).

Parish ministry is called to understand clearly what this means. In most Christian traditions, only those who are duly called and ordained are authorized to offer representatively these means of grace (Thomas

Aquinas, *ST*, vol. 2, p. 2503; Luther, *WLS*, vol. 2, pp. 810 ff.). Such a limitation is required in order to provide the believing community with full assurance that this act is offered in a way thoroughly accountable to the apostolic witness (Hippolytus, *ANF*, vol. 5, pp. 1 ff.; *Seven Ecumenical Councils*, *NPNF* 2nd, vol. 14, pp. 460 ff.). Even though there have been many differing interpretations of the Supper through many languages and symbol systems, the faithful have communed with Christ through radical cultural changes and historical reversals. Even though various parts of the service have been arranged in different sequences at different times, people have received bread and wine in the awareness of the communion of saints standing in a historic chain of witnesses to the death and resurrection of Christ.

The End Time Banquet

The meal over which the pastor presides is an eschatological supper. It is as if we were at the end time sharing a banquet with Christ himself as host. What is being celebrated at this feast is the final judgment and reckoning of God that is known already in an anticipative way in Jesus' resurrection. What is known in the general resurrection is precisely God's final coming, the end event of judgment and consummation. Jesus' resurrection anticipates the end time when God is expected finally to judge and redeem the distortions of history and bring to consummation the hopes of Israel. What is remembered in the Supper is that even while we were yet sinners, Christ died for us and was raised to attest that he was God's own Word to us. Resurrection, by definition, occurs at the end time. Jesus' resurrection therefore was interpreted as an anticipation of the final word of God at the end of history (Pannenberg, 1968, 1970–73). So Holy Communion brings the common believer into an extraordinary eschatological consciousness.

Holy Communion is a highly compacted liturgical event. It involves the offering by the people of the results of their common labor, bread and wine, for sacred use. In it we receive the feeding of Christ, the shepherd. It embodies God's offering of himself to us and our self-offering in response. It looks back in time toward the remarkable, saving event of Christ's death and resurrection in order to look forward in time to the end time itself, the consummation of all things in Christ. It awakens in believers the awareness of their reconciliation with God. It communicates the grace of God's atoning action, and invites here-and-now reconciliation with our neighbors. This is celebrated in the awareness that at table with the Lord we are at one with God through him and at one with others in him (Basil of Caesarea, *LCF*, pp. 88 f.).

The Supper embodies God's real presence with us. Through it we discover our real presence to each other. Out of it we learn to manifest God's love amid the darkness of the world. All of these meanings and nuances coalesce in a simple but marvelous event of eating and drink-

ing, where God takes the ordinary and communicates himself exceptionally clearly through it (Cyril of Jerusalem, *LCF*, pp. 44 ff.).

It is indeed possible at special times for the pastor to offer the Lord's
Supper without preaching, but ordinarily in the apostolic tradition, the
Supper is offered in the context of the preached Word (Luther, *WLS*,
vol. 2, pp. 793 ff.). The best way to clarify this relationship is to show
how the eucharist is an enacted commentary on the salvation event declared in Scripture. With remarkable fidelity, the sequence of acts in the
eschatological drama of the Supper follows directly the sequence of
events recalled by Paul in his astonishing précis of the heart of the
Christian tradition.

The Liturgical Drama

There are four acts in the drama reported in 1 Corinthians 15:

- He took
- He gave thanks
- He broke the bread
- He gave

These correspond to the four key phases of the celebration of the Supper:

Oblation
Eucharist
Fraction
Communion

They are complementary and interpenetrating (cf. Abba, 1957). If
one is held to the exclusion of the others, then the liturgy remains
incomplete, or at least imbalanced. We are not suggesting that there
must be an absolute uniformity of language for the proper celebration
of Communion, although Christians in each tradition of recollection
will give due respect to the intergenerational effort of their tradition to
preserve the apostolic memory authentically. Various rites use slightly
different sequences. But any ordained minister who is charged by the
church to break bread with integrity should know the central consensual tradition that recalls and re-enacts these four key moments. It is not
as if the minister is completely free to pick and choose privately preferred language or to express his or her poetic creativity so as to revise
independently the content of the sacramental act.
The deepest modern misunderstandings of Communion hinge
largely on the overemphasis on one or more of these four dimensions
to the neglect of another. Imbalances may arise from temperamental
inclinations or alleged special inspirations or prejudice or the historical
ignorance of those who quickly imagine that they might helpfully re-
arrange the traditional service and easily improve upon it. We are not

quarreling with serious consensual efforts at scripturally based liturical renewal, but with self-expressive individual experimentation heralded by balloons, banjos and the facades of intimacy. The ministry of Holy Communion must not be left in the unpredictable hands of self-appointed "creative persons" who may or may not know the tradition, so as to leave the *laos* bereft of what ordination essentially has promised them—an authentic ministry of word and sacrament (Justin Martyr, *ANF*, vol. 1, pp. 185 ff.; Clement of Alexandria, *ANF*, vol. 2, p. 322).

Oblation

He took bread.

The first thing the minister does in the service of Holy Communion is to receive from the people their offerings or oblations, which symbolically include bread and wine (*Seven Ecumenical Councils, NPNF* 2nd, vol. 14, pp. 594 ff.).

The offering of materials for Communion, bread and wine, was a crucial part of the earliest stratum of primitive services of the Supper (Justin Martyr, *ANF*, vol. 1, p. 219). Symbolically it is even implicit in the words of institution: He took, and therefore received, bread. The Supper was very early conceived as a thank offering, much like thanksgiving at a church night supper, where everyone brought gifts to the Lord's table, the fruits of their labor—including bread and wine, a portion of which was set aside for holy use with some food also set aside for ministry to the poor (*Apostolic Constitutions, ANF*, vol. 7, pp. 476 ff.).

This aspect of the service has been obscured in a money economy where we tend to view our offertory in terms of money rather than food. The eastern church liturgy early provided a splendid procession in which the offerings of the people were gloriously presented and received. The reception of gifts remained well-preserved in the English tradition as late as 1549, when the Book of Common Prayer rubrics called for families of the parish to make an offering each Sunday that would amount to at least roughly the price of a loaf of bread. But shortly thereafter, in the 1552 edition, this participatory aspect of the Oblation was stripped away and confused when the church warden was instructed to provide bread and wine at the expense of the parish (Abba, 1957, p. 161). So the symbolic act of the people offering bread was slowly diminished by the growth of a money economy.

Although it may seem an obscure connection, the pastor does well to remind the people occasionally that their bread and wine represent the work of their hands and therefore serve in a sense as a symbol of all the offerings, coins, checks, and bequests that they may have given in their support of the church's mission. The Holy Spirit is invoked to bless them to proper sacramental use (*Seven Ecumenical Councils, NPNF* 2nd, vol. 14, p. 610). Intercessions are then made for the people and the world.

Eucharist

He gave thanks.

Just as Jesus gave thanks as he broke the bread, so does the minister offer thanksgiving (*eucharistia*) to God as a representative act on behalf of the people of God.

By the fourth century, these eucharistic prayers had a fairly regular pattern that echoes even in modern Communion services (*Apostolic Constitutions, ANF*, vol. 7, pp. 422, 470 ff.; Early Liturgies, *ANF*, vol. 7, pp. 540 ff.). There was a salutation ("The Lord be with you"), followed by the *sursum corda* ("Lift up your hearts") as an antiphonal preface to this great act of Christian thanksgiving.

The words of institution may be rehearsed by remembering what Luke wrote of the risen Lord, that when he was at table with them, he took bread and blessed and broke it and gave it to them. And their eyes were opened and they recognized him (Luke 24:30–31). In many traditions the words of institution are recalled within the context of the prayer of consecration and thanksgiving, or eucharistic prayer. This prayer ascribes glory to God, who out of mercy gave his Son Jesus Christ to suffer death upon the cross for our redemption. Christ made "a full, perfect and sufficient sacrifice, oblation and satisfaction, for the sins of the whole world" (*BCP*, p. 190). He instituted, and in the Gospels commanded us to continue, a perpetual memory of that sacrifice until his coming again.

Ordinarily the words of institution include a specific recollection of "the night in which he was betrayed," in which "he took bread and when he had given thanks, he broke it, and gave it to his disciples, saying, 'Take, eat, this is my Body, which is given for you. Do this in remembrance of me.' Likewise, after supper, he took the cup" (*BCP*, 1979, pp. 334–35). It is an act of *anamnēsis*, "memory," remembering Jesus' words and acts, a recollection of the upper room gathering and its meaning as illumined by the empty tomb, a commemoration of the death and resurrection of the Lord (Chrysostom, *LCF*, pp. 173–75; *CC*, pp. 225 f.; *ATP*, pp. 457 ff.).

The gathered community prays to the triune God (in these or similar words): "bless and sanctify . . . these thy gifts and creatures of bread and wine; that we, receiving them according to thy Son our Savior Jesus Christ's holy institution, in remembrance of his death and passion, may be partakers of his most blessed Body and Blood . . . that, by the merits and death of thy Son Jesus Christ, and through faith in his blood, we, and all thy whole Church, may obtain remission of our sins, and all other benefits of his passion" (*BCP*, 1979, p. 335). We present ourselves as a living sacrifice (Rom. 12:1), humbly beseeching that we may worthily receive, and that "all we who are partakers of this Holy Communion may be filled with thy grace and heavenly benediction" (*Book of Worship,*

1964, p. 22) and "made one body in him, that he may dwell in us, and we in him" (*BCP*, 1979, p. 336).

Fraction

He broke the bread.

If the bread signifies Christ's body, the fraction (or breaking) of the bread signifies the brokenness of that body for us. It is not surprising that for many centuries the entire rite of the Supper would be known by many Christians as simply "the breaking of bread." From the earliest resurrection appearances, Christ has been "made known to us in the breaking of bread" (Luke 24:35).

What does it mean that Christ's body is broken for us? When we receive the broken bread, it is as if we are saying: our old idolatrous self-understanding is broken. The old will, the old Adam, the old self-assertive orientation to life is dead. We are risen anew to participate in the wholeness of new life in Christ.

Food must be masticated and "destroyed" before it can be of any use to us. This is a powerful analogy to death and resurrection. Food must be broken up before it can enter into our body for usefulness. Similarly we break (fracture) the bread for higher use. We must have food to live. Every day we eat the broken bodies of what were once living plants and animals. We cannot survive without these plants and animals literally giving up their bodies in brokenness to us. We recall as we eat that God himself through his Son is willing to be broken on our behalf and in a metaphorical sense become food for our nourishment. No nurture or spiritual feeding is possible without this brokenness. This is why it is appropriate in the service for the minister actually to physically and visibly break the bread in the presence of the congregation.

Similarly, Jesus took the cup and said, "This cup is the new covenant sealed by my blood" (1 Cor. 11:25). Wine comes from squeezed grapes, tender plants that have in a metaphorical sense bled for us, given their living juices for our life and nurture. It is not Christ's body alone that is broken, but his heart as well, symbolically participating in all human anguish.

Bread and wine succinctly symbolize the whole Christ, body (*soma*) and soul (*anima, psychē*, "living energizing spirit"), given for us. In ancient physiology the part of the body that is pre-eminently alive and most deeply symbolic of life is the circulating blood. In Jewish worship it is an axiom that there is no remission of sins without the shedding of blood. So in the manual acts of breaking bread and pouring out wine, the minister is performing a representative act on behalf of the whole people of God in symbolically re-enacting and remembering the atoning work of Christ in the crucifixion.

This reasoning will help the minister understand better why tiny pre-cut individual portions of mechanically stamped out bread or individual glasses are less appropriate vehicles for the celebration of the Sacrament than are a whole loaf broken visibly and a chalice from which all drink commonly.

Communion

He gave.

Jesus himself served the bread and wine. So does the liturgist give this nourishment to each person individually in the act of Communion. This is the last of four parts of the service: Oblation, Eucharist, breaking of bread and Communion. Having offered the fruits of our labor to be consecrated, having given thanks and remembered Jesus' last night, and having broken the bread, we now come to the climactic moment of mystical communion with Christ.

Communion is less a tribute to a dead founder than a participation in the present, resurrected life of the Lord. As the fracture recalls his crucifixion, the Communion shares in his resurrection. It is a real communion with a truly present Lord who has promised, "Lo I am with you alway, even unto the end of the world" (Matt. 20:28, KJV). Through it, God strengthens faith, reconciles us to himself, and forgives sin. It is Christ's own presence that is celebrated and received. It is far more than a memorial, although remembering is a crucial part of it (Cyril of Jerusalem, *NPNF* 2nd, vol. 7, pp. 151–161; Luther, *WLS*, vol. 2, pp. 796 ff.).

We come as the family of God and sit down at the meal of God to enjoy the living presence of God's elect Son. The Communion points toward the end time when the communion of saints will share the completed vision of human history with the glorified Lord. It is as if that is already anticipatively present in our small circle, as if it is already happening in this Holy Communion (Luther, *WLS*, vol. 2, pp. 814 ff.).

All of this can be affirmed without implying a physical miracle of transmutation of bread and wine into outwardly manifested body and blood. The church prays that the Holy Spirit will consecrate these lowly elements to their higher use, so that Christ will be present to us in no different way than he promises to be present (Gregory of Nyssa, *LCF,* pp. 141 ff.; Chrysostom, *LCF,* pp. 173 f.; Calvin, *Inst.,* 4.18).

We are enacting something analogous to, but distinguishable from, a sacrificial expiation of our sins. In the Jewish tradition, it is never human acts that propitiate God, as if our sacrifice of animals or whatever would gain us merit so we could stand in God's presence feeling accepted. Rather, it is God who expiates our sin, covers over our sin through a sacrificial act. In the Jewish tradition the sacrificial act ordinarily involved the shedding of blood, usually of animals (never human sacrifice, which was sharply rejected from the early prophets on). Even though animal sacrifice may seem repulsive to modern consciousness, it is useful to try to understand what this meant. In ritual sacrifice, the one who brought the sacrificial victim was metaphorically identifying with the victim, offering himself symbolically through giving something of real value to him as a visible sign of his repentance and desire for reconciliation. By identification with the victim, he was in a sense dying, confessing his guilt, praying for atonement, and seeking reconciliation with God. These ritual sacrifices were burned, and the smoke, it was felt, rendered a kind of purifying fire for the believer and an incense that rose to heaven. At the same time there was a ritual community meal in which the faith of the historical community was recalled and brought into public expression through this act of sacrifice (cf. Basil of Caesarea, *LCF*, pp. 70 ff.; Thomas Aquinas, *ST*, vol. 2, pp. 2483 ff.; Calvin, *Inst.*, 4.18).

Whatever happened in Jesus' death, it was clearly interpreted by analogy to such a sacrifice, yet one made by God himself on behalf of the whole world. Jesus viewed his own death as a sacrifice for others. So when we receive the broken bread and poured wine, we are incorporating into our very bodies the broken body of Christ, and the sacrificial blood shed for us and for all. We are then called to offer ourselves, our souls and bodies, as a spiritual sacrifice in response to Christ's sacrifice for us (Rom. 12:1 ff.; cf. Chrysostom, *LCF*, pp. 174 ff.; Luther, *WLS*, pp. 809 ff.).

The Supper happens with others. No one receives the sacrament alone, ordinarily. It is a rehearsal of the unity of Christ. The body is one, not many, loaves. "When we bless 'the cup of blessing,' is it not a means of sharing in the blood of Christ? When we break the bread, is it not a means of sharing in the body of Christ? Because there is one loaf, we, many as we are, are one body; for it is one loaf of which we all partake" (1 Cor. 10:16,17).

Conclusion

If we ask what clergy do and why, we cannot circumvent or neglect the sacramental life. It penetrates the heart of ministry. No activities of clergy are more definitive of ministry than these representative acts of cleansing, baptizing, receiving and consecrating the fruits of the community's labor, recollecting and giving thanks for Christ's death, breaking bread, and offering it to all who would commune with the living Christ.

REFERENCES AND FURTHER READING

For classical texts on the ministry of the sacraments, see Ignatius (*ANF*, vol. 1), Epistle of Barnabas (*ANF*, vol. 1, pp. 142 f.), Justin Martyr (*ANF*, vol. 1, pp. 185 ff.), Tertullian (*ANF*, vol. 3), Cyprian (ANF, vol. 4), Hippolytus (*ANF*, vol. 5), *Apostolic Constitutions* (*ANF*, vol 7), Eusebius (*NPNF* 2nd, vol. 1), Gregory of

Nyssa (*NPNF* 2nd, vol. 5), Cyril of Jerusalem and Gregory Nazianzus (*NPNF* 2nd, vol. 7), Ambrose (*LCF*, pp. 184 ff.), Augustine (*NPNF* 1st, vols. 3,4), Chrysostom (*NPNF* 1st, vol. 12), *Seven Ecumenical Councils* (*NPNF* 2nd, vol. 14), Hilary of Potiers (*LCF*, pp. 57 ff.), and Thomas Aquinas (*ST*, vol. 2, pp. 2382 ff.). See also collections by Kidd (1911), Ayer (1913), Schaff (1931 ed.), Schroeder (1937), Quasten (1950 ff.), Bettenson (*LCF*, 1956), Denzinger (1957), Stevenson (NE, 1957), and Leith (CC, 1973).

For sixteenth- and seventeenth-century discussions, see Luther (*WML*, vol. 6, *WLS* vol. 1) Calvin, (Inst. 4.6 ff.), Menno Simons (d. 1561), Chemnitz (1595), Hooker (*ATP*, pp. 407 ff.), Gerhard (1610), Wollebius (1622 ff.), J. Taylor (*ATP*, pp. 428 ff.), Barclay (1678). For more recent discussions of the ministry of the sacraments, see Wesley (*WJW*, vol. 7), Bridges (1847), Brightman (1915), Forsyth (1917), Dunkerly (1937), Heppe (1950 ed.), Seeberg (1952 ed.), Leeming (1956), Abba (1957), Kelly (1958), Rahner (1963a), Sullivan (1965), Lampe (1967), Powers (1973), Meyendorff (1974), Cooke (1976), Käsemann (*RGG3*), *Bornkamm (TNDT)*, Moltmann (1977), and Hopko (1982).

For recent discussions of the ministry of baptism from various points of view, see Barth (1948), Cullmann (1950), Bonhoeffer (1953 ed.), Bromiley (1953), Aland (1963), Delling (1964–65), Jeremias (1971b), and Moltmann (1977). For discussions of the ministry of the Eucharist, see Kierkegaard (1849, 1940 ed.), Rogers (1912), Jungmann (1959), Holmes (1971, pp. 8–92), Schuetze and Habeck (1974), Newbigin (1977), and Wainwright (1980). For a selection of pastoral writings on the relation of confession and penance to the ministry of Eucharist, see Raymond of Pennafort (d. 1275), Morin (1651), Fuller (1647), Berg (1841), Gaumé (1854), Pusey (1878), Lea (1896), McNeill (1923, 1932), Ryan (1931), McNeill and Gamer (1938, 1965), L. J. Sherrill (1945, 1951), and Oden (1980).

9. The Ministry of the Word Through Preaching

Admittedly, the ministry of the word is a larger category than preaching. It includes also pastoral conversation in which the word is being communicated personally in one-to-one dialogue. In this chapter, however, we are focusing on the proclamation of the word in a public way, usually set in the context of worship of the revealed God.

What Is Preaching?

Preaching is among the most important topics of pastoral theology. For preaching is the most public of pastoral acts. The quality and depth of Christian discipleship in a congregation depend heavily upon it (Ambrose, *NPNF* 2nd, vol. 10, pp. 13 ff.). For that reason, a distinguishable area of study in theology has developed called homiletics (from *homileo*, "to speak, converse, address someone"). Homiletics is the study of the process and act of listening to the Spirit speak through Scripture so as to engender an appropriate here-and-now witness to God (cf. Chrysostom, *NPNF* 1st, vol. 9, pp. 346 ff.; Bridges, 1847, pp. 171 ff.; *DPT*, pp. 1–97).

Proclamation of the coming age of God was crucial to Jesus' ministry. We see him preaching everywhere—on the Mount, on the plain, from a boat, near the temple, in the market place. When the apostles were sent out, and later the seventy and many more, their assigned task was public proclamation of the coming kingdom of God that had dawned with the preaching of Jesus.

Paul makes clear the necessity of preaching: faith comes by hearing and hearing comes through the word of God. And how do you hear this word of God unless you have somebody to declare it, and how do you do that without a preacher? (Rom. 10:11–15).

Preaching (*kērugma*) means proclamation of the good news that

Jesus Christ is Lord. Preaching is the continual and public testimony which the church is constantly seeking to make to all who would hear it, most conspicuously in the context of worship, witnessing to the church's faith in Christ. Preaching consists substantially in the clarification, exposition, interpretation, and re-appropriation of the written word that witnesses to the revealed word (Calvin, *Inst.*, 4.3). It is a public exposition of Christian truth, addressed to the here-and-now community of faith, and to all who would hear it.

Already implicit in that definition is an assumed threefold correlation between the revealed word in Christ, the written word of Scripture, and the proclaimed word in our own contemporary language. God addresses us personally through Christ in history as revealed word. The proclaimed word witnesses to the revealed word (Luther, *WLS*, vol. 3, pp. 1125 f.). Before it became a written word, the proclaimed word was first an oral tradition. In time, a written tradition of apostolic teaching emerged that subsequently became universally recognized as canon to which the church could constantly return for the nurture of its continuing oral witness (Tertullian, *ANF*, vol. 3, pp. 610 ff.).

The revealed word, the preached word, and the written word all cohere in mutual interdependence (Barth, *CD*, vol. 1). The revealed word of God is communicated through speech, expressed through ordinary human languages, spoken, written, remembered, translated, and respoken.

The gospel itself is thought to be a word (*logos*), an address to us from God Himself. The notion of *logos* can be translated not only "word," but "reason." It is by means of words, through ordinary language, that reason is expressed. There is an intrinsic correlation between reason and speech. As I struggle for words, I struggle to express reasonings. Preaching seeks to clarify that self-revealing word of God in the pulsating contemporary, local, here-and-now situation (Luther, *WML*, pp. 79 ff.).

Christian worship contains both prophetic and priestly dimensions. The prophetic aspect deals essentially with God's address to us. The priestly aspect focuses on the gathered community addressing God responsively in prayer, praise, and intercession. Preaching emphasizes the prophetic side. Ordinarily, Christian preaching does not, like Old Testament prophecy, say directly: "Thus saith the Lord," as if the revealed word were coming immediately through our preaching. Rather, it has the more modest task of saying, "Let us listen to the Scripture together. We will talk about the way in which the word of God the Father through the liberating Son meets us with the help of Spirit through the Scripture."

Preaching declares this good news, inviting persons to Christ (its evangelical dimension). It also seeks to comfort, encourage, and inspire devotion, dedication, loyalty, and discipleship to Christ (its pastoral dimension). Preaching wishes to impart clear, understandable Christian teaching (its doctrinal dimension). Finally, it wishes to build moral sensitivity and awareness and elicit changed behaviors (its morally formative dimension). These four dimensions of preaching—evangelical, pastoral, doctrinal, and moral—have elicited different styles in the history of homiletics: exegetical sermons, pastoral sermons, doctrinal sermons, and morally instructive sermons. All of these elements are implicitly embedded or assumed in every act of preaching. In a year of preaching they all should stand in a thoughtful balance.

Laypersons as well as ministers have the duty and the possibility of witnessing to the gospel. Every Christian believer has not only the potential capability but also at certian times the duty and right to declare openly the meaning of the Christian faith. Private witness does not exclude or deny the importance of this more public and representative act. But careful, well-instructed preaching of the apostolic witness by an ordained clergyman differs markedly from lay witness, in that it is (one hopes) better prepared and duly authorized to speak representatively for the whole body of Christ.

No amount of technical instruction or objective data gathering can finally call preaching into being. It cannot be reduced to an art or natural talent. Nonetheless, it can be compared in some ways to an art or artistic competency that is not taught by rote learning but by example, practicum, and experience. The spirit and energy of preaching can, with God's help, be experientially "caught," in the sense that one may experience oneself as grasped inwardly by the claim and power of the gospel, and its search for expression can be nurtured. Just as the teacher of art can teach drafting, composition, and color, hoping that the learners in time may become artists, so also there are some things that can be outwardly taught and studied about preaching: sequential organization, linguistic knowledge, the rules of rhetoric, and clear communication skills. Even the greatest talents need coaching for elementary instruction, for correction, for allowing native energies to develop (Gregory of Nazianzus *NPNF* 2nd, vol. 7, pp. 205 ff.).

Preaching points to the truth of God's self-disclosure in a way that is hearable (Luther, *WLS*, vol. 3, p. 1129). The New Testament thought of Jesus as the truth revealed (John 14:6). His resurrection became the principle clue through which all other truths were to be grasped and clarified (1 Cor. 15).

Yet preaching remains vexed by continuing problems. Several creative tensions must be affirmed without falling into latent contradictions. The polarities of preaching are represented in these questions: Is preaching addressed to the single individual or to the corporate body? Does the person preaching infuse the office with one's own personal style, or does the office of the preacher strictly determine the mode of address? Does preaching change with the times, or does it remain the same?

To Whom Is Preaching Addressed?

At first glance preaching seems to be pre-eminently a public act. Yet it intends to address the heart. Even though it is personal, preaching cannot attempt the sort of intimate, interpersonal encounter that is possible in pastoral counsel. The preached word addresses the whole community, yet by this means hopes to penetrate the heart of each individual in the community as if alone before God.

Even though many are present, what matters most, as Kierkegaard (1851) knew, is the inner address of the word to the hidden conscience of the hearer before God. Many will hear the publicly spoken word in many different ways. Preaching, to be complete, requires hearing. Yet each act of hearing is highly individual, even though addressed to many (Kierkegaard, 1849).

Preaching speaks from experience to experience. Yet in the preached word one is not simply speaking on one's own authority or individual experience. Admittedly one's own personal story is the lens through which the larger Christian story is seen. But it is not just private experience that deserves to be reported. The funded experience of a worldwide, historical community of faith is the mine to which preaching returns. That includes Scripture, tradition, and personal experience. Tradition is precisely an amalgam of Spirit-led experience, rooted in revelation, enduring through time (Wesley, *WJW*, vol. 8, pp. 283 ff.; Outler, 1968).

Admittedly, the Christian community has other ways than preaching to communicate the truth known in Jesus: the enacted word in the sacrament, the sung word in hymns, the embodied word in the laying on of hands. These are not preaching. Preaching is definitively a spoken word that builds a bridge between hearer and Scripture. Scripture may be read, but that is not preaching. We have the creeds and theology in each era of history, but that is not preaching. The gathered community needs more than Scripture read, creeds recited, hymns sung. It needs that personal address that brings the word of God to us "plain and home" (Wesley, *WJW*, vol. 11, pp. 486 ff.).

The Holy Spirit is at work to bring the preached word home to the hearer. The fact that preaching is a public event does not make it any less an inward event before God (Kierkegaard, 1850). It is a public event precisely because it has the heart of the individual as its aim— every individual present. It is a problem of both spiritual preparation and rhetorical imagination to do both of these things well—the *public* address to the *inner* heart. The best preaching prays earnestly that the Holy Spirit will illumine the hearer through our frail attempts to speak

God's own word through human language (Chrysostom, *NPNF* 1st, vol. 13, p. 461; Barth, *Church Dogmatics*, vol. 1, part 1).

Person or Office?

Is preaching primarily a personal encounter or a representative, official act? If either personalized insight or official identity is misplaced or absent, the hearing of the word may be impaired. Person and office in the act of preaching belong in the most practiced balance and creative tension.

When you go before your congregation, you go with an official commission (Luther, *WML*, vol. 4, pp. 79 ff.). You are a duly authorized officer of the church. You are appointed to the office of preaching. This is the reason why vestments in preaching have had much historical significance (Clement of Alexandria, *ANF*, vol. 2, pp. 453 ff.; cf. *Seven Ecumenical Councils, NPNF* 2nd, vol. 14, pp. 140 ff.); they are a public way of identifying the purpose and responsibility of the office. They are analogous in some ways to a judicial robe or a peace officer's uniform. Judges must exercise their responsibility within a frame of reference that they have vowed to uphold. But judges are required to bring the law to bear on unique, situational issues. That requires the best personal insight and humane judgment. Yet these analogies pertain to the administration of justice in the temporal sphere. Liturgical vestments point beyond all temporal powers to the ground and end of temporal power (Clement of Alexandria, *ANF*, vol. 2, pp. 452 ff.; Gregory, *ACW*, pp. 11, 49 f.; Thomas Aquinas, *ST*, vol. 3, p. 2706). There have been many different types of vestments in the history of Christian preaching. They have changed the way all human garb changes. However varied, they seek to point beyond all human powers and loves to the power of eternal love.

Person and office are united in the preaching ministry in a subtly nuanced way. Taken seriously, the office of ministry reduces our temptation to speak idiosyncratically as if well-informed private opinion constituted preaching. In that sense, the office of ministry distinguishes the preacher from a lecturer or an attorney or a politician (Calvin, *Inst.*, 4.3.3).

We take this office and bring to it our personal being, our unique experience, our existential life and language, and we then infuse the office with our personality. The office of preaching needs the imprint of personality, without being reduced to it (Wesley, *WJW*, vol. 8, pp. 283 f., 317 ff.). You must risk telling your own story, not as an end in itself, but rather as a sharply focused lens through which the whole Christian story is refracted. That requires a delicate balance, a creative tension, a dialectic that can easily become imbalanced. It will test your insight and ability as a preacher of the word to hold person and office together in fine balance. There is no easy formula. It requires an intuitive wisdom that has on it the stamp of your personality and sense of vocation.

Is Preaching Unchanging or Ever-changing?

Preaching changes and yet remains ever the same. For there is indeed an assumed continuity in the word to which preaching constantly refers. Christ is the same yesterday, today, and forever. Yet the task of public restatement in the present is always new and necessarily different in each proclamation. Good preaching is in touch with the specific hungers, the current aspirations, the sociocultural presuppositions of the contemporary audience. But it should not just mirror them slavishly, or cheaply accommodate to them. Preaching must come through with a vital recollection of the historical Christian memory so as to illuminate and challenge the alienated present by means of Scripture and tradition (Chrysostom, *NPNF* 1st, vol. 10; *Formula of Concord*, 1577, *BC*, pp. 531 ff.).

Christian pastoral wisdom at its best has relied heavily upon the written canon of Scripture. Without it the proclamation remains uncentered. The apostolic witness is the norm of preaching, just as it is the norm of theology. Yet preaching is not simply fixated on the now archaic language of the first century A.D. or the sixth century B.C. It is by definition essentially contemporary, a here-and-now event. How are we to make clear the seemingly remote connection between a text written twenty-five hundred years ago and this here-and-now audience? God's own Spirit works cooperatively with our intelligence and attentiveness to make that otherwise improbable connection (Tertullian, *ANF,* vol. 3, pp. 613–16).

Kērugma and *Homilia*

This leads us to another familiar distinction between two kinds of preaching. From its earliest beginnings preaching has had two distinguishable concerns. On the one hand, it reaches toward those who are already baptized communicants yet who need the continuing nurture of the preached word. Preaching is therefore concerned with both the widening of the community through evangelical witness and the deepening of the community through spiritual formation.

Consequently, two kinds of preaching have emerged. The distinction has arisen between what might be called missionary or evangelical preaching on the one hand and pastoral or congregational preaching on the other. Each of these has its own Greek terms. The *kērux* ("proclaimer," from *kērugma,* "proclamation") is one who publicly announces the good news of Jesus Christ to the world. *Homilia,* from which our word *homily* comes, points more often toward the pastoral, nurturing, didactic side of congregational preaching.

These two types of preaching are often interfused, and rightly so.

For the same community that needs to hear the gospel proclaimed also needs instruction and pastoral preaching. It depends on the audience at a given time as to which side of that equation one will give relatively greater emphasis. There are few situations that will require only one side to the absolute exclusion of the other (Gregory, *ACW*, vol. 11, pp. 23 ff.; Calvin, *Inst.*, 4.3, *DPT*, pp. 99 ff.).

The *kērugma* is addressed to a situation that is prone to distort and resist it. When this good news is announced, it is often perceived as a profound challenge to our idolatries, and so we may fight it or be offended by it. The best preachers have always sought to penetrate the self-deceptions of their hearers and work their way skillfully through hardened layers of defense. Christian preaching tries to announce the judgment and grace of God to those who may not want to hear its full force. Its promise must be presented without Pollyanna hopes or false assurances. Preaching tries to get through these obstacles, not in coercive or overbearing ways, but through skillful persuasion under the guidance of Scripture and Spirit (Augustine, *SAOE*, pp. 383 ff.).

Preaching as Gift and Task

Christian preaching is a free act that confronts and appeals to responsible freedom. It wishes to call forth freedom in Christ by finding a way of obtaining a hearing for the self-disclosure of God against our resistances. To do this effectively, a preacher has a delicate task analogous to that of an ambassador delegated to an embassy in a remote, perhaps hostile, area who tries to get across the message of the home government in whatever ways possible.

There is a powerful equalitarian motif in historical Christian preaching. Most ancient traditions of oratory were thoroughly elitist, not interested in addressing the propertyless, the family, or women. Christian preaching has been from the beginning addressed to all. It has had a distinctly universal and consistently international mission. It is no small point, in the context of the ancient world, that women came equally under the deliberate address and claim of the Christian proclamation. We may caricature preaching under stodgy, Victorian stereotypes as overbearing and authoritarian. But in its primitive Apostolic forms, molded by martyrdom and the struggle for a universal hearing, Christian preachers contributed greatly to a fundamental sense of human equality before God. All were addressed. From all parts of society people came to believe and respond. The poor and the unlearned were crucial contibutors to the primitive Christian mission. It was not an elitist proclamation addressed to power brokers and pacesetters only. Far more often it was addressed to the poor by the poor (John Climacus, d. 649; Chrysostom, *NPNF* 1st, vol. 9, pp. 340 ff.).

Christian preaching in its better exemplars has sought the language of the common people, rather than in a special technical language or an

academic jargon. With many accretions of history and through many
cultural transformations, it eventually acquired a scholastic style and
academic defenses. But the best empathic preaching strives to overcome
all esoteric tendencies by seeking to practically grasp and use the best
technical distinctions of scholastic theology put in the simplest language. Christian preaching wants to address its word in such forceful
and clear terms that anybody present can get the point. If that is done
well, then the most astute minds in that congregation are going to respond to it as well.

The church celebrates good preaching as a gift of the Spirit (1 Cor.
12:8). It is not an easy matter to do this task well, to take hearers deeply
into the meanings and claims of Scripture and to bring ancient wisdoms
into a contemporary context in good humor and spirit, and in such a
way that not only the least educated person in the congregation can
understand, but the wisest also be moved and edified (Augustine,
SAOE, pp. 374 ff.; Wesley, *WJW,* vol. 2, pp. 486 ff.).

Gifts in preaching are an essential qualification for ministry. Ordination committees try to make a serious preliminary assessment of how
well one will be able to carry out this difficult, skillful, subtle communication task (Luther, *WLS,* vol. 3, p. 1116; Chemnitz, 1593, pp. 28 ff.;
Vinet, 1853).

Yet preaching is not only a gift, but also a task to be studied and
improved upon. Its being a gift does not reduce the level of energy,
intelligence, and commitment that are required to receive and develop
that gift. Like other gifts of the Spirit, it involves a cooperative relation
between the Spirit's awakening guidance and our best human efforts.

Great preaching, from its beginnings, has been viewed as a profound mystery, a treasure in earthen vessels, God's own address
through our fragile, distortable language. God the Spirit cooperates
with our human competencies, talents, languages, abilities, and imagination to enable our speaking and hearing (*Formula of Concord, BC,* pp.
531 f.; Bridges, 1847, 38 ff. 171 ff.)

The Form and Matter of Preaching

In the spoken word, one has the opportunity to express one's own
personal appropriation of the delivered tradition. The whole apparatus of nonverbal communication (body language, eye contact, ges-
ture, tone of voice) contributes to the intensification of the communication. If the revealed word in Christ is to be made plausible it needs the
stamp of a personal witness; it must be channeled through the experience of a living believer. When preaching dwindles into philosophical
speculation, literary criticism, free verse, political manipulation, or lath-
ered sentimentalism, the laity know that the commission of ordination
has somehow been misplaced.

To some we offer milk. To others, meat (1 Cor. 3:2). To preach "in wisdom" is to draw out of the fund of scriptural wisdom the particular insight that applies most clearly to this circumstance here and now (1 Cor. 2:6).

Paul spoke wryly about the "foolishness of preaching" (1 Cor. 1:21). When he reflected on his own vocation as preacher it had a ringing, clear sound: "Christ did not send me to baptize, but to proclaim the Gospel; and to do it without relying on the language of worldly wisdom, so that the fact of Christ on his cross might have its full weight. This doctrine of the cross is sheer folly to those on their way to ruin, but to us who are on the way to salvation it is the power of God" (1 Cor. 1:17,18).

The style or form of a homily must be consistent with its substance or material. What it is determines how it is approached. What is the substance of preaching? Most classical Protestant discussions answer straightforwardly: the word of God (Luther, *WLS*, vol. 3, pp. 1125 ff.). That involves telling a story, in fact a sequence of stories that add up to an interpretation of the meaning of history. Scripture is not just woodenly quoted, but interpreted to contemporary hearers in meaningful symbol systems. Preaching involves a personally grasped, experienced affirmation of these meanings, a clarification of what they signify in our times and how they address our own situation.

When Ezekiel was called to his prophetic office, he was commanded, oddly enough, to "eat the book"—a dramatic metaphorical way of saying: totally digest this given canonical tradition (Ezek. 28:11). So in preaching we are called to consume fully the word of Scripture, to let it be a "lamp unto our feet" (Ps. 119:105). Preaching that has lost touch with the vitalities of Scripture is easily captivated by egocentric faddism, pretentiousness, and sentimentalism.

The pastoral tradition has placed unparalleled importance upon the careful, meditative, study of Scripture that leads toward a unique event, the proclamation of the word. Only then is one prepared to offer the divine word. Biblical preaching is more than rational demonstration or logical argument. It wishes to freight God's own address through human language and to reach deeply into the emotive life so as to move the hearer to behavior change and new self-understanding.

The older pastoral tradition spoke often of the pastor's duty to "declare the whole counsel of God." That means that the whole range of the historical self-presentation of God is to be made available to the congregation. You are not to withhold large portions of self-selected Scripture. There may indeed be a deliberate process of selectivity when searching the Scripture for a text. All texts are not equally fitting for a given moment. Yet through a whole season of preaching, the pastor is called upon to make accessible the wider range of the wisdom of Scripture. The lectionary will help prevent subjective, biased selections of texts.

In the Protestant tradition it is generally held that we never need fear the consequences of genuinely preaching from Scripture, but rather we stand in fear and trembling if we should withhold Scripture from the gathered community. Our task is not, strictly speaking, self-expression, but allowing the word to be faithfully articulated and powerfully expressed. The minister is not to be an obstacle to the word, but its channel to the congregation. Leave it to the Spirit to enliven the process of hearing. We can only intercede for the Spirit to be present in our preparation and delivery, and in the hearer's reception of our preaching (Calvin, *Inst.*, 4.8 f.).

Preaching is God's own way of converting, redeeming, and changing behavior. It is God's own "foolishness," an ordained instrumentality, God's own idea for ordering the ecclesia so as to provide a means by which his word becomes hearable amid the changing scenes of history. We might imagine many "better ways" (had we been asked) through which God might have desirably communicated his word, such as philosophical argument or some harder data base or direct inspiration or meditative *koans*. But, odd as it may seem, it is through this foolishness that God awakens new life.

To experience inwardly the address of the word and to communicate it relevantly to others takes courage, no less than would be required for political action or therapeutic encounter. The apostolic tradition presents us with a claim that is risk laden, yet well ordered to its purpose. It calls us to go ahead and risk letting the Word be sharply heard by the congregation.

Admittedly, Scripture is distortable by us. Our self-assertiveness can prevent our hearing its profound address or delivering it to others. We can and do prematurely assume that our own native impulses and natural predispositions are easily confirmed by divine revelation. Yet despite our resistances and hypocrisies the most significant thing we can do for our people is to try earnestly to let them hear Scripture clearly. Nothing we do in preaching is more powerful or significant or beautiful. This does not rule out the use of any rhetorical, poetic, or intellectual resource. It does not rule out a theology of culture or political analysis or philosophical wisdom. It does not squelch any human insight. It simply asks for fidelity to that center.

The Unity of Preaching

What constitutes the unity of many acts of preaching? Christ himself, the archetypical event of God's self-disclosure, the event that renders all other self-disclosures of God more fully understandable. Paul wrote: "I resolved to know nothing while I was with you except Jesus Christ and him crucified" (1 Cor. 2:2, NIV).

Reformation theology assumed that this involved the preaching of both justification and sanctification (Calvin, *Inst.*, 3.11 f., 3.19 f.). That is shorthand for God's act for us in Christ, as distinguished from the Holy Spirit's act in us to reshape our behaviors (Wesley, *WJW*, vol. 5, pp. 56 ff., vol. 6, p. 45, vol. 8, pp. 361 ff.).

To say that Christ is the center, however, does not imply that we must be systematically ignorant of everything else. Rather, it asks us to try to understand each discrete insight in relation to that incomparable divine self-disclosure. Nor does this require that preaching suddenly become encyclopedic so as to pretend to know everything and cover all subjects. There is much of which we should never speak in the pulpit, yet which we do well to know. The preacher's knowledge of poetry, theater, science, politics, and philosophy can be refracted through the lens of the central revelatory event, Jesus Christ. All human events gain sharper focus through the Father's revelation in the Son through the Spirit (Gregory, *ACW*, vol. 11, pp. 90 ff.).

Suppose you have in your congregation people of very high intellect and astute education, yet also people with little or no education. How do you preach to that congregation? Most traditional pastoral literature asks for spare, simple communication, on the assumption that if you attend carefully to plain, ordinary wisdom you will include all listeners in your address. "What for the ignorant is necessary is not unsuitable to the wise, but what is proper for the wise is not suitable to the ignorant. A man who understands his subject and his work can speak to the ignorant in a manner interesting and instructive to the wise. Depth and simplicity meet at the same point. Have you an audience composed of forty-nine wise and one ignorant? Speak for that ignorant one" (Vinet, 1853, p. 206). The best preaching is wise in its simplicity, not its complexity (Kierkegaard, 1851–52; Bonhoeffer, 1948).

Authority in Preaching

The authority of the preacher is grounded in the depth of the speaker's correspondence with the revealed word. This is the basis of the preacher's right to be heard and believed. Subjectively it is the hearer's consciousness of this right. The *kērux* ("proclaimer") speaks with authority only when the hearer perceives in the preacher's speech an intrinsic sense of rightness, namely, that it should be believed (Augustine, *SAOE* pp. 121 ff. Cooke, 1976, 411 ff.).

Through ordination the minister is authorized to preach. But just having that authority assigned in the formal sense does not make it subjectively appropriated, in the consciousness of either the preacher or the hearer. To be taken seriously the preacher has to say something right, to utter something worthy of belief. The hearer must be conscious of the rightness of that word. Only then is the circle of authority completed, when both phases coincide. Then you have a speaker with something significant to say and those who hear will be prepared by experience to trust what that person has to say.

The working pastor soon learns of the fragility of that authority. It is all too easy to lose the trust that parishioners usually hope to offer their pastor. It can be destroyed in an instant of intemperate language, or by distorting facts that are known to be true, or by abusing in other ways the trust that parishioners tend implicitly to invest in ministry (Ambrose, *NPNF* 2nd, vol. 10, p. 3 ff.).

The hearer wants to have some modest assurance that what the preacher is saying is plausibly manifested in the preacher's own life. To talk glibly about reconciliation or peace or justice and then to belie that talk through one's behavior is to undermine pastoral authority (Gregory, *ACW*, vol. 11, pp. 232 f.; Kierkegaard, 1846a).

A certain dignity properly attaches to the office of preaching, which outwardly manifests this inner sense of intuited authority (Baxter, 1656, pp. 129 ff.). By analogy, the judge does not just walk into the court in a casual way, but comes in vested and empowered with authority. Dignity accompanies the office. It is not characterized by idle chatter. Important decisions are being rendered. The judge says nothing except that which is truly critical to the case. When the judge speaks, it is with authority, an authority that would have been diminished had he injected his private sentiments or idiosyncratic opinions. There is an analogy here to ministry. Authority is diminished when the divine self-disclosure is ignored or overlooked in the interest of personal opinion-making. Humble submission to the authority of the word is central to the authority of preaching. One cannot make up for its absence by personal charm or rhetorical flair.

Prophetic Preaching

The older pastoral writings viewed preaching as closely connected with the "duty of reproof" ("correction, discipline, and admonition"). Teaching must correct; otherwise, false assumptions may be reinforced. The pastor must "reprove with full authority" (Titus 2:15). In this way, Christian preaching stands in continuity with the prophetic tradition.

Corrective preaching cares enough to be capable of negation in the context of love. We are not speaking here about private reproof, but that which belongs intrinsically to the pulpit. Pastoral courage is needed to identify accurately the particular deficit or injustice or lack of awareness in the flock at a given time. But if you are going to offend the flock, offend them with the truth. You have it turned around if you yourself are the offense. Let the gospel be the offense; let the word be the scandal; let the truth be the offense. That is good preaching in the prophetic tradition.

Prophetic preaching addresses human need not just on an individual scale, but in terms of ingrained social injustice (Amos 5:7 ff; Isa. 3:13–15). This is the unavoidable point at which the pastoral task clearly confronts systemic evil in social processes and seeks to articulate practical, biblically grounded social wisdom. There are times when the preacher must have the courage to stand up as the conscience of the community, as an unintimidated critic of a corrupted society.

Unction

This strange word *unction* comes from *unctio*, "to anoint." Unction in preaching is a subtle quality of spirit and language that expresses religious affect in the highly accurate way that is most appropriate to its subject matter—God with us, the Holy in our midst, the Spirit addressing our hearts. Unction in preaching is anointed speech. The word has an honorable history. Few today would think of applying such an archaism to preaching, even as a compliment. But in the older treatises it was a frequently used term to point toward this subtle, compassionate, firm, set-apart quality of blessed speech—when firmness is accompanied by tenderness, when awe is engendered in common worship, when moral commitment is bound with love. Its quality is only felt in rare moments when "Mercy and truth have met together, righteousness and peace have kissed each other" (Ps. 85:10, KJV).

We are speaking about something complex and beautiful: an intense awareness of the holy in the midst of our concrete life revealed through human speech. It involves the confluence of judgment and grace, of depth and warmth, of reason and affect in due proportion. For this to occur, one must grasp inwardly the depth and relevance of those truths of which one speaks. One is attempting to call truth into speech in a way that elicits in others the same emotive qualities felt in oneself. Anointed speech lives out of the Anointed One. The key reference is 1 John 2:27: "The anointing which you received from him abides in you, and you have no need that any one should teach you; as his anointing teaches you about everything, and is true, and is no lie, just as it has taught you, abide in him" (RSV).

We know good preaching when we hear it. It touches us viscerally. It is a profound, subtle mode of communication that somehow makes the transcendence of Yahweh appear palpably immanent. It mixes courage and comfort, candor and sympathy, strength and vulnerability, in the kind of delicate blend achieved by an excellent cook. Most worshipers know that there have been rare and beautiful times when they have been privileged to hear such a word. When it happens, it is a remarkable event. It is a treasure in earthen vessels.

REFERENCES AND FURTHER READING

Classical texts on the ministry of preaching include Irenaeus (*ANF*, vol. 1), Clement of Alexandria (*ANF*, vol. 2, pp. 452 ff.), Tertullian (*ANF*, vol. 3. pp. 610 ff.), Origen (*ANF*, vol. 4), Lactantius (*ANF*, vol. 7), Chrysostom (*NPNF* 1st, vol. 9), Gregory of Nazianzus (*NPNF* 2nd, vol. 7, pp. 205 ff.), Ambrose (*NPNF*

2nd, vol. 10, pp. 13 ff.), Augustine (412), *Seven Ecumenical Councils* (*NPNF* 2nd, vol. 14, pp. 140 ff.), Gregory (*ACW*, vol. 11, pp. 11 ff., 49 ff.), Ephraim Syrus (*NPNF* 2nd, vol. 13), Aphrahat (*NPNF* 2nd, vol. 13, pp. 383 ff.), Thomas Aquinas (*ST*, vol. 3, pp. 2703 ff.), Luther (*WML*), Calvin (*Inst.*), Melanchthon (1521), Major (1544), *Formula of Concord* (*BC*, pp. 531 ff.), Latimer (d. 1555), and Knox (d. 1572).

Post-Reformation texts of some importance include Baxter (1656, pp. 129 ff.), Voetius (d. 1676), Henry (d. 1714, *Aphorisms*), Doddridge (*LP*), Massillon (d. 1742), Wesley (d. 1791), Sailer (1791), Watts (1813 ed.), Asbury (1958 ed.), Newman (1837), Simeon (d. 1836), Bridges (1847 ed.), Jewel (1845–50 ed.), Kierkegaard (1846a, 1854–55), Vinet (1853), Brooks (1877), Bernard (1880), Ellicott (1880), Smith (1882), Fuller (1891 ed.), Jefferson (1905), Forsyth (1907), Jowett (1912), Garvie (1921), Blackwood (1942), Scherer (1944), Stewart (1946), Blackwood (1951), Tillich (1951 ff.), Lys (1954), Bultmann (1955), MacLennan (1955), Coggan (1945), D. G. Miller (1957), Bultmann (1960, 1969), Knox (1960), Smart (1960), Thompson (1960), Schlink (1961), Kemp (1963), Ebeling (1963), Barth (1963), Teikmanis (1964), Brilioth (1965), Kierkegaard (1967 ff. ed.), Southard (1969), Pannenberg (1971b), Hamilton (1972), Lloyd-Jones (1972), Wink (1973), Bloesch (1973), Berger and Neuhaus (1976), Switzer (1979), and Anderson (1979).

10. The Teaching Elder

The Christian community is a teaching community. In each generation it faces a new challenge: teaching emerging young minds as well as adult believers about the saving acts of God. Christianity is not only doctrine but also a life, an ethic, a mode of behavior that must be taught and transmitted from generation to generation, and beyond that from age to age. This teaching is done generally through proclamation, worship, Eucharist, and pastoral care, but more particularly through catechesis, confirmation, and deliberate efforts at Christian education. In all these the pastor is commissioned as a teacher of Christianity (Ambrose, *NPNF* 2nd, vol. 10, pp. 16 ff.).

Ordained ministry has been more deeply involved in this teaching process in some periods of history than others (cf. Augustine, *LCC*, vol. 6, pp. 39 ff., 114 ff., 150 ff.; Baxter, 1656, pp. 172 ff.; Wesley, *WJW*, vol. 2, pp. 378 ff.). In our time ordained ministry has often tended to shy away from entangling involvements in the teaching ministry, either viewing it as a lay activity or turning it over to staff professionals in Christian education. Without firm pastoral guidance, programs in Christian education can easily become diminished in quality or plagued with compulsive experimentalism.

Pastors often are shocked at the number of their parishioners who do not know the difference between Genesis and Revelation, or between Peter and Paul. Yet seldom do we attribute this deficit to a failure of pastoral initiative over several generations. The continuing presence of a biblically unschooled laity serves as evidence that Christian education has stumbled, if not collapsed entirely, in our time, despite bold hopes and brave assurances.

There are many who occasionally attend church and who are trying experimentally to be Christians, yet are unable to identify well or define accurately the central truths of Christian teaching. The knowledge they have of the Christian tradition may have come chiefly through hymns.

Their strong and sincere feelings about religion are not matched with serious biblical or historical reflection on those feelings. Religious feelings are, indeed, crucial to the deeper learning of Christian truth, but they easily become superficial and narcissistic if the mind of Christ is not a mentor to natural religious impulse (Augustine, *SAOE*, pp. 16 ff.; Calvin, *Inst.*, 3.1,2). The loss of center in Christian education is arguably due to a serious default of pastoral leadership; when the teaching elder does not teach, the effect is felt throughout the entire Christian congregation (*Formula of Concord*, 1577, *BC*, pp. 506 ff.).

The call to teach Christian truth is a significant part of the call to ministry. "Aptness to teach" (2 Tim. 2:24) is traditionally thought to be a precondition of inner calling and an important criterion applied to the church's outward assessment of the call to ministry.

The pastor not only teaches directly but is responsible for the development and guidance of a system of lay Christian education. But note carefully the complexity of the particular kind of educational process that the pastor is trying to encourage: It is not one that solely relies on human intelligence or technical competence on ingenuity. It prays for God the Spirit to be present through a teaching and learning process so that the divine word will bear fruit in due season (Cyril of Jerusalem, 348; Thomas Aquinas, *ST*, vol. 2, pp. 2247 f.; Calvin, *Inst.*, 3.1, 4.4). A Christian pedagogy that either fails to invoke God's Spirit for inspiration in teaching or fails to utilize human intelligence, insight, and commitment will fail in the teaching mission of the church.

Jesus as the Model of the Pastoral Teacher

Jesus was often addressed as teacher. Those who seek to embody Christ's mission do well to learn pedagogy from Jesus' own teaching ministry. He spent a great deal of his time teaching not only his own disciples—a close, small, intimate group—but teaching the multitudes as well, even those who might hear him only once. When he commissioned the church to go into all of the world and make disciples of all nations, a decisive part of that commission included "teaching them to observe all that I have commanded you" (Matt. 28:20).

The risen Lord's charge to Peter is metaphorically simple and profound: "Feed my sheep. Feed my lambs" (John 21:12–17). By analogy this has been thought to refer to the Christian nurture of the adult believing community and also the lambs—the little ones coming on, the ones who are eminently teachable and prone to trust (cf. Clement of Alexandria, *ANF*, vol. 2, pp. 212 ff.; Gregory of Nazianzus, *NPNF* 2nd, vol. 7, pp. 444 ff.).

There seems little doubt that this teaching process is extended not only to little children, from the beginnings of their consciousness, but also to adults, as a lifelong process. No wise adult is beyond learning. The aim of this complex developmental process is to help people to "grow in grace and in the knowledge of our Lord and savior Jesus Christ" (2 Peter 3:18). New Testament texts suggest a process of maturing from milk to meat, from strength to strength, with the hope that one will become fully established in the word (Rom. 1:11; Eph. 4:13; Col. 1:28).

But maturity has small beginnings. The teaching ministry reaches out for the smallest (Luther, *WLS*, p. 137; Baxter, 1656, pp. 100 ff.). If we examine the texts in Matthew alone that deal with Jesus' particular interest in children, the cumulative impact is nothing short of astonishing, indicating that from the outset children have been a special concern of the Christian mission (Chrysostom, *NPNF* 1st, vol. 14, pp. 468, 471, 479). When the disciples asked Jesus who is the greatest in the kingdom of heaven, "he called a child, set him in front of them and said, 'I tell you this: unless you turn around and become like little children, you will never enter the Kingdom of Heaven. Let a man humble himself until he is like this child, and he will be the greatest in the kingdom of Heaven. Whoever receives one such child in my name receives me. But if a man is a cause of stumbling to one of these little ones who have faith in me it would be better for him to have a millstone hung around his neck and be drowned in the depths of the sea' " (Matt. 18:2–6).

Later a minor crisis arose when people "brought children for [Jesus] to lay his hands on them with prayer. The disciples rebuked them." Jesus' reversal of this decision is accompanied by an eschatologically oriented view of the promise of children: "But Jesus said to them, 'Let the children come to me, do not try to stop them; for the kingdom of Heaven belongs to such as these.' And he laid his hands on the children, and went his way" (Matt. 19:13–15). Similarly, when Jesus was criticized by the chief priests and doctors of the law who were offended by the fact that small boys in the temple were shouting hosannas to the son of David, Jesus replied sharply: "Have you never read that text, 'Thou hast made children and babes at the breast sound aloud thy praise'?" (Matthew 21:16).

From these texts alone, from only one Gospel, the point is nailed down powerfully: Jesus regarded children in their simplicity, trust, and innocence as heirs of the Kingdom. He invites them into his presence, he blesses them, and he angrily rebukes those who try to hold them back. From these passages we have good grounds to conclude that the pastoral office, in response to Jesus' commission, has a significant mission to young people, and to "little ones"—to those who are not yet fully formed—to offer them the truth of the Christian faith in ways they can grasp.

A Competent Teaching Ministry Is an Expectation of the Church

The Second Letter to Timothy calls the pastor to "use argument, reproof, and appeal, with all the patience that the work of teaching requires" (2 Tim. 4:2). This work of teaching is assumed to be a part of "all the duties of your calling" (2 Tim. 4:5). Most of the classical pastoral writers dealt with the central place of the teaching office, notably Clement of Alexandria in his work on the teacher, Augustine on the catechizing of the unlearned, and Thomas Aquinas on the teaching office, followed by Luther, Calvin, Comenius, Wesley, and others. We have a strong body of literature on catechesis as a pastoral task. Origen of Alexandria was noted for his catechetical teaching, as were Chrysostom, Cyril, and Ambrose. Protestant pastors like Baxter, Owen, Bridges, and Loehe have stressed the critical importance of the teaching office in ministry.

That a competent teaching ministry is an expectation of the church is demonstrated by a brief review of the ordinal examinations of various traditions:

In the traditional Anglican rite of ordaining deacons, one of the duties of ministry is "to instruct the youth in the catechism" (*BCP*, 1662). The ordinal examination for priests asked: "Are you determined, out of the said scriptures to instruct the people committed to your charge; and to teach nothing necessary to eternal salvation but that which you shall be persuaded may be concluded and proved by the scripture?" As a part of the teaching office, the pastor was strongly charged with combating error and false and speculative teaching about Christianity parading as the truth: "Will you be ready with all faithful diligence to banish and drive away from the church all erroneous and strange doctrines contrary to God's word?" (*BCP*, 1662). The spiritual jurisdiction of the parish is in the hands of the rector (from *regere*. "to lead straight, guide"), who has the duty of instructing children. This responsibility extends also to parents and godparents, who have accepted nurturing obligations in connection with baptism and confirmation.

In the rite of the ordination of a priest in the Roman Catholic tradition, the candidate is instructed in this way: "Apply your energies to the duty of teaching in the name of Christ, the chief Teacher. Meditate on the law of God, believe what you read, teach what you believe and put into practice what you teach. Let the doctrine you teach be true nourishment for the people of God" (*Rites of the Catholic Church*, vol. 2, p. 62 f.).

In the ordinal examination for presbyters in the Church of South India, the ordinand is asked: "Will you faithfully teach and preach the word of God to the people committed to your charge. . . . Will you be diligent in the reading of the Holy Scriptures and in such studies as help to the knowledge of the same?" (*BCW*, p. 169).

And so it is in the ordinal examination of varied traditions. Most assume that the pastor is the principal teacher of Christian truth in the local congregation. Teaching is not something that is incidentally or optionally added on to the task of ministry. Rather, it is intrinsic to ministry.

Since every Christian community is by definition a teaching community, that implies that the pastor is by definition the head of a teaching institution. The pastor may delegate some of this responsibility, but essentially it falls to the one who has by calling and preparation, by ordination and experience, been set apart as teaching elder (Calvin, *Inst.*, 4.4).

If the pastor does not diligently strive for high quality in the church's wider teaching ministry, it is not likely that others will be prepared to maintain high standards. The pastor has a major responsibility in developing teaching leadership among the laity so as to involve the entire congregation in the work of Christian education and in overseeing the form and content of the entire effort. Whereas the whole community is involved in the educational mission of the church, it is the pastor to whom the overall accountability is assigned to insure the authenticity, reliability, and depth of Christian teaching in that locale (Cyprian, *ANF,* vol. 5, pp. 301 f.; Ambrose, *NPNF* 2nd, vol. 10, pp. 67 ff.; Baxter, *Works,* vol. 15).

The pastor's educational responsibility involves these diverse areas: the family, the worshiping community, the church school, and catechetical instruction (in some parishes responsibilities in a parochial school or in higher education may be added). The effectiveness of all of these efforts depends significantly upon the direct involvement of the pastoral leader as spiritual shepherd of the whole flock. This occurs through liturgy, proclamation and pastoral care and, more specifically, through direct teaching—in the various levels of the church school, in bible study groups, summer church camps, and lay theological academies.

The pastor whose congregation has significantly experienced some or all of these forms of Christian education in the home, in the congregation, in the church school, and perhaps even in a good quality Christian college or campus ministry, will find that the congregation will be all the better prepared to receive the word of God in preaching and sacrament, and to implement the church's mission. When parishioners have not had some or all of these educational opportunities, the pastor may find burdensome obstacles in the way of an effective ministry of word, sacrament, and pastoral care.

Family as Educational Context

We focus now upon the pastor's responsibility for Christian education in the home and the family. This is doubtless the most far-reaching and significant of all teaching contexts: the primary relation of parents and children. No teacher can quite match the importance of the rich gifts that parents can give children in spiritual foundations. No subsequent teacher can easily correct central mistakes made by parents. No teachers following the parents have a right to such a high level of implicit trust from the child. The earliest teachers often have the longest influence. Their actions and attitudes become the building blocks of all subsequent understanding. There the self receives primary layers of impressions that will continue throughout the entire history of its development. This conception, sometimes attributed to Freud, was familiar to many centuries of Christian wisdom before Freud (cf. Augustine, *LCC*, vol. 7, pp. 74 ff.; Luther, *WLS*, vol. 2, pp. 140 ff.; Comenius, 1657).

Thus, it is said that parents are missioners, the first communicators of the Christian message (Gibbons, 1896, 314 ff.). This occurs not only through words but also through other means at unconscious and implicit levels. The trustability of the strange cosmos becomes more plausible when parents are trustable, refracting the trustworthiness of God.

Parents have both extraordinary influence and extraordinary responsibility in the religious education of their children. Not only may moral virtues be taught early, such as courage, honesty, prudence, compassion, and temperance, but also intellectual virtues, habits of consistency and of looking for good evidence, habits of order and precision of thought. These are basic patterns that can be engendered more effectively by parents than anyone else.

Leading figures in the Christian tradition have often credited their own parents with unparalleled influence in their spiritual formation. John the Baptist is remembered as one born of pious parents, Elizabeth and Zechariah, who by their hope prepared the way for his calling and ministry (Luke 1:5–80). Timothy also was the son of parents remembered for their virtuous life. A special tribute is paid in Scripture to the parents of Susanna, that they were just and that they instructed their daughter well in the Torah. In subsequent Christian history, there are many such cases: Augustine, Chrysostom, Basil, Gregory of Nazianzus, John Wesley, and many others who largely credited their parents either with bringing them by example into the Christian faith or giving them excellent patterns of spiritual discipline.

The biblical maxim: "Train up the child in the way he should go and when he is old he shall not depart from it" (Prov. 22:6, KJV). Wordsworth stated succinctly that "the child is the father of the man" ("My Heart Leaps Up"), perhaps recalling Alexander Pope, "as the twig is bent the tree's inclined" (*Moral Essays*, I).

In early experience the inner self is more impressionable than later, less dulled by the attrition of neglect or cruelty. There is less garbage to be cleared away, fewer obstacles to be circumvented, less prejudice, less pretense, less sophistry. Young Christians are compared to "newborn infants": "You must crave for pure milk (spiritual milk, I mean) so that you may thrive upon it to your soul's health" (1 Pet. 2:2).

Learning Through Worship

There are several ways in which the pastor can influence family values, most notably through preaching. The preaching ministry is properly viewed also as a teaching ministry, with the Christian family one of its main audiences. Preaching has a responsibility to encourage a genuinely Christian family existence. When we talk about the Christian community we are not just talking about a collection of autonomous individuals, but rather about what the New Testament calls "believers with their children," that is, Christian families. The Christian life taught through preaching must finally be practiced on the toughest of all firing lines: the primary family situation, the most crucial of all interpersonal arenas (Calvin, *Inst.*, 4.9).

Special events invite special opportunities for teaching: marriage, birth, baptism, confirmation, and death (Baxter, *PW*, vol. 6, pp. 109 ff.). In all of these the minister is present with the family, teaching both verbally and through nonverbal means about Christian covenant, the incomparable value of human life and the ministry of Christ for us.

Pastoral visitation is intrinsically a part of the pastoral teaching office vis-à-vis the family. The older Protestant practice was to have the pastor visit and teach the children the catechism while he was in the home and hear confession, offer the forgiveness of Christ, direct family prayer, and perhaps even do a modest bit of preaching. Visitation was viewed as a personalized extension of Christian worship (Baxter, 1656, pp. 87 ff.). Despite its formidable tone, it still may have something to teach us. We can study it in the works of Herbert, Baxter, Taylor, and Owen. Even though it is not likely that we will return slavishly to that pattern, given the assumptions of the modern world, we will find much of it meaty and suggestive by analogy.

The weekly service of public worship is potentially a powerful context of Christian education for both the individual and the family. For in the early Christian tradition as well as in Protestantism of a later time, public worship has been thought to be a family event, not just a place for adults, but a place where believers and their children—the whole family of God—gather. One should not underestimate the importance of the whole family, including children, listening to the pulpit instruction, sharing in praise and song together, and being a part of the awe and mystery of worship (Thomas Aquinas, *ST*, vol. 2, pp. 1922 f; Luther, *WLS*, vol. 1, pp. 140 f; Calvin, *Inst.*, 4.16).

Admittedly, public worship in recent decades has been viewed as a hopelessly irrelevant context for children. There is no denying that children are often bored in common worship and that they do not seem to be enjoying themselves in a place where special constraints are put on self-expression. There is good reason, though, to continue to put strong emphasis on family worship. The family at worship is a significant educational event in itself, for there children are learning the hymns of the church, they are learning how to pray, they are learning what happens in the Christian community, they are hearing Scripture even though they may not fully grasp it, and in some places they are hearing children's sermons. But even if there is no specific portion of the service addressed to children, many benefits nonetheless derive from having the family together amid the gathered community. What other occasions are there in modern society in which families do things together in a deliberately religious frame of reference?

Parents who think of nurturing spontaneity and self-expression as the central task of parenting will doubtless disagree. The pastoral nurture of those parents may require some careful dialogue, leading perhaps to thoughtfully challenging some of their assumptions.

Pastoral Guidance of the Church School

The pastor's responsibility for Christian education takes special focus in the church school. By "church school" we mean an educational system sponsored by the church for its children, youth, and adults that, through a regular curriculum and program of educational activities, wishes to be a significant instrument of Christian learning in that congregation. Even though the work of the church school is heavily dependent upon voluntary lay teachers and administrators, it is nonetheless to the pastor that the church looks for the overall supervision and oversight of the church school. The whole church has responsibility for the school, and therefore it deserves the whole church's support under pastoral guidance.

It can not be the responsibility of the state in a pluralistic society to teach Christian education. Only the church can do it. That is why it is so important for the church to do it well. For Christian education is not just a means toward better patriotism or democracy or civil religion or the generalized values of modern civilization. Rather, the purpose of Christian education is life in Christ, which involves learning to embody the Christian faith in one's behavior. Christian education in this sense must be seriously undertaken distinct from the other deserving educational tasks of public schools. Yet in pursuing its unique aim, Christian education may also make significant contributions to democracy and to the humanization of a society (Reinhold Niebuhr, 1932b, 1959, 1965).

It may take spirited pastoral initiatives to gather and energize the support of the laity for excellence in this educational venture. This may require serious efforts from the laity for financial support—for buildings, materials, periodicals, teaching materials—and also a serious claim of time upon the laity to teach and work supportively to enable significant learning. All of this requires energetic pastoral motivation, regular supervision, and thoughtful instruction.

This effort searches for modes of communication and education

that will be intelligible to every person, even those of less clearly perceived potential or apparent capacity. Christian education does not despair over any age, any class, any condition. Every person presents a
challenge and an opportunity for Christian education. Even the oldest
and most mature in the congregation still have much more to learn. We
all have yet to reach our intellectual, moral, and spiritual capacities.
What Christian education wishes to do is to release these energies, to
open up potentialities that were not perceived before, and to see every
person—from any class, any condition or point of entry—as a potential
learner of the way, the truth, and the life.

The young, who are most teachable, are going to learn whether we
teach them or not. The question is what will they learn and whether
they will be able to have the opportunity to incorporate Christian assumptions and values into their available fund of human wisdom.

We struggle against considerable odds in this effort because of the
small amount of time that is spent in Christian education as compared
with learning from one's peers, learning from electronic media, learning from the world at large. The quality, depth, and ethos of Christian
education must therefore be unusually humane, sympathetic, imaginative, and resourceful in order to compete with these alternative claims.

Yet ministry is given exceptional opportunities to teach people at
teachable moments when their whole life is at stake. Every encounter in
Christian ministry is a potential teaching context. When we deal with
the whole person amid life and death issues, what we struggle with is
not just objective knowing, but the search for a meaningful life (Wesley,
WJW, vol. 7, pp. 83 ff., 266 ff.; cf. Comenius, 1657).

The Pastoral Catechist

Clearly one of the most important educational tasks of the pastor is
to prepare young people for re-affirmation of their baptismal vows, to
prepare them for Holy Communion by rehearsing holy history, ex-
plaining the confession of faith, discussing the Apostles' Creed, and
helping the baptised person, who has now come to a point of accountability, to think clearly and articulately about what happened to him or
her in baptism, in order to respond to it more fully and explicitly.

Readers from the worldwide tradition of believer's baptism may prefer to view the catechetical task not as one of re-affirming pedobaptism,
but of preparing for, or more directly conjoined with, voluntary, deliberate adult baptism. But whether adult or infant baptism is assumed,
catechetical instruction of some sort cannot be avoided as a continuing
pastoral duty (Cyril of Jerusalem, *NPNF* 2nd, vol. 7, pp. 1 ff.).

Pastoral catechesis does better to focus on a few things well rather
than many haphazardly, that is, not to try to cover every theological
issue in detail but a small number of central Christian teachings deeply.
This is the reason you have a catechism, to center down, to highlight

the heart of faith, to focus in on the elementary affirmations of Christianity (Calvin, *Inst., LCC,* vol. 22, pp. 83 ff.).

The pastor is called to be resourceful in spurring the interest of inquiring minds in both moral awareness and religious formation, seeking to arouse the sleeping abilities and competencies of young persons to stimulate a searching attitude toward Christian faith and a willingness to listen and learn from Scripture and tradition (Cyril of Jerusalem, *NPNF* 2nd, vol. 7, pp. 19–32; Gregory, *ACW,* pp. 89 ff.).

This is why a continuing project of reading and intellectual exploration is essential to the health of ministry. For if ministers are expected to infuse others with a vital knowledge of God, they themselves must be nurtured. We are speaking of a lifelong task, one that transcends shortcuts, avoids faddism, and mines the best of what is old and what is new. When pastors become intellectually moribund, they are not likely to awaken awe, prophetic vision, or rigorous self-criticism.

Teaching of the Christian faith to young minds requires patient love. The pastor does well to take one crucial subject at a time, presenting it in familiar language and not at too great length. Even adults do not like long discourses, but young people, especially, are easily burdened with more than can be readily digested. In appealing to the young imagination, use illustrations, mental pictures, storytelling, and parables that will imprint themselves easily upon the memory (cf. Augustine, *SAOE,* pp. 131 ff., 177 ff.). In the Scriptures one will find many resources that have this imaginative story quality.

Since the heavens declare the glory of God and the firmament shows God's handiwork (Ps. 19:1), there is much in the natural sphere that can assist Christian learning. We can grasp the majesty and glory of God by analogy with the sun, the omnipresence of God by the innumerable stars, the eternity of God by thinking about the fleeting nature of time, the unlimited reach of God by the incredible space of the cosmos, the boundlessness of God's love by the breadth of the ocean, the glory and beauty of God by the visual beauty of the world. These are natural analogies that are constantly at hand, so that creation becomes a means through which to look to the presence and goodness of God. These natural object lessons should be freely, yet carefully, used within the frame of reference of Christian revelation, not as if Christianity were purely a naturalistic religion (Augustine, *SAOE,* pp. 152 ff., 160 ff.).

Confirmation and Re-affirmation of Baptismal Vows

The rite of confirmation in many traditions offers an opportunity to confirm what has been sealed in earlier baptism. If baptism is the token and seal of God's promise, confirmation celebrates that promise as having been deliberately and thoughtfully received by its principle recipient, the baptized individual. Confirmation assumes growth toward self-determined choice, now more personally understood and embraced as covenant, with its consequent obligations and privileges (cf. Cyprian, *ANF*, vol. 5, pp. 376 ff.; Thomas Aquinas, *ST*, vol. 2, pp. 2423 ff.). The commitment is to re-affirm baptismal vows, to renounce evil and follow Christ (*BCP*, 1979, p. 415). The Apostles' Creed is affirmed. One commits oneself to support the Christian community with one's prayers, presence, gifts, and services and seek to embody the Christian life (*Book of Worship For Church and Home*, 1964; *Book of Common Worship*, 1963, pp. 123 ff.). The church prays that the confirmands will be empowered by the Spirit to service, that their baptismal covenant shall be renewed, and that grace shall increase in them all the days of their life (*BCP*, 1979, p. 418). "Be sealed with the Gift of the Spirit," the church prays (*Rites of the Catholic Church*, 1976, p. 308).

The rite of confirmation, even though it is not directly of New Testament origin, was derived from very early apostolic practice (Tertullian, *ANF*, vol. 3, pp. 669 ff.; Cyril of Jerusalem, *NPNF* 2nd, vol. 7, pp. 8 ff.). Calvin argued that confirmation was a custom of the ancient church (*Inst.*, 4.19.4). Although Luther rejected the medieval sacramental conception of confirmation, he did in his small catechism provide for an instruction of youth that soon became a confirmation service.

In 1573 the classical Lutheran theologian, Martin Chemnitz, stated the prevailing Protestant viewpont: "Our theologians have often shown that the rite of confirmation, when the useless, superstitious, and unscriptural traditions respecting it have been laid aside, may be used piously and to the edification of the Church in this way: viz., that those who were baptized in infancy, when they come to years of discretion, should be diligently instructed by a clear and simple setting forth of the doctrines of the Church; and, when they seem moderately grounded in the rudiments, they should be presented before the bishop and the church; and ... make a personal and public profession of this doctrine and faith" (Schmid, 1961, p. 551).

The question may arise as to just how much a young person should know about faith before he or she is confirmed and how thoroughly this knowledge is to be tested. The most common guide is the meaning of the Apostles' Creed as a kind of core affirmation of scriptural truth. It is not usually thought to be necessary for the young person who is being confirmed to have studied all parts of the Scripture or to have understood detailed doctrinal issues or to have read extensively in theology, but one would expect the confirmand to know the central affirmations of the Christian faith as defined by the Apostles Creed and/or other traditional confessions.

Conclusion

Teaching elders bring all of these varied educational efforts into fruition. The range of the task includes providing resources for Christian learning in the family context, preaching to the worshiping community, a wide-ranging local church curriculum and program of church school education, and, finally, catechetical instruction leading to full accountability to one's baptismal vows.

REFERENCES AND FURTHER READING

See further the Didache (2nd cent.), Tatian (d. ca. 160), Clement (*ANF*, vol. 2, pp. 207 ff.), Cyprian (*ANF*, vol 5, pp. 301 ff.), Cyril of Jerusalem (348), *Apostolic Constitutions* (*ANF*, vol. 7, pp. 450 ff.), Jerome (*NPNF* 2nd, vol. 6, p. 324), Chrysostom (*NPNF* 1st, vol. 10), Ambrose (*NPNF* 2nd, vol. 10, pp. 67 ff.), Augustine (394, 399–400, 397–426), Gregory (*ACW*, vol. 11, pp. 89 ff.), Rabanus Maurus (d. 856), Thomas Aquinas (*ST*, vol. 2, pp. 2423 ff.), Luther (*WML*, vol. 4,5), Calvin (1559, 4.1 ff.), Comenius (1657), Fuller (1891 ed.), Baxter (*PW*, vol. 15, pp. 492 ff.), Wesley (d. 1791), Sailer (1807), Bushnell (1847), Gibbons (1896), Filson (1941), H. S. Smith (1941), Jaeger (1943), Smart (1954), Miller (1956), Torrance (1959), Muirhead (1965), Vieth (1965), Colin Brown (1969), Westerhoff (1970), *Rites of The Catholic Church* (1976, 1979), and Neuhaus (1979).

11. Equipping the Laity for Ministry

The pastoral administrator is also liturgist, preacher, teacher, visitor, and at times, solicitor and distributor of relief for the poor (Gregory, *ACW*, vol. 11, 32 ff.). Here lies the key to the proper conception of pastoral administration. Liturgy requires planning and organization. Preaching requires a gathered, listening congregation, which requires planning and organizing. The role of pastoral educator requires skill in administering a program of lay teaching. Visitation requires resourceful time management. Christian care of the poor has since its inception required some organizational apparatus for the collection and distribution of resources. None of these critical pastoral duties can be accomplished well without some administrative competencies (Calvin, *LCC*, vol. 22, pp. 48 ff.). Even though administration many not be one's forte or special interest, nonetheless every pastor confronts the challenge of administration as a means to ministry.

We are less concerned with the *how* than with the *why* of church administration. Pastoral theology seeks to understand the work of the pastor as steward of the church's human and temporal resources. Since pastoral theology is a unifying discipline, it seeks to integrate church administration into a larger vision of theological wisdom. It hopes that pastoral leadership will be viewed in the light of its biblical, historical, and theological roots.

Administry—Toward Ministry

To be a minister one must administer; ministry therefore requires what was once called "administry." The prefix *ad-* in front of *minister* in Latin simply meant "toward ministry" or "an intensification of ministry." "Administry," an old English word worthy of resurrecting, referred to all those tasks that contribute *to* ministry or lead *toward* ministry. In this sense the work of ministry is inseparable from certain tasks of administration. In fact the key Greek word for ministry, *diakonia*, has at times been translated "administration" (1 Cor. 12:5, 2 Cor. 9:12, KJV). Elsewhere, *kubernēsis*, or "governance," was regarded by Paul as one of the gifts of the Spirit to the church (1 Cor. 12:28, *kubernēseis*, variously translated as administrators, governors, organizers, managers, or those who have the power to guide).

Yet seminarians are prone to approach the study of ministry with a strong anti-administration view, prematurely associating this facilitative side of the ministry with manipulation and crass business practices, and perhaps with corruption and loss of integrity. Insofar as this occurs, the task of "administry" or administration has not been well grasped biblically and theologically. Experienced clergy, on the other hand, know all too well that they must function effectively as leaders in the church and community and be responsible for complex organizational processes. They are not just pastors to individuals, but to a community that hungers for a wise and useful ordering of itself. Since working pastors intuitively sense the importance of this task of community building, they look for help, for effective ways of facilitating the building up of the community. At times they may turn to business practices that have little or no grounding in the church's traditional understanding of itself but seem to be applicable by analogy to the life of the church. How, then, are these to be integrated into a well-grounded ecclesiology?

Just as in pastoral care there has been a tendency in some quarters to take over psychotherapeutic approaches and to uncritically welcome them directly into the practice of ministry, so in pastoral leadership there has been a tendency occasionally to look inordinately toward modern business techniques and industrial management principles as the sole guides for church administration. Meanwhile, church administration and temporal governance, having misplaced its biblical and theological roots, has tended to become something of an orphan discipline in the family of theological learning. The study of pastoral leadership urgently needs to relearn from its own pastoral tradition the essentials of the ministry of governance. In doing so it will rediscover a solid tradition of reflection and will then be on firmer footing to adapt as needed from contemporary management theory and business practice.

In the interest of recovering the tradition of administry, we need not completely set aside, where useful, the best contemporary resources for organizational management: budget planning, time management, and democratic decision making. Rather, these resources are analogous to the ways in which psychotherapeutic insights can be critically appropriated by pastoral counseling. They can be integrated into ministry, but only if they are received from within the context of a scripturally firm grasp of pastoral identity. It is difficult to obtain the balance for which we strive, however, when the modern strategies tend to spawn messianic pretentions, and illusions about their own omnicompetence. Nonetheless, we can begin to redress the balance by trying to establish anew a sound theological context and basis for pastoral leadership in church administration.

Theological and Biblical Basis of Church Administration

The pastor's call is to proclaim the gospel, administer the sacraments, and provide a well-conceived order for spiritually caring for the flock. Church administration is not an addendum to these requirements but, rather, deeply latent and implicit in them. For the Christian congregation is by definition a visible, socially palpable fellowship, an organization capable of being sociologically described and logistically cultivated (Calvin, *LCC*, vol. 22, pp. 102 f.; Wollebius, *RD*, pp. 135 ff.). The church exists in time and space, not in ethereal realms alone, and thus requires temporal governance (Hooker, book 3, chap. 1, sec. 14).

Since New Testament times the church has had to struggle against docetic views of Christ as ephemeral and nonhistorical, lacking a body. That christological heresy almost always tends to speak of the church strictly as an invisible community, a bodiless ideal, not an actual community of warm-bodied, passionate human beings. The heresy that fails to see Christ as a living body has its counterpart in an ecclesiology that fails to see the church as a visible community (Augustine, *NPNF* 1st, vol. 4, pp. 326 ff.; "Apology of the Augsburg Confession," 1531, *BC*, pp. 106 ff., 169 ff.; cf. Oden, 1970, chap. 3).

It is precisely because the church has a ministry of word, sacrament, and order that it needs adept leadership, well-defined goals, financial planning, and wise administration by an efficient organization. These "management" tasks are never separable from the central imperatives of preaching, sacramental life, and pastoral care. Rather, they are needed for no other reason than to more adequately embody the body of Christ, to enable lay mission, and to make more effective and efficient the fundamental mission of the church as *marturia, diakonia,* and *koinōnia* ("witness," "service," and "community").

Since the church is not a profit-motivated business organization, but rather a spiritual fellowship, its style of organizing itself, its way of structuring its life together, deserves to be commensurable with the way in which it fundamentally understands itself. The church does not view itself purely as a natural or sociological process. It exists in response to the divine call. It misunderstands itself if it fails to respond to the wisdom of the historical apostolate, which places its own unique stamp on the church's organizational style.

What then is church administration as a discipline? It is the study, among the disciplines of theology, of the means of organizing and planning, guiding and promoting the church's activities that lead to the better proclamation of the Word, celebration of Christ's presence and care for the flock, and service to the world. It looks for fit means to embody these missional efforts that are consistent with the proper ends of ministry (Calvin, *LCC*, vol. 22, pp. 74 ff.).

Equipping the Laity for General Ministry

A memorable text for reflection on pastoral administration is Eph. 4:11–12: "These were his gifts: Some to be apostles, some prophets, some evangelists, some pastors and teachers, to equip God's people for work in his service, to the building of the body of Christ." Note carefully the reason why all these gifts are given the ministry. The critical phrase is: "*pros ton katartismon tōn hagiōn eis ergon diakonias*"—"for the equipping of God's people for the work of serving" (or "for the perfecting of the saints for the work of the ministry"). The purpose of the whole complex effort of ministry: the building up or edifying of the body of Christ. For this reason some persons are appointed "pastors and teachers" (jointly understood), to *equip* (*katartizō*) the laity, to enable the whole body to build itself up in love, to prepare it inwardly and outwardly, to get it ready for its task, and to provide logistical support for the mission to be accomplished. In this sense of an "equipping ministry," there is no doubt that administration is intrinsic to and definitive of ministry itself (Calvin, *Inst.*, 4.1).

The pastor had best not do anything that the body itself could do. The pastor's primary task is to equip the body, not try to do everything for the laity. It is pride and an overweening need to control that causes the pastor to attempt to do the work of the entire congregation.

An intriguing biblical text often referred to in this connection is the story of Jethro, the father-in-law of Moses, who, when Moses was under considerable pressure, helped him grasp the leadership task more effectively. Moses had been hearing and settling disputes endlessly. The people had been standing in line to see him all day. Jethro asked,

What are you doing for all these people? Why do you sit alone with all of them standing around you from morning to evening? . . . This is not the best way to do it, you will only wear yourself out and wear out all the people that are here. The task is too heavy for you; you can not do it by yourself. Now listen to me; take my advice, and God be with you. . . . You must yourself search for capable, God-fearing persons among all the people, honest and incorruptible persons and appoint them over the people as officers over units of a thousand, of a hundred, or fifty or of ten. They shall sit as a permanent court for the people; they must report difficult cases to you but decide simple cases themselves. In this way your burden will be lightened, and they will share it with you. If you do this, God will give you strength and you will be able to go on. And, moreover, this whole people here and now will regain peace and harmony. (Exodus 18:14 ff.)

This text implicitly states both the problem and the proper vision for pastoral administration. The pastoral temper easily wears thin when every activity must be pastorally controlled. The Jethro principle enables more people to share the leadership load, so that God's grace works through many and spares any one excessive heaviness (Calvin, *Inst.*, 4.11.8; 4.20.8). It requires searching for honest and effective persons to do this important work at various levels—thousands, hundreds, and tens—attempting to find places where people's gifts can be used to benefit the whole community.

To their peril pastors misplace this useful distinction: The pastor is accountable for seeing that things are done, not for unilaterally doing them. Instead of following this preferred pattern, many pastors do the opposite—not delegating anything, trying to put their own personal stamp on every activity—so that the whole burden of the mission rests awkwardly upon not the general ministry but the weary shoulders of the single ordained minister in charge. Little effort is made to discover, enlist, and instruct new leadership or develop potential leadership or inspire deeper commitment.

Much modern pastoral work requires skills for guiding a democratic process. It is true that the detailing of democratic procedures awaited many centuries to come to flower, but they are implicit in much of the spirit of Scripture in its respect for the community as a whole organism, with its diverse gifts and its capacity to establish goals and share meaningfully in the division of labor according to the Pauline view of diversity of gifts. This requires that the pastor engender a process in which laypersons accurately listen to one another, honoring each other even in the midst of deeply felt differences of opinion; taking time to think through differences; and allowing the organization to take its own shape with a concern for the fairness, courtesy, and orderliness that is implicit in a good democratic process.

The pastor does well to avoid taking credit that can be passed on to others. Help others feel the importance of their contribution rather than channeling accolades toward yourself. Never do the work of general ministry that can be done by others, and look long and hard for those who can do neglected tasks. People often have a hunger to serve the church and a greater readiness to be called upon than is often recognized by ordained ministry. The good pastor will challenge people in patient, reasonable, tactful ways to see the needs, to recognize how these needs correlate with their own inner sense of the claim of Christian mission, to grasp how their gifts can be used in the context of specific needs, and to see how each person can take an equitable share of the load the whole body bears.

Many ministers who are otherwise excellent preachers and pastors fail at this point of equipping the laity for service in the general ministry of the church. Pastoral leadership consists principally in learning how to <u>empower, enable, and enrich the leadership of others</u>. It often seems simpler for the pastor to do the job alone according to self-defined criteria. But when the jobs become heavier than one person can bear there emerges a growing sense of irritation, isolation, and perhaps desperation. The smoke of burnout may be seen years later. The patterns of Exodus 18 and of Ephesians 4:11–12 will better enable the mission of the people of God (Gregory Nazianzus, *NPNF* 2nd, vol. 7, pp. 205 ff.).

Arenas of Mission

There are three basic levels or types of administrative responsibilities with which the pastor must necessarily deal: general, educational, and temporal. If avoided or misunderstood, the echoes of confusion will be heard at inconvenient times.

- First, there is general administration of the local church, which includes planning, organizing, guiding, and periodically reviewing the mission of the church. This is ordinarily organized on an annual basis. Objectives are set and monitored. These policies are best formed not unilaterally but by means of a democratic process. The pastor as enabler of that process becomes a resourceful theological consultant and teaching elder in relation to lay committees that do long-range planning and those that seek to achieve shorter range objectives. To receive a "pastoral charge" is to be charged with this task of overseeing both the temporal and the spiritual welfare of the whole congregation or parish (Wollebius, 1626, *RD*, pp. 141 ff.).
- Secondly, the pastor is also an educational administrator, who must learn how to facilitate the church's teaching ministry, especially through motivating, training, and enabling good lay teaching in church schools. This means organizing and overseeing an educational enterprise in the church with significant biblical and theological study at appropriate levels. It concerns not only the education of children, but also that of young and older adults. In a wider frame of reference, the pastor as educational administrator may play a key role in the development of proper support for schools, colleges, and seminaries.
- Thirdly, the pastor is charged with oversight of the temporal, the business and financial administration of the local parish (William Laud, 1634, *ATP*, pp. 702 ff.), even though much of the regular responsibility will be duly assigned to committees. Pastors need to learn either to lead this effort effectively, or to motivate wise lay leadership to do so. If you are to have a significant mission in the church, it necessarily will involve some efforts to provide funding or resources, staff support, and budget programming. This requires learning how to manage and utilize the church's limited

temporal resources astutely as means to the proper ends of Christian mission (Luther, *WLS*, vol. 3, p. 1338). That task requires enlisting persons of high character; giving the process clear order and effective organization; and finding trustees who will take responsibility for overall financial accountability: church treasurers and financial secretaries who will keep accurate records and a financial planning board to coordinate these committees. The object is that through a democratic process the due consideration of these temporal affairs in the church can be rightly made. Through all of this the minister must learn to offer timely but spare guidance, to teach the life of stewardship, and to help propose appropriate goals and hold to them (cf. Gregory, *NPNF* 2nd, vol. 12, pp. 149 f.; *ACW*, vol. 11, pp. 182 ff.; Calvin, *Inst.*, 4.4.5–9).

All of these activities are means, not ends, aimed at implementing the church's mission. Pastoral leadership seeks to insure that the means used are honestly commensurable with the ends. To prepare for this, it is appropriate to meditate on the biblical mandates and tradition's practical wisdom concerning pastoral leadership and church administration. The church would not be the church if it did not exist in mission. The embodiment, the actualization, the funding, and the organization of that mission is an intrinsic part of the mission itself (Wesley, *WJW*, vol. 8, pp. 252 ff., 301 f.).

Biblical Mandates for Temporal Accountability

Jesus himself called the church to mission, to preach the gospel, which requires coming together in some place to sing, to speak, and to pray. In most cases this means that a building is required, or at least some place to meet. That requires organization.

"We ought to see how each of us may best arouse others to love and active goodness, not staying away from our meetings, as some do, but rather encouraging one another" (Heb. 10:24). This suggests that the problem of persuading people to be serious about coming regularly into the gathered community and being accountable to an organization is not just a recent dilemma. Apparently it has challenged the church from its beginnings.

The church is called to teach, baptize, welcome strangers, care for the sick, and preach the gospel to all the earth (Acts 1:8 and Matt. 28:19). This mission will not occur willy-nilly. It has to be organized and guided. That is in part what pastors are for. Not everyone in the church is equally and indiscriminately accountable for organizing this mission. In most historical and contemporary Christian communities, the accountability is specifically assigned to ordained ministry (Chrysostom, *NPNF* 1st, vol. 14, pp. 518 ff.). In order to implement this ministry God the Spirit has provided the whole church with varied and necessary gifts (Eph. 4:11; Acts 20:28). The administrative task requires the recognition of these gifts, finding ways of structuring, planning, and organizing life together in a Christian community so that these gifts may be best put to use.

Scripture does not give specific directives in detail about how to organize or structure or design a church organization (Thirty-Nine Articles, 1563, CC, pp. 177 f.). Assuming broad scriptural guidelines, we are to use our reason, common sense, and experience to help find the best contextual means of implementing these immediate objectives of the church's mission. In doing so we are free to use management skills, human relations training, democratic procedures, group processes, and so on to implement these ends, provided they are kept within a firm scriptural understanding of church and ministry. They are means, not ends.

Jesus called the apostles to enlist and train others in order to carry out the mission of the church. Jesus thereby provided an exemplary model of pastoral leadership and organizational and administrative shepherding as he called the twelve together, taught them, and later expanded his effort to send out seventy others (and later many more) to accomplish the mission.

There is evidence that there was in fact an administrative center in the early church—Jerusalem. There is some indication that James was the ruling elder, or chief administrator of the Church of Jerusalem. Acts 15:13–23 gives us an intriguing example of how decisions were made. In this instance, it was a very important decision about how the church was to develop its mission to the Gentiles. The administrative decision was made with good order, facing conflicts and allowing various viewpoints to be heard and thought through in relation to the delivered tradition, the guidance of the Spirit, and impinging contingencies (Calvin, Inst., 4.10.17 ff.). A consensus emerged that has powerfully affected all subsequent church history. If James, Paul, and Barnabas and others had not been willing to work through their differences toward consensus in understanding the divine imperative, the church might never have mounted a mission to the Gentiles, and the reader would not be reading this page now.

The capacity for domestic management was a major criterion powerfully applied in the New Testament to the choice of church leadership. "He must be one who manages his own household well" so as to win responsiveness from children (1 Tim. 3:4). The phrase "manage well" or "govern well" (proistemi) was used to speak of both parental and pastoral duties. Verse 6 put the issue bluntly: If a person "does not know how to control his own family, how can he look after a congregation of God's people?" Thus, a domestic analogy of home managment and parental accountability was deliberately applied to pastoral leadership.

Pastor and Organization

There is a subtle dialectic here between the Holy Spirit's call and the sociology of organization. To be sure, God the Spirit is not captive to our organizational designs. God is free to work both within and without our organizations. We see in history examples of how God the Spirit has freely moved to transcend widely held assumptions of a given organization, in some cases undermining demoralized and corrupt institutions, plowing deep and sowing new seeds. The Spirit calls us to use all our available knowledge of human motivation, democratic procedure, and social process to order and enable Christian mission.

Using the organic analogy of the church as a body with members, all of these parts cohere interdependently in the body of Christ. They all complement one another. Each works best only when all work. No part can exist separately. Christ is the head, the willing, directing center of the organism (1 Cor. 2; cf. Origen, *ANF*, vol. 4, p. 595). Within this body, the pastor is expected to help the whole organism to work together for good; to strengthen its cohesiveness; add to its integrated self-understanding; help provide a unified interpretation of its mission; and discipline, direct, train, and guide it where necessary. That is pastoral leadership.

Good pastors do not accomplish this through an aloof, self-sufficient, independent attitude, on the assumption that they are capable of doing it all. That, in fact, is not the case. You will not accomplish this cohesion by keeping yourself at a distance from the flock or considering the flock stupid or unattractive, or too slow-witted to follow your superior guidance. It is intrinsic to the analogy of pastoring that shepherds are daily with their sheep, intimately participating in their crises and respectfully involved at close hand with them. But the pastor does not simply go impulsively wherever the flock wants to go. That is not pastoral leadership. The shepherd is the one who leads them step by step to better pastures than they would have found otherwise. This guidance occurs in response to Christ's guidance of the proclaiming church. We as undershepherds, rather than wandering aimlessly, are trying to guide the flock away from danger. Therefore, every step the pastor takes in guiding the flock should be purposeful, with long range intent, astutely sensing where the green pastures are, how long it takes to get there, and the logistics of how to go from here to there.

If the flock had no dangers ever to face, there would be no need for such a shepherd. It is precisely because of these dangers that the flock learns to listen to the voice of the shepherd. Legitimate authority is accredited to the pastoral office by call and ordination, yet the pastor cannot simply count on ordination as such to legitimize anything he or she says. Respect must be again and again earned by the pastor through trustworthy behavior.

Wisely understood, the shepherding analogy does not imply that the congregation never has any opportunity to contribute its own views in the design of the local church mission or policy formation of the local church. When there are differences among the congregation about how the church's mission is to be defined or accomplished, the pastor has a important role in trying to encourage the mutual discernment of the truth, reconcile differences, and awaken native energies to fruitful use.

Spirit and Organization in Eschatological Perspective

One major difference between the church and other voluntary or business or governmental organizations hinges on Christianity's eschatological perspective. Voluntary and business organizations generally have hedonic goals. They wish to accomplish objectives that are visible within this temporal sphere, often those that fit within a five-year plan, a fiscal year, or a three-week sales blitz. The church also has a bottom line at the end of the fiscal year, but that is not the only way it assesses itself. Christian congregations also try to get things done, organize things decently, and achieve objectives, but the Christian community has a larger historical perspective on all of these activities— larger in fact than this fiscal year, this political regime, or even this civilization. Universal history, amazingly, is the horizon of Christianity's perspective. The meaning of universal history is theology's special interest.

Pastoral theology does not set aside that perspective as it makes fiscal decisions or examines the implementation of the church's mission. It knows that its goals will not be completed in a short time but only in the *eschaton*, the "end time," when God will make right the wrongs and distortions and sins of this world (Irenaeus, *ANF*, vol. 1, pp. 561 ff.; Tertullian, *ANF*, vol. 3, pp. 447 ff., 545 ff.). Jews and Christians celebrate that end time as a promised resolution of the distortions of history.

This eschatological perspective elicits, at its best, a deeper sense of patience toward organizational limits and dilemmas (Thomas Aquinas, *ST*, vol. 3, pp. 2874 ff.; Wesley, *SJW*, vol. 7, pp. 311 ff., 474 ff.; vol. 8, pp. ff.). In our secular organizations we are frustrated when we cannot accomplish everything now and change the world immediately. The Christian community also wishes to change the world. It would like to do it as soon as possible. But in the light of God's patience, there is time for hope, which entreats our patience as we continue to work within the conditions of sin and alienation to behold the slow-growing seeds of providential activity taking shape in their own way and time (Augustine, *NPNF* 1st, vol. 2, pp. 93 f.; Calvin, *Inst.*, 1.17). So, well-grounded Christian thinking about organizations has not often been mesmerized by a revolutionary frenzy that assumes that immediate change is the only way to judge God's presence in the world.

When we are persistently frustrated with the way God put the world together, we have probably forgotten something important about creation. A right understanding of providence seeks to elicit change, to help things grow in their own way and time, but knows the difference between we who plant, and others who water, and God who gives the increase (1 Cor. 3:6).

Our attempts to give order to our small spheres of influence are seen within the context of God's own design for the whole of history. We know, even when we pray, "Come, Lord Jesus," that history is not likely to be completed in our time. At best, there is a kind of lightness, a joyful unseriousness, about Christian participation in organizations and historical achievements. We need not take either our organizational successes or failures with absolute seriousness. For the organization is not the end, even though it is needed proximately for the Christian mission. The patience that wishes not to change nature, but to nurture change, stands in relation to a wider providence that works with different timing schemes than we have in our heads or political ideologies (Luther, *WLS*, vol. 3, pp. 1150 ff.).

Another difference between the church as an organization and business or voluntary organizations is that many of the church's objectives, goals, and plans are not easily subject to quantifiable measurement. In a business you have to judge annual success in terms of productivity, growth, security, and profit at limited costs. Usually you try to apply some means of quantifiable measurement to the success of the organization. But how do you measure the success of pastoral care to an elderly parishioner or preaching of the word to her grandson or of the presence of Christ in the midst of the sacramental life to her daughter? These are not readily subject to quantifiable measurement. They are not absolutely without any means of quantifiable measurement, for it is possible to report the number of baptisms, confirmations, pastoral visits, and so forth, but the outward and quantifiable aspects that are so evident in most social organizations as criteria for judging their effectiveness are often less important in the church—though, again, they should not be completely neglected.

There are pitfalls on either side: we can avoid the risk of trying to discern whether what we are doing is effective, or we can overestimate the importance of our shifting data bases. The appropriate balance is to freely use measurements of growth sparely and fairly within a clear, long-range vision of the church's mission.

Effective Governance

In seeking effectively to equip the laity for general ministry, the pastor will attend carefully to the formation of certain habits that mark good administrative leadership; among these are a capacity to use intelligence and foresight to plan ahead, and an ability to set priorities so that the important things do not slip through the cracks. Learn to correlate means with ends in their proper order.

Think of your administrative tasks as problems of exegesis. Learn how to make a biblically responsible analysis of the situation so that you can help a committee or a task force grasp its direction clearly without being tempted to take over the task yourself.

It must have been with some amusement that Jesus remarked:

Would any of you think of building a tower without first sitting down and calculating the cost, to see whether he could afford to finish it? Otherwise, if he has laid its foundation and then is not able to complete it, all the onlookers will laugh at him. "There is the man," they will say, "who started to build and could not finish." Or what king will march to battle against another king without first sitting down to consider whether with ten thousand men he can face an enemy coming to meet him with twenty thousand. (Luke 14:28–32.)

Accurately assess costs. Do not start what you cannot finish. Finish what you start.

Yet however astutely we plan, we nonetheless remain at risk with the future. James 4:14 pointedly reminds us that whatever we do we "do not even know what will happen tomorrow." We must plan, always with a wry smile, a wink at contingencies, a sense of all our plans as penultimate. We must make forecasts, anticipate conditions, make projections; but these are best done with a chastened awareness that we cannot control the future and may have to go to plan B. A large part of astute administrative skill involves not only setting objectives but learning where and how to shift them when necessary. We do well to calculate modestly how these objectives may be accomplished through a staged sequence of actions—a schedule, a calendar—and through the careful budgeting of resources. But there are always surprises.

We have not served the church well by using purely pragmatic, functional images to think about this administrative side of ministry if we thereby inadvertently cut ourselves off from sound biblical, theological moorings. Part of what an integrated pastoral ministry will seek to do is to again bring the work of church administration and pastoral leadership into practical working dialogue with Scripture, reason, tradition, and experience so that church administration is an expression of sound theology, the life of prayer, the study of Scripture, and sacramental life.

Preaching can help shape the vision of the organization. Worship grounds it in hope. Counsel enables individual growth. Pastoral teaching can provide perspective and direction for members of the body at various stages along life's way. Pastoral leadership wants to show how faith can become active in love. All these tasks intermesh in the challenging work of "managing well," or active governance (*kubernēsis*), of the Christian community.

REFERENCES AND FURTHER READING

See Irenaeus (*ANF*, vol. 1, pp. 561 ff.), Clement of Alexandria (*ANF*, vol. 2), Tertullian (*ANF*, vol. 3), Origen (*ANF*, vol. 4), *Apostolic Constitutions* (*ANF*, vol. 7), Cyril of Jerusalem and Gregory Nazianzus (*NPNF* 2nd, vol. 7), Ambrose (*NPNF* 2nd, vol. 10), Gregory (*NPNF* 2nd, vol. 12), *Seven Ecumenical Councils* (*NPNF* 2nd, vol. 14), Augustine (*NPNF* 1st, vols. 2, 4), Chrysostom (*NPNF* 1st, vol. 9), Thomas Aquinas (*ST*, vol. 3, pp. 2874 ff.), Luther (*WML*, vol. 6), Calvin (1559, 4.1 ff.), "Apology of the Augsburg Confession" (*BC*, pp. 214–224), Chemnitz (1595), Zepper (1595), Hooker (1594–1618, book 5), Wollebius (*RD*, pp. 135 ff.), Laud (*ATP*, pp. 702 ff.), Wesley (*WJW*, vol. 8, pp. 252 ff.), Gladden (1911), Fenn (1938), Blackwood (1949), Kantonen (1956), Ross and Hendry (1957), Leach (1958), Brattgard (1963), Küng (1964), A. M. Adams (1964), P. R. Jackson (1968), Moltmann (1971), Oden (1970), and J. Adams (1979).

IV

PASTORAL COUNSEL

12. Pastoral Visitation

Are the doors open?

A unique opportunity is given the pastor that is not offered the psychological counselor or psychotherapist. For the pastoral office carries with it the extraordinary privilege of calling upon persons in the parish at almost any time. This opens unparalleled opportunities for social service, intimate dialogue, and Christian witness.

To no other profession are such doors open. No matter how ill the patient, the physician waits until the patient comes to the office to request medical treatment. No matter how urgently a legal client needs to write a will or know his rights, the attorney waits in his office until the client makes an appointment. It would be bad professional ethics for the dentist to knock on the door and ask if some one had a toothache. But for the minister—and among professionals the minister only—the doors of parishioners are open. No special invitation is required. Most are honored when the pastor visits, and some feel neglected if pastoral visits are long delayed. *?*

Why is ministry so different from those professions that have a strict ethical code against self-initiated home visits? Among the professions, ministry is the only one that by moral conviction and tradition does not take fees for services. The Council of Chalcedon stated the early ecumenical consensus that no member of the clergy shall "engage in business or . . . worldly engagements" (*Seven Ecumenical Councils, NPNF* 2nd, vol. 14, p. 269). That assumption drastically distinguishes ministry economically and sociologically from other fee-based professions. Ministry depends entirely on free congregational and wider church support (Rom. 12:13; 2 Cor. 9:1–15). Members of the congregation by tradition have implicitly issued an unwritten standing invitation to their minister to come on behalf of their spiritual welfare whenever it is felt to be in their interest. The pastor is ordained and commissioned to do precisely that: to visit from house to house, call upon those in need, give spiritual counsel in due season.

theoretically so.

Visitation requires much grace, patience, and commitment. The faithful pastor is willing to go unnoticed in the newspapers while quietly following the poor to their barrios, the sick to their bedsides, the melancholic to their isolation, the alcoholic to their dregs, the sincerely inquiring to their wrenching questions, the grieving to their hope, the dying to their rest. It is only by this outgoing watchfulness that one can "make full proof" of one's ministry (2 Tim. 4:5).

Obstacles and Encumbrances

Even though in principle the duty of the pastor to "visit from house to house" (Acts 5:42) is widely recognized as intrinsic to the pastoral office, nonetheless it is often neglected and sometimes awkwardly discharged. It is plagued with several recurring difficulties:

- The unreasonable demands of some to be compulsively cared for;
- The complications of ordering one's valuable time for a complex organization of sequential appointments, while remaining flexible for emergencies and faithful to other commitments;
- The demands on-time made by large congregations. Many parishioners are geographically spread out so broadly. So many come to the pastor in times of personal crisis. There may be little time left for the "rounds";
- The large number of people working—fewer are at home, and even when they are free, the pastor may not be because of so many scheduled evening meetings;
- The intense inner resistance pastors themselves often experience toward risk-laden encounters with parishioners on their own home turf.

Old Fashioned

Ideally, pastoral visitation calls for <u>a regular round</u> (traditionally at least once a year) <u>of individual consultation</u> with every communicant or family in a parish. Only by this means can the pastor learn firsthand of parishioners' aspirations, struggles, and challenges (Baxter, 1656, p. 177). Only there can realistic shepherding be brought in touch with parishioners' actual loves and aversions, joys and sorrows, hopes and fears. There the pastor can enter empathetically into the ground floor of currently lived human experience, offer timely assistance and encouragement, and minister to changing needs (Herbert, 1652, p. xiv).

Yet to many sincere pastors, this is among the most difficult and distasteful aspect of their work. Some feel that they have no time for it. Some have great difficulty even pretending that calls are meaningful. Sometimes these aversions and resistances are accompanied by curious rationalizations. A review of the biblical understanding of pastoral visitation is needed to recover the underlying meaning of this commission.

Theological Foundation: God Has Visited and Redeemed His People

We visit like God visited

As God himself came to visit and redeem his people (Luke 1:68), so we go on behalf of God's Son to visit and share that redemption in our own arena of service. As God himself becomes personally and bodily present in the incarnation, so are we called to be personally present to those in our charge, especially those in urgent need. As God the shepherd goes out to the lost sheep and leaves the ninety and nine, so at times we must leave the secured flock and pursue the lost one who is at risk (Matt. 18:12). Pastoral visitation of persons is one way of reflecting the glory of God's own visitation of humanity in Christ, seeking the lost, redeeming sin, mending pain.

A parish is defined as the immediate area in which a pastor visits, or sojourns. Parish comes from *paroikia,* "sojourning" (from *para,* "beyond," and *oikos,* "the house"). It is a defined geographical area to which the pastor is accountable on behalf of the apostolic mission. Leaving one's own house, one's own secure and controlled surroundings, is therefore essential to the definition of a visit.

The Hebrew root of visit, *paqad* (rendered in Greek as *episkopeō* and in Latin as *visitare*) has two complementary nuances:

- to examine or prove by testing
- to see that all is in order.

Traditional pastoral visitation has both qualities: an inquiry to see if faith is present and growing; and an on-site review to check on current developments.

This outreaching, self-extending side of visitation is expressed in the two active verbs of Matthew 25:36: "I was sick and you visited (*episkepsasthe*) me, I was in prison and you came to (*ēlthate*) me." Both are initiative-taking, energetic verbs. The very nature and social dynamics of ministry require active pastoral visitation. "After some days," having preached the gospel to many in the vicinity of Antioch, "Paul said to Barnabas, 'Come, let us return and visit (*episkepsometha*) the [brothers and sisters] in every city where we proclaimed the word of the Lord, and see how they are' " (Acts 15:36).

The pastoral office is by definition a shepherding task that involves not just a single meeting with the flock, but continuing oversight and feeding. The analogy suggests a deeply involved relationship. It requires vigilance, constancy, at times "watching through the night," and above all, a caring heart.

This is why shepherding cannot be done at a sterile distance, with automated telephone answering services, computerized messages, and impersonal form letters. By definition there cannot be an absentee shepherd. There can be no mail order or mechanized pastoral service because pastoring is personal. It is not just public talk, but interpersonal meeting where richer self-disclosures are possible.

The pastor's very title and vocational identity stems from this shepherding metaphor, which assumes visiting. The flock is dispersed and scattered vulnerably about in a hazardous world. They will be shielded from thieves and led to fresh water only if the pastor is in the same field with them.

During the period of the rebuilding of the Temple (520–518 B.C.), Zechariah gave a withering description of the "worthless shepherd" who "abandons his sheep," who does not even notice those that are lost, who when notified of a crisis fails to go out and "search for those that have gone astray," who persistently neglects to "heal the injured or nurse the sickly" (Zech. 11:15–17). Earlier, Jeremiah had quarreled with the religious leadership of his day: "You have scattered and dispersed my flock. You have not [visited, KJV] watched over them. . . . I will appoint shepherds to tend them; they shall never again know fear or dismay or punishment" (23:1–4).

When Yahweh visits the people, he "puts them on trial," "exacts a reckoning" (cf. Jer. 14:10, Hosea 4:9, 1 Sam. 15:2, Ps. 89:32). When God "makes a visit" amid human history, there is personal encounter and correction, because the holy God will not abide sin (Exod. 32:34; Amos 3:2). The purpose of Yahweh's visitation is not merely to vent wrath or express some arbitrary purpose, but rather that the people may examine their own conscience and ultimate accountability.

Jesus as Model for Visitation

The Hebraic memory of God's visitations to human history came to a momentous climax in the ministry of Jesus of Nazareth. Through him it was later said that God himself had in person "visited and redeemed his people" (Luke 1:68). We can learn most of what we need to know about pastoral visitation simply by looking carefully at the interpersonal ministry of Jesus:

- A large part of Jesus' ministry was directed toward individuals in face-to-face interactions. Jesus engaged in many conversations— some brief, some sustained—with hurt and troubled individuals. It was precisely through personal meeting that it began to dawn on people that the governance of God was beginning to occur through the ministry of Jesus. Jesus visited individually with

  Nicodemus (John 3:1–9)
  The Samaritan woman (John 4:1–42)
  The centurion (Matt. 8:5–10)
  The nobleman whose son was sick (John 4:47–50)
  The widow whose son was dead (Luke 7:11)

>A scribe (Matt. 8:19,20)
>The woman of Canaan (Matt. 15:21–28)
>The parents of the demoniac (Matt. 17:14–21)
>The rich young ruler (Matt. 19:16–22)
>The adultress (John 8:2–11)

Demoralizing life patterns and disablements were reversed, often through probing, one-on-one conversations.

- Healing, in Jesus' ministry, was generally accompanied by significant life-changing personal interactions, as in the cases of

>The leper (Matt. 8:2–4)
>Bartimaeus (Mark 10:46–52)
>The man born blind (John 9:1 ff.)
>The man with a withered hand (Matt. 12:9–14);
>The impotent man (John 5:5–9)

- Jesus visited in succession the towns and villages of Judea, Samaria, and Galilee. He often entered into the houses of willing hearers, whether rich or poor, learned or lowly. He ministered along the way to people where they were in their places of joy or travail (Mark 1:39, 17:11, 23:5; John 12:3).
- Jesus characteristically addressed people in the ordinary locus of their usual or typical activity, where they lived or worked:

>The seashore (Mark 4:1)
>The well (John 4:6)
>The highway (Mark 10:46)
>The marketplace (Matt. 20:3)
>The tax office (Matt. 9:9)
>The temple (Matt. 26:55)

- Jesus witnessed to the coming governance of God to all sorts and conditions of people. He intentionally reached out for persons of decidedly different backgrounds, social strata and opinion:

>Sadducees (Matt. 22:23–33)
>Pharisees (Matt. 12:2–6)
>Herodians (Matt. 22:15–22)
>Romans (Luke 7:2)
>Zealots (Luke 6:15)

Similarly today, well-grounded pastoral visitation does not limit itself to the immediate flock, but reaches out to persons of all dialects, political parties, economic ideologies, and social classes.

- Some of Jesus' most important disclosures (such as those on the

Span of Care

Mount of Transfiguration) occurred in extended retreatlike settings that allowed unhurried, intimate conversations with his disciples (Matt. 5:1 ff., 12:46–50, 17:1–13, 26:17–29; Mark 9:2–8,
14:12–25; Luke 9:28 ff.; 22:7–38).

- The frequency with which the Synoptic Gospels report that Jesus
  visited persons in their own homes makes it evident how important
  this context was for Jesus' ministry:

  The home of Levi the publican (Luke 5:29)
  The wedding at Cana (John 2:1,2)
  The houses of Pharisees (Luke 7:36–50, 14:1–24)
  The house of Mary and Martha (Luke 10:38–42)
  The house of Simon the leper (Matt. 26:6).

- When Jesus met people in their homes and work settings, he cut
  through to the marrow of their lives, exposed their idolatries, awakened a living sense of the presence of God, looked deeply into their
  souls, heard them empathetically, and called them to repentance
  and faith. Jesus remains the pattern for all who would converse or
  counsel in his name (Gregory, *ACW*, vol. 11, pp. 45 ff.).

The Apostolic Patterns of Visitation

Did the apostles deliberately continue this one-on-one interpersonal
ministry of Jesus? And did they visit "from house to house"? Paul suggests as much in his recollection of his own ministry at Ephesus: "I did
not shrink from . . . teaching you in public and from house to house"
(Acts 20:20, RSV).

The antiquity of this practice is evident from the account in Acts 5.
The apostles had just been released from prison following the speech of
Gamaliel. They had been severely flogged and ordered to give up
speaking in the name of Jesus. Yet courageously they returned immediately to do what they had been doing: "daily in the temple, and in every
house, they ceased not to teach and preach Jesus Christ" (Acts 5:42,
KJV).

The apostles' practice had its root in Jesus' commission, in which
visitation was assumed to be intrinsically connected with preaching: "As
you enter the house, salute it. And if the house is worthy, let your peace
come upon it; but if it is not worthy, let your peace return to you. And
if any one will not receive you or listen to your words, shake off the dust
from your feet as you leave that house or town" (Matt. 10:12–14, RSV).

The pastor must learn to "change his tone" with varying circumstances, as Paul suggested amid a frustrating conflict with the Galatian
church: "I desire to be present with you now, and change my voice"
(Gal. 4:20). Such subtle, contextual modulations of voice tone and body
language cannot be accomplished through the written word or formal
address, but can occur through responsive personal encounter.

Now the tradition is small groups

Confession in the Protestant and Catholic Traditions

Auricular confession provided medieval Catholicism with a regular sacramental means of engaging in one-to-one interaction between pastor and penitent prior to Holy Communion (Thomas Aquinas, *ST*, vol. 3, pp. 2590 ff., Council of Trent, 1545–63; Borromeo, 1701). Luther's attack on the abuses of a routinized doctrine of penance foreclosed the practice among Protestants (Luther, *WML*, vol. 1, pp. 13 ff.). But it took only a short time for Protestant ministry to discover the form and style of its substitute. By returning to the apostolic practice of pastoral visitation from house to house, Protestantism devised an effective replacement for auricular confession that preserved the best aspects of personal pastoral dialogue, yet tended to protect it from familiar medieval abuses (Baxter, "Special Directions for Holy Conference, Exhortation, and Reproof," *PW*, vol. 6, pp. 246 ff.).

Medieval penance rested upon a sound psychological principle: the need of the human spirit to unburden itself in the presence of a trusted companion who could mediate the forgiveness of God amid human sin. Protestantism sustained that value while at the same time resisting the potential distortions of sacramental penance.

The pastoral counseling movement since the mid-1920s stands in direct line of continuity (although unselfconsciously) with both the achievements and the limitations of Protestant pastoral visitation as a surrogate mode of confession. Modern clinically oriented "pastoral counselors" sometimes view their chief mentors as Freud, Jung, Rogers, Maslow, or Berne (each one with various implicit roots in Jewish or Christian piety). But the deeper resonances in the Clinical Pastoral Education movement often hark back unconsciously to seldom read but still archetypically remembered and socially transmitted pastoral models such as Luther, Baxter, Francis de Sales, Fenelon, Wesley, and Asbury.

Just as a priest hearing confession needs patience, wisdom, and a good ear, so the Protestant pastor's task in visitation is far less to become a good talker than it is to become a gifted listener. Earlier pastoral writers long before Carl Rogers knew that often the pastor's greatest possible service was to listen accurately without predisposing judgments (Gregory, *ACW*, vol. 11, pp. 54 ff.; Luther, *WLS*, p. 326; Wesley, *WJW*, vol. 7, pp. 733 f.).

But visitation is hardly a Protestant invention, even though Protestants gave greater attention to its practical implementation. Long before Luther we hear Chaucer (*Canterbury Tales*, lines 348–352, *LLE*, p. 41, 1386–90) writing of that "good man of religion" that he like his Master went about doing good:

> His cure was wide, with houses far asunder;
> But never did he fail, in rain or thunder,
> In sickness and in mischance, to visit all,

> The furthest in his parish, great or small,
> Upon his feet, with staff in hand for aid.

The preparation for this sort of pastoral ministry begins in the heart. If it is an irksome duty, the trouble is in the pastor's heart and must be attended to first at the most interior level of understanding of pastoral calling (Herbert, 1632, chap. 17.).

A Word in Season

The purpose of visitation is to bring Christian truth to bear upon the personal situation of the believer. Truth announced from the pulpit depends upon the willingness of the hearer to credit it as trustworthy. Truth well spoken in the pulpit may be made doubtful if the hearer never sees evidence of the preacher's active caring (Ambrose, *NPNF* 2nd, vol. 10, pp. 15 ff.). Visitation seeks to authenticate the proclaimed word through a personalized word.

However full may be the pastor's scholarly life or homiletical brilliance or skill in reasoned argument or organizational ability or depth of devotional life or dignity in worship (all of which justify considerable attention) none of these can substitute for being out there with the flock. This implies engagement, openness, availability, presence. How else shall the pastor acquire an intimate awareness of the personal needs to which preaching is addressed?

But how does the pastor offer the truth in highly individualized applications? There is no rule that can replace good judgment, proportional reasoning, and careful listening. This is presupposed in what the Bible calls wisdom (*hokmah*, cf. Ps. 90:12, 111:10; Prov. 2:6 ff., 4:5 ff.). Wisdom knows the right time for a particular word. How? The answer itself requires wisdom. No wonder wisdom is so often thought to be a secret (Job 11:6; 15:8).

In preparing pastors for ministry, the church hopes and prays that by grace each one may "get a heart of wisdom" (Ps. 90:12; Eccl. 2:3; Prov. 4:5). The study of theology may help, but not assure, wisdom. The simple recollection of an apt Scripture can powerfully mediate pastoral wisdom. But how does one recognize what is apt? Simply citing Scripture routinely or out of context is hardly wise. One must "get a heart of wisdom" through a lifetime of prayer, scriptural wrestling, and faithful study of universally acknowledged church teachers.

Some Guidelines

With these disclaimers in mind, it is still possible to state some guidelines for those who are seeking to grow in pastoral wisdom. This section will gather up some general guidelines pertaining to visitation. These will be followed in the concluding section with a visitation practicum, which will develop more specific logistical and strategic suggestions.

- Each conversation is specific, borne out of a particular context, and singular. Listen intently to the situation. Each situation is unique and cannot be anticipated specifically (Gregory, *ACW*, vol. 11, pp. 90–92; Barth, *CD*, vol. 3, p. 4; Bultmann, 1952, vol. 1, chap. 1).
- On the question of how intimate a pastoral conversation should be and how closely addressed to the core issues of spiritual growth, the Swiss pastor Vinet offered this wisely balanced maxim: Pastoral visitation should proceed "in a manner sufficiently indirect not to alarm their liberty, sufficiently direct to act upon them closely and strongly" (Vinet, 1853, p. 248). The dialectical energy of that maxim is intricate. It proceeds according to the rule of apt proportion: not too passive, not too aggressive; not too overbearing, not too withholding—all depending on the circumstances.
- The biblical term for visitation includes the dimension of discipline. This is an aspect of pastoral care that is grossly eroded by modern hedonic narcissism. Good pastoral care was "tough love" long before that phrase gained currency. The excessive emphasis on conflict-avoidance and positive "stroking" almost certainly will lead to defaulting the disciplinary task.
- In visitation as in pastoral prayer, the minister acts as a representative of the whole congregation, acting not merely on his or her own authority or inclination, but offering sensitive expression to the faith, hope, and love of the living community. The pastor does not visit on behalf of the local congregation alone, as if abstracted from the historical church, but on behalf of the whole church, understood historically and ecumenically. In visiting, the pastor is doing nothing but what the office of ministry and obligation to parishioners necessarily implies and requires. Christ and the church have called, chosen, and authorized the pastor to visit. Through deliberate channels of support the pastor has been sent out in the parish to care for souls. There need be no apology for knocking on a door. One often discovers that people have long been waiting for the knock.
- Pastoral conversation includes but transcends mere sociality. It wishes to consecrate the art of conversation to a higher end. It wants to retain the skills and pleasures of good social intercourse but through them to nurture the life of the Spirit. This is why pastoral visits are neither purely coffee klatsch social chats nor rigid official visits, such as an auditor might pay to a bank or a scoutmaster to a troup.
- The pastoral visit celebrates human friendship in the light of God's friendship. Its pastoral aspect need not diminish its essentially friendly character. Its final aim is not social talk but spiritual improvement. Analogously, one would not expect from a surgeon only friendliness in the surgery room. To say that the pastor should

be friendly and socially apt is a truism. Like Jesus, the pastor will take delight in being with friends, and enjoy repartee. But at times friendship is transmuted into spiritual communion. The right balance is struck by Paul: "Let each of us please his neighbor for his good, to edify him" (Rom. 15:1,2, RSV).

Visitation runs the dual risk of either turning in the direction of an overbearing inquisition or reducing itself to an awkward routine of social trivia. The first error prevailed in the seventeenth century; the latter in the twentieth. Either extreme comes out of a misunderstanding of the fine balance between friendly concern and evangelical witness that is intrinsic to a proper view of pastoral visitation.

A pastor who is perceived as either inwardly bored or outwardly officious, as if this were merely the dismal discharge of a distasteful obligation, will rarely provide significant ministry through visitation. The visit should be recognizable as the visit of a pastor, as distinguished from a precinct politician, civic club representative, or ice-cream vendor. Yet it will be infused with personal warmth, genuineness, and skilled listening. The pastor is best recognized as one who by common consent is sent as a representative of the whole church to enable spiritual growth. When this is clearly grasped by parishioners, the visit will have clearer definition, and in most cases people will happily cooperate to help fulfill its intention. It is not a bad idea to preach a sermon early in one's ministry on the church and the pastoral task, so as to include a brief description of the purpose of visitation and thus prepare the minds of the congregation for a richer expectation of pastoral dialogue.

Why Visit?

From the outset, Christianity has been an intensely conversational religion. With Jesus as its pattern, what else could it be? From his ministry has come a style of malaise through conversation. What are some of the principle benefits that have accrued through this unparalleled dialogical style of religious leadership? Why is visitation so often commended as one of the assumed ways that Christian ministers offer soul care?

- Only by visitation does the pastor acquire direct and immediate knowledge of the flock on a current basis. Pastoral dialogue opens closed doors, illumines hidden needs, penetrates resistances, heightens pastoral consciousness.

     Many parishioners will carefully hide their anguish, irresponsibility, and in general their conflicted feelings behind a tight-lipped facade of routines and formalities. Visitation is more likely to break through the deadly silence of formality than anything else the pastor can do. It invites people to open up about their feelings, uncertainties, hopes, and limitations. Lonely despair is brought back into contact with hope. The spiritually depressed are revived. Mourners are comforted. Young people are given the opportunity to examine vocational choices.

- The purpose of visitation is precisely to search out these who need spiritual counsel. No office-bound psychiatrist is free to do this. This is why, at the level of accessibility, good pastoral counsel is potentially far more effective than secular, time-cramped, fee-based, medically modeled psychotherapies. Its accessibility offers it the opportunity to serve prior to the crisis. A timely intervention may prevent unnecessary hurt while promoting needed growth.

- The aged, the infirm, and shut-ins depend heavily on the adequacy, consistency, and quality of pastoral visitation. Without it their only access to ministry may be the electronic media with their temptations to sentimentalism, exploitation, and fanaticism.

- A high degree of sustained pastoral influence cannot be expected if visitation is neglected. With regular visitation, however, the pastor receives ever new opportunities to get acquainted with growing families, new neighbors, new inquirers, and ever-changing young people maturing through various stages. Marriages can be nurtured. These possibilities can be discovered only by going out among the people and being there to see and hear for oneself. A period of visiting may reveal that there are lonely people out there who have long waited for the pastor to open up a potentially significant conversation concerning a daughter or a parent or about a business failure or a lesson learned.

- One purpose of visitation is to teach the minister better to pray personally for each member. We may not follow in detail Cotton Mather's pattern, but he had the right idea. He made a list of all his parishioners, and went over it periodically, interceding individually for each member one by one. At times he would set aside a single day of fasting and prayer for a particular member by name (Mather, *Manuductio ad Ministerium,* 1728).

  The benefits of personal intercession are great. Before God ask: What am I grateful for concerning this person? Where does this person's current struggle lie? Are there urgent needs? What can I do on this person's behalf? Preparing for visitation in this way broadens the liturgist's sympathies, infusing pastoral prayer with pulsating human concerns.

- Although study and other pressing duties may indeed compete with visitation for time, it may be shortsighted to forever pit them against each other. For the effective results of long hours of study are often best brought to practical result in pastoral conversation. There Scripture is unpacked, tradition re-appropriated, the church's teaching probed, the Christian ethic made experiential. From there one may return both to one's books and meetings with more penetrating questions (Baxter, *PW*, vol. 14, pp. 283 ff.).

Visitation is difficult and character building. Every experienced pastor knows that. It exposes the pastor to risks that could be otherwise avoided. It puts the pastor in direct touch at times with mean tempers, explosive conflicts, and compulsive fears. It requires a wide repertoire of insights and interpersonal skills, instantly accessible. But it puts a seal of authenticity upon all other pastoral endeavors in a way that nothing else can.

- One of the most palpable benefits that most pastors will realize from visitation, however, is the kindling of the homiletical mind. Let us assume that due confidentiality will be maintained. Pastoral conversation will furnish the mind of the preacher with a pregnant train of ideas and kernels of insight. Biblical subjects will be animated by rich experiential vitality. Calvin was particularly critical of immobile, nonvisiting preachers: "It is as if their voices were shut up in the sanctuary, since they become completely dumb as soon as they come out of it" (Calvin, *Commentary on Acts*, p. 175; cf. Hoppin, 1869).
- Even if a congregation largely disagrees with one's prophetic preaching or administrative style, if one visits significantly as a pastor to all the people, they will accept all kinds of otherwise prickly ideological differences. There is nothing that endears a pastor to the flock like sustained, personalized, caring visitation. When people see the energy, empathy, and sincerity of the pastor personalized in their own home, they are more likely to be ready to take seriously pulpit appeals for social justice or evangelical commitment (Murphy, 1877, pp. 224 ff.; cf. Gladden, 1899).

Paul strongly enjoined pastors to act so as to be worthy of the affections of the people (1 Thess. 5:1 ff.). Only on this basis does he call upon believers to "acknowledge those who are working so hard among you, and in the Lord's fellowship [as] your leaders and counsellors" (1 Thess. 5:12).

There is a poignant image of face-to-face meeting embedded quietly in Proverbs 27:18–19 that is easily missed: "He who guards the fig-tree will eat its fruit, and he who watches his master's interests will come to honour. As face answers face reflected in the water, so [one's] heart answers another's." In face-to-face personal dialogue with God's people, especially those who manifest spiritual maturity, pastors may be astonished to learn how deeply they themselves are being instructed, fed, and enlivened.

Daniel Kidder, the first Protestant missionary to the Amazon (1837–40) and my remarkable predecessor in this discipline over a century ago at Drew Theological School, aptly enumerated these benefits that accrue from pastoral visiting that are "difficult if not impossible to be otherwise acquired."

1. A practical knowledge of human nature in its religious and non-religious aspects
2. A particular knowledge of the condition and moral necessities of one's own people, and consequently, of the subjects and modes of address by which one may do them the greatest good
3. Sympathy with the trials, the difficulties, and the afflictions of those to whom one ministers
4. The capacity to testify from personal observation (Kidder, 1871, 462 f.). It would be difficult (and unnecessary) to present a stronger and sounder case for pastoral visitation.

Practicum

It remains for us to note a few logistical and practical points on the practice of visitation. So unlike are the circumstances under which pastoral visits take place that it seems impossible to set down any reliable guidelines for approaching them. "No strict rules can be laid down for pastoral visiting, for there is no profession so irreducible to mechanical working as that of ministry" (Upham, 1898, p. 21). Special occasions "will bring their own rule with them" (Shedd, 1867, p. 392). Although good sense and experience are the best guides, these few suggestions may help:

- Many of the classical Protestant pastoral texts emphasized the importance of becoming and remaining systematic (regular, methodical) in visitation, and of proceeding by some definite design. The pastor may not enjoy calling at first, but can usually acquire a liking for it and in time will recognize its effects and benefits. When the pastor occasionally meets with deadly boredom or harsh rejection, it is still best to persevere. To plan is to ensure that you will not visit only those with whom you feel personally comfortable, neglecting those with whom you might feel some discomfort.

    It matters less what the plan is than that there be some plan. Pre-order printed materials you expect to distribute. Visit by neighborhoods or districts or some other rational scheme. Make memoranda of visits.
- It is also important to be open to "hunches," which may be the nudging of the Spirit. At times you may feel a strong urge to see someone. Even if it is not in the plan, you may find it timely to be there.
- Some pastors effectively use brief personal, handwritten notes as a visitation followup. I know an experienced pastor who for many years tended to make rather short calls, but after many of them he

wrote a brief, penetrating personal note pointed especially to the perceived edge of that person's spiritual growth. He left behind him a trail of notes long treasured by recipients.

- Pastoral confidentiality must be scrupulously maintained. "A minister's breast should be like the old lion's den in the fable, into which many strange things were seen to enter, but out of which none ever returned" (Meade, 1849, p. 185).
- The interpersonal tone of the visit is better affectionate and caring than nosy or provocative. The intention is to become a soul friend, not to hold court. If the pastor is irritable or resentful about having to make a visit, it will likely be communicated through body language. Others will get the point and may politely help the pastor withdraw. The pastor who thinks visitation is drudgery may become the unintended object of help instead of the intended helper.
- The call need not be wearisomely long, nor should it be so quick as to seem perfunctory. Within reasonable bounds each call will set its own length when one is attentive to circumstances. Lengthen the stay with the lonely individual upon whom time hangs heavy; shorten it with the busy and harassed.
- Whatever the length of the visit, it is always made in the name of Christ. Yet, it may be through eye contact or touch more than what one says that the Christ-imparted meaning of the visit is conveyed. It is an indefinable something that signals clearly to the parishioner that the pastor is empathic in response to God's empathy.
- "If [the pastor] arrives inopportunely, say in the midst of housecleaning, or just as his hosts are preparing to go out, or when other company is present, he will make everyone happy by wishing all 'good day' and leaving in a moment or two. Let him not be deceived by assurances that he must stay." For the host is likely to "conceal, if possible, any embarrassment which a guest unwittingly may cause" (Beebe, 1923, p. 280). Such confusions can be avoided by indicating in advance when one expects to call.
- Talk is not the only purpose of a visit. Simple "presence" or "being with" may be more crucial, as in the case of the shut-in who is cut off from fellowship or the dying faithful too weak to talk.
- These priorities should be considered: The sick claim early attention—those irreversibly or gravely ill more urgently than those recoverably ill; and those whose illness is accompanied by pain or personal crisis, than those whose illness is not. The aged often need regular more than urgent attention and will often make the pastor feel most welcome and needed. Don't forget members not in dire necessity. The very point of regular visitation is precisely in order that these ordinary members of the flock not be wholly neglected over the long term.
- The logistics of modern transportation, urbanization, changes in

sexual patterns and family life do not outmode the practice of visitation, but they may change its form. A century ago, when the extended family was the assumed normative core of the social process, pastoral visitation focused almost exclusively on gathered families. Today, when more are living alone or in surrogate families, pastoral visitation must adjust to that reality and treat it imaginatively and with care.

It seems to be an unwarranted rationalization, however, to say that having automobiles and telephones and computers makes pastoral visitation more difficult than it must have been for those who walked or rode long distances on horseback over parishes far wider than ours today.

The telephone can be used as an instrument of pastoral calling once the relationship has been established. The telephone can make communication easier, eliminating travel time and worry about awkward timing. It may facilitate routine and immediate interaction, but it is not likely ever to become a permanent or an adequate substitute for personally present one-on-one interaction, since the voice alone is not as complete as the whole sensory apparatus.

Our inner resistances to visitation are treated in the older literature under the quaint category of "diffidence"—to be unduly timid or inordinately hesitant. Classical treatises urged pastors to work deliberately to overcome inordinate diffidence, even though in modest proportion it was regarded as a virtue.

Our deeper obstacles in pastoral visitation are often more inward than external. They are less a matter of managing time than managing ourselves. They involve interpersonal blocks we feel as we approach an unknown risk. Reinhold Niebuhr as a young pastor in Detroit wrote pensively: "I am glad there are only eighteen families in this church. I have been visiting the members for six weeks and haven't seen all of them yet. Usually I walk past a house two or three times before I summon the courage to go in. . . . I don't know that very much comes of my visits except that I really get acquainted with the people. Usually after I have made a call I find some good excuse to quit for the afternoon. . . . I need the afternoon to regain my self-respect" (Niebuhr, 1929, p. 21). Every working pastor has probably experienced similar reticence.

There is nothing neurotic about being diffident or bashful or slow to strike up a conversation. But the task of ministry ordains and commissions persons to initiate and engage in significant relationships with people through empathic, witnessing encounter. Diffidence surely must also be a problem for insurance agents, attorneys, teachers, physicians, salespersons, and anyone who comes into contact with the public at significant levels of emotive engagement. It is potentially a special problem for ministry because the call to encounter is built into the very definition of parochial ministry. One is ill advised to enter parish ministry if one recognizes in oneself an exaggerated need to withdraw. For the office of ministry itself may intensify such an inclination in the direction of neurotic avoidance. Ministers, like others, may be affected by mild or severe forms of agoraphobia that make them more inclined to stay in than to risk uncertain encounters. Such phobic responses will be more hampering vocationally for a minister than for a home craftsman, a machine worker, or an auditor, who works more with things than with people.

• The pastor can reduce visitation anxieties by standard relaxation techniques—deep breathing, tensing and relaxing various muscle groups, using the quieting reflex, and meditation—as well as through intercessory prayer for the person to be visited.

• In calling, the pastor looks for fit moments to unveil the religious assumptions of a supposedly secular dialogue. The pastor learns in time to grasp where false gods are crumbling, where sin has elicited self-deception, and where grace is hidden in ordinary relationships, and then to be courageous enough to speak the overtly religious word, to proclaim God's goodness amid our all-too-human struggles. That is the purpose of pastoral visitation. If it fails that purpose, it may succeed in being pleasant conversation, but hardly pastoral dialogue.

This does not imply that the pastor need begin every interaction with overt religious talk. But if the pastor is not equipped to recognize where profoundly religious assumptions are lodging quietly in seemingly worldly concerns, the pastor has not thought enough theologically about the body, the family, politics, the environment, sexuality, or the economy—the kind of things people talk about when they do not think they are talking religion.

• It is often wise toward the end of a visit to look for some clarification of specifically targeted behavioral changes (Baxter, 1656, p. 104 ff.; Wesley, *WJW*, vol. 1, p. 92, vol. 7, pp. 269 ff., 301 ff., vol. 13, pp. 304 f.). It is better to take one or two small steps than to attempt none; if too many are projected, the imagination becomes cluttered.

• The traditional pastoral practice has been to end the visit with a fitting prayer of thanksgiving and intercession personally related to each individual present. Although this practice has deep meaning and needs to be re-appropriated in the modern context, it should not be taken as an inflexible rule, but rather should be commended wherever it seems fitting, and should be done often. It should not be forced, however, since prayer is the least appropriate of all acts to intrude upon people. In most cases it will be appropriate.

Conclusion

Social responsibility and evangelical witness are both crucial to the work of pastoral visitation. There are good reasons to appeal to both liberal and evangelical pastors for the recovery of pastoral visitation: to social liberals because this is the best opportunity the culture gives to the pastoral office to relate Christ to the concrete, evolving world of social and personal change, and to evangelicals because this is the richest context in which to make personal witness to Christ vivid and experiential.

No experienced pastor will deny that visitation has its peculiar difficulties and discouragements. To perform it well requires situational wisdom borne out of hard-won experience. In one call, the pastor may find a quiet bereavement; in another, a hardened cynic who testily rejects all God talk; in another, a sedate board member dissatisfied with the way the flowers were arranged; and in the next one, a genuine chance to touch the frayed edges of the parishioner's real guilt and mediate the forgiveness of God.

The whole range of human experience will be laid open. A wide compass of resources for ministry may be required at any moment. But in each varying situation, the central task remains the same: embodying Christ to the world, mediating the love of God to humanity.

REFERENCES AND FURTHER READING

For classical discussions of visitation see Ambrose (*NPNF* 2nd, vol. 10, pp. 15 ff.), *Seven Ecumenical Councils* (*NPNF* 2nd, vol. 14, p. 269), Gregory (*ACW*, vol. 11, pp. 54 ff.), Thomas Aquinas (*ST*, vol. 3, pp. 2590 ff.), and Council of Trent (1545–1563).

For classical Protestant discussions of visitation, see Luther (*LW*, vol. 40), Calvin (1559, 4.3), Bucer, (1972 ed., pp. 429 ff.), Herbert (1652), Gouge (1664), Bayly (1669), Taylor (*TPW*, vol. 2, pp. 105 ff.), Bunyan (1870 ed.), Owen (d. 1683), Baxter (*PW*, vol. 4, 90 ff., vol. 15, pp. 497 ff.), Burnet (1692), Mather (1728), and Wesley (*WJW*, vol. 7, pp. 117 ff.). Nineteenth-century pastoral writers on visitation include Vinet (1853), Cannon (1853), Shedd (1867), Kidder (1871), Murphy (1877), Hoppin (1884), Upham (1898), and Gladden (1898).

For related issues see also Kierkegaard (1850), Beebe (1923), Niebuhr (1929), Holman (1942), Barth (*CD*, vol. 4), Stumpff (1934), Kemp (1948), Bonhoeffer (1948), Cameron (1954), Wynn (1957), Nuttall (1957), Tournier (1957), Hulme (1962), Oden (1969, 1974, 1976a), and Jackson (1975).

For various writings from the tradition of moral theology that impinge on pastoral visitation and the care of families, see Lechleitner (1776, 1789), Liguori (1834 ed.), Fulton (1872), Slater (1908), Schnackenburg (1965), Häring (1966), and Dailey (1970).

13. The Care of Souls

Soul care is one way of describing the pastor's entire task, including the ministries of preaching and sacrament, teaching and administrative leadership. For the whole work of ministry has been called *cura animarum*, "the care of souls" (Nemesius, *LCC*, vol. 4, pp. 257 ff.; Augustine, *SAOE*, pp. 126 ff.).

But in a narrower sense, the care of souls has come to refer to a more intensive part of that larger task, a personal ministry of conversation (Gregory, *ACW*, vol. 11 pp. 251 ff.). A regular and demanding part of Christian ministry lies in the quiet sphere of one-on-one meeting with persons who look to pastors for interpersonal, moral, and spiritual guidance (Baxter, 1656, p. 239 ff.).

Soul, Psyche, Anima

What do we mean by soul? If soul is that which is committed to the pastor's care, can we say more about what it is?

Soul, according to its classical Christian conception, is the unitive center of the inner powers of the person. To do something "with all your soul" (Deut. 13:3) is to act from the center of your personal being. Job spoke of the soul in crisis as "poured out" in tears (30:16) and "made long" in patient endurance (6:11).

Soul is that by which we most deeply feel, know, and will, and by which the body is animated. The soul lives out of God, and its life transcends this mortal sphere (Tertullian, *ANF*, vol. 3, pp. 181 ff.; Augustine, *LCF*, p. 199 ff.). It is to the soul that the truth is made known (Augustine, *NPNF* 1st, vol. 3, p. 356).

Soul translates the Greek *psuchē*, which in Latin is rendered *anima*. Both terms were used to translate the Hebrew *nephes*. The primary meaning in Hebrew is "possessing life," or "that which lives." It is the living, energizing center of anything alive (Nemesius, *LCC*, vol. 4 pp. 257 ff.). *Nephes* is that which moves and animates a body, whether human or animal, and distinguishes a living from a dead being. *Nephes* is also considered the seat of physical appetite (Ps. 78:18), the source of emotion (Isa. 1:14), and the seat of longing (Ps. 63:1). Soul is closely intertwined with the will and moral action (Gen. 49:6; Job 7:15; cf. Augustine, *NPNF* 1st, vol. 5, pp. 315 ff.). Tragically, soul is capable of stumbling and falling, of abusing freedom, of being led into captivity.

In the New Testament, psyche is the seat of the religious life and of the person's relationship with God. It is this religious center of human existence of which John referred when he wrote to Gaius: "I pray that you may enjoy good health, and that all may go well with you, as I know it goes well with your soul" (3 John 2). At times the soul needs rest, according to Jesus (Matt. 11:29). When Paul used the term "psyche," he most often referred to the *life* which is in the body, that which activates responsiveness. Psyche also referred to the center of desire or emotion (Phil. 1:27; 1 Thess. 5:23). According to early Christian psychology, the soul may be subjected to temptation (cf. Origen, *ANF*, vol. 4, pp. 337 ff.) and can become separated from the spirit by sin (cf. Origen, *ANF*, vol. 4, p. 296).

Care of souls therefore means the care of the inner life of persons, the mending and nurturing of this personal center of affect and willing. God is the chief carer of souls (Origen, *ANF*, vol. 4, p. 313). Our interpersonal soul care seeks to understand and respond to God's active caring. Pastoral counsel is soul care in this sense. It seeks to address the inner wellsprings of personal decision making with wisdom, prudence, and love. To be given care of souls means to be accountable for shepherding the inner life of people through the crises of emotional conflict and interpersonal pain toward growth in responsiveness toward God (Gregory, *ACW*, vol. 11 p. 210).

The Uniqueness of the Pastoral Relation

The pastor/parishioner relation is therefore different than the usual relation that prevails between

physician/patient
teacher/student
leader/follower
attorney/client
public official/citizen

All of these roles are in some sense analogous to various aspects of ministry, yet none encompasses ministry, because none accepts the full responsibility of soul care. The difference between ministry and its closest counterparts hinges closely on a crucial assumption of soul care, although that assumption is likely to be stated in many different ways in the modern period. The crucial premise is that the pastor is more likely to compassionately behold the parishioner's whole existence—physical, moral, and spiritual—in the context of salvation history or universal history seen in relation to eternity. However competent, other professions do not share that operative assumption.

This has made ministry far more like a bond of kinship than any other profession. So the pastor, by tradition and unwritten invitation, is often intimately present with individuals and families amid critical situations of birth, marriage, sickness, and death, a presence that is not expected of salespersons, bureaucrats, mechanics, and brain surgeons, however dedicated they might be.

The Christian community is a covenant community bonded not by race or blood or kinship but by covenant with God and spiritual relationship to Christ. Jesus regarded his disciples as sisters and brothers, the Christian community as a nurturing family, and the faithful as children of God. In a local congregation the pastor is called to encourage and guide this family in spirit, to care for each member and to wisely parent the process, seeking to help each member of the family of faith grow to fuller maturity (Acts 1:15 ff.; 1 Thess. 5:15 ff.; Eph. 4:13; Col. 1:28). Such a task requires some special personal qualities that can be sought, studied, cultivated, and improved, although at times these qualities seem more like a gift than a task.

Personal Qualities Needed for Care of Souls

What excellent personal qualities and interpersonal competencies are most desirable for someone who assumes the responsibility of care for souls? Even though our answer to this question will be based largely on historical Christian pastoral sources (Gregory, *ACW*, vol. 11; Luther, *LCC*, vol. 17; Bucer, 1538; Herbert, 1652), we find that they anticipate much contemporary psychological insight into "the necessary and sufficient conditions of effective psychotherapy" (Rogers, 1961; Carkhuff, 1969; Bergin and Garfield, 1971).

- Deep insight and extensive self-knowledge are prerequisite to soul care. The pastor who has reliable knowledge of him- or herself is best prepared to offer good counsel (Augustine, *SAOE*, pp. 138 ff.; Calvin, *Inst.*, 1.1, 2.1; Wesley, *WJW*, vol. 11, pp. 521 ff.). One must come to understand oneself inwardly, to knows one's own driving passions, skewed motivations, neurotic edges, latent doubts, and emerging struggles. To know oneself is a central premise of knowing others helpfully. The more clearly we grasp our own experience, the better we can understand and respond to the experience of others (cf. Baxter, "The Mischiefs of Self-Ignorance and the Benefits of Self-Acquaintance," *PW*, vol. 16, pp. 1–280; Kierkegaard, 1846a).
- Secondly, though it may seem trite to say it, a genuine caring for ordinary people—a love of people—is a crucial prerequisite to soul

care. Neither analytical skill nor theoretical knowledge can have positive effect if there is no genuine love and compassionate care for others. This interpersonal care lives either implicitly or explicitly out of God's care for us (Thomas Aquinas, *ST*, vol. 1, pp. 121 ff.; cf. Oden, 1966, chaps. 1, 2).

- Accurate empathy is another universally acknowledged interpersonal competence required for effective soul care. This is an imaginative capacity for listening that is able to enter into another person's frame of reference and feel one's way into their emotive responses. Learning to get clear readings of another's motivations and inner feeling-states is quite different from objective psychological knowledge. Rather, it requires astute listening to the contours of perceived experience, acute sensitivity to internal dynamics, and keen attentiveness to newly emergent feelings (Gregory, *ACW*, vol. 11, pp. 79 ff.; Luther, *LCC*, vol. 18; *LW*, vol. 40; *WLS*, pp. 553 ff.).
- Situational wisdom is a principal component of soul care. It seeks reasoned judgment grounded in a wide data base, but more. It also requires adaptability, flexibility, and sensitivity, but even more. Essentially it requires that one be ready and able to speak the right word at the right moment. This requires that we not superimpose upon the situation some preconception of what it is, but allow ourselves to be freshly addressed by the ongoing process or developing encounter (Augustine, *LCC*, vol. 6, p. 376; Thomas Aquinas, *ST*, vol. 2, pp. 1380 ff.; Wesley, *WJW*, vol. 7, p. 43, vol. 8, pp. 275 ff., 299 ff.; Kierkegaard, 1847).
- The capacity for trust includes both being trustworthy and trusting the resources that are already present in the partner in dialogue. The trust that parishioners invest in a spiritual guide must be based on trustworthiness. Any hint of abuse of that implicit trust will undercut the ground of the relationship. This is why coercive and manipulative acts must be strictly ruled out of pastoral care. If you are to be worthy of the parishioner's confidence, you must disavow the temptation collusively to use relationships for other ends than that person's good or to permit deceptions to take root in the relationship (Baxter, 1656, p. 150).
- The pastoral advisor must advise. Advice is best given sparely, chiefly on invitation, and with full respect for the conscience and self-directive resources of the other person. Few things have diminished the effectiveness of contemporary pastoral care more than the constant polemic against advice-giving of any sort. This tends to handcuff the pastor, inducing guilt about offering the guidance that the pastor alone is commissioned to offer. Yet do not assume that every parishioner should take your advice (wise or not) simply because you hold the office of pastor. Do not get yourself carelessly into a rigidly defensive, officious posture. Be willing to offer rather than

hold back useful counsel when the timing is right, without creating unnecessary guilt or resistance. But if you altogether withhold wise advice from a parishioner at a critical time when it would make a difference in his life, you may by omission be doing that person a serious injustice (cf. *The Rule of St. Benedict, LCC,* vol. 12, pp. 294 ff.). The pastor *owes* fit counsel to the parishioner (Baxter, *PW,* vol. 15, pp. 299 ff., Bridges, 1847, pp. 337 ff.).

- Genuineness, candor, honesty, and internal congruence (feeling your own feelings accurately) will help build trust relationships necessary to the care of souls. Effective pastoral care occurs in a friendly, open, and accepting style of interpersonal meeting, with a vibrant sense of personal availability and readiness to listen to subtleties (*The Sayings of the Fathers, LCC,* vol. 12, pp. 175. ff.; Baxter, PW, vol. 16, pp. 45 ff.).
- Among other attitudes or actions that will significantly help to engender interpersonal justice, improved psychological functioning, and spiritual health are: hope, courage, humor, and the willingness to face limitations.

The operational assumption is that life has God-given meaning. It is not that our dialogue must invent or create that meaning, but that we must discover it as already providentially latent and growing like tiny mustard seeds planted deeply in emergent experiencing.

These qualities cannot be readily acquired merely through objective teaching of empirical facts. But they can to some degree be modeled and practiced. The art of caring is hard won. It is best approached through realistic case studies, role playing, practice in role reversal, and rigorous community accountability.

The General Ministry of Care

Why isn't care of souls assigned to the whole laity? Don't all Christians have this duty of watching over others, caring for others, providing watchful concern for others in this Christian family? What is special about the pastor's care?

Indeed, all baptized persons do have the task of caring for others in need, feeding the hungry, visiting the imprisoned. But in ordained ministry something different is meant by care of souls since the ordained minister is exercising this care not only as a personal friend, but through an office, not only in a small circle of associates, but in the gathered flock that the shepherd is commissioned to oversee. It is done not on one's own private authority, but on the authority of Christ's ministry and calling as recognized by the church. The ordained minister reaches out for the congregation, not merely on the basis of personal warmth or sympathy, but as the representative of the whole church. If the ordained minister were exercising this care only in his or

through an office

her own name, it would more likely take place within a limited circle of acquaintances. But being a pastor specifically means undertaking the care of souls of the whole body of Christ in that place. Ordained ministry is a representative function that speaks *to* the faithful on behalf of the apostolic witness, and *for* the faithful to God in intercessory prayer. The layperson is not so authorized or called or prepared or commissioned.

The pastor is freed from other burdens precisely to do these crucial services without distraction. Admittedly the lay Christian carpenter, clerk, or janitor also has a clear duty to care for others, but such is not their principal lifelong vocational task. Care of souls is not a side interest in the pastor's life and work; it *is* the pastor's life work. This in part is why the pastor offers a differently determined spirit of soul care. It comes to the recipient on behalf of the whole church through one whose life energies are not broadly diverted elsewhere. Amid sickness or guilt or death, the pastor is authorized to speak under discipline in the church's name, whereas an individual lay Christian is more likely to be reticent to do so under the same circumstances. The congregation has a right to have pastoral services delivered fittingly by a pastor who can provide a straightforward biblically grounded clarification of their meaning.

The Personality of the Minister and the Office of Ministry

What happens to compassionate caring when it becomes an official duty? Does it not result in an unintended reduction in the quality of care? Does dialogue tend to become depersonalized when empathic listening and guidance are contracted as a full-time stated obligation? Does this not undermine some of the inner energy of the Christian ministry?

The church hopes to deepen and improve the quality of care by setting apart and supporting persons whose entire lives are committed to ministry. There are instances where this hope is disappointed, however.

The office does not self-evidently imply the loss of personalization, but it usually means some rechanneling of it. Much of the effectiveness of ministry depends upon the quality and integrity of the personal existence that shines through the office (Gregory, *ACW* vol. 11, pp. 56 ff., 68 ff.; Baxter, 1656, pp. 900 ff.).

There is a paradox here. Even though the pastor has a representative office of caring, still the caring process is not best embodied strictly in cold, impersonal, official ways. Rather, it must come radiantly alive and show through the unique personal being of the pastor (Ambrose, *NPNF* 2nd, vol. 10, pp. 15 ff.). Thus the best pastoral care will likely seem more personal than official, yet the personal side of the task is always being infused by the profound expectations associated with the office. All personal meeting from within the pastoral office is understandably colored and affected by perceptions of it as a sacred duty and a representative service.

The pastor cannot lay aside the office at inconvenient times. If the pastor tries to reduce all encounters to purely personal interactions so as to disavow pastoral identity, confusions will abound. Friendship, however valuable, is not in itself sacred ministry. Yet when pastoral interactions become purely official, they easily lose the personal vitality and presence that the office itself requires.

Care of souls was often thought by the pastoral tradition to be both an art requiring gifts and a science requiring study (Ambrose, *NPNF* 2nd, vol. 10, pp. 1 ff.; Erdman, 1924). The latter aspect of pastoral care (the so-called scientific side, in the sense of a discipline of objective study) is the part that is susceptible to investigation, data gathering, objective knowledge, experiential testing, rules of consistency, and rational cohesion. Pastoral care indeed constitutes both an academic discipline and a professional practice that can be studied critically as a discipline at the university or seminary. Indeed there is a vast literature that treats pastoral care as a discipline or "science." Yet the actual work of pastoral caring is best learned through pastoral practice.

For centuries before clinical pastoral education, pastoral care proceeded by thinking concretely out of case studies, with complex data and practical intent. Since the time of Gregory the Great (and implicitly before him, in Cyprian, Nemesius, and Augustine), the study of the care of souls has often proceeded by means of something resembling a case study method, showing patiently, as Gregory does, how one case is to be treated differently from another (*ACW*, vol. 11, pp. 89 ff.). The physician of souls, like the physician of the body, does not apply the same spiritual remedies to all patients, but listens carefully to different symptoms of emotional, moral, or spiritual malady. In fact, the modern case study method derives from a very old theological discipline, *casuistry*, which studied cases of conscience in penitential conversations prior to Holy Communion (McNeill, 1923).

When we overstress the outward, official, side so that the personal side is misplaced, we fall into the trap that in the New Testament is called "lordliness," against which Peter warned his fellow elders, when well-intended pastoral care tends toward arrogant, dictatorial self-righteousness and is accompanied by a tendency to find fault. On the other side, one hopes to avoid excessive personalization, to the neglect of the representative ministry. Here one may be content simply to be a crony or boon companion or everybody's pal, to the neglect of the representative priestly and prophetic ministry to which the pastor is called.

Pastoral Accountability

The daily round of pastoral conversations is left largely to the pastor's own internal sense of accountability to God and the people. Nobody stands over the pastor's shoulder to record time and motion data. The district office or judicatory official may ask for periodic reports on attendance, new members, finances, marriages, and so on, but *cura animarum* is never finally quantifiable, and mostly is done on one's own initiative; it comes basically out of the inward commitment and motivation to be a pastor, not out of any external constraints. The way in which pastors order and regulate their own schedules for pastoral care is largely a matter of need assessment, good judgment, and pastoral conscience.

The practice of ministry will present challenging and difficult experiences and agonizing situations at inconvenient times. When dog-tired, hurried, and distracted, just then will come the urgent call to go an extra mile on a dark night. Only God will know the specific contours of pastoral accountability on such a night.

Classical treatises on *cura animarum* have all marveled at the great difficulty and subtlety of caring for souls, its highly nuanced, problematic character, its need for wisdom in crucial situations. Who can do it? Traditional pastoral wisdom has answered: Nobody can do it or should try to do it alone. It is only in the companionship of grace, drawing on resources beyond one's own, that wisdom will be found for this task.

The working minister is in a co-working ministry day after day with Christ's own ministry, supported and energized by the Holy Spirit (Chrysostom, *NPNF* 1st, vol. 13, pp. 407 ff.). This is the centerpiece of care of souls: Jesus the overshepherd of our shepherding. God the Spirit is the comforter in all of our attempts to provide comfort. It is not what the pastor is out there doing that finally counts, but what Christ is doing through the pastor. How is Christ's own ministry at that moment funding and challenging our own words and deeds? How is Christ's own ministry to that person already at work and how may one assist? Does this relieve us of responsibility? From final responsibility, yes. But it calls us always to look for footprints of Christ's presence before us, all along the way.

Jesus as Pattern for Caring

No method or approach to caring is more vivifying, enlightening, and reliable than Jesus' own approach to people. It is clear that he saw each person as incomparably valuable in God's eyes. He took time for each one. He listened deeply for the particular needs of each person in each situation, and awakened latent possibilities in that person, not through massive programs, but for that very person (Gregory, *ACW*, vol. 11, p. 263).

Jesus did not coerce anybody into discipleship or belief. He was willing to view human growth patiently in the context of slow-ripening time. He was able to offer the truth of God's presence in ordinary language. His interactions were like seeds left to germinate later according to the proportional receptivity of the individual. He was willing to allow the developmental process to take its own pace, yet he often stimulated decisive change in those he met. He did not disguise the cost of discipleship. He made it clear from the beginning that the way is narrow and few enter it.

This is the style of caring that centuries later was recalled and commended during the church's struggle through its period of martyrdom, its taking responsibility for society with Constantine, its crisis in the fall of Rome, and through early monasticism. Slowly yet firmly it developed a sense of historical pastoral identity. From the Shepherd of Hermas, through Clement of Alexandria, Ambrose, Augustine, and Gregory the Great, the pattern of Jesus remained decisive for Christian pastoral identity.

While preaching became more particularly directed to the whole gathered community, soul care became more often directed to the single individual or in some cases to small, intimate groups, marriage partners, or families. Yet the same Word was addressed, whether to one or many. Preaching can nourish only those who come to hear it. Pastoral care was needed because it had extensive freedom to reach out even to those who may not set foot in the worshiping community.

Some pastors are more capable of public witness than private soul-searching. But since both are necessary, the working pastor should improve that competence for which there seems to be less natural aptitude and not allow any one pastoral activity to be artificially separated from the others. Neither preaching nor pastoral care should be detached from the cohesive body of pastoral duties as professional specialties. When separated, one loses precisely that creative dynamic elicited by the tension between them. The congregation will be more attentive to the preaching of one whom they have known in confidential, significant, intimate personal interaction. Pastoral care will be put in proper context only by constant Scripture study and by the good news of Jesus Christ, which is the subject of preaching.

To Whom Is the Cure of Souls Directed?

Pastoral writers have often said that the care of souls is properly directed to all persons in a parish, not just some. And yet in practice it is always some fewer who are either ready or motivated or hurting enough to benefit from intensive pastoral care. By what criteria shall the pastor decide where the needs or possibilities are the greatest?

Here the term "cure of souls" is instructive. In the English tradition it was said that when a minister was sent to a parish, the pastor was given a "cure" or curacy or "care for souls" (*cura animarum*) in that local area. In doing so the pastor took on a well-defined responsibility to God for the people.

But today we must ask: for which people? Is the responsibility for the whole parish, for everyone whether in one's own denomination or not? Is one responsible for the whole civil population, or in a more precise and specific sense only for one's own congregation? To answer, we must thread our way between an excessively broad, nondescript "multitudinism," and a too narrow spiritual elitism.

The first extreme to be avoided is an exaggerated idealistic equalitarianism that argues that pastoral care must of necessity reach out for everybody equally, even if this results in a lowering of standards of pastoral care for some. Practically, this works out as a shallow accommodation to the cultural environment. For such a "multitudinism," the only ideal of churchmanship is "a population of one hundred percent church people" (Thornton, 1958), regardless of how superficially they might understand the Christian life.

The opposite view has the advantage of being more realistic by seeking to offer more intensive pastoral care to those who are more receptive to it. It does not pretend to reach out to everybody in the parish, but rather is attentive to those who show readiness for the ministry of care. It tends to limit its attention to respondents of its own congregation, and even more sharply upon those within a given congregation who are relatively hungrier for the guidance and care that can in fact be offered within the time and energy limits that constrain all pastoral caring. Although more realistic, this may result in an unintentional spiritual elitism or an exclusive attitude that is alien to the very idea of Christian community.

Both of these extremes are to be avoided. One way reaches out too broadly so as to loose the Christian center. The other may become so narrowly introverted as to lose touch with the surrounding world. We are not looking merely for a clumsy synthesis of two errors. Rather, pastoral care seeks to nurture small communities and persons within those communities who will contribute to the redemption of the whole society. Anything less than the whole seems to misunderstand the hope of Christian mission for the world; yet a modest realism is required in order to offer more substantial time to those who are more ready for spiritual direction and may as a result better serve the commonweal.

Anyone who has worked with people in crisis or worked for societal improvement knows that the spiritual commitment needed for significant change only comes from a sensitized conscience and inner discipline. These often grow out of a creative struggle with limitation, through sacrificial suffering, self-criticism, and dying to the old Adam. Practically, the working pastor finds that this always applies to less than the whole congregation, and more intesively to a very few. So it is difficult to keep the balance between the small circle of persons intimately involved in significant pastoral care without ending in elitism, and at the same time channel the limited resources of the committed community to benefit the larger society.

No chapter on Evangelism ~church
whole model based on state - Christendom
196   PASTORAL COUNSEL

Whenever there has been a genuine recovery of the Christian life in history, it has been accompanied by a deepening of pastoral care for souls that seeks to engender new life in some on behalf of all others. This impulse we see in monasticism, the Reformation, the Counter-Reformation, and most remarkably in the evangelical revivals of Protestant pietism. One of the key evidences that the life of the church is being renewed by the Spirit is the quality and depth of soul care, which does not just play at dressing wounds "skin deep only, with their saying, all is well" (Jer. 6:13), but effectively works to cure the despair of unbelief. The best evidence of the fruits of such inner renewal is its outward effect on the larger society.

The logic of the pastoral office leads to the surprising conclusion that no pastor should accept an appointment to a parish in which he or she can not properly care for the souls in that place. No flock should be so large that it cannot be cared for, either by the pastor personally or by a well-ordered staff under rigorous pastoral direction. The logic of the office moves against so dividing the pastoral office into specializations that its unity and integrity become lost. In a large church staff where one is visiting, another preaching, another educating, another doing youth work, another administration, it may be more difficult to identify the unity of the pastoral office. When the office of pastor is integrated in a single person, it can manifest that intrinsic unity of the office better than when it is divided up into staff specializations. Although we cannot redo history, it seems better, where possible, to keep local congregations small enough that a single pastor can look after them. Many congregations are too large for this. In larger congregations the staff should be sufficiently integrated to bring the whole ministry in that parish into a single, unified focus.

The Principle of Variability

Curacy requires learning how to treat different persons in different ways. This is a long-standing principle of pastoral care. Nowhere is it better stated than in its earliest version in the following lengthy quote from Gregory of Nazianzus: "What great skill is required to treat various persons responsively so as to change their lives." Different pastoral counsels and encouragements are needed for

men as distinguished from	women
young from	old
rich from	poor
the happy from	the depressed
sick from	healthy
governors from	the governed
the weakhearted from	the courageous
the angry from	the serene
and the achievers from	the failing.

Gregory of Nazianzus continues:

How great is the difference, between pastoral counsel for the married and the unmarried. Significant differences remain between those who live alone compared to those who live together. And even among religious celibates who live in a community, there are still important differences in counseling those advanced and those beginning in the art of contemplation. Differences abound between pastoral care for urban and rural people, between the simple and the crafty, between the person of leisure and the person of affairs, between those who have met with reverses and those who in their prosperity have never experienced misfortune. If you compare the temperaments of these persons you will see that they differ more widely than they differ even in physical features. So to give pertinent guidance to them is no easy task.

The principle is this: just as the same food and medicine is not appropriate to every bodily ailment, so neither is the same treatment and discipline proper for the guidance of souls. Those with wide pastoral experience will best know how to recognize the differences. Some persons are better motivated by words, others by example. Some who are sluggish and dull need to be stirred up to the good, while others are already inordinately fervent and so rushed about that they need to be calmed. Praise will benefit some, while correction will benefit others, provided that each is administered in a seasonable way. Out of season your counsel may do more harm than good.

Some respond best to confidential correction, while others seem unmovable except by public rebuke. Some pay no attention to a private admonition, but are easily corrected if it risks public embarrassment, while others cannot bear a public disgrace and would, if publicly rebuked, grow morose and impatient, yet they would be happy to accept quiet correctives in response to sympathetic treatment. Some persons make it necessary to watch them closely even to the minutest details because they prefer to hide their faults and arrogate to themselves the praise of being politic and crafty. Toward others, however, it is better to take no notice "as if seeing we do not see and hearing we do not hear." For if we call their faults to their attention, we may bring them to despair so that even with repeated reminders they tend recklessly to lose self-respect and grow in their guilt. In some cases it is necessary that the pastor show anger in the interest of love, or seem to despair of a parishioner as if a hopeless case, even though from another perspective he is far from hopeless.

Each pastoral response hinges strongly on the particular temperament of the person. Some we must treat with meekness in order to encourage them to a better hope. Others seem to require that we combat and conquer them and never yield an inch.

The pastoral principle: variability. All persons are not to be cured in the same way. We do not simply say this is virtue and this is vice noncontextually. For one spiritual remedy may prove dangerous in some cases and wholesome in other cases. The right medicine must be applied for the right occasion as the temper of the patient allows and as the time and circumstance and disposition of the individual indicates. This, of course, is the most difficult aspect of pastoral wisdom, to know how to distinguish which counsel is needed in which situation with a precise judgment so as to administer appropriate remedies for different temperaments. Only actual experience and practice are the basis for skillfully developing this art. (Gregory Nazianzus, Oration 2, paragraphs 28–33, my rendering, adapted from *NPNF* 2nd, vol. 3, pp. 210–11 and from the Greek text in Migne, *MPG,* vol. 35, Oration 2, pp. 406 ff.)

This testimony from the fourth century of Christian pastoral care expresses, better than anything I know, the reasoning of the early tradition about the central challenge of pastoral counsel. This is the reason it is impossible to write a strict rule-oriented casuistry of pastoral counseling. It is toward the development of this sort of practical, contextual, interpersonal wisdom that the pastor has for centuries studied what we now call psycholgy (motivation, passion, the psychosomatic interface, freedom, guilt, and anxiety), as well as Scripture and tradition. The pastor listens hard for the Spirit searching out the deep things of God in us.

The Holistic Concern of Pastoral Care

The several simultaneous levels of human caring—physical (temporal), moral (volitional), and spiritual (eternal caring)—are best seen in creative tension with each other in pastoral care.

Good pastoral care does not ignore the *bodily* needs or hedonic concerns of the whole person. At times good curacy will need to pay primary attention to physical comfort, economic necessity, and temporal happiness. There is nothing in the biblical mandate that requires the pastor systematically to ignore these pressing forms of human need. Prior to hedonic psychotherapies, pastors were seeking to increase happiness and to improve the ratio of benefits to costs among persons in their charge. Prior to welfare politics and utilitarian ethics, pastoral care was far more concerned than it now is with the actual administration of poor relief. No pastor is in a parish long before seeing the needs of the poorest of the poor and experiencing the call of the truly sick and needy for assistance. Yet the pastor will soon learn that many occasions are improper for active intervention. Only with experience will the pastor intuit those situations in which the pastoral office will be more effective than its secular bureaucratic alternatives (Gladden, 1898; Holmes, 1982, pp. 77 ff.).

Beyond the physical and material well-being of the parishioner, the pastor has traditionally had an even more deliberate concern for *moral development,* yet one that still lies short of intensive spiritual formation proper. There are value choices, ethical deliberations, and moral judgments that parishioners make in which a sensitive ministry is rightly involved.

The idealistic tendency in ministry sometimes loses sight of the fact that ministry is directed toward fallible people, not ahistorical angels, who face crucial questions and tragic choices with limited vision. Ministry at its best does not just pronounce a cheap word of blanket forgiveness on these complex scenes, as if all moral choices were in the long run the same from God's point of view. Rather, justifying grace prays for sanctifying grace. Faith seeks to become active in love. Though Christianity is not reducible to a moral system, it funds moral awareness and gives spiritual depth to conscience.

The responsible pastor will not tilt quixotically with every windmill on the moral horizon, but with patience and discretion will look for those ripe moments where good moral sense can be brought to personal and social decisions. Especially in the political sphere, the pastor should not try to do all that needs to be done unilaterally, but rather, should try to inspire others to meaningful efforts at political justice.

The hedonic and moral aspects of soul care, however, should never eclipse the pastor's intense concern for *spiritual formation*. It tempers, shapes, and affects all that the pastor may do at other levels of physical need or ethical counsel. The cup is offered, not wordlessly, but in the name of Christ. Temporal happiness is seen in relation to eternal happiness. If this crowning and undergirding element does not take central focus in its own time in pastoral conversation, then both the material and the moral interests will be diminished and misunderstood (Cyril of Jerusalem, *NPNF* 2nd, vol. 7, pp. 6 ff.).

Maxims of Effective Pastoral Counsel

One of the most reliable rules for pastoral guidance has also been familiar to medical practice for two millennia:

* Do no harm.

This is said in the sober awareness that it is, regrettably, possible for the pastor to do great harm by either ignorance or malice. If you agree to take responsibility for the soul (the most inner self, the God-relationship) and the spiritual growth of another, it is your task to make sure that you do not lead that vulnerable person into "a state worse than before" (Luke 11:26).

Irresponsible shepherds have been known to lead flocks to barren hills. Indeed, some forms of self-expressive, self-actualizing "therapies" have been known to increase psychological dysfunction. Some abuses of Reichian, Gestalt, and psychoanalytic practice have been shown to be associated with harmful "deterioration ratios," according to "outcome studies" of the effectiveness of psychotherapy (cf. Oden, 1974a, "Response"; 1974b, chap. 3; 1980, chap. 1). When these are imported uncritically into pastoral practice, the result may be harm that comes under the guise of healing.

* Respect the parishioners' right and responsibility to choose their own spiritual guide.

The pastor should be available as a soul friend or spiritual guide for every member in the parish, yet great respect should be shown for those subtle differences that may move one to affirm and another to leave a particular spiritual guide. The pastor does well to encourage every person to seek out some spiritual guide, confessor, confidant, or soul friend, but not to expect it always to be a pastor (cf. Wesley, *WJW*, vol. 7, pp. 112 ff.). The pastor will be available for such a relationship, without needing always to pre-empt it possessively.

- Allow people time to arrive at long-awaited moments of insight in which their self-perception or interpersonal life elicits growth not previously thought possible.

There is a profound, subtle relation between the timing of pastoral guidance and its effectiveness. Learning how to read the subtle moments, the irrecoverable times when a bit of empathic caring or advice or confrontation or analysis or a parable or story is uniquely fitting and nothing else will do—that is precisely what is meant by pastoral wisdom. Do not expect all parishioners to be ready for significant insight just anytime, or just at the instant you happen into their lives. Personal spiritual growth occurs according to its own timing, just as a plant grows in its own season (Herbert, 1632, chap. 18).

- Do not woodenly assume that either quiet listening or active confrontation is always the obligatory way to engage in pastoral conversation.

There are times when empathic listening is far more helpful and necessary than any kind of assertiveness or advice giving. But there is also a time when people desperately need trustworthy, soundly reasoned advice. Much modern pastoral counseling theory has too absolutely ruled out advice, as if it were always bad. Experienced pastoral wisdom prays that it will be Spirit-led to know when to confront entrenched deception and when to listen acceptingly.

- View spiritual formation not merely in terms of short-term crisis management, but rather in terms of the long-term development of the whole person.

The person is seen in the larger context of social environments and even historical developments surrounding that person. That slice of history is then beheld within the context of universal history, which in turn is celebrated from within the larger context of the awareness of God's purpose in creation, redemption, and consummation.

Good pastoral care seeks that sense of due proportionality in finite human conflict which does not ignore suffering or pretend it does not exist, but rather views stressful, tragic, flawed freedom in the context of ever-widening spheres of providential awareness. These horizons extend finally to universal history, the meaning of which is the unique interest of theology (Pannenberg, 1970–73; Oden, 1974a). Theology is the university's only discipline that takes as its stated subject matter the meaning hidden in that universal historical frame of reference of human choosing and consequence suffering.

Patience is therefore a weighty factor in pastoral care. If you listen carefully and wait for the proper moment in spiritual guidance, the person will, in his or her own way, lead you to the depths of the moral dilemmas and spiritual temptations that impinge inwardly. Admittedly, there will be avoidance patterns, unconscious blockages, and neurotic circumventions. But patience in empathic listening will eventually bear fruit by revealing the hidden edges of despair and the scenarios of responsible freedom (Kierkegaard, 1843).

- View the pastoral caring process as taking place within a community of caring, rather than just as an isolated interaction, as if the believing, supporting community did not exist.

Caring for souls means caring for torn persons in vulnerable friendships, in important sibling and family intimacies, in palpable primary relationships, in concrete social and interpersonal entanglements. It should not be considered out of bounds in pastoral counseling to invite troubled persons to church for worship and celebration, to experience more immediately the support of the believing community.

These maxims may be found explicitly or implicitly in the pastor literature of many centuries of crisis and experience. They remain as valid in modernity as in premodern settings.

The Pastor as Friend

A valuable gift in pastoral care is an unaffected, natural, personal openness that tends to invite encounter rather than habitually defend against it. The pastor is, indeed, far more than a gregarious, civic club gladhander or greeter of a welcoming agency. Nevertheless, it is necessary for the minister to be accessible and friendly enough to be perceived as an approachable person.

Since person and office intertwine, the kinds of friendships that the pastor will have within the parish will, to some degree, have the stamp of the pastoral office softly imprinted on them. Many good parish friendships will be shaped, even if slightly, by the fact that the pastor is representative of the Christian community. The pastoral office in fact will open up friendships that would not otherwise be open.

This makes it all the more important to take care to make good pastoral judgments in initiating, developing, and responding to friendships. They are best sought with all classes of people in the community, not simply with an elite group, or "our kind of people." Pastoral friendship will reach out for the resourceful and the resourceless, possessors and dispossessed. Friendships in ministry do well to embody a class-transcending, inclusive hope for human society so far as possible. In a small town the pastor will often be on good terms with the mayor and the courthouse janitor, the service station attendant and the person who owns the business. The pastor may know troubled street kids by name and the police counselor that works with them.

Ministers who limit their friendly accessibility only to their congregation may be offering a flawed example of Christ's ministry to the world. If Jesus is taken as the prototype of shepherding, then it is clear that Jesus was friend to publicans and sinners, insiders and outsiders, children as well as adults, the poor as well as the wealthy. This blatantly open style of ministry in fact created several conspicuous crises in Jesus' ministry.

The pastor seeks to build bridges between Christ and the world, to all classes, dialects, and skin pigments. If a pastor does not have a friendly demeanor, the bridge may be blocked or hazardous.

The sanctity of ministry is not enhanced by withdrawing from engagement in the world, but by enmeshing oneself in the life of the world. God himself expresses the incomparable divine holiness not by withdrawing from the world but by dwelling within it. Some parishioners would sooner die than utter a four-letter word in the presence of the pastor, yet in the locker room there seems to be no such inhibition. There is social meaning in this special treatment of ministers, however quaint, that should not be too quickly debunked. One reason for this curious behavior is that people expect ministry to exemplify the life to which Christian preaching witnesses. There rightly should be some tension between the morality of the minister and herd morality, just as there rightly should be some difference between the Christian layperson and the moral common denominator in society—but one hopes not at the cost of withdrawal from the ordinary world.

The very meaning of the incarnation is that God is engaged in the world without ceasing to be God. By analogy, ministry does not deny its faith by engaging in the real world. Rather, it embodies its faith only through engagement in the world.

Yet, in doing so, ministry should avoid the type-cast roles of credulous pushover, Milquetoast, or starry-eyed sentimentalist. They invite collusions in which manipulative people easily entangle the naive minister in any one of the many games parishioners play.

Conclusion: The Listening Ministry

In any given parish, there is a great deal of trouble and heartbreak that the minister will soon know about. He or she will know about it in a deeper way than gossip knows about it. For what gossip does is repeat bad news in a blaming, damning way. Constant love is more likely to try to find a way to conceal malicious semitruths that will eventually hurt people (Kierkegaard, 1847). Ministry resists gossip in order to more meaningfully be available for the disclosure of the truth in its own time (Wesley, *WJW*, vol. 12, p. 446).

The pastor should not complain if he or she has to listen to these problems. Put simply, that is the pastor's task. It comes with the territory. Though at times emotionally draining, it remains the work of clergy. The kinds of misery and conflict that finally find their way into the hearing of the minister are often not the kind that make the newspapers. They are not public problems or grand issues the minister will get a prize for confronting. It is not even likely that the pastor's record of achievement will be immediately affected by the handling of these situations, even though in time they will have cumulative effect. This is what the older tradition called personal ministry or the ministry of friendship.

This kind of ministry is not easily engineered or manipulated or put into packages as if you could schedule it for a given hour each week. It is an odd and recent misconception that one might assume that at ten o'clock Tuesday one is going to have a significant pastoral conversation with a person because an appointment is on the book for that time. That is not the way personal ministry works. It occurs seldom on cue, often unexpectedly and at odd hours. One must be alert to the serendipities when they develop, whether between the acts of a school play or on a jogging track or after a tense committee meeting. Such encounters may occur at a backyard barbecue or after a funeral or over a second cup of morning coffee.

But they will not happen if the parishioner does not have confidence in both the office and the person of the minister. That trust is gained mostly through trustworthy encounters. Learn patiently to open up the wedge of possibility for significant encounters. That is an important part of what empathic pastors often are doing, even when they look like they are doing other things.

The readiness to reach out for the hurt is an important mark of those who share Christ's ministry. Sometimes the cry for help will come with an uncertain handshake or labored glance after a church service, or when someone knocks on your door unexpectedly. The nonscheduled social format is hardly at all like psychotherapy or legal service or business relationships—precisely because it is ministry.

REFERENCES AND FURTHER READING

Classical texts on the care of souls include Clement of Rome (ca. 96, *LCC*, vol. 1, 43 ff.), Clement of Alexandria (*ANF*, vol. 2), Tertullian (ca. 200b, 208),

We operate without authority

Origen (*ANF*, vol. 4), Cyprian (*ANF*, vol. 5), *The Sayings of The Fathers* (*LCC*, vol. 12, pp. 175 ff.), Nemesius (*LCC*, vol. 4, pp. 257 ff.), Chrysostom (*NPNF* 1st, vol. 13, pp. 407 ff.), Cyril of Jerusalem (*NPNF* 2nd, vol. 7, pp. 6 ff.), Gregory of Nazianzus (*NPNF* 2nd, vol. 7, pp. 210 ff.), Augustine (*NPNF* 1st, vol. 1), Gregory (*ACW*, vol. 11), John Cassian (d. 435), Bonaventure (d. 1274), Luther (*WML*, vol. 1, pp. 105 ff.), Calvin (*Inst.*, 3.20, 4.9), Bucer (1538), Post-Reformation writings on pastoral care and counsel include Francis de Sales (1628), Herbert (1632), Baxter (1656), Taylor (*TPW*, vol. 2, pp. 2–19), Bunyan (d. 1688), Olearius (1718), Law (1728), Wesley (*WJW*, vols. 6–8), Edwards (d. 1758), Zinzendorf (d. 1760), Kierkegaard (1847), Bridges (1847 ed., pp. 337 ff.), I. Spencer (1851–53), Hardeland (1897–98), and Pusey (1901).

Monographs on figures and movements in pastoral care include Nebe (1892), Heinrici (1910), Benoit (1940, 1947), McNeill (1941), Schempp (1949), Bachmann (1949), McCoy (1957), and E. Thornton (1964). Philosophical and psychological works on the psyche or soul include Plato (d. 347 B.C.), Aristotle (d. 332 B.C.), Descartes (1649), Hegel (1806), Freud (d. 1939), Rohde (1925), Pegis (1934), H. S. Sullivan (1953), Reeves (1958), Scharfenberg (1959), Pannenberg (1970–73), and Bouyer (1974).

By far the most significant study of soul care in this century is that of Lake (1966). Modern writers on the theory of pastoral care and the underlying theological ground of care of souls include W. Webb (1892), Maclaren (1896), Watson (1896), Holman (1932), Hoch (1937), Box (1938), Bonthius (1948), Spann (1951), D. Williams (1954), M. Thornton (1958), Tillich (1959), Oates (1961a, 1962, 1974), Hostie (1963), Muller and Stroh (1964), Brister (1964, 1978), Uhsadel (1966), Offele (1966), Halmos (1966), Stollberg (1969, 1971), Holtz (*RGG3*, vol. 5, pp. 1640 ff.), Hulme (1970), Thilo (1971), Ridley (1975), E. Jackson (1975), C. Bruce (1976), Hulme (1981), and McLemore (1982).

Modern pastoral writers whose concern is directed relatively more toward praxis in pastoral counseling include Cameron (1931), Bonnell (1938), Hiltner (1945, 1949), Riecker (1947), Wise (1951), Godin (1965), Clinebell (1966), Kemp (1971), Patton (1976), and Gerkin (1979). Many pastoral writers have sought to appropriate the learnings of modern psychology. Various approaches include Stoltz (1940), Waterhouse (1940), Goulooze (1950), Bergsten (1951), Johnson (1953), and Hiltner (1959). Among pastoral writers who have given attention to biblical themes in pastoral care we note Oates (1953), J. Adams (1970), Crabb (1975), and Oglesby (1980). Psychologists who have had a significant impact upon pastoral practice are, among others, James (1897), Freud (d. 1939), Jung (1959 ff.), C. R. Rogers (1951, 1961), Sullivan (1953), Mowrer (1961), Szasz (1961), Truax and Carkhuff (1967), Menninger (1972), and Pruyser (1976).

Among many writers in the Christian tradition who have approached pastoral care as a task of ascetic discipline we mention the following: The Desert Fathers (*LCC*, vol. 12), Antony (1975 ed.), Basil (d. 379), Macarius (d. 390), John Cassian (*NPNF* 2nd, vol. 11), Syriac Apophthegmata (1934 ed), Dorotheus (6th cent.), John Climacus (d. 649), Bernard of Clairvaux (*Letters*, 1953 ed.), Francis of Assisi (d. 1226), Thomas Aquinas (*ST*), Theologica Germanica (14th cent.), Hilton (d. 1396), Thomas a Kempis (d. 1471), Ignatius Loyola (d. 1556), Calvin (*Inst.*, 3.3), Teresa of Avila (d. 1582), John of the Cross (d. 1591, 1962 ed.), Francis de Sales (1608), Baker (d. 1641), Fenelon (d. 1715), Grou (d. 1803), John of Kronstadt (1967 ed.), Macarius (d. 1860), Faber (d. 1863), Scaramelli (1924), Pym (1928), Fedotov (1948), O. Chadwick (1950), Guibert (1953), Kadlovborsky and Palmer (1954), Chitty (1966), Merton (1973), and Dunlop (1975).

14. The Work of the Holy Spirit in Comfort, Admonition, and Discipline

The theme of pastoral admonition weaves relentlessly through all classical pastoral literature (Cyprian, *ANF*, vol. 5, pp. 311, 335 ff., 369 ff.; Eusebius, *NPNF* 2nd, vol. 1, pp. 229 ff.; Augustine, *NPNF* 1st, vol. 1, pp. 219 ff.; *Seven Ecumenical Councils*, *NPNF* 2nd, vol. 14, pp. 63 ff., 125 ff.). Yet it is conspicuously absent in modern pastoral writings. Our purpose here is to look anew at the ways in which God the Spirit works not only to console but, in the context of a ministry of love, to correct and discipline. We will clarify the biblical basis of this corrective work of the Spirit, its theological rationale and psychological meaning. We will ask why it has been neglected and how it might be recovered.

Nouthesia

The Greek *nouthesia* is usually translated "admonition," "counsel," "warning," or "instruction" (*noutheteō*, "to warn, advise"; cf. *DNTT*, vol. 1, pp. 567 ff.). Admonition is a duty owed by the pastoral guide to the parishioner (Wesley, *WJW*, vol. 7, p. 297). It involves correction when things go wrong and may require confrontation when they go amiss repeatedly. It is not a coercive act that would manipulate change, but a respectful dialogue that holds up possibilities for the voluntary redirection of behavior (John Cassian, *NPNF* 2nd, vol. 11, pp. 280 ff.; Benedict, d. 550; Thomas Aquinas, *ST*, vol. 2, pp. 1338–40).

Admonition can only properly take place in the context of love. Paul urged Christian leaders at Thessalonica "to admonish [*noutheteite*] the careless, encourage the fainthearted, support the weak, and be very patient with them all" (1 Thess. 5:14). The corrective temper is best rooted in love, mutuality, and trust (Cyprian, *ANF*, vol. 5, p. 355). One does not find in it harsh tones or blaming, despairing, judgmental negation, but rather, a patient, hopeful capacity for conflict and correction that is placed in the context of encouragement, support, and compassion (Gregory, *ACW*, vol. 11, pp. 66, 249).

Paul wrote similarly to the Roman Christians: "My friends I have no doubt in my mind that you yourselves are quite full of goodness and equipped with knowledge of every kind and well able to give advice [*nouthetein*] to one another" (Rom. 15:14). He assumed that such admonition would be embedded in good intent and situational wisdom. It is not merely an act of self-expression or an outburst of frustrated energies. "Instruct and admonish with the utmost wisdom" (Col. 3:16). Admonition is linked inseparably with the pastoral task of teaching, tempered by careful listening.

The corrective task has long been thought to be a central pastoral duty. It recurrently appears as an essential dimension of virtually all classical descriptions of care of souls (Gregory of Nazianzus, *NPNF* 2nd, vol. 7; Ambrose, *NPNF* 2nd, vol. 10, pp. 50 ff.; Gregory, *ACW*, vol. 11, pp. 89 ff.). Most agree that it is necessary to ministry and that the task must be approached with great care, concern, sensitivity, and delicacy—and that it is fraught with hidden dangers.

Paul stressed the need for gentleness in admonition and for a healthy self-criticism that would accompany one's critique of another: "We must not be conceited, challenging one another to rivalry, jealous of one another. If a [person] should do something wrong . . . on a sudden impulse, you who are endowed with the Spirit must set [that person] right again very gently. Look to yourself, each one of you: you may be tempted too. Help one another carry these heavy loads, and in this way you will fulfill the law of Christ" (Gal. 5:26–6:2). Wherever the duty of admonition is mentioned, it is often deliberately coupled with the need for empathy. It is only the combination of gentleness and strength that enables the negation to be stated in a fitting time and wise manner (Wesley, *WJW*, vol. 6, p. 116).

The Duty of Reproof

Jesus set the pattern for Christian counsel by calling the apostles to admonish in the context of God's forgiving love. "If your brother goes wrong, reprove him. If he repents, forgive him. Even if he wrongs you seven times in a day and comes back to you seven times saying, 'I am sorry,' you are to forgive him" (Luke 17:3,4).

In time the duty of reproof became connected theologically with the doctrine of sanctification, and practically with the pastoral effort to bring life in Christ to actual behavioral fruition. Accordingly, reproof is not something I can charitably withhold from my neighbor. It is something I owe in good conscience. It cannot be justly neglected. If my neighbor fails to see a shortcoming that injures others or an obstacle to his or her own spiritual growth, and I have the possibility of clarifying the misjudgment in a wise, fair, and helpful way, I cannot justly be silent. The neighbor similarly owes that debt to me, if we are to live together significantly in the body of Christ and share mutually in the gifts of the Spirit. "Smite me friendly," wrote Mr. Wesley (*WJW,* vol. 8, p. 20; vol. 6, pp. 297 f., vol. 8, pp. 269 ff.; cf. Ps. 141:5).

Well conceived admonition will not elicit a defensive response. The receiver will welcome it, recognizing that it is for his own betterment. We desperately need each other's empathic perceptions and best judgments on our misconceptions and misdeeds. Although this corrective task is generally required of all Christians, it remains a special concern and responsibility of the representative minister, whose counsel (*nouthesia*) is given to one on behalf of all.

The counselor is not like a detective, assigned to go about ferreting out misdeeds. Nor should the counselor encourage gossip or faultfinding, which are unnecessarily destructive to the community. For they blame and deride others apart from the context of compassionate care, which is the premise of good brotherly and sisterly admonition.

In what follows we will attempt to offer a re-interpreted traditional clarification of this pastoral task, asking how far it can be viewed as relevant to our contemporary practice of ministry. Admittedly, by most recent pastoral writers the task of admonition has either been ignored or considered passé or destructive. Few writers of this century have considered it to be a crucial or even interesting part of pastoral counseling.

Why Admonition?

Why is admonition a requirement of love? Because freedom is prone to sin, because correction needs the wider perspective of a caring partner, and because solitary self-correction is prone to self-deception.

If we are going to live out our lives together in responsible community, we ask accountability from each other commensurate with our varied capacities for accountability. This presupposes some shared assumptions about what behaviors are expected for serious entry into and meaningful maintenance of that community. Even if a community were to attempt to be little more than a mutual toleration society or group for the preservation of permissiveness, such norms would themselves require surveillance, social conditioning, and eventually, mutual correction when abused. If a community is to nurture accountability in a just way, it will try to make clear the norms against which behavior is to be viewed.

Since the church is primarily a moral and spiritual body, it will eschew external coercive penalties and rely solely on moral suasion, based on caring and talking-through the moral implications of one's behavior. No bone fide classical doctrines of Christian admonition or discipline have presupposed coercive power on the part of the spiritual advisor. It is an important principle of admonition that one must not harm the body of another allegedly on behalf of the person's soul. That principle was abused in the period of witch-hunts and inquisitions. In the central pastoral tradition, the only leverage we have for discipline is moral reason based on the inner claims of conscience, and the witness of Scripture. In order to have moral power, pastoral admonition must disavow illicit use of other types of power. It should be completely free from compulsion.

The purpose of *nouthesia* is the awakening of self-critical reflection and the reshaping of behavior toward greater proximate good, and thus, it is hoped, toward greater personal and social happiness. Put more traditionally, its purpose is penitence, purification, pardon, reformation, and restitution.

This interest in deliberate behavior change in the individual is correlated with a concern for proximate purification of the believing community. For the believing community does well to keep itself as free as possible from elements of demoralizing corruption. For Christ "loved the church and gave himself up for it, to consecrate it, cleansing it by water and word, so that he might present the church to himself all glorious, with no stain or wrinkle or anything of the sort, but holy and without blemish" (Eph. 5:25–26). Christ filled the church with gifts of the Spirit, yet every member of the body remains exposed to temptation, anxiety, and risk of freedom's falling into sin. Though Christ is guileless, undefiled, and holy (Heb. 7:26), the church, which includes sinners, is both holy and always in need of purification and thus constantly pursues repentance, announces forgiveness, and seeks reconciliation (*The Pastor of Hermas, ANF,* vol. 2, pp. 38 ff., 360; Tertullian, *ANF,* vol. 3, pp. 657 ff; Cyprian vol. 5, pp. 592 ff.).

The well-instructed Christian community is aware of its own sin, but this is not inconsistent with the desire to present itself holy before the Lord insofar as possible. Church discipline is thought to be an important part of the proximate purification of the church. Without it, how could one envision a church that hopes to stand in good conscience before the Holy One?

The other side of admonition is the redemptive concern for the person, the reformation of the misguided, the restoration into fellowship of persons estranged from the body of Christ.

The assumption is that persons who enter into the Christian community do so voluntarily. They do so because they wish to share in the life of Christ and they seek earnestly to embody life in Christ in their own behavior. When that does not occur, is there not a duty owed to such a person to help nurture and support a redirection of behavior, a maturing process, in order to help behavior move incrementally toward a greater responsiveness to Christ? The Pauline tradition hoped that we shall "all at last attain to the unity inherent in our faith and our knowledge of the Son of God—to mature manhood" (*andra telion*, "fullgrown personhood"). How is this measured? "By nothing less than the full stature of Christ" (Eph. 4:13).

This corrective dialogue depends greatly upon a sense of shared intent and upon the implicit trust of both parties toward each other. One member of the body of Christ looks to another to help him or her grasp where misdeeds or misjudgments may lie, in order to mature more fully toward humanity in Christ.

The desired outcomes are awakening, restitution, improved behavior, and reconciliation to God and neighbor. If I have done something wrong to someone, even if unintentionally, I may need another's perspective even to grasp what needs to be done. I may need to do something more than say I am sorry. Something may need to be done actively to change the objective situation, to redress grievances, to repair hurts, to repay debts, to seek reparation, not merely to change my inward understanding of it. For that I may need another's counsel (*nouthesia*, "admonition") grounded in empathy. I may need another's interpretation of the data or sense of the situation in order to learn how best to make restitution (or, as the medieval phrase suggests, "do penance," do something to upright the wrong).

But if one is predisposed to defensiveness, one may protect oneself from the very feedback needed to repair the brokenness. The problem of pastoral admonition often hinges just here: learning precisely how to penetrate that defensiveness, but do it in a patient, caring, empathetic way so that in time the wrong can be righted and the person reconciled. This requires deep grounding in a "love that covers a multitude of sins" (1 Pet. 4:8).

Timely admonition was viewed as a gift of the Spirit. God's own Spirit loves us enough to search our hearts for correctives when we go awry. Pastoral admonition at its best only wishes to give active form to the Spirit's own heart search.

The very need for admonition, however, is evidence that the believer needs to continue to learn more deeply of personal self-accountability before God. It is assumed that each believer in the community is going to be trying hard to listen to the guidance of the Spirit so that admonition will be less frequently necessary.

Admittedly the possibility of excommunication (blocking a person off from communicating, from Holy Communion) has frequently been a part of classical discussions of pastoral discipline. Although withholding Communion may be an alternative to be considered in extreme cases of impenitence and recalcitrance, it holds far less pastoral meaning today than when it was regularly viewed as the prevailing means of pastoral discipline. It is best not to employ this alternative even as an implicit threat because the sacrament itself, rightly viewed, has the power to instruct conscience, break through deceptions, and heal inner wounds. Self-responsibility in the light of conscience and Scripture is the principle assumption underlying the Pauline phrase that we should not "bring judgment upon ourselves" by communicating unworthily (1 Cor. 11:27).

Yet some question remains as to whether the truly recalcitrant are able to exercise self-responsibility. The argument for withholding communion on certain occasions of repeated or sustained impenitence hinges on this point: the shepherd may consider withholding communion as a way of keeping the sheep from hazardous grounds.

Admonition in Preaching

The classical treatises on preaching often spoke of admonition as intrinsic to the office of the preaching of the word. The purpose of preaching is not simply to preach what people want to hear. The purpose of preaching is to preach the word so that the word itself, not the speaker, becomes its own offense where it needs to be.

The choice of subjects for preaching should have a great deal to do with the pastor's sense of where the congregation at that moment needs correction, prophetic vision, reproof, or discipline. Pastoral discipline is misunderstood if it is thought only to function on the level of one-on-one counsel. For scriptural preaching will offer many opportunities to bring the divine address to bear upon our corporate limitations and frailties.

The intent of admonitory preaching is, again, not public tongue-lashing or indiscriminate blaming but, rather, listening to Scripture address our actual misdeeds with its word of hope, correction, and reconciliation. Preach on those texts of Scripture that accurately target the neglect or misdeeds of the community at the time. The preacher who assiduously avoids this corrective task will have fewer serious listeners, because they know inwardly how much they need correction.

Pastors may be tempted to assert their own private interest under the guise of some alleged divine claim of God's will for the church. When that happens, the pastor will be fortunate to be able to sort this out with wise and understanding laypersons. In this case pastors themselves may urgently stand in need of a corrective word (*nouthesia*) from the laos.

Whatever Became of Pastoral Reproof?

Has Christianity lost something of its power and influence by misplacing this dimension of discipline? One could argue that in the political sphere, the admonitory function has expanded rather than been reduced by modern Christianity. For in the preaching of the church on social justice one might say that a broader arena of admonition has developed in the period of Protestant liberalism. But on the whole, with that exception, it seems clear that the admonitory function of the modern pastor has been relatively neglected. In the interest of an overweening ethic of toleration, the pastor more and more has appeared in public view as one who dares not offend or appear "judgmental."

Admittedly, the tradition of pastoral admonition is subject to great abuse. One need only think of the Spanish Inquisition or of the potential abuses you might experience if you were a slightly dissenting member of a seventeenth-century Puritan church to imagine the dangers. Reinhold Niebuhr has reminded us that every time we correct someone else we are prone to see the other person's misdeed from the vantage point of our own tendency to self-justification (Niebuhr, 1941, chap. 1). However well instructed we are, it remains difficult for most of us to see the planks in our own eye; it is far easier to see the specks in others (Matt. 7:4), their passing ill tempers and temporarily reduced motivations to do good.

In addition to its temptations to hypocrisy and excessive zeal, admonition may carry with it the tendency to divisiveness. Congregations may be fragmented and polarized by its excess (Gregory of Nazianzus, *LCF*, pp. 124 f.).

In seeking to renew the tradition of pastoral admonition, we must not lose the best equalitarian and tolerationist values that have been hard won in the last two centuries. They spur us to more refined, more humane, more democratic forms of admonition.

With all these caveats in mind, it is now possible to try to state the other side of the case, that the long-standing neglect of church discipline and pastoral admonition leads to a breakdown and demoralization of Christian community. The church in Corinth offers the key biblical example of the need for discipline and the consequences of its neglect. Paul thought the root problem at Corinth was precisely their failure to admonish each other in love, and avoidance of the duty of compassionate reproof. With more caring admonition, Paul thought that the Corinthian church would not have spawned the confusions that eventually required the Corinthian Epistles to be written.

The reasons we have not made the attempt to recover admonition in our time are complex. We have accommodated to many of our contemporary culture's shallow, facile assumptions about the nature of truth and reality. One of the key assumptions of our culture is unconstrained individual freedom: Let each one do one's own thing (and in a very tiny parenthesis we add: as long as others do not get hurt). The narcissistic edge of our culture is inordinately concerned with individual hedonic self-actualization. Doubtless all cultures to a certain degree have had that concern, but few have carried it to the lengths of modern hedonists, with their feather massages, frenetic self-improvement strategies, upwardly mobile individualism, bed-hopping, and high juvenile suicide statistics.

As long as Christian community and ministry accommodate to these hedonic assumptions about life's purpose, there is no room for or even perceived need for mutual correction. There is only pretended toler- ance and the inner condemnation we feel when we do not fully "actual- ize ourselves."

Good pastoral care will strongly affirm the freedom of the Christian. It is for responsible, Spirit-led freedom that Christ has set us free (Gal. 5:1). Justification is by grace, not our achievements in fulfilling of the law. But the gospel does not make void the law (Rom. 3:31). Life under grace is not a normless life without any moral accountability. It is a life in which moral accountability is transformed, deepened, and renewed in the light of Christ's forgiveness (Rom. 12:1 ff.).

Some contemporary theology has been enamored with the heady idea of an imagined freedom that functions without any law or norm or rule of obligation. The technical name for this idea is antinomianism. This yen for freedoms other than Christ's freedom has compounded the problems in pastoral theology. Pastoral practice has at times been exceedingly ready to be guided by this antinomian tendency in theology that implies: if God loves you no matter what, then your own moral responses to God's absolute acceptance make little or no difference; God is going to love you anyway, so assert your individual interest, express yourself, do as you please, and above all do not repress any impulses. It is on the basis of this normless, egocentric relativism that much well-intended liberal pastoral practice has accommodated to nat- uralism, narcissism, and individualism. It has therefore steered consis- tently away from any notion of admonition, hoping to avoid "guilt trips." But ironically, guilt is more likely to be *increased* by the lack of timely, caring admonition (Harsch, 1965, pp. 20 ff.; Oden, 1980, chap. 1). For if there is no compassionate admonition, we tend to hide our guilt in ways that make it worse.

In modern society we have permitted a "pass the buck" attitude toward moral accountability, social obligation, and personal duty. What- ever goes wrong, it is society's fault, not mine. Don't ask me to be ac- countable. Who am I, poor victimized me? Ask social determinants. Ask parents. Ask institutions, policymakers and governments why they fouled up on me, but do not ask me. If we accommodate to this philos- ophy, the effort of supportively calling each other to mutual account- ability will be endlessly avoided. This assumption is finally demeaning to freedom, even though it appears to speak in the name of freedom.

The Crisis of Professional Ethics in Ministry

The pastoral office would be more trusted today if it had diligently maintained and more subtly understood the task of sensitive admoni- tion. Without it, ministry has tended toward innocuous accommodation to the prevailing culture.

Those who see professional standards in ministry at a low ebb today offer these points of evidence: mail order diploma mills for quick and painless "ordination"; the highest divorce rates in the history of Protestant ministry; the frequency of adultery among the clergy; unparalleled political naiveté of either the extreme right or left; overprotection of petty institutional self-interest; the deterioration of Christian mission abroad, to the urban poor and to the university; the general corruption of standards of clerical morality; the non-use of freedom of the pulpit; the lack of administrative skill; the uncritical accommodation of secular psychotherapy into pastoral counseling; the increasing neglect of biblical languages and exegesis; the boring nature of preaching; and a miscellany of other charges. Ironically, at a time in which our progressive assumptions would lead us to think that a new era of unexcelled achievements should be just around the corner, much evidence suggests deterioration.

These charges vary in their seriousness. Although a full inquiry into them cannot be our concern here, they should be investigated nondefensively by clergy. It seems evident, however, that if ministry had policed itself better, shown its own determination to nurture a higher quality of intellectual integrity, biblically grounded leadership, and rigorous moral self-expectations, its identity crisis would not now be so acute.

The morality and language of professionalism can hardly be a substitute for ministry. For ministry is not reducible to professionalism. Professionalism itself is in trouble today. The paradigm of professionalism has been applied to ministry in some ways that are instructive (Glasse, 1968), yet its relevance is limited. In an era in which "professional real estate ethics," for example, tend to protect realtors more than they protect the public, and when physicians on ethics committees tend first to protect fellow physicians against investigation, we cannot look to the general ethics of modern professionalism for the reform of ministry. Ministry must be reformed by standards intrinsic to ministry, not by feebler standards familiar in the sociology of professionalism.

Efforts at reform are hampered by our sentimental attachment to the outmoded assumption of automatic progress in history, which tends to relieve us of responsibility for individual change. We have discovered many ways freshly to rationalize our way out of responsibilities long committed to ministry. We have shifted our responsibility for the poor, for example, to society at large. We blame our failures on "history" or "sin."

A central premise of this book is that with an excellent ministry, the gifts of the Spirit will work powerfully within the church for its upbuilding. With an ill-informed, weakly committed, or heretical ministry, the church is in deep trouble. We cannot predict which way the next century will lead us. Each generation of ministry probably stands at something like this same crossroad: courage or timidity, apostolicity or novelty, watchfulness or ease.

Who shall watch the watchers? Who counsels the counselors? How are the pastors to be shepherded? Who will admonish the admonishers? Some say that it is impossible to achieve discipline in ministry and still maintain pulpit freedom and the ethics of toleration. Yet imagine a case) in which a pastor in charge is doing an incredibly bad job in ministry. Suppose the pastor is really hurting people, tearing up church after church. That is not unthinkable. Things like that indeed happen. What modes of defense do congregations have against that called, ordained, and appointed pastor? It is exceedingly difficult in some polities to challenge entrenched pastoral authority, once appointed, anointed, and blessed. In some traditions, it is almost impossible to put a minister on ecclesiastical trial, because of the understandably high value we place on freedom of the pulpit and toleration of differences. So where does that leave the laity? Often, with little redress. The point: If ministry does not constantly seek to surveil its own standards and reform itself in the light of Christ, its mistakes compound and havoc is created in the life of the church.

The Corrective Spirit

Meaningful admonition cannot be based on a vague or ill-defined sense of social responsibility. In the biblical tradition, admonition presupposes a clear, socially shared consensus concerning well-defined moral accountability. The divine requirement on Israel, however, was viewed from within the frame of reference of the grace of God, refracted through a supportive, caring community.

In Scripture the tradition of admonition assumed clear accountability to clearly stated law. Before speaking of admonition, Lev. 19:11–18 stated straightforwardly the conditions for assessing behavioral responses. They were not impossible requirements. Listen to their clarity and specificity:

You shall not steal; you shall not cheat or deceive a fellow countryman.
You shall not swear in my name with the intent to deceive and thus profane the name of your God. I am the Lord.
You shall not oppress your neighbor, nor rob him.
You shall not keep back a hired man's wages until the next morning.
You shall not treat the deaf with contempt, nor put an obstruction in the way of the blind.
You shall fear your God. I am the Lord.
You shall not pervert justice either by favoring the poor or by subservience to the great. You shall judge your fellow countryman with strict justice.
You shall not go about spreading slander among your father's kin nor take sides against your neighbour on a capital charge. I am the Lord.
You shall not nurse hatred against your brother.

It is within this specific background of stated covenant accountability that the key Old Testament passage on admonition appears: "You shall reprove your [neighbor] frankly and so you will have no share in his guilt. You will not seek revenge or cherish anger towards your kinsfolk; you shall love your neighbour as [one] like yourself. I am the Lord" (Lev. 19:17–18). Reproof is set in the context of a covenant community that has amazingly clear rules and assumptions about what behaviors are decent, fair, and equitable.

In a remarkable instance of apostolic admonition, when Paul not so gently counseled Peter in Gal. 2:11–14, the whole fate of the Christian mission to the Gentiles seemed to be at stake: "When Cephas came to Antioch, I opposed him to his face, because he was clearly in the wrong . . . because he was afraid of the advocates of circumcision. . . . But when I saw that their conduct did not square with the truth of the Gospel, I said to Cephas, before the whole congregation, 'If you, a Jew born and bred, live like a Gentile, and not like a Jew, how can you insist that Gentiles must live like Jews?' " Without Paul's willingness to confront, we might not have had a Christian community in the non-Jewish world at all.

Later Timothy was given specific instructions to counsel, admonish, and correct where needed as a part of his pastoral ministry (1 Tim. 1:11, 5:13; 2 Tim. 2:2, 3:16, 4:2). This tradition of pastoral admonition was rigorously continued among church fathers such as Tertullian, Cyprian, Ambrose, and Augustine. In each ensuing century it encountered new cultural contexts in which to further define and clarify itself. The assumption is that the church is called to holiness of heart and life, to reflect the holiness of God amid the life of the world, and to manifest responsive behavior that is accountable to the mercy of God toward us.

During the period of martyrdom, the issues of corrective discipline became a life and death matter, essential to the very survival of the harassed church. By the time of the General Ecumenical councils we see a determined effort not only to define an orthodoxy of doctrine, but just as carefully to establish an orthopraxis of discipline. Ironically, the amount of time spent by the councils debating matters of church discipline equalled or exceeded that spent on the doctrinal formulations for which they became famous (*Seven Ecumenical Councils, NPNF* 2nd, vol. 14, pp. 25 ff.).

A new genre of writings on penitential discipline appeared in the early medieval period, in an effort better to order the pastoral direction of Christian conduct (McNeill, 1923, 1951). Highly specific acts of penance became an assumed precondition for receiving Holy Communion. Later, in assimilating the Pauline teaching about justification by faith alone, the same concerns for sanctification continued in Protestantism (in figures like Herbert, Baxter, Taylor, the Puritan divines, and Wesley), although without the apparatus of auricular confession and the sacrament of penance. But the reformers were equally concerned to try through pastoral guidance to bring the behavior of the Christian believer into a fit and active response to the love of God.

The Protestant tradition quarreled mightily with medieval penitential discipline, especially when church and state became uncritically intermeshed in applying civil penalties, corporal discipline, imprisonment, and even capital punishment to matters of faith and moral behavior. These misjudgments rightly were rejected in the Protestant tradition and in the nascent democratic tradition of separation of church and state.

Yet meanwhile, the Protestant tradition developed its own misconceptions of pastoral admonition, especially in the self-righteous and picayune legalism that continue in much popular Protestantism. Luther had hoped for a church that could distinguish between law and gospel, between what God requires and what God does on our behalf. Regrettably, Protestantism did not fulfill this hope. But the best representatives of pastorally oriented Protestant theology such as Baxter, Owen, Wesley, and Edwards continued to try to engender communities of sanctification grounded in the preaching of justification by grace through faith.

By the time we get to Protestant liberalism, which flowered in the middle of the nineteenth century and continues to the present time, the mood had sharply changed. The tradition of Protestant liberalism has had as one of its key notions the idea of the innate goodness of the human self. Therefore, there was a consequent neglect in responding pastorally to human self-assertiveness, pride, and the inveterate tendency of the self to assert its own interest inordinately against the common interest. Another assumption of liberal Protestantism was the progressive evolutionary assumption that things are getting better and better so eventually, even if we do have some vexing human problems now, they will doubtless work themselves out either naturally, rationally, or technologically. This is why liberal Protestantism divested itself almost completely of the task of admonition.

When sin is reduced to social determination, when history is viewed as having an inevitable trend upward, and when uncritical tolerance is the centerpiece of all human values, do not expect the gift of admonition to be happily received or nurtured. Rather, you had best expect the act of confession to drop entirely out of the service of worship, as it did in pietistic liberalism.

The Administration of Discipline

What are the sins or offenses for which one conceivably would be admonished? In the traditional literature there is a distinction between *adiaphora* ("issues on which salvation does not depend") and fundamental Christian teaching. Admonition may focus on these fundamental issues, denials of core doctrinal affirmations such as the triune God, the atoning work of Christ, or salvation by grace through faith. According to some pastoral writers, moral misdeeds and ethical judgments may also require careful examination and compassionate admonition. If you are going to have a community of prayer that seriously seeks to be a holy community, you cannot, according to this classical ecclesial understanding, simply ignore either doctrinal or moral discipline. So, undesirable behaviors like theft or blasphemy or fraud or adultery, which are by consensus regarded as contrary to Christian character, are therefore subjects of sensitive corrective dialogue.

If we lay aside excommunication and ecclesial trial as objectionable contemporary strategies, how should admonition proceed? The main work of pastoral admonition centers on intimate one-on-one interactions between the pastor and parishioner in pastoral visitation and counsel. It may also find fit expression in preaching. Look for the right moment, whether public or private, for timely admonition. You may need courage to confront recalcitrant defenses. The compulsive avoider of conflict cannot be a good pastor.

The essential sequence of the administration of discipline was well stated in Matt. 18:15–18. "If your brother commits a sin, go and take the matter up with him strictly between yourselves. And if he listens to you, you have won your brother over. If he will not listen, take two or three others with you so that all facts may be duly established on the evidence of two or three witnesses. If he refuses to listen to them report the matter to the congregation and if he will not listen even to the congregation, you must treat him as you would a pagan or a tax gatherer." The purpose is not simply to cast the person outside of the community but, through reproof, eventually to bring the person back into the reconciled community. The purpose is not exclusion but correction and reconciliation.

If an individual believer requires discipline, one does not immediately proceed publicly, but instead privately, confidentially, and with good evidence. You do not start with prejudicial assumptions against the person, but listen to what the person has to say.

The pastoral literature strongly urges that the whole process of admonition be tempered with discretion. One had best not be too slow—or too hasty. Some persons who dearly delight in blaming others will abuse this otherwise legitimate and needed function. Others may be overtimid and unrealistically hope that the problem will vaporize on its own.

We are looking for balance in this delicate task. Do not listen to gossip or irresponsible charges. Sort out the overlay of anger and defensiveness so to assess accurately alleged misjudgments. The pastoral tradition urges on us a prudent reserve so that through this scaled sequence of conversations, one is brought through private interaction to accountability in relation to the community. In this way the Holy Spirit works through the human spirit to correct, redirect, and redeem fallen human freedom.

REFERENCES AND FURTHER READING

Classical pastoral texts on admonition and discipline include The Pastor of Hermas (*ANF*, vol. 2, pp. 38 ff.), Tertullian (*ANF*, vol. 3, pp. 657 ff., *ACW*, p. 17), Cyprian (*ANF*, vol. 5, pp. 437 ff.), Eusebius (*NPNF* 2nd, vol. 1, pp. 229 ff.), Gregory of Nazianzus (*LCF*, pp. 124 ff.), Ambrose (*NPNF* 2nd, vol. 10, pp. 50 ff.), Augustine (395, 396a, 399–400), John Cassian (*NPNF* 2nd, vol. 11, pp. 295 ff.), *Seven Ecumenical Councils* (*NPNF* 2nd, vol. 14, pp. 63 ff., 125 ff.), Gregory (*ACW*, vol. 11), and Thomas Aquinas (*ST*, vol. 2, pp. 1338 ff.).

Reformation and scholastic Protestant texts on pastoral admonition include Luther (*WML*, vol. 6, pp. 215 ff.), Bucer (1538), Calvin (1559, 2.5, 2.7, 3.4), Perkins (1611), Herbert (1652), Baxter (1656), Taylor (d. 1667), Fox (1911 ed.), Wilson (1708), Wesley (*WJW*, vol. 6, pp. 297 ff.), and Woolman (1922 ed.).

For modern treatment of these issues, see Kierkegaard (1851–52), Vinet (1853), Cannon (1853), Hoppin (1884), Henson (1905), Keedy (1912), O. Chadwick (1958), Rensch (1963), Bieler (1963), Glock (1967), Dittes (1967, 1979), C. Brown (1969), Browning (1970), Scharfenberg (1972), and Drakeford (1978).

V

CRISIS MINISTRY

15. A Theodicy for Pastoral Practice

Theodicy means to speak justly of God amid the awesome fact of suffering. Its task is to vindicate the divine attributes, especially justice, mercy, and love, in relation to the continuing existence of evil. It wishes to speak about God (*theos*) with justice (*dikē*) precisely at those points at which the divine purpose seems most implausible and questionable, namely, amid suffering. We will seek to provide the essential rudiments of a pastoral theodicy.

THE PERENNIAL ISSUE OF A CARING MINISTRY

Obviously, pastors are not the only ones who think about these issues. Much insight can be derived from folk wisdom, drama, literature, psychology, and philosophy. But no profession faces the direct question of the meaning of suffering more frequently than ministry. And no theological dimension of the pastor's work is more difficult. Theodicy remains among the most perplexing, practically pressing, and difficult of the theological issues of pastoral practice. Ultimately, it affects every other dimension in one's ministry.

No pastor can avoid these questions. They come with the territory. They arise inevitably as a result of the confluence of one's preaching ministry and caring ministries. Let us narrow our issue: What is it essential for the pastor to know theologically amid the parishioners' struggle with suffering and its questions?

The quality of a pastor's understanding of theodicy will have an effect upon a host of pastoral activities: care for the physically sick, the spiritually depressed, the dying and the bereaved, and the poor. It will also impinge on the minister's own suffering, both as a personal dilemma and as a problem of preaching and teaching. Anywhere parishioners experience the pain, torque, and stress of human suffering, these questions will emerge directly or indirectly out of the pastoral scene.

These are not theological questions that the minister will bring to the people. They are theological questions that the people bring to the minister.

Nor are these questions reducible to intellectual debate. Questions about the dubious meaning of human life amid intense or irreducible sufferings are not merely abstract, theoretical reflections. They are asked out of the depths (Ps. 130). They cannot be answered casually or dealt with purely as a reflective exercise. Nonetheless there remain important intellectual dimensions in these issues that the pastor does well to think of clearly in advance, before knocking on the hospital door or arriving on the scene of an accident.

The parishioner has a right to expect that the pastor has thought deeply about the coalescence of God's power, love, and human suffering. These issues are intrinsic to ministry, intertwined with the heart of the gospel.

Our purpose is less to offer a philosophical discussion of the source and ground of evil that it is to be accountable to the pastoral situation and to the Christian tradition in our meeting with the prisoner, the cancer patient, the unemployed provider, the alienated youth, the victim of a broken life. Such situations, though they differ in specifics, are often similar in the tone of the human cry: How can we make sense of the power and goodness of God if we open our eyes to the terrible presence of radical suffering and evil in the world and in our own lives?

The Perplexing Triangle and Some Premature Solutions

There are three sides of the perplexing triangle of any serious theodicy:

> God is unsurpassably good.
> God is incomparably powerful.
> Suffering and evil nonetheless exist. Why?

Three premature and deficient, but tempting, "solutions" must be rejected:

- One false solution is the failure to look candidly at the reality of evil. This is the most frequent pastoral default in theodicy: pretending that evil does not have any psychological power or social resilience or durable reality. Out of good intention the pastor may so affirm the power and goodness of God as to look away from the throbbing pain or pretend that suffering has no power to demoralize. That does not aid the sufferer but, rather, intensifies the problem by avoidance.
- Second, in the presence of protracted suffering, the pastor may be

tempted to prematurely give up on the Christian affirmation of the insurmountable goodness of God. The pastor may have become so beaten and demoralized by the wearing power of sin, evil, and suffering that they may seem to have assumed an ultimacy that properly belongs only to God.
- The third premature "solution" is prone to "limit" (so to speak) God's power. Admitting the good intentions of God amid the awesome power of evil, the hurried conclusion is that God tries hard to conquer evil, God struggles for the good, but he is without final power to overcome it.

Each of these premature answers grasps two sides of the triangle, but misses the full affirmation of the third. Classical Christian theodicies are far harder to argue than any of the above three familiar "discounted solutions." For the tough-minded premise of classical pastoral theodicy is to find a way of strongly affirming all three simultaneously: the Almighty God, unsurpassable in benevolence, allows conditions and contingencies to occur that by the abuse of freedom result in real evil and suffering, yet God's incomparable love and power are not diminished. But how can all three be held together? The answer involves patient reflection on Scripture and tradition and a careful examination of freedom abused.

The Question Biblically Stated

God suffers with us (Heb. 2:9). We are not alone in our struggle (2 Cor. 1:1–8). God promises to be present with us in our struggle (Phil. 3:10). God promises victory over temporal suffering in eternity (Rom. 8:18). This is made known in the suffering, death, and resurrection of Jesus Christ for us (Matt. 27,28).

We moderns are not alone in our struggle to understand human misery. Even in the isolation of pain, we stand in the presence of the God who suffers with us and knows pain personally. We stand in the presence of a lively company of witnesses to God's almighty power and love precisely amid the darkest evils (1 Pet. 4:12 ff.). We stand in the presence of a historical community with a long memory that has thought deeply and prayed often for disclosures of providential meaning amid our seemingly absurd struggles (Augustine, *NPNF* 1st, vol. 2, pp. 361 ff.). Here we face a choice: either to deprive ourselves of the benefit of the reflection of those who have gone before us or to learn to listen, pray, and think out of the rich matrix of this historical experience.

The young person may ask (in more modern language): "Why do the wicked prosper?" The same powerful question reverberates deeply from within the biblical story: "O Lord, I will dispute with thee, for thou art just; yes, I will plead my case before thee. Why do the wicked prosper and traitors live at ease? Thou hast planted them and their roots strike deep" (Jer. 12:1,2). The believer who feels alone and alienated may or may not recognize in himself an echo of Christ's own cry, "My God, my God, why hast thou forsaken me?" (Mark 15:34), which itself is an echo from Ps. 22:2.

When parishioners wonder despairingly about the brevity of their years, when life burns out as quickly as summer grass, when good things are so fragile, we hear the same cry sounding from Psalm 90. When we as pastors are tempted to rail in outrage against God for having allowed evil to come to the people to whom God has promised good, we may again be standing unaware in the shoes of Moses, who angrily "went back to the Lord, and said, 'Why, O Lord, hast thou brought misfortune on this people? And why didst thou ever send me? Since I first went to Pharaoh to speak in thy name he has heaped misfortune on thy people'" (Exod. 5:22,23).

No simple, flat, noncontextual answer can be imposed on varied situations. But we cannot say nothing. Christian ministry must not be forever benumbed by suffering. It must learn to speak wisely out of a wide data base of historical experience.

What we say will not put an end to suffering, but it may put us in touch again with these classical pastoral reasonings about the One who gives us life under even difficult conditions and challenges us to trust an ultimate hidden goodness beyond all historical evils.

THE PASTORAL CONSOLATIONS

We now proceed to clarify a series of interrelated arguments, or pastoral consolations, from the Christian tradition of soul care. No one of these arguments is in itself sufficient, but taken together, they constitute a powerful reflection on God's purpose amid suffering.

They do not end suffering. That is not their purpose. Rather, their sole intention is to speak accurately and justly of God amid suffering, to not speak amiss of God or in an imbalanced, thoughtless, or impious way under circumstances that stand as an apparent challenge to God's goodness and power. No single consolation, taken abstractly, has compelling force to elicit faith in God, but together they constitute a rich constellation of insights that have given heart to pastoral care for centuries.

None of these consolations is less than five centuries old, and most are nearer two thousand. Our task is merely to state them plausibly, accurately, and in contemporary language, not to pretend to improve upon them. They require much serious study and meditative reflection before being implemented pastorally. Here are the twelve most applied, most recalled classical pastoral consolations:

God Does Not Directly Will Suffering

The first consolation: Suffering is not directly willed by God, even though it occurs by the divine permission as a consequence of finitude and sin (Irenaeus, *ANF*, vol. 1, pp. 502 f.; Origen, *ANF*, vol. 4, p. 638). We have a duty to say that clearly to our parishioner, and our parishioner has a right to hear it accurately.

What God gives is good (Gen. 1:31; Tertullian, *ANF*, vol. 3, p. 305). The evil that emerges as a result of sin, and the suffering that is caused by it, is indeed permitted by God (for how could human freedom otherwise be affirmed?), but it is far from God's original intention or direct will for humanity (Origen, *ANF*, vol. 4, pp. 328 ff.; Novation, *ANF, vol. 5, pp. 611 ff.*).

Origen argued that God works in each situation to amend what has become broken in his creation:

For although, in the creation of the world, all things had been arranged by Him in the most beautiful and stable manner, . . . He does at each particular juncture what it becomes Him to do in a perverted and changed world. And as a husbandman performs different acts of husbandry upon the soil and its productions according to the varying seasons of the year, so God administers entire ages of time, as if they were, so to speak, so many individual years, performing during each one of them what is requisite with a reasonable regard to the care of the world. (*ANF*, vol. 4, p. 528.)

God cares for the world as a gardener cares for a garden. But the gardener has a broader view of the garden than does the wilted strawberry blossom.

God's original wish for us, God's primordial will for humanity, is unmitigated good. The natural order, with time, causality, and finitude, is the setting in which God's own goodness is to be received and experienced insofar as human finitude proportionally is able to experience it ("Recognitions of Clement," *ANF*, vol. 8, pp. 120 f., 136 ff.; Augustine, *NPNF* 2nd, vol. 4, pp. 146 ff.). However, in the light of our personal and social sin, it happens that guilt, anxiety, and suffering enter into the otherwise good world (Kierkegaard, 1844b, chap. 2; Reinhold Niebuhr, 1941, chaps. 4–6). These are not directly what God wills, but God nonetheless responds to these conditions of distortion with healing initiatives and proportional goods that still can be received, even under the conditions of sin and alienation (Augustine, *NPNF* 1st, vol. 4, pp. 351 ff.).

The Free Will Defense

The free will defense is the prevailing argument in the pastoral tradition that enables us to speak well of God's unfathomable goodness and power amid suffering. When God chooses to give us the extraordi-

nary gift of finite freedom, that carries with it the possibility of abuse
(What alternative is conceivable? How could you have a freedom that
could not be abused?). The necessary condition of moral virtue is free
will (Clement of Alexandria, *ANF,* vol. 2, pp. 361 ff.; Thomas Aquinas,
ST, vol. 1, pp. 417 ff., 819 f.). How could moral accountability be required if all free wills were protected against falling, or if sin should be
made impossible?

Creation would have been spared sin only at the cost of giving no
creature free will. Without will, there could have been no virtue. God
did not choose to create that more simple universe with just rocks and
algae and no freedom. Rather, God took the higher risk of creating
human beings with finite freedom, consciousness, intelligence, conscience—that is, self-directive, morally responsible persons (Irenaeus,
ANF, vol. 1, pp. 521 ff.; Augustine, *NPNF* 1st, vol. 1, pp. f.; vol. 4, pp.
351 ff.). The fact that God created not just inorganic matter but human
beings is clear evidence that God wished to have some part of his creation share to some degree in his own infinite freedom, power, and
goodness.

God apparently would have done less than the best if God had
created a whole world without any free beings capable of moral activity
and therefore without some proportional capacity for communion with
God himself (Irenaeus, *ANF,* vol. 1, pp. 368 ff., 522 ff., 544 f., 556). But
you cannot have freedom without risking the abuse of freedom. God
chose the more perilous, but potentially rewarding, route of giving
some of his creatures free will, even with its hazards (Clement of Alexandria, *ANF,* vol. 2, pp. 361 ff.; Augustine, *LCC,* vol. 7, pp. 395 ff.).

Setting aside for the time being the so-called naturally caused evils
like earthquakes and floods, the free will defense essentially argues that
God does not create evil; human freedom spawns the evils from which
suffering emerges, but keep in mind that the goodness that accrues
from finite freedom is greater proportionally than whatever it is able to
jeopardize. Augustine is the principle exponent of the free will defense
(Augustine, *LCC,* vol. 7, pp. 342 ff.). Tertullian before him astutely
argued that although the abuse of freedom was foreseen by God, it
could have been prevented only by taking away from human existence
its most noble attributes: intelligence, moral accountability, and responsible freedom (*ANF,* vol. 3, pp. 80, 218 ff., 299–310).

This can be a profound and practical consolation for suffering if we
can grasp it deeply enough and learn to articulate it ourselves through
our own experience: that even though we do suffer from the consequences of social evil and our own individual sin, that evil in itself
points back to a greater gift God gives us, namely, free will (Augustine,
NPNF 1st, vol. 1, pp. 103–111). God honors us with that amazing gift,
even if we abuse it and even though it cannot be given without also
being subject to potential abuse.

God's Power Can Draw Good Out of Any Evil

The third pastoral consolation: God would not have permitted any evil at all unless he could draw good out of evil (Augustine, *LCC*, vol. 7, pp. 342 ff.).

The most dramatic expression of this logic is the *felix culpa* theme: It was thought to be a "happy fault," a blessed disaster (seen from a long-range view), that Adam fell, in order to become the occasion of a greater redemption (Wesley, *WJW*, vol. 6, pp. 232 ff.). If Adam had not fallen, God would not have had the occasion of his fall out of which to bring a far greater good, in fact history's greatest good, redemption in Jesus Christ.

Repeatedly Jewish-Christian historical experience has discovered that God draws the greatest goods out of the greatest disasters. When perversions of power or natural calamities lay human societies low, the human spirit is powerfully challenged to re-seed and re-root. The evidence is abundant: bondage in Egypt, the struggle for the promised land, Babylonian captivity, Job's calamities, the crucifixion of Jesus, Paul's thorn in the flesh, the blood of the martyrs, the fall of Rome, and so on—a song of many verses (Augustine, *NPNF* 1st, vol. 2, pp. 226 ff.).

It is a reliable premise in Christian pastoral care that the goodness of God would not have permitted an evil to exist in the first place had not God foreseen in some way (transcending our own finite vision, perhaps beyond our death, even through unseen millennia of social processes), that a greater good could come out of it than if freely chosen evil had not been permitted to emerge at all (Augustine, *LCC*, vol. 7, pp. 353 ff.).

That does not imply that God necessarily draws some greater good for me individually or immediately out of my evil, as I might view it egocentrically. Rather we do better to view the mystery of evil as a social reality, an intergenerational process, an affair of the whole of humanity (Adam) seen together. Everything that happens to my family, happens to me. Everything that happens to Adam happens to me. Everything that happens to my society in some sense happens to me. We suffer socially for social sins and individually for individual sins and individually for social sins and socially for individual sins (Ireneaus, *ANF*, vol. 1, p. 502; Clement of Alexandria, *ANF*, vol. 2, pp. 361 ff.; Origen, vol. 4, p. 631). Sorting out the differences is like trying to find a glitch in a pile of discarded computer tape.

Yet even though we may suffer in particular ways now, God sees the possibilities for humanity that we see dimly if at all. God has in mind larger goods and exquisite value configurations that could come about only through the exercise of our vulnerable, sin-prone, finite freedom, which itself leads to social suffering, but then points toward a presently unknown greater good. Faith in God's providence involves an act of trust that somehow, despite our limited vision, God knows what he is doing in history (Augustine, *NPNF* 1st, vol. 2, pp. 337 ff.).

Pastoral care is always wrong to try to console sufferers that God directly sends suffering upon us, as if it were God's absolute, unambiguous, original will for us. Rather, God permits a set of conditions to emerge such that, given free will, the suffering that comes from freedom is permitted by a divine grace that sees farther than we can see (Origen, *ANF*, vol. 4, pp. 289 ff., 303 ff.).

A word about so-called natural evils: When misdeeds occur, God does not suddenly halt all natural causality. That would require an abrupt break in the vast order of natural intelligibility. Better than this is God's permission that allows natural causality to be felt at times as suffering. Even earthquakes and floods are a part of that natural intelligibility. If this intelligible order were arbitrarily broken by God or capriciously circumvented, then the basis for many more human goods would be undermined, and evils would then increase proportionally. This natural intelligibility governs the shrinking crust of the earth that results in quakes and the great rains that fall on the just and the unjust that in lowlands result in floods (Thomas Aquinas, *ST*, vol. 1, pp. 391, 491 f., 577).

Suppose you invented a universe in which you ruled out floods. Do you thereby rule out running water and lowlands? Better to use human intelligence to prevent harm wherever possible. No reasonable person can justly make a special pleading with God to be exempt from the conditions for life that prevail on this planet, which are so relatively rare in the vast universe.

Let us not misplace the central thread of argument: God does not will evil, but permits free agency. It is only from a good freedom that evil deeds emerge. It pleased God to create just such beings, beings who have free self-determination. This pleased God more than if all creatures had been harnessed in absolutely under strict causal determinations without any self-determination. Yet out of the abuses of our freedom, God still elicits goods that could not have been otherwise elicited (Thomas Aquinas, vol. 1, pp. 249 ff., 927 f.; Erasmus, in *Erasmus & Luther*, 1960).

Evil Does Not Limit God's Power

Is it a limitation on God's power that God permits sin? It is hardly to be called a limitation that God freely welcomes other freedoms. Rather, it is creation's most remarkable expression of God's power. A less powerful God would not have permitted other challenging powers. Only an almighty God could permit alternative freedoms (Thomas Aquinas, *ST*, vol. 1, pp. 111 f., 135 ff., 413 ff.).

The fourth pastoral consolation: Only God is so unsurpassably powerful that he is willing to take the "risk" (i.e., within the limits of history, which God creates and transcends) of living in intimate dialogue and communion with a foreseeably fallen, sinful, self-alienating creature, and all this without any threat to God's own identity or holiness! Surely only God could create such a world (Wesley, *WJW*, vol. 7, pp. 228, 265 ff.; vol. 10, pp. 229 ff.).

God is not threatened with loss of self when he permits the free self-determination of his historical creature to proceed, to act, and to live with the consequences of abused freedom. God continues to struggle against sin within the sphere of history that he transcends, but in a way analogous to the way a good, secure, nondefensive parent may face conflict with a growing child: The parent does not wish to squelch all, even the most remote, possibilities of falling or wrongdoing at the cost of destroying the very freedom in which a young personality essentially consists.

The biblical idea that at times God "hardens our hearts" when we have been already long recalcitrant to his will does not deny human freedom but rather allows freedom so radically as to permit it to put itself in bondage. When God raised up Pharaoh, his purpose was to show his power even through the perversity of Pharaoh (Exod. 9:16). The power of Pharaoh, according to the Exodus account, was primordially God-permitted, as are all historical powers. When Pharaoh abused that power so as to cause suffering to Israel, God did not arbitrarily inhibit this exercise of unjust, pain-laden human choice. To say, metaphorically, that God hardened Pharaoh's heart simply means that God allowed him to abuse his own freedom and did not restrain the outcome of freedom abused. Pharaoh was not forcibly protected from the consequences of his own choices, nor are we. The suffering Pharaoh's freedom caused was not directly caused by God, but God used even that distortion of freedom to reveal his incomparable power and steadfast love (Calvin, *Inst.*, 2.4.3, 3.24.13–14).

Even though God permits the free will to act irresponsibly (otherwise how could it be free?) and to live with the tragic social-historical consequences of those choices, nonetheless God does not simply stand by forever and watch history deteriorate. That is what the story of Israel is about. God continues to work to redeem the consequences of freedom abused. This work occurs through intelligible natural law, through moral awareness and conscience, through the revelation of his commands in the Decalogue, and through the prophets, but finally and convincingly through Jesus Christ and the guidance of the Spirit (Augustine, *NPNF* 1st, vol. 2, pp. 284–361). Even through the most disastrous human deprivations, sufferings, and sins, God wishes to call individuals and societies back to their original intention, to God's original will for them prior to the self-chosen fallenness of their freedom.

The Lessons of Affliction

The pastor is often asked: Why does God allow suffering? The fifth strain of pastoral consolation has plainly answered: Evil and suffering are at times experienced as a purgative, like a needed medication that clears out the system, or a regimen that in the short run is rigorous but in the long run promotes health (Cyprian, *ANF*, vol. 5, pp. 501 f.). They can be the occasion through which conscience becomes awakened, the spirit becomes in time strengthened, the moral fiber toughened (Calvin, *Inst.*, 3.8.8). "At ease in Zion" we do not grow. Through trial and testing we may grow. Then we are asked to trust in providence even when we cannot immediately see its benefits.

The underlying question is: How are we to be coaxed or weaned away from idolatries? Hasn't it often taken some startling deprivation or limitation or loss to call our gods into question? Gregory the Great rightly argued that suffering may tend toward the increase of virtue, not because suffering is good in itself, but because it is the necessary means of a greater good, namely, moral courage (*ACW*, vol. 11, pp. 120–29).

The pastor is often privileged to behold persons growing through suffering. There are times when the capacity for compassion is increased precisely through facing some difficult or limiting situation. We then learn to reason by analogy from our own suffering to the suffering of others. Without this training, where would our capacity for sympathy be? So the alcoholic grasps what compulsive behavior is far better than those who have not been street-schooled by alcoholism.

This is a distortable point that must not be carelessly misstated so as to make suffering look good in itself or so as to ignore the latent temptations that painful limitations may offer the human spirit. Wise pastoral reasoning about suffering tries patiently to thread this needle: God never intends suffering as an end in itself, but only as a means. Means to what? To awareness of our finitude and sin, so as potentially to lead to greater trust in God's power and benevolence precisely amid worldly loss (Pastor of Hermas, *ANF*, vol. 2, pp. 6, 49; Athenagoras, *ANF*, vol. 2, pp. 129 ff.; The Recognitions of Clement, vol. 8, pp. 136–40; *The Clementine Homilies, ANF*, vol. 8. pp. 229 f., 284–300).

In a detailed investigation by William Goulooze (1950, 65 ff.), parishioners were asked to identify significant lessons they had learned from illness. Among the most frequent statements made were these: They learned that God had a purpose in permitting suffering that they did not understand at first and may have understood later only in a mysterious way, but nonetheless felt was in some way made known to them. They learned that in due time God "gives grace sufficient for every need"; that they could face death and suffering with calmness; that Scripture at times became unspeakably comforting to them in ways not previously recognized; and that when they prayed from the heart, "Thy will be done," they found that God answered their prayer "in a way that is best" even if unexpected. They learned that faith helped them not to give in or accede to suffering, but rather to struggle against illness for health, and to be patient when a long-term healing process was required.

Further insights were reported by Goulooze: that God can work through medical technology, surgery, and nursing; that cooperation with medical regimens can at times present itself as a clear Christian duty; and that though with suffering comes the temptation to unbelief, despair, and bitterness, yet the trial of affliction is never greater than the grace of God. They also discovered that they belonged to a fellowship of suffering, not only with others nearby in the hospital or in the local community of faith, but even more so with a wider historical fellowship—with the apostles and martyrs and finally with God himself. They learned that by entering the unwelcome sphere of suffering, they unexpectedly felt a deep bond of fellowship with suffering humanity everywhere, the poor, the sick, the hungry (Goulooze, 1950).

None of this learning necessarily diminishes the reality of pain, but it may help people endure it. None could pretend to "solve" the riddle of evil, but they helped put it in more meaningful perspective.

The Cleansing and Educative Elements of Suffering

When people ask, "Is suffering a chastisement?" they expect a straight, informed answer. It is important to recall that the root meaning of chastisement is not direct punishment. Rather, it essentially means to purify, cleanse, or make chaste. The maxim "Whom the Lord loveth he chasteneth" (Heb. 12:6, KJV) does not imply that God directly afflicts those he loves with a case of hives. Such a God one had best not be loved by.

This question brings us to the sixth consolation: To chastise, in scripture, does not mean to hurt but to help through cleansing. God's purpose in suffering is not to increase pain, but rather to increase our capacity for joy by making out of pain something that would have been less good without it. The key biblical text is better translated, "The Lord disciplines those whom he loves' (Heb. 12:6, NEB), or, "It is where he loves that he bestows correction" (Knox translation).

Jesus himself strongly repudiated the notion that material calamity is a punishment directly sent by God. Jesus was specifically asked about his interpretation of an actual tragic event, the tower of Siloam that fell so as to kill eighteen innocent people. "Do you imagine they were more guilty than all the other people living in Jerusalem? I tell you they were not" (Luke 13:4,5). Jesus then used this incident as a context in which to call all persons, not just those who might be suffering, to repentance.

It is ill advised for a pastor to enter the scene of suffering and announce on New Testament grounds that God is punishing the sufferer for sin. If chastisement means purification from blemish (from Latin *castus*, "spotless, pure"), then we have no right to leave in our hearer's mind the implication that God is causing direct punishment for sin. We do better to stress that through suffering the Spirit wishes to work toward the cleansing of the human spirit, to purge it from sin, to scour it clean, to wean us away from idolatries toward trust in God's care precisely amid wrenching events that temporarily may make it seem doubtful (*DNTT*, vol. 1, pp. 161 ff.; vol. 3, pp. 776 ff.).

When it is said in the pastoral tradition that suffering is a discipline, the term discipline (*paideia*) also needs to be precisely grasped, not as legalistic regimen, but rather as inner education (*discere*, "to learn"). God wishes to use all human events to educate us, to introduce us to ourselves as finitely free, responsible, fallible moral agents. Thus, whatever occurs as a consequence of freedom can become a part of our moral education, potentially teaching us to trust in the One who is beyond all human goods. No experienced pastor would deny that suffering can become a spiritual discipline in that sense.

So whereas chastisement wishes to cleanse us, discipline wishes to teach us. It is the educative, leading office of the Holy Spirit that seeks to make us more faithfully intelligent, stronger, more fit for mission (Cyprian, *ANF*, vol. 5, pp. 309 f.; *Recognitions of Clement, ANF*, vol. 8, p. 178). So although suffering is never masochistically to be sought, neither is it to be compulsively avoided.

Individual Suffering Is Socially Rooted and Socially Redeemed

Anyone who reflects deeply about the conjunction of suffering, omnipotence, divine benevolence, and social sin will realize that theodicy stands at the confluence of many layers of mystery. By mystery we do not imply complete absurdity, but rather, an enigma mostly hidden but whose meaning is partially being revealed. Yet amid suffering we recognize more clearly than elsewhere that we humans have very limited knowledge. We are born and die within a short time. We experience only a tiny glimpse of history. We taste only a small slice of human experience. But even within these slender boundaries, we remember God's self-disclosure in the history of Israel and Jesus. We may not understand it all, but we can be graced by enough of it to enable us to trust God's undisclosed purposes even when the evidence of evil seems piled high to the contrary. Trust in providence means precisely that: to rely on God's promise when all seems otherwise hopeless. Amid suffering that test is stiffened. From suffering something can be learned about providence that may not be accessible to learning in good times (Thomas Aquinas, *ST*, vol. 1, pp. 121 ff.; Outler, 1968).

Even the best of human willing occurs in this social history in which much evil is systemically diffused in social structures and intergenerationally transmitted (Calvin, *Inst.*, 2.8, 3.3; Reinhold Niebuhr, 1941).

Others suffer from my sins, and I suffer from the sins of others. If we simply try to grasp the meaning of suffering on a strictly individual basis (as if it were morally self-evident that only I should suffer for my sins and only you for yours), the problem of suffering is mired in hopeless contradictions. Individuals are socially shaped and socially harmed. Sin cannot be reckoned strictly individually, and neither can suffering.

Reinhold Niebuhr once wryly affirmed that "the doctrine of original sin is the only empirically verifiable doctrine of the Christian faith" (Niebuhr, 1965, p. 24). Few theological ideas are more readily testable than the hypothesis that others suffer for my sins. One need only ask oneself whether one knows what it means to suffer for someone else's sins, in order to verify that assertion. I have never met a person yet who seriously holds that he or she has never once suffered because of something someone else did. Only a simplistic individualism would maintain the point that the doer suffers only for his or her own deed, never for anyone else's.

Not only do I suffer from others' sins and others from mine, but also we may suffer together for things that happened some time ago in our parental or ancestral histories and over which we had no direct control. Granted that, the dilemma of theodicy follows: Why would God have created circumstances in which future persons, even generations hence, may suffer for our misdeeds, or in which we in fact suffer because of the injustices or biases or stupidities of those who have gone before us?

The answer can only be grasped by considering what the possible alternatives to this state of affairs might be. Solipsism is impossible. When I imagine that only I exist, I play with a fantasy that could only live in a world of discourse, a world of others which ironically denies the very premise of the fantasy. No human consciousness comes into being apart from human interaction. If we assume that people influence each other, then we can hardly escape the conclusion that something good done by one generation can benefit the next generation. Similarly, something that is evil can harm a subsequent generation. How else could you posit responsible, historical, transgenerational influence? If you grant that point, you have given up already on the idea that only an individual can suffer for his or her own misdeeds. Without risking the potential cost (of being badly influenced from the past), we could not enjoy the potential benefits of freedom and of being positively influenced by others. This is the price of historical existence. One would have to destroy human freedom to "achieve" a situation in which the social transmission of sin would be impossible. One would also have to deny the fact that we human beings are historical beings who influence each other and that therefore sin can be transmitted from one time or era to another (Augustine, *LCC*, vol. 7, pp. 395–405).

The echoes of my neuroses will doubtless reverberate in my children, howevermuch I wish otherwise. They will inevitably suffer for some of my finite limitations (of knowledge and moral awareness) as well as from my willed, sinful negations of significant values—values that they later may perceive more clearly than I am able to at this time.

Many layers of mystery may obscure precisely how my finitude and sin affect others. Elaborate psychoanalytical or sociological or historical analysis may reveal some aspects or layers of that mystery, but it is doubtful that all of its complex dynamics could be fully revealed even by the most exhaustive empirical analysis.

This leads us to formulate this seventh pastoral consolation: Christian faith does not despair over the social mysteries of evil and suffering. It faces them in the hopeful awareness that God, whose complete will is beyond our knowing, has nonetheless become significantly revealed in a special history that culminates in Christ, which gives us the possibility of trusting the unfolding divine will even while portions of it remain stubbornly opaque (Augustine, *NPNF* 1st, vol. 2, pp. 90 ff.; Luther, *WLS*, vol. 3, pp. 150 ff.; Calvin, *Inst.*, 2.5.3; 3.8; Wesley, *WJW*, vol. 6, pp. 78 ff.).

Even while we cannot understand all of God's good motives or larger intentions in allowing sin-prone history, we do not despair. For our trustful response to this mystery tends to transmute it, to change its face from enemy to friend. The response we make to the mystery of evil to some degree determines its power. For "nothing is so light that it does not appear heavy to him who bears it unwillingly, and nothing appears so heavy that it does not appear light to him who bears it with good will" (Salvian, *FC*, vol. 3, p. 2).

Let us retrace the trajectory of our argument: We are trying to state concisely the recurrent modes of reasoning from the pastoral tradition that attempt to speak well of Almighty God, unsurpassably good, under the conditions of suffering, especially when the suffering is implacable and calls for honest religious interpretation, and especially when it is the suffering of the faithful. All of the arguments of pastoral consolation that we are proposing are long-remembered traditional approaches to the pastoral care of suffering. Contemporary ministries can benefit practically by a fresh re-appropriation of them. They may serve to correct some of the faltering views of theodicy that have prevailed more recently under the influence of faddish styles of pastoral care that have too easily accommodated to the assumptions of narcissistic hedonism, utilitarian ethics, and naturalistic reductionism. Recent pastoral psychological faddism has not achieved notable breakthroughs on the question of theodicy.

Suffering May Put Goodness in Bolder Relief

We now proceed to another more controversial, but nonetheless potentially significant, classical pastoral consolation. It is an aesthetic argument that views suffering as a creative dissonance or transitional discord within a larger, harmonious symphony of meaning. Evil and suffering are not denied, but seen as passing incongruities that are later resolved in a larger, but as yet only partially perceived, concord (Pastor of Hermas, *ANF*, pp. 9 ff.; *Recognitions of Clement, ANF*, vol. 8, pp. 118–20, 139 ff., 178 ff.). In musical composition, the unrestful chord functions to increase, not decrease, the aesthetic pleasure in a transitional phrase between two chords. The analogy is that temporal sin-laden suffering is, within providence, something like a meaningful dissonance that flows into a new strain of harmonious integrity (Clement of Alexandria, *ANF*, vol. 2, pp. 498–504; *Recognitions of Clement, ANF*, vol. 8, pp. 168–73).

By analogy, suffering puts goodness into bolder relief. We would all prefer to live without any suffering. Never should it be sought. But when it must be faced, it may increase our capacity for joy.

Although venerable, this is a limited argument, to be used selectively. For if sin and suffering are logically or psychologically necessary to happiness, then one might ask what need there is for redemption from them. This analogy is best used sparingly also because it may tend to ignore the harsh reality of suffering. Since this point of consolation is so incomplete, it greatly needs the complement of other modes of pastoral reasoning about theodicy.

The Values Intrinsic to Struggle

The ninth approach to pastoral consolation focuses on the essential nature of growth: Opposition, tension, and struggle are necessary to growth, development, and healthy formation. If a muscle is to grow strong, it must push against something, be strengthened by exercise—the more, the stronger, as any athlete knows (Thomas Aquinas, *ST*, vol. 1, pp. 806–12). Without tension or testing, it atrophies.

The same is true of societies, according to Toynbee. It is when the society is challenged that it must either show its mettle or deteriorate. No growth occurs without struggle It is similarly the case with moral and spiritual development: Without the challenge or opposition that creates moral fiber, the muscle grows flabby (Toynbee, 1946, pp. 60 f., 75 ff., 140 ff., 363 ff.).

Hegel saw this as the key to the logic of history. The whole of history is an unfolding of struggling reason, discovering itself only through conflict, by working through antitheses. Once some idea or nation or mode of consciousness is established, it must face the challenge of some antithetical view or power, but out of this challenge comes a richer synthesis, a higher expression of historical reasoning. Only in this way is social change or historical development even possible. Social conflict has positive value (Hegel, 1806, passim).

Change does not occur without pain. Yet the incidental pain is func-

tionally necessary to constructive change, which would not have occurred without it. There is no way to achieve higher refinements of
value by avoiding conflict. Any increase of value must come up against
the foil of suffering and perceived evil, which, even though felt as pain,
may yet become a stimulus to personal insight or moral virtue or social
improvement. This high valuation of historical conflict for spiritual
growth is to be distinguished sharply from the Buddhist view that
would seek release from historical conflict by self-transcending meditation that rises beyond the tensions and opposites that vex historical existence.

Patristic writers such as Irenaeus (*ANF,* vol. 1, pp. 485 ff.), Cyprian
(*ANF,* vol. 5, pp. 469 ff.), and Augustine (*NPNF* 1st, vol. 2, pp. 361 ff.)
echo elements of this conflict-affirming consolation. They thought that
the best moral and spiritual learning would come only by working
through frustrations and overcoming obstacles. Without these, free
moral agency would become so soft and flabby that it could not respond
to the real conditions of life, with its hard choices and, at times, seemingly tragic value negations.

God apparently prefers a life-toughened, time-tested human freedom, rather than a flimsier, more fragile freedom, or a merely theoretical freedom that has never been subjected to the struggle with
fallenness. God did not want to protect human existence from the possibilities of growth that can come only through being challenged, facing
conflict, and struggling with divergent powers. This type of theodicy
concludes, therefore, that perceived evils and suffering do not simply
or necessarily corrupt and impede but, rather, form a significant part
of our human education, permitted by God for a greater good—the
nurturing of responsible free moral agency (Nemesius, *LCC,* vol. 4, pp.
352 ff., 409 ff.; Augustine, *SAOE,* pp. 31 ff.).

Proportional Receptivity of the Good

The medieval writers developed an argument of proportionality
that has influenced pastoral theodicies ever since. God gives his complete and incomparable goodness to finite creatures in proportion to
their capacity to receive it. Since we are finite—limited in time, space,
reason, imagination, and moral capacity—we are incapable of fully beholding or receiving God's goodness to the entire extent of its reality.
We can receive it only within the limits of our imperfection, myopic
vision, and moral dullness (Hugh of St. Victor, 1134, pp. 69 ff.; Thomas Aquinas, *ST,* vol. 1, pp. 248 ff., 662 ff.).

Such are the principle approaches to pastoral consolation, except for
two, to which we now turn: the Augustinian view of evil as a privation
of the good, and the view of Leibniz that the world God has chosen to
create, with the gift of freedom that regrettably is prone to self-aliena-
tion, is the best of all conceivable worlds. We will argue that these two

consolations deserve careful attention in the practice of ministry. Although distortable and easily misunderstood, they have power to console the sufferer who is willing to think deeply about them. Although not empirically verifiable, they are profound and richly suggestive a priori arguments worthy of extended meditation.

Evil as a Privation of the Good

No consolation has had greater influence on the Christian pastoral tradition than that developed by Augustine, the chief exponent of pastoral theodicies that hinge on the coupling of the free will defense with the idea of evil as a privation of good (*privatio boni*).

The heart of Augustine's argument is concisely stated in the *Enchiridion*:

All of nature, therefore, is good, since the Creator of nature is supremely good. But nature is not supremely and immutably good as is the Creator of it. Thus the good in created things can be diminished and augmented. For good to be diminished is evil; still, however much it is diminished, something must remain of its original nature as long as it exists at all.... As long, then, as a thing is being corrupted, there is good in it of which it is being deprived; and in this process, if something of its being remains that cannot be further corrupted, this will then be an incorruptible entity [*natura incorruptibilis*], and to this great good it will have come through the process of corruption.... Wherefore corruption cannot consume the good without also consuming the thing itself. Every actual entity [*natura*] is therefore good; a greater good if it cannot be corrupted, a lesser good if it can be.... From this it follows that there is nothing to be called evil if there is nothing good.... This leads us to a surprising conclusion: that ... every being, in so far as it is a being, is good.... This is because every actual entity is good [*omnis natura bonum est*]. Nothing evil exists in itself, but only as an evil aspect of some actual entity. Therefore, there can be nothing evil except something good. Absurd as this sounds, nevertheless the logical connections of the argument compel us to it as inevitable.... If there were no good in what is evil, then the evil simply could not be, since it can have no mode in which to exist, nor any source from which corruption springs.... Evils, therefore, have their source in the good, and unless they are parasitic on something good, they are not anything at all. (Augustine, *LCC*, vol. 7. pp. 343–45.)

But why did God order things in this unusual way, according to Augustine's reasoning? Because "God judged it better to bring good out of evil than not to permit any evil to exist" (*LCC*, vol. 7, p. 355).

Even though this argument may seem to neglect the reality of pain or evil and to some degree ignore human agency, it nonetheless has an important role to play in a practical pastoral theodicy for persons suffering loss or limitation. For it shifts consciousness away from immediate pain and from the preoccupation with subjectivity and instead speaks a priori (prior to experience, purely on the basis of rational deduction from reasonable premises, rather than on the basis of empirical evidence) about the nature of being, showing how it is logically impossible for anything to be evil unless it depends upon something that is good. That does not remove the pain, but places it in a vastly different context. Some examples will point to its pastoral relevance.

In bereavement, the very malaise that is experienced depends wholly upon something good, very good in fact—the life that has been lost. One is experiencing a profound awareness of loss of value, otherwise one would not feel the pain of bereavement. That loss would not be a disvalue unless there were some value being negated upon which that disvalue depends. The truth of this may be grasped by recalling that the greater the life is valued by a loved one, the greater is the sense of loss in bereavement. Those who are bereft, at some point in the later stages of the grieving process, deserve to see that the evil they feel is dependent upon a premising good and that evil does not exist independently of a very great good.

Suppose the parishioner is immobilized in traction, feeling trapped and depressed. Subjectively the experience is so limiting that it seems an unmitigated evil. Immobility can be a distinct mode of suffering, particularly for persons whose lifestyle is highly active. Yet it would not be immobility unless there were some good previously experienced as mobility. This is not just an innocuous verbal dispute, but a potentially significant insight. One cannot even have a sickness unless one first posits some degree of health. One cannot experience the dysfunction of an organism unless there is first a functioning organism that can become dysfunctional. There is no way one can imagine a completely sick organism with no semblance of health in it. That would by definition be a dead organism. Every sick person, insofar as he or she is sick, already shares in some mode of health that is the precondition of malaise. No sickness exists except that it depends on something to some degree healthy. By analogy no suffering exists except as it depends upon something that has being and is in some sense good. If there were absolutely no being or goodness in an organism, even a sick one, that organism could not be said to exist. Whatever sickness it experiences exists as a parasite on some good function, otherwise the sickness would not even be recognized as sickness.

Augustine came to a profound theological conclusion about this curious state of affairs: God judged it better to bring evil out of good than not to permit any evil to exist (*LCC,* vol. 7, p. 355; cf. *NPNF* 1st, vol. 2, pp. 215 ff.). Translated into the pastoral care of the physically ill: God judged it better to bring health out of the risks of illness than to create what some might call a "better world" in which there was no possibility of sickness at all. God judged it better to allow physical limitations, suffering, and pain to exist dependently, because he judged it better to work toward bringing good functioning out of dysfunction than not to permit any sort of dysfunction at all. God chose to employ human effort to bring well-being out of disease rather than to create finite conditions in which no disease were even possible or conceivable.

The body exists only in space and time. If we were angels, it would be otherwise. Angels were posited as intelligent spiritual beings that were not bound by the bodily limits of space and time (Augustine, *NPNF* 1st, vol. 2, pp. 180 ff.). But our bodies are temporally and spacially defined (Augustine, *NPNF* 1st, vol. 2, pp. 253 ff.). We could not have human existence without a circulatory and a respiratory system, skin and bones, a digestive tract, neural responsivity, and so on, that is, without a body of some kind. Yet since all these functions exist within space and time, they by definition are subject to corruption, to deterioration of the good, to potential loss and decay of optimal functioning. In the real world that God has apparently created, God has graciously allowed these bodily forms to exist under the conditions of potential decay and deterioration (Augustine, *NPNF* 1st, vol. 4, pp. 267 ff.). These are the specific limits of finitude. God permits human bodies to exist, amazingly, rather than not allowing them to exist. Why? Suppose the contrary were true. Suppose there were no such things as bodily deterioration, pain, and suffering. Would not one thereby also have to give up the very idea of having a body at all in time and space with a circulatory, respiratory, glandular, and digestive system—precisely all those things that can go awry?

If you posited a perfect body, not subject to any forms of deterioration, corruption, or decay, and thus not subject to death, then with all the time in the world, time would obviously be meaningless, for any decision could be indefinitely postponed. So freedom and responsibility would then be meaningless, and you would thereby give up on the very idea of human existence, which by definition is finite freedom existing in space and time. (Nemesius, *LCC*, vol. 4, pp. 262–80; cf. Frankl, 1955).

The pastoral relevance of this consolation is that it is always possible to celebrate that which is good even when it has partially slipped into dysfunction. There is no evil that does not depend for its badness upon something better.

This pastoral consolation will not appeal to unreflective people who are not prepared to explore the hazards of its alternatives, but it can be grasped by the reflective parishioner who is already reasonably well instructed in Christian teaching about God's goodness, power, will, and creation.

Let us take an even more hazardous example. The pain of a divorce is different from a broken leg, for it involves working through the suffering of a relationship, and through an interpersonal history that involves many free acts of will. The pain of divorce, however, exists in direct relationship or proportionality to various perceived goods: a personal relationship that once bore hope; the interests of children who may have been spawned by the promise of that relationship; the positive values of stability, mutual trust, and continuity that now are threatened. If there had been no such hopes or no children or no fragments of stability, then the divorce would be less likely to be experienced as wrenching. It is painful only in relation to these aspirations to value, these intimations of good things, these hoped-for meanings now being threatened or negated.

How can such an idea or reflection possibly help the person facing divorce? It cannot end the pain, but it can put the pain in a quite different context, the positive sphere of aspirations to meaning and value. This may modestly salve the pain. But even more, does not the aspired-to value itself, however distorted in practice, deserve to be beheld, proportionally valued, appropriately affirmed?

The physiology of cancer also illustrates the point poignantly. Cancer is a dysfunction of cellular division, overactive cellular reproduction. A cancer cell does not keep its genetically imprinted signals straight so as to limit itself. It continues to reproduce without constraint. The evil that results is correlated with and dependent upon good cellular functioning, which by definition has limits. Ironically, at one level cancer is too much of a good thing (the capacity for cellular division). It would not exist at all were it not for the good it is trying inordinately to express and actualize. Cancer tends toward disorder, but as a misguided dysfunction of a much more complex larger bodily order.

Is This World the Best God Could Do?

Leibniz argued that God, if all-powerful, is surely able to envision an infinite number of possible worlds. But by virtue of his insurmountable goodness, God is bound by a moral necessity to express his own goodness, and therefore bound to create that world which, considering all things, contains the greatest amount of potential and actual good possible (Leibniz, 1686, pp. 3 ff.).

That does not imply "the greatest good from my private, personal point of view," or from the point of view of my family, nation, or social class. But taking the whole cosmos, all past, present, and possible times and places into consideration, which an omniscient God alone would be able to do, Christianity posits that God, being infinitely good, would choose that world which is best for the whole, even though some part may not participate as fully or consciously in the good as some other parts. If you have a complex world, all parts do not function the same way or on the same level of consciousness. So we have grounds to conclude, on the basis of the Christian teaching about God's power and goodness, that this very world we are in, despite its problems, recalcitrant evils, and imperfections, because it is God's world, considering everything (some of which we cannot understand from our own finite perspectives), is the best possible world (Leibniz, 1686, pp. 5 ff.).

Note carefully that this is not argued empirically, on the basis of observed evidence, but a priori, on the basis of the logic of God's goodness and power. For the best of all possible worlds must be a world in which finite freedom exists rather than does not exist. If finite freedom exists, it must be a freedom subject to abuse (otherwise, unfree), and if subject to abuse (like Murphy's Law writ large), everything that is free to go wrong, will, in time, go wrong. Freedom will miss its mark (*hamartia,*) inevitably, although not by necessity (since it is precisely freedom that is directing itself).

> That God always acts in the most perfect and the most desirable way possible, is in my opinion the basis of the love which we owe to God above all things. . . . God has chosen that world which is the most perfect, that is to say, which is at the same time the simplest in its hypotheses and the richest in phenomena, as might be a geometric line whose construction would be easy but whose properties and effects would be very remarkable and of a wide reach. . . . This is the cause for the existence of the best, which his wisdom causes God to know, his goodness makes him choose, and his power makes him produce. . . . If we could sufficiently understand the order of the universe, we should find that it surpasses the desires of the most wise and that it is impossible to make it better than it is. (Leibniz, *TGS*, pp. 206–11.)

Here in summary are some of the achievements of the Leibnizian and Augustinian theodicies that are adaptable to pastoral practice:

- They affirm natural causation (they do not look always to miracle for a solution).
- They do not dodge the subjective reality of evil or pain (unlike Mary Baker Eddy or various spiritualist idealisms).
- They provide a placement of subjectively conscious suffering within a larger order of being, meaning, and value.
- They steadfastly preserve all three affirmations of the triangle of Christian theodicy: God's power, God's goodness, and the proximate reality of evil and suffering.

Before leaving Augustine and Leibniz, it is well to point out some limitations or pastoral deficits in their theodicies, fully respectful of their achievements. If one were to take them indiscriminately into just any hospital room, one would court disaster. A deeper pastoral sensitivity looks for times in which just this word is needed and hearable. Do not stretch them beyond their limited usefulness. None of these arguments can substitute for caring, empathy, and Christian presence. Yet even with these limits, these arguments have time and again been found to be comforting in pastoral practice and should not be too quickly dismissed on purely psychological grounds.

The notion that sin is essentially a deficiency of the good may not grasp the full extent of sin. It may underestimate the biblical teaching that sin involves an overt, willful act of disobedience to God, an active negation of the divine will. Sin is not finitude. It is willed rebellion and rejection of divine goodness. It is more than a lack of moral goodness. It is an assertive, knowing disobedience, a self-deceptive egocentricity that results from pride, lust, self-centeredness, or ambition. Sin cannot be fully ascribed to limitations of knowledge or mistaken perceptions of the good, apart from willed evil. There is a strong and persistent emphasis in Scripture on culpable moral will that freely and deliberately falls from grace, that is not fated but freely chooses rebellion against the unsurpassably good One.

Another liability of any of the pastoral consolations, however valuable otherwise, is that they may appear to the person weeping over a bereavement or languishing in a hospital like an impersonal, cold, logical debate that amounts to being insensitive to the actual suffering of the person present. If inappropriately used, the consolations may feel like an ontological catch 22 or metaphysical gamesmanship. The sufferer may be saying inwardly: "So what? Who cares if evil is a deprivation of the good? What have you done for me lately?" Subjectively, pain and suffering are felt as a positive assault on the goodness of bodily function, not just as an absence of value.

So the empathetic pastor will employ these consolations with caution, aware of their limits. They are not panaceas. None should be used without careful attention to the situation. But the pastor who listens carefully to the feelings of people will find many opportunities to adapt this traditional wisdom to actual situations of the human quandary amid suffering. Learning how to make this adaptation is a major part of the challenge of pastoral wisdom.

PRACTICAL OBSERVATIONS

Correcting Oversimplifications

No pastor works long without encountering demoralized parishioners who plaintively shrug their shoulders with the throwaway comment that their disease or suffering is simply "the will of God." That may be the only way they can find meaning in it and keep their faith. This may become an important pastoral occasion to teach that although God permits sickness, God does not directly will it. Although sickness, disease, and their consequent sufferings are clearly permitted within the larger providence of God, nonetheless God blesses merciful efforts to reduce suffering.

Jesus' messianic ministry featured a constant struggle against illness yet paradoxically was willing to take the path of voluntary redemptive suffering. But the reason Jesus took up his cross was not to increase suffering but, from a longer view, to reduce it.

Although it can be admitted that certain illnesses may be a direct result of one's own or another's sin in some cases, such as the peptic ulcer that may result from chronic anxiety, or the staph infection that may result from poor sterilization procedures, there are many other cases of innocent suffering, the Down syndrome infant, for example. At this point there is good reason pastorally to affirm the positive side of the order of natural causality, which on the whole is beneficial to human history, even though it is subject to regrettable distortions, like missed genetic signals that skew normal infant brain development, or infections that live only by destroying functioning cells.

The pastor who is both skilled and wise may be able to help the parishioner see, amid loss or suffering, how God draws good even out of evil, and how the evil itself is dependent upon some good for its existence. But never should it be implied that the affliction is desirable in itself. Pastoral care has too often been perceived as encouraging masochism, and we need not further re-inforce that perception.

It is a fine line the pastor walks, that risks a clumsy tumble on either side: Affirm the creative possibilities within suffering without becoming fixated on the value of suffering in itself. Take the familiar examples of Beethoven and Milton: No one would charitably wish deafness on a Beethoven. But who can deny that it was only as Beethoven became increasingly deaf that he seemed to grasp ever more profoundly his musical vocation and with his inward harmonic ear heard the deeper strains of melody that made him great. It was as if the sensory apparatus, as it lost its power, paradoxically challenged itself to greater genius or perfection. How else can one account for the irony that Beethoven's most awesome compositions were written only following the severe limitation of deafness? The same irony applies to Milton's blindness. Yet that is no reason to conclude that deafness or blindness are somehow valuable in themselves. Rather, they only offered to incipient genius the challenge of enriched and matured genius.

Pastoral consolation does not woodenly respond the same way to varying circumstances. At one moment pastoral consolation may take the form of an act of quiet, self-effacing mercy, at another, palliating a tough-minded confrontation, a gentle nudge at another, or a word of witness at yet another.

It is not the pastor's role to suggest to others: "You ought to feel this way or that." Rather, it is to show how this particular situation or effect corresponds with latent, unrecognized possibilities for spiritual growth. Whether joy or sorrow is being experienced, the pastor will be looking for ways to understand how either can become a means of communion with God and heightened moral awareness. Artificiality backfires. Pastoral consolation can only be well grounded when it sincerely enters accurately into the sphere of current emotion, moral perplexity, and spiritual struggle in risk-taking encounter.

The young pastor is often amazed that even within a small parish there are so many instances of genuine suffering, so much real sorrow lived out by real people under his or her care. In time the question will turn on the extent to which the pastor will become vulnerable to these hurts, rather than remain carefully defended against any real meeting with bitterness, hurt, chronic despair, and cruelty. The pastor cannot proceed in ministry by pretending these hurts are not there. But it will take some risking to open one's eyes to see the pained glance of the one who has lost his job, or hear the silent cry of the parent who can find no way to communicate with children, or touch the cool hand of the dying, or feel at home while walking through crumbling, demoralized neighborhoods, or smell the stench of rotting, atrophied institutions. Facing suffering is a primary pastoral responsibility. In all of these arenas, the pastor will pray for pastoral wisdom to open up whatever possibilities for growth may be latent in the context. Where else can one begin? Ministry, after all, is not done in heaven, but on earth.

The image often appears in pastoral wisdom that only when fields are plowed up can the seeds be planted. So in human experience, as the securities and reliable conditions of our familiar orders break up, the time comes to sow seeds. It is God who plows. It is God who desires new growth. It does not occur without disruption and burial of the old.

This is a fragile analogy that must be carefully applied without attributing evil directly to God, but viewing the disruption as divinely permitted in order to bring about a proportionally greater good. Any garden that remained forever unplowed would remain ill planted and unproductive.

Jesus did not say "blessed are those that mourn" in order to elevate mourning as an end in itself but, rather, to show that loss of worldly value can elicit increased spiritual awareness. To mourn is to be intensely aware of the loss of some creaturely values. But those that mourn have the possibility of becoming blessed, and perhaps even more blessed than before. For through their mourning after creaturely values that fail, it may be more possible for them to be comforted by trust in the eternal source and end of values in the One who does not fail, since that One is not subject to loss or deterioration.

It may take an extended sequence of pastoral conversations to unpack meaningfully the ways that the movement through affliction can strengthen moral toughness and charity. It may take a long pastoral dialogue to grasp how loss elicits faith, how weaning the self from idolatrous trust may open the way to trust in God. The Spirit's address may be faint. The will of God may look opaque. Amid accidental injury, sorrow, folly, crime, absurdity, or suicide, it can be hard to speak or hear any note of plausible consolation. Indeed, the parishioner may rightly be protecting her- or himself vigilantly against cheap consolation.

The Eschatological Note

Given these obstacles, the most pertinent form of pastoral consolation may have an eschatological note, looking completely beyond all earthly, historical reassurances toward the end time, the last word in history, which surely must be God's own word. It lifts the parishioner's vision above and beyond the limits of temporality. It beholds the suffering in relation to the beginning and end of history, and to Christ as the center of history. Even if there is no hope of grasping the meaning of a particular affliction, the pastor looks for ways to teach, nonetheless, that "all things work together for good to them that love God" (Rom. 8:28a, KJV), even when it is difficult to see how, and even when the working out can only be viewed intergenerationally and historically. The fuller meaning of skewed personal histories may only be understandable generations or centuries hence. But God continues to work patiently within the limits of our tedious histories, and his design is trustable, even though not fully visible.

This is the eschatological dimension of the practice of pastoral consolation: It is consoling to affirm that in the final time, or end time, the time of final historical judgment and decision, when no more time is left for subsequent revisions—in that time God's will surely will be done. If the problems of evil and suffering are not solved within history, they will (in some manner beyond our historical vision) be solved at the end of history. This faith of the prophets and apocalyptic writers can also be our faith, if we choose, even amid the most massive absurdities of present human suffering.

For as long as history exists there will be human freedom, since history is an expression of freedom. Yet as long as freedom chooses, it is likely to be abused, to fall short—this we can predict even by looking at our own abuse of our own freedom. But these abuses of human freedom cannot speak the last word in history. Only God can.

The hope of resurrection is that God will set right what has fallen, that God will vindicate whatever has been left amiss, that somehow evil will be judged and overcome at the end, and that the full intention of God for creation will, despite our worst abuses, be brought to fit completion. This hope is connected with the faith that God would not create a world with explosively powerful human freedom and then simply leave it to spawn evil and do nothing about it finally, so as to allow evil to succeed finally in corrupting the original good intent of creation. That is unthinkable for Jews and Christians who celebrate the resurrection as end time event.

The Blessed

The moving prayer of an anonymous confederate soldier captures the heart of these insights:

I asked God for strength, that I might achieve;
I was made weak that I might learn humbly to obey.
I asked for help that I might do greater things;
I was given infirmity, that I might do better things.
I asked for riches, that I might be happy;
I was given poverty that I might be wise.
I asked for power that I might have the praise of men;
I was given weakness that I might feel the need of God.
I asked for all things that I might enjoy my life;
I was given life that I might enjoy all things.
I got nothing that I asked for, but everything I had hoped for.
I am among men, most richly blessed.

REFERENCES AND FURTHER READING

For recent discussions of crisis ministries, see Hiltner (1949), Clinebell (1966), Oates (1969), Switzer (1974), Jackson (1974), Stone (1976), Gerkin (1979), and Dittes (1979).

For discussions of classical Christian pastoral consolations see Irenaeus (*ANF* vol. 1), Athenagoras (*ANF*, vol. 2, pp. 129 ff.), Pastor of Hermas (*ANF*, vol. 2.), Origen (*ANF*, vol. 4), Cyprian (*ANF*, vol. 5), The Clementine Literature (*ANF*, vol. 8), Nemesius (*LCC*, vol. 4), Augustine (*NPNF* 1st, esp. vol. 2,3, and *LCC* vol. 7), Salvian (*FC*, vol. 3), Theodoret of Cyrus *NPNF* 2nd, vol. 3), Boethius (524), Gregory (*ACW*, vol. 11, pp. 120 ff.), William of St. Thierry (d. 1148), Thomas Aquinas (*ST,* vol. 1, pp. 248 ff.), Erasmus and Luther (1960 ed.), Calvin (*Inst.,* 1559, 2.5, 3.8), John of the Cross (1959 ed.), Leibniz (1686), and Wesley (*WJW,* vol. 6, pp. 232 ff.).

For modern discussions see Kierkegaard (1843a, 1843b), Bushnell (1905 ed.), Temple (1917), Mathews (1930), R. Niebuhr (1941), Harkness (1945), Toynbee (1946), Baillie (1948), Goulooze (1950), Frankl (1955), Hazelton (1958), Boisen (1960 ed.), Farrer (1961), Luethi (1961), Bertrangs (1966), Hick (1966), Outler (1968), Ahern (1971), Burkle (1977), Lake (1981a, 1981b), and T. Bonhoeffer (1982).

16. Ministry to the Sick

The purpose of pastoral theology is to reflect biblically, historically, and systematically on the work of the pastor. Care of the sick is widely regarded as a regular and important ingredient of the practice of ministry.

Soul care for the physically ill requires mental and spiritual preparation, interpersonal gifts, and a wise spirit of discernment. It assumes that one has already thought through the perplexing issues of pastoral theodicy developed in the previous chapter.

The General Ministry to the Sick

Pastoral caring for the physically ill is set in the context of the general ministry of the laity to all who suffer. For all Christians, not clergy only, are called upon to visit the sick, after the pattern of Jesus and the apostles (Matt. 4:23, Mark 6:13, John 4:46, 11:1–6). In doing so, Christians express and embody the mercy of God to those in need, even as God has been merciful to us in our need (Matt. 8:1–17). Yet beyond this general commissioning of the laity to care for the sick, ordained ministry has a special representative role in visiting the sick, which involves not just conversation, but teaching, praying, healing, and consoling in Christ's name on behalf of the whole community (Matt. 10:1, Luke 9:1–2, Mark 3:13–14).

Our focus is not on the laity's ministry to the sick, important as that is, but more particularly upon the twofold duty of ordained ministry: (1) to facilitate, organize, and equip the ministry of the laity in its care for the sick; and (2) to serve purposefully and intentionally as representative minister for Christ's whole body in meaningful pastoral calling upon the sick. *[handwritten margin note: teach it / do it]*

The pastor reaches out for the physically ill on several distinct levels of concern that go beyond ordinary expectations of lay concern. This may include:

- palliative physical comfort where needed
- astute, well-prepared spiritual direction amid the inner challenge of the struggle with illness and limitation
- sacramental and liturgical service to the ill when appropriate
- family assistance and spiritual guidance for the family when indicated
- general support of the medical and nursing facilities, including temporal aid when necessary
- intercessory prayer, commending to God the struggles, discomforts, and hopes of the ill

In Christ's Name

"When I was sick, you visited me," Jesus says poignantly in his parable of the Last Judgment (Matt. 25). In visiting the sick neighbor, we are in effect visiting Christ himself incognito, hidden silently in the needs of the neighbor. When the cup of cold water is held to parched lips, it may be offered in the name of Christ (Mark 9:41, Matt. 10:42).

A major biblical instruction for ministry to the ill is found in James 5:14: "Is one of you ill? He should send for the elders [*presbuterous*] of the congregation to pray over him and anoint him with oil in the name of the Lord."

By analogy to God's own visitation of us in our sickness, we call upon the physically ill. As God calls us to care for the poor under the analogy of God's own caring for us amid our poverty (2 Cor. 8:9), so it is amid sickness. Sickness and poverty are structurally similar: bodily and physical resources are strained and constricted (Chrysostom, *NPNF* 1st, vol. 13, pp. 191 ff.). In such vulnerable times we may more powerfully learn how God befriends us (Gregory, *ACW*, vol. 11, pp. 122 ff.).

An unknown third-century Christian wrote that a bedside visit in Christ's name should be:

> without deception
> without covetousness
> without noise or empty chatter
> rooted in reverence for God
> without haughtiness
> without elegant or well-arranged words of learning
> but with the meek and lowly spirit of Christ
> confidently, with prayer and fasting
> by those who have received the gift of healing from God
> [adapted from *Recognitions of Clement, ANF*, vol. 8, p. 59]

Does Sickness Have Meaning?

Christianity teaches that all things have meaning, especially when seen in the light of the meaning of universal history disclosed by God in

Christ. Even though sickness may be physically painful or morally wrenching, it is not without meaning (Boethius, 524; Thomas More, 1535; Baxter, *PW*, vol. 15, pp. 492 ff.).

Pain and illness have been a challenge to human beings from the beginnings of evolving human history. Christians participate like everyone else in this vulnerable human condition (Chrysostom, *NPNF* 1st, vol. 13, p. 335). Religion does not arbitrarily exempt anyone from potential illness, for grace does not mean disembodiment.

Unlike much religious wisdom, Christianity speaks boldly of God's own active participation in our suffering, God's empathic intention to be with us as fully as possible as humans, even unto death. That word was uniquely clarified in Jesus' death and resurrection. Though sickness and suffering remain a reminder of finitude and a challenge to patience, they are not absurd (John Cassian, *NPNF* 2nd, vol. 11, pp. 445 f.). The journey through illness can occur in companionship with God, where it can become a means to growth and the enrichment of values. Christians "take up their cross and follow" Christ, not morbidly, but affirming God's own companionship in the journey all human beings make (Luther, *LCC*, vol. 18, pp. 38 ff.). Far from a masochistic fascination with pain, Christianity manifests a persistent and practical desire to transcend pain both by medical palliatives and cures and by beholding it from a reference point larger than its sheer physical discomfort (Chrysostom, *NPNF* 1st, vol. 14, pp. 499 ff., 517).

There can be little doubt that sickness is at times enmeshed, consciously or not, in the complexities of sin, personal and/or social. But this does not imply that sickness is a direct punishment for individual sins (a view that Jesus himself repudiates in Luke 13:3–4). Nonetheless my choices may contribute to social sins that cause discomforts for others. Others choose social evils that elicit discomforts that I must endure. This is a social fact that stands at the center of the Hebraic understanding of illness.

The relation of sin and sickness may be more apparent in some illnesses than others. It seems relatively more evident in the statistical correlation between overeating and heart disease, or between sexual license and venereal disease. Compulsive drinking, once freely chosen, may eventually elicit liver disease. One who chooses to drive recklessly may have to lie for weeks in traction in a hospital bed. These are relatively obvious correlations. But even in these cases the intricacies of whether and to what degree these choices are "free" remain debatable. Yet there are still other instances where the correlation is far less apparent because the sin is socially engendered and not the direct "fault" of the suffering individual. In these cases we do well to keep in mind the Hebraic assumption of the social matrix of both sin and suffering. I may drive carelessly and someone else may get the broken nose. You may fail to take precautions against the spread of infection and I may

get the infection. The chemical company from whom I buy pain-reduc-
ing medication may have thoughtlessly disposed of their chemical
wastes thirty years ago in a way that carcinogenically affects my neighbor's water supply.

In the real world, the sufferer may never get a direct chance to
make a clear-cut decision for good or ill but nonetheless will suffer
because of the diffusely hidden collective irresponsibilities of Adam
("humankind"). It would be far easier for ministry to the sick if this fact
were not as persistent as it is. This contributes to the sense of the profound mystery of evil upon which pastoral wisdom has reflected for two
millennia.

Consequently, good pastoral care does not fix its gaze individualistically on the direct effect of a particular sin on suffering. But it need not
therefore close its eyes completely to the intergenerational mystery of
social sin, with its attendant collusions and self-deceptions. There will
be times when the pastor will deliberately try to help individuals grasp
how their own distorted behavior or skewed responses may affect an
illness, or the causes leading to it.

However complex may be the variable correlation between sin (corporate or individual) and suffering, ministry works to comfort, assuage,
palliate, and cure, on the theological assumption that health and full
functioning are God's basic intention for us. When God permits us,
through our corporate lives together, to abuse freedom so as to cause
others and ourselves to suffer, the illness is not to be viewed as fate or
an end in itself, but as a permitted means to growth, correction, and
learning from and about our finitude and corporate accountability
(Basil, *NPNF* 2nd, vol. 8, pp. 132–36, 200–204).

Christian ministry prays in good conscience for healing, although it
does not tempt God by making faith contingent on a particular healing.
Ministry never prays that sickness or pain be increased. Ministry consistently is on the side of fighting affliction, not increasing it. Meanwhile,
it does not view pain as an absolute evil out of which no good could ever
come (Luther, *LCC*, vol. 18, pp. 241 ff.).

Except where resistance must be made to medical abuses, the pastor
cooperatively supports and prays for medical services (Nemesius, *LCC*,
vol. 4, pp. 206–18, 271 ff.). Pastors view themselves as providing the
kind of spiritual and moral guidance for physically ill parishioners that
the hospital and medical professionals are not mandated or able to provide.

Often the sick think of themselves as completely useless, and their
lives therefore seem meaningless under the conditions of sickness. The
classical pastoral tradition has pointed to three ways in which human
behavior may be seen as purposeful during illness:

- The purpose of the sick is to get well. It is therefore purposeful
  activity to rest or recuperate, in order that other purposes that

cannot now be actualized can in due time be sought. Without rest they cannot even be attempted (Thomas Aquinas, *ST*, vol. 1 pp. 352 ff.).

- Purposeful activity amid sickness should not only include a pharmacological and physiological therapy or regimen, but also a spiritual regimen, since so much spiritual learning is by wide consensus, uniquely possible under the limitations of sickness (Nemesius, *LCC*, vol. 4, pp. 350 ff.; Calvin, *Inst.*, 3.20, 4.20).

- It is also a purposeful act during illness to witness to faith even amid weakness, maintaining a quiet hope that never succumbs to despair and never ceases to love and show mercy even in small ways (Wesley, *WJW*, vol. 4, pp. 47 ff.; vol. 5, pp. 115–29; vol. 7, p. 366). These may become powerful means of grace to silent beholders. Even terminal illness cannot finally undercut faith, hope, and love, for these abide (1 Cor. 13).

The Immediate Sufferer

It is generally expected that the pastor will go promptly to the sick. The pastor who waits to be sent for may miss significant opportunities to minister.

However important other tasks of ministry may seem—sermons, committees, administrative planning, social service—a significant claim upon the pastor's time is the immediate sufferer. Even if the task at times becomes burdensome or distasteful or irksome, visitation of the sick remains a primary duty of representative ministry. Based on the example of Jesus, reinforced by the ordination commission and by centuries of social expectation, the pastor is ill advised to neglect this ministry (Baxter, 1656, pp. 102 ff.).

To many parishioners, the significance of other efforts in ministry will hinge importantly on the quality of one's grasp of this task. The pastor who is ineffective here may discover that the effectiveness of other social or preaching ministries will be undercut. The pastor who promptly, steadily, and adeptly serves the sick and their families will be almost disproportionately cherished and welcomed, however uneven the quality of other efforts.

Calvin thought that sickness was a time of the "greatest need" for pastoral services. For when persons are facing afflictions, "whether of disease or other evils, and especially at the hour of death . . . there [one] feels more strongly than ever in [one's] life before pressed in conscience" both by God's judgment and the temptation to despair. Calvin thought of sickness as a unique opportunity for ministry to help better to disclose to people a "good providence, who sends nothing to believers except for their good and salvation" (Calvin, "Visitation of the Sick," p. 127; cf. *LCC*, vol. 22, pp. 64 ff.).

When the person is confined, limited, alone and perhaps demoralized and frightened—familiar conditions of illness—there is often a deepening of self-reflection and a potential for rechanneling of energy. The parishioner may have few other resources for moral support than the pastor, may dread grave illness, may compound physical problems with emotional crises or financial troubles. A deep sense of misery may accompany the crisis of illness that far transcends physical symptoms alone (Taylor, *TPW*, vol. 2, pp. 106 ff.).

Into this situation the church's representative ministry comes not to gain profit or do research or enhance institutional power, but to serve, to palliate, to cooperate with whatever healing resources are available. This ministry is undergirded not by technology, medications, or computer readouts, but by Scripture, prayer, and the presence of Christ (Siirala, 1964).

The analogy between Christ's suffering and ours has pervaded classical Christian reflection on sickness. Gregory the Great developed this analogy in an exceptionally detailed way. He noted that when we are sick, we face a whole series of discomforts, humiliations, and dangers that are similar to Christ's struggle. We are bathed by others. We get stuck with needles and cut into with scalpels. We feel thirst, and our mouths get dry. In each of these discomforts, Christ has preceded us, observed Gregory, by himself participating in our fleshly existence with its dangers and pain. Thus, when we are being washed helplessly by a nurse, we may recall our radical dependence upon God, and the cleansing of baptism. When we have to spend many hours in isolated silence, we are in a position like that of Jesus who endured suffering silently. When we feel the buffeting of thorns, Christians recall that God's own Son wore a crown of thorns. When we are thirsty, we recall Christ's thirst upon the cross (Gregory, *ACW*, pp. 126 f.). And even as we meet death, we may recall how Christ himself prepared for his impending death by prayer, commending his spirit to the Father. If Christ endured so great an evil as a result of his own good deeds, Gregory asked, why should not the believer be willing to endure passing temporal discomforts for which to some degree he may have been responsible?

Degrees of Pastoral Risk

Should pastors visit when diseases are infectious or life-threatening? Even though we expect a minister to use prudent discretion in such instances, there is an unwritten rule in curacy that wherever pastoral services are genuinely needed, the pastor will make a good faith effort to be there. Particularly when urgently needed, the minister has no more "right" than a fireman or a combat soldier to avoid the arena of immediate risk-laden need, even if it involves bodily peril, provided reasonable protections and safety measures are exercised.

Risks should be reduced by prudent precautions. Use masks. Wash hands. Avoid infectious contact when severely fatigued. (Otherwise the

virtue of courage may turn into the vice of foolhardiness.) Fairbairn
stated the classical ethic of pastoral risk concisely: "Unless in very extreme cases, the shrinking of the minister from the region of danger is
viewed as a dereliction of duty, since there appears in it an unwilling-
ness to venture for the sake of men's souls where others readily go for
the sake of their bodies" (1875, p. 300). Paul wrote to the church at
Corinth: "As for me, I will gladly spend what I have for you—yes, and
spend myself to the limit" (2 Cor. 12:15).

Preparing to Minister to the Sick

Alert the congregation to the importance of their role in notifying
the pastor when a parishioner falls ill. Even though they may be reluc-
tant to trouble the minister, they will help by offering prompt and accurate information in order that the pastor can respond appropriately.

The first visit to an ailing parishioner may be more difficult than
subsequent ones. The pastor may need to work through obstacles within, or initially skewed expectations of, the parishioner. Some have cynical or sinister preconceptions about what occurs in a hospital visit.
These obstacles, it is hoped, will be surmounted after the first visit.
Inquire beforehand about the patient's current condition, either by going to the nurses' station for information, or by asking family or
friends. A home visit is best preceded by a courtesy call to set a mutually
convenient time.

An irritable, anxious, or pressured entrance is hardly the way to
begin. When the patient is sleeping or otherwise disposed, wait for the
proper time. Conform the visit to the sick parishioner's needs. In most
cases the pastor will be welcomed and received as a valued guest, without hesitation or embarrassment. In some cases the pastor's very presence will be instantly perceived as already a palpable blessing, even
before anything is said.

A simple intercession before entry may serve to center consciousness. It was Augustine who wondered why ministers should make such
great efforts in the preparation of sermons but "never take care what
they should say to sick people" (quoted by Doddridge, *LP*, p. 107).

Pastoral Conversation with the Sick

Our purpose is not to provide a "how to" approach to pastoral conversation with the physically ill, but to lay bare the biblical-historical-
theological reasoning underlying pastoral practice amid illness. Some
aspects of pastoral reasoning are based on an ethic of simple personal
courtesy: thoughtfulness to the patient, minimizing of inconvenience,
reduction of potential friction. These in turn are rooted in a larger
vision of Christian love. Some are maxims of professional courtesy,
such as the rule that the pastor will not interfere with medical directives
or medication routines or standard nursing procedures. There may be

some exceptions to these maxims, but ordinarily they will serve the patient's interests. They should not be treated cavalierly by ministers who may imagine that they have easily transcended law with gospel. For the gospel itself elicits such maxims of moral sensitivity to guide behaviors in critical situations.

Obviously there is no single rule to apply to varied situations, yet we are not thereby totally lacking all norms or practical principles. Apply a given rule only to the situation to which it applies. How does one recognize the situation to which a given rule applies? As we have stressed throughout, only the foolish imagination tries to answer that in advance. Only wisdom can answer in context.

Here are some traditional guidelines, gleaned chiefly from Doddridge (*LP*, pp. 107 ff.):

- "Let your visits be frequent, but not too long."
- Visit with the parishioner alone if possible, to encourage more personal dialogue.
- Attend where needed to physical discomforts.
- Warmth in prayer is more important than rhetorical content. An attitude of gentleness, hope, empathy, and honesty is fitting for prayer in crucial situations.
- It is a misconception to assume that prayer is addressed to the ailing parishioner rather than to God. The minister seeks to give language to the Spirit's searchings, to the deep, unspoken prayer of the individual, and to the church's intercession for the individual before God. The essential prayer for the sick, Pascal rightly argued, is that God will enable us to make good use of sickness. It need not be long, but it must be from the heart.
- Scripture, better than rational argument, will connect directly with felt needs. Return often to familiar affirmations like John 14, Romans 8, Isaiah 41, 2 Corinthians 5, or various psalms of consolation (Pss. 23, 27, 38, 42, 77, 91, 103, and 121). These are among the most powerfully renewing words of biblical faith. The Spirit through Scripture can often penetrate the heart more quickly and deeply than our own words.

Qualities of Pastoral Interaction

Good pastoral conversation is spontaneous, quick-witted, attentive, and correlated accurately with the precise feeling contours of the moment. It seeks to draw out the undisguised condition of the heart at that instant as the person stands before God. Its purpose is to console and strengthen in the struggle with pain and limitation and, at times, to allow the unburdening of the heart in confession.

The older pastoral tradition assumed that the minister's task was to help the physically afflicted grasp the will of God or the hidden purpose of God through whatever troubles were occurring. That may need some translation for modern hearers, but its deeper intent remains valid.

There will be times when intricately layered questions of guilt will arise, and will need careful sorting out. Listen empathetically, without defensiveness. Do not hesitate to offer the good news of divine forgiveness at the right time. Link pardon to practical steps at reparation and behavioral change designed to try to redress whatever wrong has been done.

It is fitting that the pastor bring some good cheer, warmth, joy, and positive emotional energy into the sickroom, yet without overdoing it with Pollyanna-like "positive thinking." The experienced pastor will recognize to which situation humor belongs and to which belongs sobriety.

We get a glimpse of the depth of encounter in traditional Protestant pastoral visitation by looking at this stark series of questions that Philip Doddridge plainly asked of sick parishioners: Do you struggle with the corruptions of your own heart? Have you seriously attempted remedies? What have you done to change your behavior? Have you experienced the power of the Spirit supporting these efforts? How have you sought to use these limitations for good? (Doddridge, *LP*, pp. 108 f.). These questions reveal the steady determination of a seventeenth-century pastor to crack through defenses to the real inner world of the afflicted in risk-laden interaction.

The purpose is not to crossexamine but to enter into personally penetrating pastoral dialogue. The pastor does not need always to control or set the direction of the conversation. With patience, the dialogue will offer its own opportunities.

Do not be afraid of silence. The parishioner may be struggling valiantly for slow-growing self-understanding or difficult language that is not ready at hand. Interruptions may be costly. One may never be able to go back to that previous matchless moment.

Pastoral conversation is more than amiable talk. It requires attentiveness and the situational wisdom of the well-educated pastoral theologian. Wisdom is needed to treat different cases appropriately. Wisdom implies the precise application of truth to the situation. Pastoral wisdom beholds the laid-bare agony of the sick from the vantage point of God's own agonizing for us.

Litanies for the Sick

We turn now to the liturgical aspect of the work of clergy amid physical illness. The pastoral tradition is well furnished with prayers, litanies, and services that have been used and revised for centuries in ministry to the sick. Many are commendable even to low church or free church ministries that normally do not use much ceremony. For these prayers often capture the essence of pastoral conversation in spare and beautiful language. It is fitting to present at least the major outlines of some of these offices as models for visitation to the sick. Among the approaches we will briefly review are the Anglican Book of Common Prayer's "Order for Visitation of the Sick," Roman Catholic revised liturgy for the sick promulgated by Vatican II, and Luther's instruction on anointing the sick.

Should Communion be offered the sick? Though some Reformed theologians have had doubts, the majority, from such widely varied quarters as Roman, Anglican, Eastern Orthodox, and Methodist, have answered yes. Calvin himself had some uneasiness with the notion of private Communion, on the grounds that the Supper is an act of the whole church, but Calvin did not directly oppose Communion for the sick. Virtually all Protestants reject the notion that extreme unction is a sacrament instituted by Christ, but many Protestant adaptations have been made to the liturgy of anointing the sick.

The traditional Anglican "Order of Visitation for the Sick" (*BCP*, 1662) has been used as the basis of many free church adaptions. Not primarily a service of Communion, the rubrics call for it to be used, all or a part, at the discretion of the minister, for anyone who is sick.

It begins with an ascription of peace "to this house and to all that dwell in it," followed by a collect for mercy and the Lord's Prayer. Scriptural selections emphasize communing with God from the heart (Ps. 77); God's searching out of the human spirit amid need (Ps. 138); trust in the "God of our strength" (Ps. 43); praise of God who forgives sin and heals infirmities (Ps. 103).

Its central petitions are that God may, first, sanctify this sickness "that the sense of [one's] weakness may add strength to [one's] faith and seriousness to [one's] repentance"; secondly, that God may restore the person to former health; thirdly, that the sufferer may be comforted and sorrow turned into joy. This does not assume that God will cure the illness immediately, but prays for deepening spiritual growth and courage through illness.

The traditional Anglican rubrics call the minister "as the occasion demands" to address the afflicted on "the meaning and use of the time of sickness, and the opportunity it affords for spiritual profit." The rubrics explain further: "Here may the minister inquire of the sick person as to his acceptance of the Christian faith, and as to whether he repent him truly of his sins, and be in charity with all the world; exhorting him to forgive from the bottom of his heart all persons that have offended him; and if he hath offended any other, to ask them for forgiveness; and where he hath done injury or wrong to any [person] that he make amends to the uttermost of his power" (*BCP*, 1662). This offers a concise picture of how pastoral sick visitation was approached in the English church tradition.

The service concludes with a prayer for mercy ("Consider his contrition, accept his tears, assuage his pain") and a benediction. Such services have been hammered out by generations of pastoral experience. They can and should be adapted to contemporary conditions, symbols, and language.

The 1979 Book of Common Prayer revision has three parts: "The Ministry of the Word," "Laying on of Hands and Anointing," and "Holy Communion," which may be used separately or together. Scriptural selections include 2 Cor. 1:3–5 (God comforts us in affliction), Luke 17:11–19 (Your faith has made you well), Heb. 12:1–2 (Looking to Jesus, the perfecter of our faith), and Psalm 23 (You anointed my head with oil).

Services of Anointing and Healing

The biblical warrants for the anointing of the sick with oil are principally:

- Mark 6:13 where Jesus gave the apostles authority over unclean spirits. "So they set out and called publicly for repentance. They drove out many devils, and many sick people they anointed with oil and cured."
- James 5:14–17: Those who are ill should "send for the elders of the congregation to pray over him and anoint him with oil in the name of the Lord. The prayer offered in faith will save the sick man, the Lord will raise him from his bed, and any sins he may have committed will be forgiven. Therefore confess your sins to one another, and pray for one another, and then you will be healed. A good man's prayer is powerful and effective!"

By the fifth century there were stated liturgies for the blessing of oil by bishops for use with the sick. By medieval times the service of anointing for last rites (or unction) had become widely viewed as one of the seven sacraments, designed to anoint all five of the senses—eyes, ears, nostrils, mouth, and hands—with a blessed oil that promised the comfort of grace to the ill.

The traditional Roman rationale for anointing was stated by the Council of Trent: Anointing mediates divine forgiveness. Anointing "strengthens the soul" of the sick person that he or she "may more easily bear the trials and hardships of . . . sickness . . . and sometimes regain bodily health, if this is expedient for the health of the soul." Anointing was a sacramental palliative that aimed more at comfort and at engendering faith than at direct, immediate healing.

Those who are to receive this service of anointing, according to the Vatican II revised rubrics, are the sick generally, but especially those who are "at the point of death." Oil, with soothing physical properties, has been used from time immemorial as a symbol of healing and consolation. In the Vatican II service of anointing, the act centers on the laying of hands by the *presbuteros,* offering prayers on behalf of the whole church that by grace the afflicted will gain new strength to fight illness and demonic temptation, and that morale will be restored.

The service is simple and powerful in its directness: Water is sprinkled to remind the sick of their baptism, and therefore of their "sharing in Christ's redeeming passion and resurrection." The mandate of James 5 is read aloud as a biblical authorization. A confession of sin and a prayer for mercy are followed by the reading of the story of the centurion's servant (Matt. 8:5–13), which recalls Jesus' healing ministry. As the priest places his hand on the head of the sick person, the triune God is invoked: The Father for the incomparable gift of life; the Son for humbling himself to share in our suffering; and the Spirit for healing our infirmities. Then "the priest anoints the sick person on the forehead and hands saying once, 'Through this anointing may the Lord in his love and mercy help you with the grace of the Holy Spirit. Amen. May the Lord who frees you from sin, save you and raise you up.'" (*Rites of the Catholic Church,* 1976, vol. 1, "Rite of Anointing and Pastoral Care of the Sick," p. 603).

That is essentially the service of anointing that Protestants sometimes find so mysterious. It ends quite simply with the Lord's Prayer, after which, if able, the sick person may receive Holy Communion.

One June 1, 1545, Martin Luther wrote a brief set of instructions on spiritual healing and pastoral anointing that deserve to be included here without comment, since they speak powerfully for themselves:

If physicians are at a loss to find a remedy . . . you should proceed as follows: go to [the person] with the deacon and two or three good [persons]. Go, confident that you as pastor of the place are clothed with the authority of ministerial office. Lay your hand upon him and say, "Peace be with you, dear brother, from God our Father and from our Lord Jesus Christ." Thereupon repeat the Creed and the Lord's Prayer over him in a clear voice, and close with these words: "O God, Almighty Father, who hast . . . encouraged us to pray . . . 'Ask and you shall receive':... We unworthy sinners, relying on these thy words and commands, pray for thy mercy with such faith as we can muster. . . . Free this [person] from all evil, and put to nought all the work that Satan has done to him. . . ." Then when you depart, lay your hands upon the man again and say, "These signs shall follow them that believe; they shall lay hands on the sick and they shall recover." Do this three times once on three successive days. Meanwhile let prayers be said from the chancel of the church. (*CHSH,* p. 74.)

The healing service of Albert E. Day, a Methodist minister of Baltimore, has become a model for informal services of spiritual healing. Meetings are held in a chapel. The minister is in liturgical robes. The service is preceded by a brief instruction stressing that genuine intercession prays essentially that God's will be done.

After instruction along such lines, we go into a period of silent prayer for about a half an hour. Opportunity is given for any who wish our prayers to come forward one at a time and whisper their request, in response to which we lay hands upon them sacramentally and offer silent prayer for their need. There are no physical manipulations or demonstration. All this while, the assembled company is also engaged in silent prayer. . . . No money is requested . . . fees are a threat to our own sincerity and devotion. (*CHSH*, p. 53.)

Readers who wish a longer historical account of the tradition of prayer for healing from biblical through rabbinic, patristic, medieval, and Reformation traditions, are recommended to read Kelsey (1963), Bouyer (1963, 1968, 1974), and Leech (1979).

The Psychosomatic Interface

That inner states of consciousness affect bodily conditions has been long recognized in classical Christian psychology (Nemesius, *LCC*, vol. 4, pp. 257 ff.). The body can powerfully affect psychic states, and the soul (psyche) can affect neural and muscular responses. This psychosomatic interface was of constant fascination to classical Christian psychologists (Augustine, *LCC*, vol. 7, pp. 206 ff.; Boethius, 524; Thomas Aquinas, *ST*, vol. 1, pp. 363 ff.).

Human freedom swims in the matrix of this interface, this delicate balance of materiality and spirituality, of causal determination and free self-determination. Human existence is not properly understood as simply a material mechanism, nor is it properly understood as disembodied psyche. Either side without the other misconceives the distinctively human. Human beings are not beasts that lack language, imagination, complex self-determination, and poetry, yet human personhood never exists without a body that lives in tension with its own capacity for self-transcendence. That is precisely what defines the human: the juxtaposition of polarities (Kierkegaard, 1849; Reinhold Niebuhr, 1941). The energies of classical Christian psychology were deeply invested in serving and grasping this interface. Pastoral wisdom has sought to apply these insights to daily pastoral caring. Psychosomatic study is not exclusively an achievement of recent empirical study but an inquiry that stretches throughout the twenty centuries of Christian pastoral tradition (Tertullian, *ANF*, 463, pp. 548 ff.; Gregory of Nyssa, *NPNF* 2nd, vol. 5, pp. 393 ff., 419 ff.; Baxter, *PW*, vol. 6, pp. 109 ff.; Alberti, 1714b).

The roots of our word *health* reflect the wholeness of that psychosomatic interface. Health means to have hale or good functioning of both quasi-independent dimensions of human existence: physical and spiritual.

Happiness is misunderstood if reduced to images of adaptation to reality, a prominent modern definition. It is disastrous to adapt uncritically to conditions of alienated, fallen humanity, to the pride and self-assertiveness of the world. That could hardly be called happiness according to classical pastoralia (Chrysostom, *NPNF* 1st, vol. 9, pp. 332, 447). Healthy personhood is more likely to exhibit a resilient determination not to adapt to distorted, sinful worldliness and social alienation. The healthy find their own ways of transcending the distortions of the world.

God loves us toughly enough not to allow us to be happy with our sins. The recollection of sin rightly brings misery of conscience. How else could moral awareness be saved from sentimentality? The deepest human happiness, we learn, is grounded in holiness—God's holy love and our responsive attempts to reflect it fittingly (Chrysostom, *NPNF* 1st vol. 13, p. 341; Wesley, *WJW*, vol. 7, pp. 314 ff.; vol. 10, pp. 364 f.).

Physicians may be less likely to see health and happiness in holistic terms, since their professional attention is often more narrowly directed toward physiological and pharmacological treatment of body dysfunctions. But that is all the more reason that the pastor is needed, and usually welcomed. The pastor is expected to bring a larger, wiser perspective on the psychosomatic interface. It is precisely because ministry wishes to see the patient as a whole rather than partially that it behooves the minister to learn seriously about physiology, symptomology, etiology, pathology, psychotherapy, and physiotherapy.

Among diseases known to have important psychosomatic dimensions are colitis, hypertension, migraine headaches, obesity, insomnia, constipation, peptic ulcer, and so on. The heart patient who needs to learn to live under limitations of schedule and reduced expectation will be dealt with in a different way pastorally than the depressed patient who needs to heighten expectations and break through assumed limitations. Wise pastoral care of the sick seeks to be attentive to the ways in which moral and religious modes of consciousness and psychological distortions are at work affecting the psychosomatic interface (Nemesius, *LCC*, vol. 4, pp. 293 ff.; Gregory, *ACW*, vol. 11, pp. 122 ff.; Young and Meiberg, 1960).

Variables Affecting Pastoral Response

We have previously stated the principle of variability in pastoral care, that spiritual remedies must be responsive to varied situations and volatile maladies. Now we wish to apply that principle to three polarities of variables that impinge strongly on pastoral care. Pastoral care for the ill differs radically in its approach (1) to chronic and acute illnesses; (2) to the maturely faithful as distinguished from the unbaptized or uncatechized novice; and (3) to unconscious as distinguished from fully conscious patients. These three polarities will illustrate how widely varied the situations may be.

1. The pastoral response will be strongly affected by whether the parishioner is chronically or acutely ill. Chronic illness is more deep seated and extends over a longer time (*chronos*). Most pastors will have some chronically ill parishioners to be visited regularly: people with long-standing, persistent ailments; invalids with low mobility—some heavily medicated, some under nursing care— who need modest levels of attention all the time; some self-sufficient but elderly who continue to live at home but with serious obstacles. These persons need long-range supportive pastoral services, a steady low-keyed ministry of hope, friendship, and consolation. Foul weather and unpredictable discomforts may deprive them of weekly church fellowship. It may become an important extension of the Christian ministry to offer them transportation when needed, and word, sacrament, and care when appropriate. It also may be possible to bring the weekly service to them electronically through video or audio tapes or closed circuit television.

The acutely ill have symptoms of more immediate severity (*acutus*, "sharp"), but of less duration. They may come quickly to a crisis and then as quickly pass beyond it. Acute illness is more likely to knock the props out from under the unsuspecting who then are faced with picking up the pieces.

The most general feature of ministry to the acutely ill is immediate responsiveness, whereas to the chronically ill response is more regularly paced, set in a longer time frame, and focused more on hope, patience, and endurance. The chronically sick need steady hope to face latent despair, more than do acute patients, who are more likely to need immediate courage in the face of severe temporary discomforts.

2. Another difference among sick parishioners to which the pastor must be accountable is that between the well catechized who have been duly baptized, instructed, and confirmed, and those quite inexperienced in faith and discipleship. The uninstructed may stand as a greater challenge to ministry amid illness. The pastor cannot assume an active prayer life (even though it may be incipient). Terms like intercession, absolution, and sacrament are best avoided. Yet these persons may be strong in native courage and should not be prematurely judged otherwise. The principle challenge is to build the personal relationship first, as a basis for the pastoral relationship. Good wit and accurate empathy will be the pastor's best resources.

3. The degree of consciousness is another important variable, ranging from fully alert, articulate consciousness to the comatose. Obviously, ministry tries to conform its communication or prayer to the actual level of consciousness that exists in the patient. A special case emerges when the pastor is called upon to visit an unconscious patient not previously known. Hold up the situation in intercession before God, asking the Spirit's guidance. Keep in mind that the so-called unconscious patient may have greater consciousness than is ascribed to him or her. When

praying with the family of an allegedly unconscious patient, it is more prudent to assume that the patient can hear your prayer. Ministry to the unconscious patient is essentially a ministry of intercession, a representative ministry praying for the whole church on behalf of the speechless person, and a ministry of calm, patient, hopeful conversation with family and friends.

In most of the above cases, a closing prayer is recommended as a general rule, but not as an inflexible absolute. Often when a visit is concluded with a brief, personal, gentle, clearly uttered prayer, the tone of the entire encounter is raised beyond the routine. Pray for what you regard as that person's most central need, whether for endurance of pain or peace of conscience or recovery of hope. Pray that God's own Spirit will work within our spirits to heal our wounds and mend our brokenness.

Confrontation: The Duty to Disturb False Peace

Up to this point we have circumvented one aspect of pastoral care to the sick that the classical tradition thought to be very important: the juncture between religious conversion and the challenge of sickness. The older pastoral tradition considered repentance, confession of faith, and conversion to be an overriding concern of ministry to the sick, at times involving an attitude of confrontation that has sometimes harmed ministry's credibility among healing professionals. How far is it appropriate to approach the sick with the challenge of new life in Christ? To seek a radical change of mind and heart amid the conditions of illness?

One may begin to answer by ruling out two opposite extremes: Although conversion should not be considered always mandatory as a primary aim of care for the physically ill, neither should it be completely ruled out in every case. Admittedly, what the sick often need most is quiet. They need a peaceful chance at recovery, not someone stirring up the waters, trying to get them to change or to take a radically new direction. Later, in due seasons of ministry, fit contexts will emerge in which to probe the need for repentance and faith. This need not always be the only item on the agenda.

Having made that proper disclaimer, however, something remains to be said in favor of re-appropriating and redefining the intention of the older conversion tradition. Writers such as Doddridge and Vinet stress candor as an important dimension of pastoral care: "Give them your own judgment plainly" (Doddridge, *LP*, p. 112). Vinet (1853) deals with this subject under the arresting title of "The Pastor's Duty to Disturb False Peace." Though specifically repudiating a "formal interrogation" that might "shut the heart rather than open it," Vinet's pastoral approach nonetheless wants to open up the sick person whose heart is closed to the gospel, seeing this in the long-range interests of the person's ultimate health. He urges the pastor not to be immobilized by the parishioner's silence, but through gentleness, persistence, and modest assertiveness, to seek a hearing for Christian truth. He warns against overly stressing deathbed conversions, which he thinks to be very rare. But recalling the case of the thief converted on the cross, he argues that it is never too late to exercise "our sacred duty to labor for the conversion of the sick."

Some have remained uncommitted, nominal Christians until, in the midst of serious illness, they discover that a deeper grasp of Christian truth is accessible to them. Our awareness of our vulnerabilities may sharply penetrate our usual armored rationalizations and self-deceptions. Ministers can help unravel those confusions if they are sensitive, gentle, and firm. "The duty of disturbing false peace is not the most difficult, but it is the most formidable; and we must either be armed by a severe fantacism, or by great faith and charity; moment by moment we must be guarded against our own weakness, in order to fulfill faithfully a mission so painful; painful indeed, since the success itself is formidable, and we must equally fear not producing disturbance and producing it" (Vinet, 1843, p. 285). Vinet's pastoral care is a "rough love" at times when "roughness being now the only form of charity" one much reach out actively on behalf of the spiritual development of the neighbor. "But the true pastor seldom finds himself placed in this stern necessity, and will doubtless exhaust all other means before he resorts to this" (p. 286). When only a tough confrontation can penetrate illusions, the pastor must be ready for this toughness. This may be required in ministry to the ill, even to the very ill, but such moments should be well timed, and full of a deeper gentleness.

The stress in James 5 is on the mutuality of confession ("confess your faults to one another"). At times it is important for pastors to communicate their own limitations to parishioners, their sense that they too stand in need of God's mercy, that the faults are to be confessed mutually.

Far from expecting earnest confession in every pastoral interaction with the ill, there are more common times when the parishioner's greater need is for positive stroking, specific affirmation, and developing of ego-strength. There are times when the pastor needs to become the assertive advocate for the parishioner's resourcefulness, power, integrity, and goodness, even against the self-effacing impulses of the parishioner him- or herself.

Whatever short-term confrontation may be required for the sake of long-term growth, keep in mind that often the sick are incapable of doing verbal battle. The pastor must not thoughtlessly irritate or exacerbate the weakness of the patient, even in the interest of evangelical witness.

REFERENCES AND FURTHER READING

Classical Christian texts on care of the sick include Clement of Alexandria (*ANF*, vol. 2), Tertullian (*ANF*, vol. 3), Lactantius (*ANF*, vol. 7), Gregory of Nyssa (*NPNF* 2nd, vol. 5, pp. 395 ff.), Basil (*NPNF* 2nd, vol. 8, pp. 132 ff., 200 ff.), Nemesius (*LCC*, vol. 4, pp. 206 ff.), Chrysostom (*NPNF* 1st, vol. 14), Augustine (*NPNF* 1st, vol. 4), John Cassian (*NPNF* 2nd, vol. 11), Boethius (524), Gregory the Great (*ACW*, vol. 11), Thomas Aquinas (*ST*, vol. 1), Luther (LCC, vol. 18, pp. 26 ff.), Paracelsus (d. 1541), Calvin (*Inst.*, 4.9), More (1535), Bucer (1538). For seventeenth- and eighteenth-century discussions see Browne (1635), Baxter (*PW*, vol. 6, pp. 109 ff., vol. 15, pp. 492 ff.), Scandeus (1635), Dickson (1656), J. Taylor (*TPW*, vol. 2, pp. 106 ff.), Alberti (1714a, 1714b, 1726), Doddridge (*LP*), Wesley (*WJW*, vol. 5, pp. 115 ff.), Morgagni (1761), Leuthner (1781, 1782), Ostervald (1781), Sailer (1788), and Gerard (1799).

Nineteenth-century texts on *Pastoralmedizin*, and on the psychosomatic relation and pastoral care of the ill include: Köhler (1800), Vering (1809, 1817), *Medicina Clerica* (1821), Schreger (1823), Bluff (1827), Bridges (1829), Harms (1830 ff.), Valenti (1831–32), Kierkegaard (1844b), Britzger (1849), Löhe (1851 ff.), Vinet (1853), Cannon (1853), *Visitatio Informorum* (1854), Ware (1864), Kidder (1871), Fairbairn (1875), Capelmann (1879), Hoppin (1884), James (1897, 1902), and Gladden (1898).

The same tradition continues in the early twentieth century with Sanford (1904), Antonelli (1904–5), Thompson (1905), O'Malley (1906), Cabot (1908), Olfers (1911), Lichliter (1931), Niedermeyer (1935, 1949-1952), Cabot and Dicks (1936), Tillich (1946), Dunbar (1947), Hiltner (1949), Heuch (1949), Schoellgen (1949, 1956), and Pfister (1949). Since 1950 the following discussions of pastoral care of the sick are worthy of note: Scherzer (1950), Weatherhead (1951), McEwen (1954), Young (1954), Doniger, ed. (1957), Reeves (1958), Hiltner (1959, 1972), Young and Meiberg (1960), Martin (1960), Dwyer (1960), *The Relation of Christian Faith to Health* (1960), Westberg (1961), Gordon (1961), Rössler (1962), Bouyer (1963, 1968, 1974), Schillebeeckx (1963), Kelsey (1963), Siirala (1964), Wilkinson (1967), Kemp (1971), Haendler (1971), Gusmer (1971), Lapsley (1972), Oates (1974), Ashbrook (1975), Pruyser (1976), *Rites of the Catholic Church* (1976), Adams (1979), and Leech (1979).

17. The Care of the Poor

Mercy to the defenseless and downtrodden remains a crucial component of ministry today no less than in the earliest church, when the diaconate was first created to seek to ensure greater fairness to dispossessed widows in the "daily distribution" (Acts 6:1). Classical pastoral writers assumed that care of the poor was intrinsic to the pastoral office. It remains a perennial theme of pastoral theology, elementary to the very definition of the diaconate.

The classical pastoral tradition has struggled with its mission to the poor from its beginnings and through many centuries of development. For "has not God chosen those who are poor in the eyes of the world to be rich in faith, and to inherit the kingdom he has promised to those who love him?" (James 2:5).

Our purpose here is not to investigate detailed issues that properly belong to Christian social ethics (political strategy, economic theory, sexual morality, international relations). Rather, pastoral theology sharpens the focus particularly upon how the pastor is accountable before God to seek social justice, and particularly to care practically for the poor. It is beyond the scope of our specific subject matter of pastoral theology systematically to analyze political influences and economic conflicts that may impinge at any given time on a situation of ministry. That is a vastly complicated and important subject; for no ministry exists apart from some political and economic context. Yet the classical tradition has argued that the pastor may improve society in no better way than by simply becoming a true pastor. It is our task to define how that necessarily involves ministry to the poor.

This discussion links together many diverse themes previously discussed: God's gift and human responsiveness, the gathered and scattered community, teaching and administration, the general and representative ministries, the relation of *kerugma* and *diakonia*. This chapter is the longest because it draws together so many previous threads into urgent, practical application.

Mercy: Divine and Human

The theological center of caring for the poor must be made clear if Christian ministry to the poor is to be properly conceived and embodied. Some church-related political actions have misfired by assuming that this biblical-theological grounding can be skipped over quickly in order to move directly into "Christian political action." But uncritical activism has spawned its own confusions. The task of this chapter is to try to build those foundations carefully.

The exercise of mercy toward those who are hungry, dispossessed, and alienated is understood by analogy to God's mercy toward us. We are called to the same kind of charity toward the broken neighbor that God has shown toward us in our brokenness (Augustine, *NPNF* 1st, vol. 2, pp. 274 ff., 529 ff.). Although Christian charity is due everyone, the poor are Christ's particular concern, precisely because they are the neediest (Chrysostom, *NPNF* 1st, vol. 14, pp. 374 f., 421 ff., 453 ff.).

The poor are by definition those who do not have needed resources in this world and cannot easily acquire them (Thomas Aquinas, *ST*, vol. 2, pp. 1972). They are in immediate need of our merciful care, just as we ourselves stand in radical need of the merciful care of God, before whom we possess nothing (Gregory, *ACW*, vol. 11, pp. 92 f., 158, 182 f., 258).

The claim of the poor on Christian conscience is rooted directly in Jesus' own ministry (Matt. 11:5, 19:21; Mark 10:21, 12:42 f.; Luke 16: 20 ff.). In the parable of the Last Judgment Jesus made this startling analogy: "As you did it to one of the least of these my brethren you did it to me" (Matt. 15:40). When we meet those who are thirsty, strangers, naked, sick, or imprisoned, we are in effect serving Christ himself through service to the neighbor in need.

Care of the poor remains a claim not only upon ordained ministry but upon the general ministry of the whole church. Yet precisely because all lay persons are properly involved in this complex mission, it requires the special energy and direction of an ordered ministry. From its beginnings the task of ministry (*diakonos*) has been directly concerned with caring for widows, orphans, the poor, and the alienated (Acts 6:1; Gal. 2:10; 1 Tim. 5:3–16; James 1:27).

Pastoral care stands to learn much from the ways in which the church has faced varied new historical situations with the word of God's unchanging mercy. From this wide historical experience we may learn better how to communicate and embody God's compassion practically and concretely toward those whom a particular economic order has treated harshly. Widely varied approaches to care of the poor have emerged in many generations of diaconal effort. These varieties invite widened freedom to our contemporary attempts to care well for the poor. Persistent historical models such as almsgiving, tithing, church-wide collections and solicitations for the poor, and equity calculations in distribution of relief remain in their basic intent suggestive guidelines for the contemporary context.

Diversity of Approaches

It should not be prematurely assumed that in the Christian tradition the range of benevolent activities was narrowly limited to food, shelter, and clothing. It also had to do with more subtle efforts to relieve psychological stress, such as that connected with the supply of dowry so that the delay of marriage would not be extended inordinately, and help to provide practical skills so the youth of the poor could obtain jobs that would enable them to come out of the syndrome of poverty. New arrivals in the community were assisted through loans from the common chest. Orphans were offered physical necessities and training (Pastor of Hermas, *ANF*, vol. 2, pp. 32 f., 52 f.; Cyprian, *ANF*, vol. 5, p. 314, *Apostolic Constitutions*, *ANF*, vol. 7, pp. 422 ff., 433 ff., Bucer, *LCC*, vol. 19, pp. 306 ff.).

As early as the *Apostolic Constitution* that were redacted in the fourth century, the elders were urging that "those who have no children should adopt orphans and treat them as their own children" (*ANF*, vol. 7, p. 433) and help children "of outstanding ability who have no patrons to be educated," as well as show concern for the "unemployed that they may make a living by their trade and feed their children." The range of their caring acts for the poor is seen in this amazing passage, wherein the churches were instructed to provide

to the orphans the care of parents;
to the widows the care of husbands;
to those of suitable age, marriage;
to the artisan, work;
to the disabled, sympathetic response;
to travelers, a house;
to the hungry, food;
to the thirsty, drink;
to the naked, clothing;
to the sick, visitation;
to the prisoner, help . . .
to young persons, assistance that they may learn a trade.
[adapted from ANF, vol. 7, p. 435]

In these twelve statements we see the breadth of activities for relief of the poor in the early church.

Relief funds were to be used for "the deliverance of slaves, of the captives, and of prisoners, of those who have been abused, and of those that have been condemned by tyrants" (*Apostolic Constitutions*, *ANF*, vol.

3, p. 435). A widely ranging social ethic and embrionic political theology were implicit in primitive Christian care for the poor, later to be more explicitly developed. Ambrose is said to have melted down the vessels for the Eucharist in order that the poor could be fed and prisoners ransomed. When reproached by the Arians for this extravagance, Ambrose replied, "The church has gold not to keep but to give, to relieve distress" (Ambrose, *NPNP* 2nd, vol. 10, pp. 419–24).

The relief work for the poor was closely connected with the worshiping community. Oblations were received in relation to the Supper; alms came through the alms box in the church; tithes were received in sabbath worship (*Apostolic Constitutions*, *ANF*, vol. 7, pp. 411, 468 ff.; *Early Liturgies*, *ANF*, vol. 7, pp. 535, 540, 554 f.).

Biblical Themes

Jesus warned, "When you do some act of charity, do not let your left hand know what your right hand is doing: your good deed must be secret, and your Father who sees what is done in secret will reward you" (Matt. 6:3). From the outset there has been a rigorous ethical concern for a correspondence between good intention and outward acts of mercy (Chrysostom, *NPNF* 1st vol. 10, pp. 433 ff., 467 ff.).

In following the command to give alms with simple, merciful intent, the church was continuing, yet transmuting, the Deuteronomic tradition of almsgiving and care of the poor. Deuteronomic law called the faithful to "tithe all the yield of your seed which comes forth from the field year by year" (Deut. 14:22, RSV). In addition to this radical social commitment there was another remarkable rule: "Every seven years every creditor shall release what he has lent to his neighbor" (Deut. 15:1–2, RSV).

The Hebraic social hope was sweeping: "There will be no poor among you . . . if only you will obey the voice of the Lord your God, being careful to do all this commandment which I command to you this day" (Deut. 14:4–5, RSV). In Hebrew law, the presence of the poor in a society was regarded as evidence that the commandment and judgment of God were still impinging on that society. "If there is among you a poor person . . . in any of your towns within your land which the Lord your God gives you, you shall not harden your heart or shut your hand against your poor brother, but open your hand to him and lend to him sufficient to his need, whatever it be. . . . You shall give to him freely, and your heart shall not be grudging when you give to him, because for this the Lord your God will bless you in all your work and all you partake" (Deut. 15:7–10, RSV). The promise of special blessing accompanied the radical duty to care for the poor.

It is in the context of this same passage that a controversial phrase appeared (which Jesus later quoted in part from a text that he doubtless knew in full): "The poor will always be with you [but the sentence does not end there!] in the land and for that reason I command you to be open handed" (Deut. 15:11). The assumption is that, given the conditions of fallen human freedom and consequent social alienation, there will always be persons who are dispossessed and treated unfairly. Yet it is for this very reason that we are commanded, "You shall open wide to the needy and to the poor, in the land" (Deut. 15:11, RSV). This bold Hebraic social ethic became a central feature of Christian pastoral care. The Deuteronomic writer doubtless would have disapproved of this phrase being employed as a rationale for inactivity toward the poor or acquiescence to the status quo of social suffering, since the opposite was intended.

The pattern of selling all possessions and distributing to the poor is found in the second chapter of Acts. The promise of the Torah that "there will be no poor among you" (Deut. 15:4) was in fact fulfilled, according to Acts 4:34, for "there was not a needy person among them . . . and distribution was made to each as any had need." This pattern was so deep in earliest Christian consciousness that it persisted for centuries as an economic ideal of Christian *koinōnia*, with especially powerful influence in monastic communities.

"Joseph, who was surnamed by the apostles Barnabas . . . sold a field . . . and brought the money and laid it at the apostles' feet" (Acts 4:36–37, RSV). The distribution was made to the poor by the Apostles. This story is then tellingly counterpointed by the story of Ananias, who sold a piece of property, and with his wife's knowledge deceptively kept back some of the proceeds. He brought only a part of it and laid it at the Apostle's feet. "But Peter said, 'Ananias, why has Satan filled your heart, to lie to the Holy Spirit, and keep back part of the proceeds?' . . . And when Ananias heard these words, he fell down and died." When his wife heard the news, "immediately she fell down at his feet and died" (Acts 5:1–10, RSV). These were regarded as signs by the early Christian community that the Holy Spirit was deadly serious about asking Christians to make a radical economic response, to disavow egocentric use of individual property, and to engage earnestly in a mission to the poor.

Pastoral Empathy for the Poor

In seeking to understand pastoral responsibility to the poor, pastors do well to begin with serious self-examination of their own attitudes, class interests, biases, potentially idolatrous relation to personal wealth, and temptations to exaggerate the importance of possessions for genuine happiness.

This is not something a pastor simply can dutifully require of him- or herself, as if to say, "Now I ought to be compassionate and merciful." Rather, it requires a long-term exercise in empathetic imagination and close-range engagement. We are speaking about an improvable pastoral habit through which one may come increasingly to care about those in deep distress, feel less anxious about being with them, and have less egocentric concern for maintenance of status (Chrysostom, *NPNF* 1st, vol. 10, pp. 340 f., 344 ff.).

This awareness is not likely to emerge vividly unless the pastor actually goes to the places where the poor are and, to some meaningful degree, participates in or at least clearly knows about their suffering (Wesley, *WJW*, vol. 12, pp. 310 ff.). Many protected, educated clergy have remained aloof from the crowded streets of the ghetto, or even the cramped apartments of less fortunate parishioners. Some have never felt more than a passing tinge of hunger. Would it not be wise for such pastors to learn how to leave economically secure surroundings and first learn how simply to be present with the poor? Empathic listening with patience to the voice of the poor is requisite to their pastoral care (Ambrose, *NPNF* 2nd, vol. 10, pp. 11 f.; Luther, *WLS*, vol. 1, p. 534). It requires specificity about where local needs lie. It requires more than mimeographed resolutions or abstractly generalized political programs, as a government policymaker might envision them from a neat office.

The Pastoral Epistles viewed riches as a snare that tends to distort a clear perspective. "There is a great gain in godliness with contentment, for we brought nothing into the world, we cannot take anything out of the world, but if we have food and clothing, with these we shall be content. But those who desire to be rich fall into temptation, into a snare, into many senseless and hurtful desires" (1 Tim. 6:6–9, RSV).

Early documents on care of the poor include those by Clement of Alexandria, Tertullian, Cyprian, Chrysostom, Ambrose, Augustine, and *The Apostolic Constitutions.* Among their recurrent issues are how to care equitably for widows, how to collect and distribute alms, whether the rich can be saved, how the episcopal office should administer relief to the poor, how the diaconate can implement the care of orphans, how adoptions are to be understood and handled, how poor youths may be put in the care of the master artisans for instruction, whether to tithe, and how money received on fast days should be distributed.

Calvin defined deacons as "stewards of the poor" (*Inst.,* 4.4) under whom subdeacons were to "assist . . . in poor relief." In his Draft Ecclesiastical Ordinances of 1541, Calvin conceived two functions for the deacon: "to receive, dispense, and hold goods for the poor, not only daily alms, but also possessions, rents, and pensions; the other to tend and care for the sick and administer allowances to the poor." Through the diaconate flowed a movement of resources from the resourced to the resourceless. Calvin was especially concerned, in this sensitive process of transferring these resources, that great care may be taken to not injure, but to improve, the poor (Calvin, 1541, p. 64). Bucer sought to devise a system of care for the needy so that aid was distributed "to each as was necessary for him to live decently and devoutly" (Bucer, *LCC*, vol. 19, p. 256).

Degrees of Poverty

In seeking clearer definition of the concept of poverty, we turn to a useful distinction made by Thomas Aquinas between three degrees of poverty: ordinary poverty, acute poverty, and destitution.

- The most prevalent type of poverty, ordinary poverty, is seen in the person who is able to provide only a minimal livelihood, has little or no property, and lives day by day at a standard of living that most persons in the society would regard as very low, barely eking out the necessities and unable at times even to care for basic needs such as food, clothing, and shelter. Such poverty is at or near a bare level of subsistence. Remedies for the poor at this level have been divided into two parts: (a) "Preventive remedies," that is, actions that would prevent the person from falling more deeply into acute poverty or destitution, and (b) "curative remedies," which would help change the outward social conditions and inward psychological patterns that reinforce such poverty (Thomas Aquinas, *ST*, vol. 2, pp. 1320 ff.).
- Acute poverty refers to a crisis in which the conditions for supporting life are temporarily but immediately threatened. If life is to continue, some external help is needed to make up the deficit. Care of the poor at this level consists of emergency relief.
- Destitution, or chronic extreme poverty, refers to a recurring or continuing state of being without the means of bare subsistence, destitute of resources or the means of acquiring them and in persistent absolute want of the necessities of life. It is an intensification of the previously described conditions with no potentiality for recovery by its own means. Care for the poor at this level consists of preventive, curative, and emergency remedies (Thomas Aquinas, *ST*, vol. 2, pp. 1323 ff., 1681 ff.).

Pastoral care of the poor traditionally has tried to sort out where the greatest extremity of poverty lies and to attend to that extremity first, while sustaining also its preventive and curative efforts at other levels. Curative remedies have also sought to heal the blocks that may reside within the sufferers themselves that might prevent them from becoming productive, self-sustaining persons in the society (Bucer, *LCC*, vol. 19, pp. 256 ff.).

All of these levels of concern have expressed themselves perennially as problems of pastoral care. These strategies include the removal of immediate want, spiritual encouragement to help persons to struggle with the unavoidable conditions they must face (including the demoralizing effects of poverty), and the fostering of a desire for work and independence, as well as providing means of employment and education for the poor so they can increasingly take better care of themselves (Calvin, *Inst.*, 4.4).

The undergirding value assumed in all of this is the incomparable value of life itself. When the person cannot self-supportively sustain life, it is assumed that human kindness in response to God's kindness must attend to urgent need, so that life at the minimal level can at least be sustained, even if on an inadequate basis (Thomas Aquinas, *ST*, vol. 2, pp. 1320 ff.).

The Jewish tradition of almsgiving provided the early church with a preliminary model for beginning to develop practical structures through which people could regularly channel their oblations, tithes, and gifts to the widow, the stranger, and the poor. Their purpose was to render social life and temporal existence more of a blessing than they could have been under the conditions of poverty.

Pastoral care of the poor has had to face complex abuses on two simultaneous fronts. (a) The church has fought the exploitation of the structures of charity by supposed agents of charity (who may on occasion pursue their own private interests). (b) The church has struggled for centuries against encouragement of inordinate dependency among the recipients of relief. There is a persistent historical concern for justice both in the giving and receiving of poor relief. There is a wariness in the pastoral literature toward a gullibility that would assume that anybody who asks for something *ipso facto* needs it. At times this calls for a realistic investigation of the actual needs of the poor, but in a way that is not degrading to the poor (Bucer, *LCC*, vol. 19, pp. 256 ff.).

Proportional Reasoning in Urgent Cases

The proportional rule to be applied contextually is the greater the degree of want, the greater is the urgency for relief. In order that those in acute and critical situations of poverty may simply be sustained in basic necessities, it may be necessary for others not in radical need to stand by until the more urgent emergencies are handled. Such an emergency ethic tries to achieve the greatest proportional good under the circumstances. The desperately destitute need to be taken care of first under circumstances of limited time and resources (Luther, *LCC*, vol. 18, pp. 171–89).

This brings up a general dilemma of pastoral care: the church's resources for helping the needy are always limited. The treasury of Jesus' disciples was never abundant. It was sadly limited, and therefore one might suppose that too they had to make hard decisions about who needed help most and who was most capable of using it meaningfully.

Widows and orphans were first priority. There was no superabundance of gifts to give. The apostles could not give even modestly to everybody who said they had need. The least protected by the customs of the day, widows and orphans, were cared for first (Augustine, *NPNF* 1st, vol. 3, pp 531 ff.; vol. 8, pp. 39, 664).

The basic analogy came from medicine. It assumed that in poverty we have something similar to social illness. We must take care not only to treat immediate symptoms and alleviate the pain, but also to take preventive measures to help those persons avoid the circumstances under which the conditions of poverty emerge. Classical pastoral care for the poor sought first to care for the most immediate needs— give the cup of cold water to the thirstiest, give the food to the hungriest—but then also to seek to counter the demoralizing effects of poverty, give moral guidance and spiritual encouragement, foster self-esteem and the desire for work and independence, and above all help people learn spiritually from their situation of alienation and destitution something about their moral and human capacities and responsibilities, so as to help keep them out of the very circumstances and social injustices that may have led to their alienation (Chrysostom, *NPNF* 1st, vol. 13, pp. 349 ff., 374 ff., 155).

Some contemporary political ideas of care for the poor have been damaging and shortsighted by overemphasizing the importance of social benevolence apart from any inward moral development or instruction. The result is an excessive confidence in state programs of poor relief and impersonally administered welfare that have eventually resulted in demoralization. Not so in the classical pastoral treatises that hold together these two parts; the immediate effort is to give the bread and cup, but it is accompanied by a second effort to help nullify the demoralizing effects of poverty and to help the poverty-stricken revise whatever behaviors they may have had that might have colluded with or contributed to their social alienation (Baxter, *PW*, vol. 4, pp. 383 ff.).

How is the pastor to know what to do in the midst of all of these dilemmas and conflicting claims? Bucer in the sixteenth century argued that the Holy Spirit instructs us through Scripture, teaching us how to distribute. This is not a matter of immediate divine inspiration, but rather of careful inquiry and of spiritual discernment, of listening to the actual situation of the poor so as to hear the Spirit's address through the situation (Bucer, *LCC*, vol. 19, pp. 257 f.).

Mother Teresa's care is more radical. She gives openhandedly and without prudential distinctions to "the poorest of the poor." But of course she makes some judgments about who are these "poorest," and therefore her ministry is more likely to be in Calcutta than Detroit, and more likely in Detroit than Grosse Pointe (Mother Teresa of Calcutta, 1975, pp. 53 ff.).

Principles Guiding Effects upon Recipients

The church's care for the poor traditionally has differed substantially from paternalistic, dependency-prone modern state poor relief. It begins with a realistic understanding of human nature. For the well-instructed church has always assumed that both rich and poor are sinners, prone to egocentric interpretations of economic interest (R. Niebuhr, 1932b, chaps. 2–5).

The poor have potential moral and spiritual advantages over the rich through their potential learning of radical dependence upon God. Nonetheless, rich and poor alike are prone to press their self-assertive interests so as not to take into account the common welfare and to rationalize their economic behavior in terms of ideals that subtly serve their private or group interest. Though care for the poor has been a consistent interest of Christian ministry, it has never proceeded on illusory assumptions of the infinite perfectability of economic life or the intrinsic good will of either rich or poor, at least not prior to the nineteenth century (R. Niebuhr, 1932a).

Some modern efforts at relief have tended to proceed on the opposite, optimistic assumption present in most evolutionary utopianisms that human nature is seldom egocentric or prone to sin, that history is getting better and better, that there is an inevitable increase of abundance due to scientific progress with no retrogress possible, and that therefore we can afford to be equally generous toward everybody who claims need, and can assume that no abuses will occur among either administrators or recipients. These are grossly optimistic assumptions about human nature that could only have prevailed in an expanding economy and which have been largely proven wrong through their subsequent history. This is the stuff that paternalism is made of (Baxter, *PW*, vol. 4, pp. 383 ff.; Hoppin, 1884, pp. 541 ff.).

It is useful to state several principles of the historical pastoral care for the poor that seek to avoid abuses harmful to the commonweal, the poor, and even those who are seeking to help them. Keep in mind that these guidelines on service to the poor are not intended to reduce, but rather to improve, the quality of relief to the poor and the long-term prospect of the poor. Far from being motivated by cynicism or penuriousness, they are, rather, motivated by the hope of finding effective and reasonable ways of channeling limited resources to those who have greater needs. They are offered in awareness of the stark fact that rich and poor as sinners are prone to assert their interests inordinately, and under the guise of absolute ideal values pitch their appeals to others. Overt claims of absolute disinterestedness from either the rich or the poor are suspect (R. Niebuhr, 1932b).

Here then are some of the principles that we find in the historical pastoral tradition that have proven themselves realistic through the test of experience and that still have much relevance to modern care for the poor. Some have been neglected in modern state-administered welfare, which has at times been informed by wildly optimistic assumptions about human incorruptibility.

The end of relief effort is the improvement of resources, competencies, self-esteem, and productive capacity of the poor, rather than the smug sense of righteousness or moral self-congratulation of the givers (Bucer, *LCC*, vol. 19, pp. 256 ff.).

The search for justice in human society is intrinsic to the prophetic task of ministry (Augustine, *NPNF* 1st, vol. 2, pp. 66 ff., 284 ff., 337 ff.; Thomas Aquinas, *ST*, vol. 2, pp. 1435 ff.; Calvin, *LCC*, vol. 22, pp. 56 ff.; *Inst.*, 4.4, 4.20; R. Niebuhr, 1931, 1941). It is expressed through preaching, but also through practical attempts to exercise due influence in a democratic society.

We best minister to the poor when we help the poor practically to seek resources in themselves. Acts of mercy should maintain and guard the dignity of recipients, respecting whatever competencies they have (*Apostolic Constitutions, ANF*, vol. 7, pp. 433 ff.). Healthy self-esteem is never best achieved by a paternalist dole without concern for developing self-initiative. That elicits a sense of dependency that diminishes self-esteem. Christian care for the poor has known this for a long time, but it has become lost in the maze of government economic policy formation. "A charity that destroys the principle of self-activity, and of personal energy and responsibility, on the part of the poor, is perhaps as bad as charity that systematizes it into a science that kills all spontaneity of heart and act" (Hoppin, 1884, p. 538).

The maxim that "idleness is the mother of famine" was repeatedly invoked in early Christian documents (*Apostolic Constitutions, ANF*, vol. 7, pp. 434 f.; Clementina, *ANF*, vol. 8, pp. 58 ff.). Oft quoted were such proverbs as, "Drink and greed will end in poverty and drunken stupor goes in rags" (Prov. 23:21) or the proverb about the sluggard who "plunges his hand in the dish but will not so much as lift it to his mouth" (Prov. 19:24). If laziness is demeaning, alms must not encourage it. "The fool folds his arms and wastes away" (Eccles. 4:5).

Idlers who could "sustain themselves by their own powers" were thought to be unjustly taking food away from the truly poor when they accept help furtively (Bucer, *LCC*, vol. 19, p. 257). "He that hath and receives in hypocrisy and through idleness, instead of working and assisting others, shall be obnoxious." Why such harsh language? Listen carefully to the reason: "Because he has snatched away the morsel of the needy" (*Apostolic Constitutions, ANF*, vol. 7, pp. 430 f.). For this reason many early pastoral instructions urged that rather than giving money in relief of the poor it is better to provide tools for self-help or material resources that will encourage self-reliance rather than dependency.

Do not provide support that will encourage people to continue in idleness leading to demoralization. There never was in the New Testament any assumption that people would simply receive charity and not give what they are able to give or not work if they are able. In fact, there is a constant awareness of the obligation to labor. "If anyone will not work" (that is, work to their ability, their reasonable capacity), "let him not eat" (2 Thess. 3:10, RSV). Paul admonished the Thessalonians to "live quietly, mind your own affairs, and work with your hands . . . so that you may command the respect of outsiders and be dependent on nobody" (1 Thess. 4:11–12, RSV).

The underlying principle of this rule was that good relief for the poor is not intended to reinforce sin but to relieve need, not to increase vice but to give persons the possibility of improvement in virtue so as to increase their happiness.

The arena of relief of the poor is subject to many deceptions, so much so that the distributor may be tempted toward cynicism and lose respect for the poor whom he is called to serve. "Beware that we do not engender poverty by the very pains by which we seek to destroy it" (Vinet, 1853, p. 298). One could inadvertently tend to encourage poverty by creating situations of dependency in which idleness and loss of self-respect become normative and expected conditions.

Relief for the poor should never be provided in such a way that it "adds the affliction of shame to the affliction of poverty" (Bucer, *LCC,* vol. 19, p. 313). Extraordinary sensitivity should be used in the administration of relief so that the recipients will not be or feel demeaned by it. Washington Gladden, the great Social Gospel advocate who tried to pursuade his denomination to turn down a large gift from Standard Oil as tainted money, wrote: "The deepest need of these poor is the need of . . . self-respect. . . . Whatever tends to lighten their sense of responsibility and weaken their self-reliance is mistaken kindness" (Gladden, 1898, p. 454).

Even when it is not within the power of either the church or society to solve massive international economic problems, it is always possible for Christians to offer faith, hope, and love. Gladden grasped this clearly: "In all pastoral care for the poor, the material must be the means, the spiritual the final aim in the labor. 'The soul of caring for the poor is caring for the soul' according to Elizabeth Fry's maxim" (Gladden, 1898, p. 455).

The Nearer the Neighbor the Greater the Responsibility

A general principle is operative in much traditional Christian care for the poor that hinges on the notion of physical or symbolic proximity. Although it is an abusable principle, it deserves thoughtful reconsideration in our time. Its central idea: The closer the neighbor is to the one who has resources, the greater the opportunity and responsibility of that person to be responsive to those needs (Luther, *LCC,* vol. 18, pp. 184 ff., 322 ff.).

Neighbor precisely means "the next one" or "nearest one," "the one who concretely claims you with immediate need" (*DNTT,* vol. 1, pp. 254

ff.). If that need is urgent, all the more equitable is it for the person
nearer at hand to respond to it. Tomorrow the situation could be reversed.

As a result of this principle there has been a persistent localization
and personalization tendency in Christian pastoral care of the poor.
Rather than plan vast programs for persons at great distances away, the
essential energy of Christian care has been the parish itself where some
live in need, others in relative abundance. The pastor is commissioned
to search out those who are in greatest need and appeal on their behalf
to those who have both conscience and resources. Pastors who rely solely on government programs to help people may have circumvented this
responsibility.

The Church is commissioned

Jeremy Taylor beautifully wrote that if you go to the poor and "minister with your own hand what your heart hath first decreed, you will
find your heart endeared and made familiar with the needs and with
the persons of the poor, those excellent images of Christ" (Taylor,
TPW, vol. 2, p. 47). Taylor argued that the precepts of charity are not
directed indefinitely to general instances of need but rather to "he that
is in thy sight." What if the pastor has no resources? "If thou hast no
money, yet thou must have mercy." Similarly Kierkegaard (1847, pp.
153 ff.) urged us to "love those we see."

The personal focus of Christian benevolent activity is not a denial of
the universal scope of benevolence to which Paul referred in Gal. 6:10,
"As opportunity offers, let us work for the good of all." Yet it is always
only in some particular locale that the neighbor can be served. It is
impossible to serve everyone at everytime, even though Christ's ministry reaches out in various times and places for all.

What if one cannot be everywhere at all times serving every needy
person? Thomas Aquinas deftly anticipated this question: "Charity
binds us, though not actually doing good to someone, to be prepared in
mind to do good to anyone." For, "Since the love of charity extends to
all, beneficence also should extend to all, according as time and space
require" (*ST*, vol 2, p. 1321). It is possible to intend good for all, yet it
is impossible actually to do concrete good all the time to every person in
the whole world. Nonetheless, it is possible to have a good will to all.
Thomas thought that this was "manifested most profoundly when we
pray for all." Augustine also held together the principles of universal
love and the immediate claim of the proximate neighbor: "All . . . are to
be loved equally. But since you cannot do good to all, you are to pay
special regard to those who, by accidents of time, or place, or circumstance, are brought into closer connection with you" (*NPNF* 1st, vol. 2,
p. 530).

Yet the proximity principle does not refer merely to physical nearness. The tradition has also had in mind symbolic types of nearness. In
kinship there is an obvious nearness of natural affinity. With fellow

citizens there is a "nearness of civic matters." Among the faithful there is a nearness felt in spiritual insight (Thomas Aquinas, *ST*, vol. 2, pp. 1298 ff.). It is by this "law of affinity" that we are called to care most immediately for those urgent needs that are nearest to us. The person in the next town is not likely to come over to our town and take care of us except for one noteworthy exception. It is kinship, which is a more compelling level of "nearness." The person in Switzerland, however well intentioned, is less likely to come and take care of the poor in our vicinity, unless we are by some means "brought near" (i.e., made a neighbor) through some personal affinity. This principle has largely been neglected in the era of humanitarian religion and centralization politics, which have on the whole shifted charitable and benevolent activity away from locales and toward state and federal capitals and distant administrative offices.

This line of reasoning must not end with the evasion that if a stranger comes into your town, you have no responsibility. Rather, it is precisely the fact that it is your town into which the stranger comes that makes it imperative that you respond. If everybody took care of their own towns, it was assumed, the poor would more likely be cared for than if everybody tried to take care of everybody else's town through an impersonal centrist philosophy.

Bucer forcefully stated the proximity principle: "If any needy persons belong to anyone's circle, either by blood or marriage or by any other special relationship or particular custom, it is certainly their duty, if they have the means of the Lord, to provide for their own the necessities of life. . . ." Why? If every family takes care of its own, the ministry therefore will have more resources to take care of those "who have no home or family" (Bucer, *LCC*, vol. 19, p. 307). "Those whom the Lord has given to us in special close relationships fall particularly under the second great commandment, in which the whole law is contained and fulfilled so that thou shalt love thy neighbor as thyself (Matt. 22:39)" (Bucer, *LCC*, vol. 19, p. 307).

If *neighbor* means the closest one, who is closer than the family? Thus, a crucial ancillary task in the teaching office of pastoral care of the poor is to teach families their responsibility in relation to the less fortunate or poor or sick within their own families (as their nearest neighbors) in order to free the church to minister to those who have no family.

Bucer does not stop at the family. The principle is extended into the community so as to help sustain "those who do not have any family assistance," and if any locality is so hard pressed that it cannot take care of its poor, then a wider organization of responsibilities may be justly involved, so that no one will be without resources for survival. Bucer regarded this as having a New Testament prototype in the example of Paul (Rom. 15:26–27) who went out to the gentile (relatively wealthier) churches to help the impoverished church in Judea. The theological principle: we are all "members one of another" (Eph. 4:25).

Not only did the early church provide for the poor in its own neighborhood. When great calamities occurred, there were often complex relief efforts for those far away. Cyprian reports that when Christian men and women of Numidia were taken captive, the Christians of Carthage at a great distance away raised money for their ransom (Cyprian, *ANF,* vol. 5, p. 355).

It was assumed in the New Testament that charity begins, but does not end, at home. It extends outwardly to members of the Christian community, to other communities, to non-Christians (Gal. 6:9–10), and to the whole world (1 John 4).

The mercy of God is to be shared with all, and without discrimination on the basis of race, sex, clan, or nationality. Charity is not just for "people like us." Nonetheless, the specific place where the claim of charity is addressed is always some particular locale. There the universality of God's love penetrates the highly specific vectors of local need (Cyprian, *ANF,* vol. 5, p. 314; Cooke, 1976, pp. 390 ff.).

Guidelines for Maintaining the Integrity of the Giver

Having collected resources for the resourceless, the ministry has been charged with very careful, aboveboard, discreet, absolutely honest management of whatever resources have been collected. The whole exchange should be above suspicion. It should be sensitive to the feelings and needs of both the giver and the recipient, so as not to increase the pride of the giver or engender the loss of self-esteem of the recipient. Deacons are admonished by Calvin to "distribute these goods to whom they are owed, with the greatest awe and reverence, as if in God's presence" (Calvin, *Inst.,* 4.4).

Funds for the poor are to be applied carefully "to the use for which they were originally consecrated to the Lord." If there is any suspicion of abuse there should be an investigation by church authorities, for in that case those who defraud would be "appropriating to themselves what belongs to the church . . . so that the poor are oppressed" (The Council of Antioch, *NPNF* 2nd, vol. 14, p. 249).

"Keep scrupulously accurate records, since some are apt to misconstrue the actions of ministers, and it is of so great moment that they should not lie open to any suspicion of misapplying charitable funds, that it will be generally most prudent for them not to desire to distribute any part of them but to persons whom they expressly name" (Gerard, 1799, p. 10).

Should money be accepted that has been obtained unjustly, from disreputable sources? There is a massive pastoral literature that argues that those funds should in good conscience be rejected. In *The Apostolic Constitutions,* the church is urged "to avoid corrupt dealers and not receive their gifts," avoid "gifts from extortioners, those that oppress the widow and overbear the orphan and fill prisons with the innocent" (*ANF*, vol. 7, p. 434). The church can live without tainted gratuities.

Pastoral Counsel of the Poor

The tone and style of spiritual direction of the poor begins with deep empathy for their predicament. The poor "ought to have a great share in the concern of [Christ's] ministers" (Wilson, 1708, p. 412). Bishop Wilson summarized the pastor's duty to the poor in three phases: "to relieve, to instruct, and to comfort" (Wilson, 1708, p. 412). The sequence begins with immediate acts of relief, but does not end there. To relief work is added the pedagogical function of instruction of the poor regarding moral conscience and spiritual growth, and to these are added a caring spirit of consolation.

A major pastoral concern in spiritually counseling the poor has to do with meeting honestly the wrenching question of why God permits poverty. That brings back into focus the issues of pastoral theodicy that we have previously discussed. They take on an especially poignant form in the case of poverty, which often has to do with economic influences that are far removed from the control of the suffering individuals involved. Innocent suffering is a persistent problem of pastoral care of the poor. The working pastor may be contextually required to offer a serious spur-of-the-moment pastoral theodicy concerning the poor. How do we speak well of God's insurmountable power and love in relation to the awesome fact of entrenched social inequities?

Such questions have troubled Christian ministry from its beginnings. In order to present at least one classical model of pastoral counsel for the poor, we will use Richard Baxter's spiritual directions for the poor as a preliminary guide.

- No condition of life is so lowly or poor but that it may become sanctified and fruitful to us, if we understand it in relationship to providence. The pastor is able to offer to the poor an even greater kindness than if he prayed simply that they be delivered from poverty and given riches. Baxter understood it to be a part of the minister's task to teach spiritual truth to the dispossessed, not on the assumption that it can be a substitute for their physical needs, but as a pastoral duty owed them. What the poor need even more than money is an understanding of their situation before God and before their neighbor (Baxter, *PW*, vol. 4, p. 379). They need to discover that they themselves are of inestimable worth, and loved by God.
- Trust providence. God "will not allow you to be tested above your powers" (1 Cor. 10:13). Since God's love toward you is greater than your love toward yourself, God will provide in ways that transcend your vision (Baxter, *PW*, vol. 4, p. 380).

- You will be saved from many self-deceptions and miscalculations if you keep in mind that riches can be as dangerous to the soul as poverty. Jesus himself remarked how few of the rich can enter the kingdom of Heaven, and that it is easier for a camel to go through the eye of a needle than a rich man to enter the kingdom of God. If the spiritual dangers of riches are greater than the dangers of poverty, the faithful may no longer pray thoughtlessly for riches, except to pray that through whatever resources may come, they may be given grace do good to others (Baxter, *PW*, vol. 4, p. 381; cf. Gregory, *ACW*, vol. 11, pp. 182 ff.).

- There are, indeed, some sins that tend toward poverty: ill-gotten gain, pride, gluttony, drunkenness, slothfulness, and idleness. The unjust acquiring of wealth is "like fire in the thatch," for precisely because it "came easy," it will tend toward wastefulness. Baxter thought that there was a subtle affinity between gluttony and drunkenness, on the one hand, and spiritual depression on the other (*PW*, vol. 4, p. 382). For gluttony and drunkenness may detract from the productivity that is itself an antidote to poverty. Several proverbs suggest that sloth tends naturally to want (Prov. 23:20; 12:24).

- The poor may be tempted inordinately to think that worldly riches will elicit happiness. The poor may tend, perhaps more than the rich, to be inordinately vexed and made anxious about the immediate future. They may also face stronger temptations to impatience and covetousness. They may need to resist more directly the temptation to be eaten away by hatred and malice toward those who are wealthy (Baxter, *PW*, vol. 4, pp. 383 f.).

- The poor may in time become tempted to use unlawful means to supply their wants. They may in extremity be driven to use otherwise deplored means, such as flattery or theft, murder or desperate revolution. They may be tempted to neglect their spiritual duties in the interest of material improvement. They may be tempted by virtue of their immediate struggle with poverty to neglect the education of children. All of these temptations must be earnestly dealt with by pastoral support and searching counsel (Baxter, *PW*, vol. 4, p. 385).

- Remember that Christ himself chose a life of poverty. So it is not a life that is dishonorable in the Christian community. Christ himself had no place to lay his head. It is well for the poor to keep in mind that at the point of death, all historical benefits end. There the rich will be just as poor as the poorest. "Naked they came into the world and naked they must go out. . . . It is no more comfort to die rich than poor. . . . The more pleasant the world is to them, the more it grieves them to leave it" (Baxter, *PW*, vol. 4, p. 388). For these and other reasons, poverty need not always be absolutely despised by the Christian. It may be endured and conceived as an occasion for potential spiritual growth and moral development.

- Any pastor who teaches these things does well to teach them out of a commitment to voluntary poverty or a willingness to live modestly on the gifts of laity, as a basis for validating and making credible the teaching that poverty can be a context for spiritual increase.

These are among the pastoral instructions offered by Baxter to the poor, not as a substitute for physical relief but as an accompaniment to it. Although modern hedonism will find many of these points objectionable, they are due for serious reconsideration. The last point leads directly into a perennial concern of classical pastoral care: the ideal of voluntary poverty.

The Psychology of Voluntary Poverty

Long before Baxter, Boethius had wisely observed that "greed is never satisfied" and that "wealth can not remove want." Wealth tends to create a gnawing desire for more wealth, which is never quite adequately fulfilled. Greed always wants more because it lives out of desire. What desire means is that one lacks something. Until one deals with the problem of desire one has not dealt with the problem of happiness. Money does not solve the problem of desire. Money tends to elicit a continuing, and even increased, desire for more things (Boethius, 524).

John Chrysostom treated this psychological syndrome in an extremely subtle and clear way. What causes pleasure, he argued, does not lie in the object of pleasure itself but in the relationship that one has to the object. So the disposition of the subject is important in whether something is experienced as pleasurable. For example, if you come to a table hungry, the food tastes better. In fact, the plainest food obviously tastes better when one is hungry than a gourmet dinner when one is not. The wealthy tend to mistake this psychological paradox. They may continue to stuff themselves with delicacies without ever becoming hungry, to spread fine condiments, delicacies, and "a thousand exquisite preparations for the palate" constantly before them, yet with little sensation of pleasure because their appetite is not excited by hunger. The ironic conclusion: you must experience hunger if you are going to enjoy the pleasure of eating (Chrysostom, *NPNF* 1st, vol. 9, p. 352). Scripture had already grasped this subtle point: "A man full fed refuses honey but even bitter food tastes sweet to a hungry man" (Prov. 27:7).

Similarly, Chrysostom argued that what makes sleep sweet is not a soft couch but the fatigue, the drowsiness, that comes from work, and therefore from the need of sleep. "Sweet is the sleep of the laborer whether he eats little or much; but the rich man owns too much and can not sleep" (Eccles. 5:12). The poor may own something that the rich do not possess. The rich want to avoid work and sleep well. The poor can not avoid work, and their sleep is sweet. The rich eat an excess of food without exercise and expect to sleep, but they can not. The poor may be capable of greater pleasure than the rich, because of their subjective relationship to the object of pleasure (Chrysostom, *NPNF* 1st, vol. 9, p. 352).

Chrysostom then turned to counsel the poor concerning the demeaning things that may happen to them. It is a counsel against collusion. "The insult is either created or destroyed, not by the intention of those who insult, but by the disposition of those who bear it. For example. Someone hath insulted thee with much language, fit or unfit to repeat. If thou shalt laugh at the insults . . . thou art not insulted. . . . Insults are constituted real and dishonorable ones, not from the folly of those who offered them, but from the [collusion] of the insulted. For if we know how to be truly wise, we are incapable of being insulted" (Chrysostom, *NPNF* 1st, vol. 9, p. 353).

Here we have a remarkable psychological argument about the power of the poor not to allow themselves to be victimized by unnecessary collusions. From this, the poor have gained an extraordinary sense of strength, self-esteem, power, and personal integrity. This is the special power of the poor, according to Chrysostom. It is not their wealth, but their pleasure, their strengthened will, and their spirits made wise by crisis (Chrysostom, *NPNF,* 1st, vol. 9, p. 353).

In a period in which there is so much talk about the poor by middle-class social idealists who have little living experience or working closeness with the poor, who know little about the poor except from books, there is much paternalistic talk about victimization and oppression. But such persons often do not understand the strength, gifts, and grace of the poor. All these things Chrysostom was saying about the poor are evident to anyone who has lived and worked with the poor and knows them well. The strong among the poor are those who are not, in an overweening sense, envious of the rich. Mightily though they struggle to improve their lot, they do not see their final self-definition in relation to the wealth of the wealthy.

Mother Teresa has often said that she feels extraordinarily privileged to care for the poor. Their hearts are educated by limitation. They are relatively freer from the corruptions of pride (Mother Teresa of Calcutta, 1975, pp. 30 f., 39 ff.).

Voluntary Poverty and the Support of Ministry

The pastor is by ordination, scriptural mandate, and long historical tradition deeply involved both in administration of funds for the poor and solicitation of funds from the wealthy on behalf of the poor. It is therefore an important part of preparation for pastoral care for the poor to have in mind the essential reasoning of the pastoral tradition concerning wealth and poverty.

Through preaching and pastoral care, the minister will have occasion to give instruction and spiritual direction to those who have temporal resources. At these times the pastor must be prepared to state clearly why the poor have a legitimate moral claim on the resources of the wealthy.

Even though the tradition is clearly aware that wealth carries with it temptations toward idolatry and pride, nonetheless, wealth has not been universally condemned outright. In fact there are substantial arguments in the tradition that have given support to the modest accumulation of wealth for survival. By analogy from nature, it has been argued that all animal life is required at times to gather and preserve what is needed for survival. Bees and ants, for example, bring goods into stores so as to help them live through seasons of want. If all life has a duty to preserve itself, it can only do so at times by means of stored foods and reserved assets. Accordingly, the prudent person is obliged to gather and store resources for winter survival and seasons of want. Hoarding is rejected as an excess of a good thing and therefore a vice. In its appropriate proportion, however, the gathering and storing instinct or natural appetite to conserve was indeed thought to be the good gift of God (Thomas Aquinas, *ST*, vol. 2, pp. 1326, 1682 ff.).

Wisdom seeks to preserve this delicate balance between survival and idolatrous pride: "Give me neither poverty nor wealth, provide me only with the food I need. If I have too much, I shall deny thee and say, 'Who is the Lord?' If I am reduced to poverty, I shall steal and blacken the name of my God" (Prov. 30:8–9).

In such scriptures we see a rule of proportionality at work. In relation to property and worldly goods, pastoral wisdom pursues a middle way between two extremes each of which may lead to corruption. Thomas Aquinas argued that extremes of wealth and destitution are both temptations to vice. "There is a virtue of liberality, which gives what should be given and retains what should be retained. But the vice of defect is illiberality, which retains the things which should not be retained" ("On Providence," *SCG*, vol. 3, p. 169). Prodigality is the opposite vice of excess in which everything valuable is thoughtlessly given away (*ST*, vol. 2, p. 1692 f.; Oden, 1976a, chaps. 4–8).

Yet we must keep in tension with this the more radical command of Jesus to the rich young ruler to "sell all and give to the poor" (Mark 10:21; Luke 18:22), which some have argued is normative for the Christian life at all times. Others argue that it can not be normative for persons with families and hungry dependents. Let us suppose that someone is going to sell all possessions and give all to the poor, following Jesus' radical call to voluntary poverty. This is not as easy to adopt consistently as one might at first think. For the funds disappear, and life is left, and cannot thereafter continue, without some food and support. Furthermore, giving away all of one's accumulated resources is a radical, symbolic act that can only be done once; then something will have to be done for food and shelter the next day. Trusting God's providence as do the lilies and the birds has not usually implied a complete neglect of rational planning, foresight, and self-initiative.

A second way of trying to obey this command to sell all and give to the poor is to have common possessions with other believers from whom provision is made for individuals according to their need. Yet disagreements may emerge among the recipients as to who has the greatest need. This may become an impediment to the very life of serenity and prayer that the shared possessions are seeking to support (Thomas Aquinas, *SCG,* vol. 3).

In the light of the deficits of these arguments, Thomas proceeded to argue for a better way, which in its basic reasoning remains applicable not only to monastic life but also to the laity's support of the church's mission to the poor. Those who are called to serve the poor through a frugal life of voluntary poverty still may live on the modest resources freely offered by others who wish to support their mission to the poor. Lay persons whose natural obligations to their families make it morally reasonable that they not give away all their wealth may nevertheless wish to make contributions to this ministry that itself is voluntarily poor. Ministry does not therefore seek to gain money for itself, but it seeks to be a channel through which the church can minister to the needy. This was the excellent way that women, according to Luke 8:2–3, ministered to Christ out of their substance.

Clergy are therefore assumed to be committed not to developing stores of wealth for their own benefit, but to looking to God for providential support from those who have jobs and resources and who wish to contribute to Christ's mission and thereby extend their offices of mercy to those whom they would not otherwise have time to serve. Ministry should not passively wait for resources to come. That would be to tempt God. Nor are ministers to ignore the necessities of food, shelter, and clothing to support the body in order that they may accomplish their moral and spiritual mission. In the central Christian tradition there is very little Docetism or Manichaeanism that would insist flatly that the body is directly evil. Rather, the body is seen as a good means to a higher end.

A well-ordered ministry deserves the support of lay Christians. It lives modestly but, one would hope, with reasonable food, shelter, clothing, and necessity, all of which must be assessed relative to changing historical conditions (cf. *Seven Ecumenical Councils, NPNF* 2nd, vol. 14, pp. 359 ff., Bucer, *LCC,* vol. 19. pp. 306–315).

It is on this basis that Thomas argued that "riches are good to the extent that they advance the practice of virtue, but if this measure is departed from, so that the practice of virtue is hindered, they are not to be numbered among goods but among evils" (*SCG,* vol. 3, p. 177). Likewise, poverty is regarded as praiseworthy insofar as it frees persons "from vices in which some are involved through riches" (ibid., p. 177).

So wealth may be useful when it is ordered to its proper end, or it may be harmful if it tempts us to pride or avarice. "Insofar as poverty takes away the good which results from riches, namely, the assisting of others and the support of oneself, it is purely an evil" (Thomas Aquinas, *SCG*, vol. 3, p. 178). The clergy who wish not to be involved in the acquisition of money but rather in the service of the poor nonetheless need food to support their lives. They have a need for modest temporal resources to support their mission. But "poverty in itself is not good, only insofar as it liberates from those things whereby a [person] is hindered from intending spiritual things" (*SCG*, vol. 3, p. 179).

Voluntary poverty is not an unmitigated good, and neither is the acquisition of wealth an unmitigated evil. Both are potential goods the use of which becomes good or evil. Thomas argues: "Riches are a definite good for man[kind] when they are ordered to the good of reason, though not in themselves. Hence, nothing prevents poverty from being a greater good, provided one is ordered to a more perfect good by it" (*SCG*, vol. 3, p. 180).

"Tentmaking ministries" constitute another alternative: living off the labor of one's own hands to support oneself in ministry, according to the pattern of Paul (2 Thess. 3:8 ff.). Its limitations: it may not get away from the heaviness of the task of making a living and owning possessions, and it may rationalize its own self-interest with an ideology of altruism.

So the moral reasoning that most often defends and explains the resolution of this dilemma is something like this: the church's ordered ministry, if well understood, is presumed to be committed to voluntary poverty. It will live from those things that are freely offered by others who wish to support its ministry. "There is nothing disgraceful in [ministers] living on the grace of others, because they make a greater return on their part, receiving temporal support, but in regard to others, contributing to progress in spiritual matters" (Thomas Aquinas, *SCG*, vol. 3, p. 186; cf. *Didache, AF*, p. 317).

Counsel of the Rich on Behalf of the Poor

Richard Baxter summarized these penetrating spiritual counsels for the rich:

- Your wealth should not be considered a part of your spiritual happiness. It does not reconcile you to God. If riches tempt you to love them above God, then they have undone you.
- Do not assume that you will never be put to the test of losing wealth once you have come into dependency upon it. That is like the

       patient who seeks to be cured by a physician but desperately hopes
       that the physician will not prescribe a difficult remedy.

- Do not make harsh or cynical judgments about the poor as if they
  were always lazy. For in such partiality you only deceive yourselves
  and misunderstand your situation before the poor and before God
  (Baxter, *PW,* vol. 4, pp. 389 ff.).

The Council of Gangra in 345 stated, "We do not condemn life
enjoyed with uprightness and beneficence; and we commend plainness
and frugality . . . and we bless exceeding charities done by the brethren
to the poor, according to the traditions of the church" (*Seven Ecumenical
Councils, NPNF* 2nd, vol. 14, p. 101). This conciliar view reflects the
biblical assumption that despite temptations to abuse, wealth in itself is
not evil, that it can be a blessing, as in the case of Abraham, that can be
regarded as the gift of God.

    However, it brings with it special responsibilities of liberality toward
the needy. It also brings with it special dangers (Clement of Alexandria,
ANF, vol. 2, p. 591). For we are tempted to trust in it (Ps. 52:7) or not
to acknowledge God as the ultimate source of all temporal blessings
(Hosea 2:8). In Jesus' parable of the sower "the false glamor of wealth"
is what chokes the word and makes it barren and unfruitful (Matt. 13:
22). 1 Tim. 6:9 f. describes not money but the love of money as the root
of many evils.

    Because of these temptations and dangers into which wealth so
often falls, the rich are more frequently denounced as a class in Scripture than the poor, who have often been seen as the object of the
special mercy and promised blessing of God. Poverty is more likely to
form the seedbed of strong faith, whereas riches may more likely dead-
en faith. The church in Laodicea was portrayed saying to itself, "How
rich I am, how well I have done. I have everything I want," to which the
writer responded, "In fact, though you do not know it, you are the most
pitiful wretch, poor, blind and naked" (Rev. 3:17).

    The crucial text of pastoral instruction to the wealthy is found in 1
Tim. 6:17–19: "Instruct those who are rich in this world's goods not to
be proud, and not to fix their hopes on so uncertain a thing as money,
but upon God who endows us richly with all things to enjoy. Tell them
to do good and to grow rich in noble actions, to be ready to give away
and to share, and to acquire a treasure which will form a good foundation for the future. Thus they will grasp the life that is life indeed."

    John Chrysostom's exegesis of 1 Tim. 6 and his treatise on the stat-
utes (*NPNF* 1st, vol. 9, pp. 348 ff.) constitute a self-examination for the
wealthy. For those who labor for wealth alone and trust in its power,
making it their god, "the labor is certain but the enjoyment is uncertain." Chrysostom was fascinated by the psychology of coveteousness,

especially the relationship of pride and financial power. "The coveteous man is not rich; he is in want of many things, and while he needs many things he can never be rich. The coveteous man is a keeper, not a master, of wealth, a slave, not a lord." The truly rich person "is not one who is in possession of much, but one who gives much. Abraham was rich, but he was not covetous; for he turned not his thoughts to the house of this man, nor prided in the wealth of that man; but going forth he looked around wherever there chanced to be a stranger, or a poor man, in order that he might succor poverty, and hospitably entertain the traveler" (p. 349).

Chrysostom argued that the poor are much more prepared for human contingencies and historical crises than are the wealthy, who tend to be perplexed by them, "wandering about, seeking where they might bury their gold." Poverty is a training ground for responsiveness, wit, alertness, and flexibility.

The pastor has the responsibility to counsel the rich that they are not proprietors but only stewards, for the earth is the Lord's (Ps. 19). Those who have received more than others have more to account for.

The Grace of Generosity

Happily we have in 2 Cor. 8 a clear biblical case study of the theological underpinnings of pastoral solicitation for the poor. Having reported to the Corinthians about the generosity of the congregations of Macedonia, Paul clearly pointed out that God the Spirit was at work in the Macedonian community to elicit the grace of generosity, even "from the depths of their poverty" (v. 2). They have not just given, but they have given "to the limit of their resources, as I can testify, and even beyond that limit . . . and their givings surpassed our expectations; for they gave their very selves."

Paul was praying for the same gift to be given the Corinthians. He promised to send Titus along to "bring this work of generosity to its completion" (v. 6). Paul did not approach this question coercively. He did not think of this appeal as "an order" (v. 8), but he recognized that it did "put love to the test." Here is the essential frame of reference in which the claim of the poor was made crystal clear: "For you know how generous our Lord Jesus Christ has been: he was rich, for your sake he became poor, so that through his poverty you might become rich" (v. 9). The meaning implicit in Christian contributions to the poor is directly linked with the gift of God in Christ who voluntarily "became poor," entered into our human situation with its limits, allowing himself to become defenseless and vulnerable.

The proportional principle: "Give according to your means" (v. 11). Paul was not even asking them to give "at the cost of hardship to yourselves" (v. 14). Rather, an indirect principle of equity was at work. Christ was asking that from their surplus somebody else's dire need should be supplied; for someday you will have a similar need, and from someone else's surplus you will be supplied. The result of this effort at equity would be that the person "who got much had no more than enough and the [person] who got little did not go short" (2 Cor. 8:15).

Paul thought it important to "guard against any criticism of our handling of this generous gift." He was aware that the process of receiving and channeling money from the resourceful to the resourceless was subject to many challenges of fraud and deception. That is all the more reason why he wanted to select persons "whose reputation is high among our congregations everywhere for [their] services to the gospel." He thought Titus to be one such person, and for this reason he was sent on this mission.

Paul's maxim of giving was, "Remember: sparse sowing, sparse reaping; sow bountifully, and you will reap bountifully. Each person should give as he has decided for himself; there should be no reluctance, no sense of compulsion; God loves a cheerful giver" (2 Cor. 9:6). There is a marvelous balance of freedom, yet moral seriousness—without a sense of coercion or heavy-laden guilt—coupled with the promise that God will bring to fruition what we provide. "He will multiply it and swell the harvest of your benevolence" (v. 10).

Conclusion: On the Guilt of Wealth and the Anxiety of Poverty

Both the rich and the poor deserve and are due pastoral counsel, but in different ways according to their special needs. One might speculate that whereas guilt hangs potentially heavier upon the rich, anxiety is a greater temptation and problem for the poor. The rich have the power to act, therefore must feel accountable for their action, and therefore must bear the weight of memory of negated values, whereas the poor have less temporal resources for which to be accountable.

These two types of pastoral instruction concerning the use of worldly goods correlate with two principal angles of vision on pastoral care: care for the guilty and care for the anxious (Oden, 1969, chaps. 1, 2). Although, obviously, rich people can be anxious and poor people can be guilty, on the whole there is reason to believe that the greater weight of anxiety would fall to the poor, and guilt, to the rich. In both cases pastoral care concerns itself not only with physical necessities but also with moral conscience, idolatry, and spiritual formation.

REFERENCES AND FURTHER READING

Among classical Christian texts on pastoral care of the poor, see Irenaeus (*ANF*, vol. 1), The Pastor of Hermas (*ANF*, vol. 1, pp. 32 ff.), Didache (*AF*, pp. 317 ff.), Clement of Alexandria (*ANF*, vol. 2, pp. 591 ff.), Tertullian (*ANF*, vol. 3), Cyprian (*ANF*, vol. 5, pp. 314 ff.), Hippolytus (*ANF*, vol. 5), *Apostolic Constitutions* (*ANF*, vol. 7), Eusebius (*NPNF* 2nd, vol. 1), Ambrose (*NPNF* 2nd, vol. 10), Augustine (*NPNF* 1st, vols. 2, 3), Chrysostom (*NPNF* 1st, vol. 9), *Seven Ecumeni-*

cal Councils (*NPNF* 2nd, vol. 14), Gregory (*ACW*, vol. 11, pp. 92 ff.), Francis of Assisi (d. 1226), Thomas Aquinas (d. 1274), Bucer (1523), Luther (d. 1546), Calvin (1559, 3.7, 4.4, 4.5), Taylor (d. 1667), Baxter (d. 1691), Burnet (1692), Wilson (1708), Gibson (1717), Wesley (d. 1791), and Gerard (1799).

Among nineteenth-century writers on care for the poor, see Kierkegaard (1847), Vinet (1853), Kidder (1871), Hoppin (1884), and Gladden (1898). For more recent discussions, see Troeltsch (1931 ed.), Reinhold Niebuhr (1932a, 1932b, 1943, 1959), Barth (1936 ff.), G. H. Williams (1962), Fensham (1962), Moltmann (1965, 1971, 1975, 1977), Keck (1965), Georgi (1965), Metz (1969), Pannenberg (1971a), Kemp (1972), Hengel (1975), Cone (1975), Segundo (1975), Mother Teresa of Calcutta (1975), Cooke (1976), and Anderson (1979 ed.).

18. Pastoral Care of the Dying

Two life moments are unparalleled in awakening a sense of awe: beholding a birth, and standing in the presence of death. The mystery of death is illumined by analogy to birth. In both cases we learn that life is not easily comparable with other values, since all other values depend upon life to make them valuable.

Whether we hold a newborn infant or touch the hand of a person near death, a fundamentally similar awareness emerges: life is exquisitely valuable. Language stretches to express it. Life belongs in a wholly different genre of value than measurable, material, temporal goods (Thomas Aquinas, *ST*, vol. 1, pp. 99 ff.).

This is why death is among the most solemn of human events. We sense immediately a radical value loss that differs from all forms of measurable, objective loss. Just as in birth it is fitting to commit to God the newly received incalculable value of life, so in death it is fitting to commit into God's hands the passing away of incalculably valuable life (Augustine, *NPNF* 1st, vol. 1, pp. 90, 138 ff.; Doddridge, *Works*, vol. 3, pp. 404 ff.; *BCP*, 1979, pp. 462–511).

Medicine and ministry tend to see death through oddly different lenses. Ministry supports the struggle of medicine to protect and extend life (Luther, *LCC*, vol. 18, pp. 241 ff.). But when death comes and medicine stands helpless, ministry acts to commit into God's hands the care of the dying and holds before that person's and that family's consciousness so far as possible the essential heart of the Christian gospel: that Christ died for our sins, that the love of God does not end on the cross but rejoices in the hope of resurrection, that grace makes perfect our weakness (*Book of Common Order*, 1940, pp. 161 ff.). To such moments the good pastor will come well prepared, with clear identity rooted in Scripture and intuitively in touch with the great pastoral tradition.

Why Do People Turn to the Minister?

Whenever an illness reaches the point of impending death, the pastor should be notified quickly and should come immediately. With the exception of a sudden death or an accident involving a stranger or a relative of a parishioner, the pastor will have already established some relationship with the person or family.

The pastor will soon learn that widely varied responses accompany the approach of death. To some the end may seem like a welcome relief after a long struggle. In some cases the dying person will experience an ironic sense of delay or wish that suffering might not be prolonged. In others, fundamental anxieties about death need to be faced and patiently worked through, if possible (Taylor, 1857 ed.; Baxter, *PW*, vol. 9, pp. 342 ff.). In still other cases, feelings of inadequacy or guilt may predominate. In these varied circumstances, the empathetic pastor does well to listen carefully and accurately to the nuances of feeling that underlie interactions and, in due time, to bring to bear the wisdom of the Christian tradition upon the all-too-real circumstances of death (Chrysostom, *NPNF* 1st, vol. 14, pp. 306, 443 ff.).

It is not surprising that individuals and families should in those times look toward pastoral wisdom, guidance, and practical support. For the pastor is, after all, the one who has already been publicly speaking of meaning in life and death, of the providence of God amid trials, and of the incomparable value of the individual before God. Indeed, it is a rare and distinctive privilege of ministry to be welcomed into the small, quiet, broken circle of the family in such critical times.

As shepherd of souls, the pastor has a different task and embodies a different social function than other professionals related to death and dying. Psychotherapists who base their services on hedonic cost/benefit calculus have less to say amid death, because such calculations seem largely irrelevant. People come to pastors not because they need a physician for the body, but because the physician for the body lacks omnicompetence and stands impotent before the power of death. Amid such circumstances it is the pastor to whom people turn for a hoped-for ministry that extends through and beyond the awesome mystery of death (Jackson, 1957; Switzer, 1970).

As body and spirit are complementary yet distinguishable, so are the tasks of medicine and ministry. The pastor's service does not neglect the needs of the body, but focuses more on serving the whole person, both the body and the self-transcending capacities of the person: the imagination, reason, moral awareness, and capacity to trust. In this less palpable realm, physicians are often all thumbs and do not view themselves as competent, and often do not wish to become entrapped in tough questions about death, meaning, absurdity, destiny, futurity, and trust in God. Modern physicians, despite exceptional technical competence, are especially vulnerable to frustration in the presence of death. For they are committed by oath to prevent or at least resist death. Their time-honored medical ethic centers upon sustaining life rather than dealing with death (Oden, 1976b). Thus there are deep avoidance patterns built into modern medical practice when death is near. Communication becomes choked with technical phrases.

Other professionals, as well, default in the presence of death. The attorney can give useful counsel about legal rights, wills, taxes, and distributions, but has little to say about the inner pain of separation and bereavement. The funeral director has an essentially material and objective function in caring for the body after death, ironically analogous to the physician taking care of the body before death. Only the fact of death is dealt with, not its meaning.

It is the minister who by tradition, by social role designation, and by common expectation, finds her- or himself uniquely enmeshed in crucial situations of counseling the dying and the bereaved where other professionals are loath to tread (Doddridge, *Works*, vol. 3, pp. 285 ff.; Paley, vol. 4, pp. 237 ff.).

What Can Ministry Do?

Even if the pastor were tempted to avoid such situations, it would be extremely difficult. The expectation is that the pastor will be personally and significantly present in the period approaching death and following death, both as an interpreter and counselor amid human brokenness and a resource for hope and faith precisely when all the ablest servants of the body are at their finite limit. Furthermore, the Christian believer turns to the pastor not as a legal requirement or a physical necessity, or merely as an act of social courtesy, but on the whole deliberately by free choice, earnestly inviting the pastor's presence, feeling the need for a word in due season.

However much we may hedge ourselves against an immediate awareness of death under ordinary circumstances, when death comes near, it breaks powerfully through our defenses. Anyone who has stood in the presence of death knows that it is not a power to quibble with. Vulnerabilities are laid bare (Gregory Nazianzus, *NPNF* 1st, vol. 7, pp. 254–69).

It is amid that sort of awareness that people turn to their pastor, who in other settings may have become their friend and trusted confidant. Beyond personal friendship, however, ministry is seen as a representative office on behalf of the whole church, witnessing to the insumountable power and goodness of God. It would seem quite out of place for a physician or a mortician to enact a service of committal, where the body in its weakness, limitation, and corruptibility is finally committed to God. That is uniquely a pastoral act. When we walk through the valley of the shadow of death, we need someone there to put that journey into context, to provide some meaningful interpretation of it beyond sheer hedonic value loss (Wesley, *WJW*, vol. 6, pp. 167–89; vol. 7, pp. 463 ff.).

The pastor traditionally has been asked to provide that service. It is not merely an act of talk, but also of wisely "being with," of attentive presence, of patient standing by. The covenant faithfulness that is willing to stay up nights and watch and pray is an expression and reminder of God's own covenant faithfulness to us (Pss. 89, 103, and 136). By analogy, God does not abandon us in the midst of our troubles. The empathic pastor will be there, will come early, be vulnerable to the hurt, and stay late if needed.

For anyone who has not served awhile as a pastor, it may seem odd that ministry to the dying is perceived as a task of exceptional dignity and importance. The young person in ministry learns to meet death only by meeting it. A treatise is hardly sufficient as preparation for ministry to the dying. For persons experienced in ministry, however, the tender, quiet, heavily weighted moments of ministering to people amid death may prove to be among the most meaningful events of a year's work, those most often dreamed about, those remembered years later, those that best offer opportunities to mediate God's love to human brokenness, those that infuse the rest of ministry with profound though inconspicuous significance (Luther *LCC*, vol. 18, pp. 53 ff.; Vinet, 1853).

Since Pentecost, when the meaning of Jesus' death and resurrection became clear to a large group of his followers, Christians have believed that through our meeting with death we are being given an exceptional opportunity to move toward greater trust in God. Long before a harsh, unexpected meeting with death, Christians should give themselves the opportunity to be instructed by Romans 5–8 as a basis for thinking scripturally about death (cf. Chrysostom, *NPNF* 1st, vol. 12, pp. 294 ff., 388 f., 393 ff.). Furthermore, through meeting with the death of others, God prepares us better for our own death (Clement of Alexandria, *ANF*, vol. 2, pp. 411 f.; Augustine, *NPNF* 1st, vol. 1, pp. 137 ff.; Gerkin, 1979, pp. 74 ff.).

The death of one person affects all with whom he or she has dealt. Death is an eminently social event. It breaks in on a community like an echoing, ricocheting sound reminding us all of our finitude. It rearranges relationships in families. Death can teach us much, if we are willing to learn. Ministry amid death is best understood, not just individualistically as care for a single person, but also interpersonally for the family, friends, and wider community as well.

Without ruling out confrontation or challenge, ministry to the dying is usually one of quiet consolation, palliation, and hope, seeking to comfort those who mourn (Matt. 5:4), "to bind up the brokenhearted . . . to give them garlands instead of ashes, oil of gladness instead of mourner's tears, a garment of splendor for the heavy heart" (Isa. 61:1,3). Jesus himself must have been fond of that passage since he recalled it in the inauguration of his own ministry (Luke 4:16–30). It is by analogy with Jesus' own ministry of comfort that we understand our ministry of comfort to be illumined and empowered (2 Cor. 1:3–7; Luther, *LCC*, vol. 18, pp. 55 ff.).

The Approach of Death

Rarely will a pastor preach a sermon to a congregation among which no one feels the throbbing ache of radical loss; there is someone out there who still feels the sting of death. Ministers who deal courageously, clearly, and sensitively with the reality of death will deepen the tone of all other aspects of their ministry. They will be at the same time dealing with the "little deaths" that every one experiences day by day—the slender losses of value that are illuminated profoundly by death, which is the loss of that inestimable, incomparable value that is the precondition of all other values (John Climacus, d. 649, pp. 66 ff.; Luther *WLS*, vol. 1, pp. 164 ff.).

The experienced minister knows that the times of approaching death and bereavement are exceptional opportunities for spiritual growth. Sensitive care is required to nurture them toward their fullest potentiality and not let them become an occasion for stumbling. They have great potentiality for demonic as well as creative growth. There is often a keen consciousness of the limits of temporal power among those whose abrasiveness has been tempered by loss. Within that context it may be far more possible to speak of trust in God than it is in a well-defended environment. When the person is distanced, invulnerable, and armored by social routines and amenities, only smaller shifts of consciousness are conceivable. Death tends to rob us of these defenses (Luther, *WLS*, vol. 1, pp. 365 f.). It is therefore dangerously powerful and at the same time potently promising. It is into this tender, susceptible situation that the pastor enters. One's personal presence should be as open and outreaching as one's language is modest and self-limiting.

A piercing analogy recurs in pastoral literature: death prepares the soil for heightened spiritual growth. The soil is harshly upturned, yet made ready for new planting (Pastor of Hermas, *ANF*, vol. 2, pp. 32 ff.; *Recognitions of Clement, ANF*, vol. 8, pp. 172 f.; Luther, *WLS*, vol. 1, pp. 368 ff.; *LCC*, vol. 18, pp. 139 ff.). Cheaply interpreted, the analogy is hazardous, since it could turn into a manipulativeness that uses grief for ends other than deep spiritual formation. Regrettably, ministry lives with the memory of a history of abuses of this sort. But properly interpreted, the analogy touches the complex meeting place of hope, loss, renewal, and providential care.

The physician Alfred Worcester has written helpfully about the approach of death. His words need to be understood by every pastor:

We are always dying; instantaneous death is rare and even when sudden the minutes seem hours, and there is usually ample warning that death is imminent. Every medical student should hand in full observations of several deaths, to learn how the process occurs and to impress himself with the duty of serving those needs. The process of dying is progressive, not a simultaneous failure of vital functions. It usually proceeds from below upwards, as reflexes are lost in the legs before the arms, the intestines and the stomach cease to function. Only water should be given in decreasing quantities, noting that thirst is the first and last craving. . . . There is no death agony except in the imagination. . . . Remarkable recoveries of consciousness occur at the last, and the loss of consciousness is usually gradual. Long after whispered words are inaudible the patient may signify assent or dissent with slight movements of the head. Still later only the eyes may speak. . . . It is the physician's duty to tell the patient and the family of death when he sees it coming. Most dying patients have the feeling that death is near. Some may prefer not to speak of it, but frankness is a comfort to all concerned. Preparation for death is needed, and death is almost always preceded by a perfect willingness to die. (Worcester, 1920.)

The same pastoral competencies that are needed amid death and bereavement are also found in effective ministry generally: empathic listening ("Weep with them that weep"—Rom. 12:15, KJV); gentle, unconditional acceptance ("Be compassionate as your father is compassionate," Luke 7:36); internal congruence, ownership of feelings ("When Jesus saw her weeping . . . he sighed heavily and was deeply moved," John 11:34); witnessing to God's comfort ("How blest are the sorrowful; they shall find consolation," Matt. 5:4); candor, honesty ("He spoke about [death] plainly," Mark 8:32); confrontation when appropriate ("Judge not that you be not judged," Matt. 7:1).

Even if significant conversation may be slow in coming and takes time to ripen, it is often weighty with meaning. Each person's season of anticipatory mourning (grieving prior to death in awareness of the coming value loss) has its own pace and internal timing. Ministry listens carefully to grasp that accurately.

The pastor's listening is more finely tuned when clearly aware of his or her own smaller griefs that stand in analogy with the greater grief of the bereaved. One taps directly and existentially into the emotional depth of the parishioner's grief by analogy with one's own griefs over current losses (Luther, *LCC,* vol. 18, pp. 53 ff.; Wesley, *WJW,* vol. 5, pp. 258 ff.).

Such moments require spare use of language and keen sense of real personal presence. It is not a time for intricate dialectics or heavy rhetoric, as if the deathbed were the final round of a debating society. Rather, it is time for well-chosen scriptural wisdom personally expressed in the language of one's own experience, enriched with compassion, sincere thanksgiving, and the courage to face reality (Doddridge, *Works,* vol. 3, pp. 283 ff.).

As pastors we are being called to "infuse ourselves . . . into our exhortations and instructions; to put ourselves on a level with those we seek to console; to show them in ourselves a sinner assisting another sinner; to relate to them, insofar as we can, the history of our souls; and, in a word, to reason with them, not from an elevation, but on the same simple plane with themselves" (Vinet, 1853, p. 289).

The parishioner may not be ready to listen to a lot of talk, but may eagerly hear a spare, fit word of Scripture or honest prayer that helps grasp the faith already latently held. To find that special word requires wisdom, knowing how to relate the wider truth to the here-and-now situation.

How does the pastor learn what to say? It might seem facile to answer too quickly: only by being a pastor. But that is essentially the right answer. Only by being there as the one who in other times is liturgist and preacher and teacher, but now is shepherd of souls in the presence of death. We learn what to say, in part, by listening to what is being said. If we let the person tell us where he or she is, we will soon learn how best to respond (Gregory, *ACW*, vol. 11, pp. 109 ff., 122 ff.).

Should the Patient Be Told?

If death is clearly approaching, should the minister be a part of that crucial communication to the patient that he or she is very seriously ill? There are two distinct views on this, and both have some merit, although the affirmative answer on the whole seems stronger than the negative.

The negative is essentially this: Often there is a strong predisposition on the part of both physicians and family not to give any potentially depressing feedback, but constantly to reassure the patient that there is a possibility of improvement, and never to hint that things may be going downhill. The medical and psychological reasons for this must be sorted out and understood. The physician wishes to muster all the patient's energy and courage, so that nothing detracts from the will to live. It is thought that a sudden announcement that "you are likely to die from this" would demoralize the patient and, in effect, cause death sooner. This is the main reason that some physicians seldom if ever tell patients they may not recover, even if the prognosis is grim.

Whereas some of the literature errs by suggesting that the patient should never be told, other writers err on the side that the patient should always be told. Neither option is always correct. Although there is no single answer, following are some reliable guidelines.

It is never appropriate for the pastor to say that he or she knows the parishioner is dying. The reason is that no pastor knows that absolutely. There are too many cases of unexpected remission amid dire circumstances to be unequivocal or absolutely certain about such announcements. It is not the pastor's role to say flatly that any illness is absolutely incurable.

The pastor has good reason to work toward open, clear, realistic communication with the physician on the prognosis, especially when death seems highly probable. It need not be assumed that the pastor will always follow woodenly the physician's intuitive assessment of the parishioner's needs, wishes, and strengths. There may be some cases in which the pastor will have to press the physician persistently in order even to obtain a clear and realistic prognosis. The pastor may interpret the parishioner's feelings in a different way than the physician does. As patient advocate, the pastor at times may vigorously support the patient's "right to know."

In most cases the initiative will lie with the parishioner rather than the pastor in significant disclosures concerning the gravity of an illness. Such a discussion should not come on suddenly or with alarming abruptness, but rather emerge out of some unfolding edge of an ongoing conversation. The pastor may have good reason to listen attentively and await, with the greatest sensitivity the right moment to nurture the conversation.

There may come a time in ministry where indeed it becomes the pastor's (as distinguished from the physician's or the family's) responsibility gently to advise the parishioner of the gravity of the situation. There may come a time when the conspiracy of concealment and deception needs to be broken through for the interests of all concerned. Such a moment will require the keenest interpersonal skill, tact, courage, and sensitivity. In most cases little more is needed to begin such a conversation than to say something like, "I am sure you are aware that you are very seriously ill." Allow the conversation to grow organically from there.

The pastor needs a balanced, proportional sense of the ethical claims that may conflict in such a situation. There is the moral requirement to assist in sustaining life versus the moral requirement to reduce suffering. Either of these may conflict with the patient's assumed right to know. Hospital communication routines have a legitimate moral claim and should be respected, yet at times the pastor may feel they conflict with the patient's overall interest.

The person may need time and a caring context to prepare for death, to gird up resources, to think about the consequences of death, to reflect on the meaning of life. The virtues of pastoral conversation in this sphere are honesty, gentleness, candor, and love, rooted in a sense of realism about limitations, yet completed by faith in providence. The intent of such a communication is not simply to boldly, baldly tell the simplistic truth (bang, pow, period) and then forget it. Rather, it is to open this person up to enable the fullest possible spiritual formation even under life's most limiting circumstances.

There are a number of potential injustices that can be thoughtlessly

done by the pastor to the parishioner under the guise of good intentions: prematurely tell too absolutely about supposed impending death;
speak too bluntly or clumsily in the interest of supposed candor; subtly
reduce the will to live by prematurely creating discouragement under
the guise of realism; or withhold from the person a truth to which he or
she is due (cf. Baxter, *PW*, vol. 6, pp. 109 ff.).

The dying are often keenly conscious of their surroundings, more
than they are able to express. When physical responsiveness is at an
extremely low level, that does not necessarily imply that consciousness is
also extremely low.

The symptoms of approaching death are almost always known by
the dying person. The person feels and experiences his or her own
body much more directly than others do. Often it comes as a relief to
the dying person to know that others at last recognize what he or she
has known for some time and may have had to bear silently (Kübler-
Ross, 1969). For this reason, the pastor should remember not to talk
with relatives or others in the presence of the dying on the dubious
assumption that the person is wholly unconscious or unaware of the
surroundings.

Never assume that the person has expired until that is medically
indicated. Do not terminate your ministry or end your efforts at palliative care until it is clear that the vital signs have ceased, for there are too
many cases known in which nonmedical persons have prematurely
thought that life has ended, while further ministries were still needed.

Can Pastors Help Prepare Persons for Death?

Traditionally, the preparation of parishioners for death has been a
crucial task of ministry. In our time, psychological, moral, and spiritual
preparation for death is generally avoided by all of the professions otherwise responsible to the dying.

The reality of death is covered up, depersonalized through sterile
hospital routine, and avoided with a fierceness that defies description.
As ministers, we may complain that we have had too much resistance
from a death-avoiding culture to do our traditional job of preparing
people for death, but that is hardly convincing. Too few have tried to
go against the stream.

If dying is something that one can fully do right only once, then we
can draw this ironic conclusion: being alive, and therefore having as yet
missed the experience of death, is, oddly enough, an intrinsic presupposition of ministry. So the minister, in not having died, is on equal
footing with members of the dying person's family but not with the
dying person, who knows existentially more than the minister does
about the experience. This is an odd point, but I am determined to
make it: ministry does well to acknowledge its critical lack of experience

and to listen carefully to the unparalleled expertise of those who are dying. This is a mode of "teaching" in which the dying "learner" is experientially ahead of the pastoral guide.

Preparation for death began to erode when religion became infused with false utopian optimism. Technology, it was thought, would ultimately conquer human limitations. But death remains a stubborn limit that finally conquers every technology. Naive optimism about progressive history has unintentionally resulted in a conspiracy of silence about death and dying. We may look back disdainfully at our seventeenth-century forebears for their seemingly morbid concern with preparation for death. But if they were to look at our death-avoidance patterns, they would perceive our society as morally limited and emotionally constricted for lack of attention to death, its significance, and its reality. They would observe with curiosity or amusement our embalming procedures, Forest Lawns, and heavy steel caskets. They would sense in us a lack of joy, a default of realism, and a loss of Christian confidence in the midst of death (Baxter, *PW*, vol. 4, pp. 403 ff.).

Preparation for death, as the pastoral tradition knew, is a lifelong process (cf. Augustine, Gerson, Luther, J. Taylor). If preparation belatedly begins only upon symptoms of terminal illness, that may be too late. Much in the prior ministries of preaching, worship, teaching, and visitation can help in a longer time frame toward preparation for timelessness. Yet, whatever preparation is made, the actual emergent possibility of approaching death may be a trial of faith equal to no previous test (Taylor, *TPW*, vol. 2, pp. 1 ff.).

Pastoral Counsel for the Dying

No experienced pastor would expect a noncontextual set of absolute rules to be laid down for care for the dying. The surest rule probably is that pastoral attentiveness must be ready to respond in sharply different ways as circumstances direct. On the other hand, the pastoral tradition has developed some reliable general guidelines for pastoral counsel of the dying:

- God does not try us beyond our strength. The dying believer has a right to hear clearly spoken the biblical promise: "God keeps faith, and he will not allow you to be tested above your powers, but when the test comes he will at the same time provide a way out, by enabling you to sustain it" (1 Cor. 10:13).
- Jesus himself is the best pattern for the Christian's meeting with death. On the Mount of Transfiguration he gave much thought to the approaching possibility of his own death. By the time he came to the Garden of Gethsemane, when death became imminent, he had already acquired the spiritual disciplines through prayer that are necessary to ready the whole self, body and spirit, for its final

encounter with the limits of finitude (Mark 9:2–8, 14:32–42).
- The pastoral duty to assist persons in their meeting with death may require diverse interpersonal competencies. Contextually it is a ministry of unpacking the layers of meaning that death may have for that person and witnessing within that context to the power and goodness of God.

Like all creatures we exist in bodies that die. If we have a bodily beginning, we will also have a bodily ending. Our existence is temporal. Our creaturehood points beyond itself to that which enlivens it, the Spirit of God. If we have been given, as Psalm 39 speculates, a finite measure of days, that deepens our responsibility to live accountably in those fleeting days. Death more than any other fact of life binds us to other bodily creatures—the snail, the crab, the antelope all face death. Death more than anything reminds us that we are not God. It invites us to praise the eternal One who stands before and after all things. It asks us to behold and celebrate our humanity as limited, and given as such by God (Augustine, *NPNF* 1st, vol. 3, pp. 240 ff., 539 ff.; Kazantzakis, 1960, pp. 125 ff.).

Christian ministry wishes to teach these elementary lessons at all times, but never more so than amid death. This is why Christianity at its best is less prone than materialistic hedonism to cover up the fact of death or pretend cosmetically that it does not involve the actual rotting and dissolution of the body. Christian hope looks beyond death to the resurrection of the body and eternal life with God, which does not deny temporal death but transcends it in hope.
- Anyone who is aware that choice implies negation knows that freedom is no unmixed blessing. Particularly persons who are aware that death may be near will understandably ponder upon regretted value negations. They care about value losses, the recollection that others may have been hurt by their freedom, that others may have had to suffer for their sins. That is not so unreasonable and they should not be prematurely dismissed or cheaply reassured. Help the person to hear the word of pardon and to seek appropriate modes of restitution or reparation.

In such a setting, feelings of guilt are best seen finally in relation to the forgiveness of God. The ministry of word and sacrament should bring a well-timed message of God's pardon to the penitent with clarity and with a kind of quiet force that is appropriate to the situation. The pastor stands ready to offer Holy Communion when asked, and to encourage its being received whenever appropriate (Calvin, *Inst.*, 4.17.43; Wesley, *WJW*, vol. 7, p. 149).

Questions Concerning Sedation and Medications

Medicine and ministry sometimes find themselves in conflict at a particular point: Suppose the dying person, who may profoundly need or wish to talk about his or her spiritual and moral situation, is so medicated or sedated that it is impossible to ask or even think about spiritual care? Although the usefulness of sedatives, tranquilizers, and painkilling drugs needs to be proportionally affirmed by ministry, nonetheless the time may come when the pastor will stand prudently as an advocate of increasing the consciousness of the patient. At times sedative drugs so reduce consciousness that there is little or no opportunity for spiritual preparation for death or Christian edification in the face of terminal illness.

The physician may do a proportional injustice to the patient by so reducing self-awareness through medication that the mind has no power to struggle for understanding, pardon, restitution, and spiritual integration. Hedonism seldom understands why it should not always be the case that pain should be avoided. A more balanced Christian understanding views pain as more than simply chemically activated neural signals. Pain and death are not simply physical enemies to be dealt with as a mechanical or chemical problem, they are also opportunities for spiritual discipline and the integration of life's meaning. The pastor who has not sufficiently worked through classical Christian teaching that views our suffering in the light of Christ's suffering will probably not have a serious rationale to offer those who may assume that the unconstrained application of consciousness-reducing sedatives amid approaching death is always unambiguously preferable to pain of any kind. Consciousness-reducing drugs do not solve everything. There will be times when the interests of the patient will be better served by the increase of consciousness even at the cost of some physical pain. Better perhaps to let nature and natural death be its own sedative.

Let no implication be prematurely drawn that we are generally opposed to sedative medications that help patients manage pain. These are great gifts of God and good medicine, and should be used proportionally and wisely. We are speaking rather of extreme and rare cases in which medications have so reduced awareness that they have limited any possibility of spiritual responsiveness, any capacity to pray or discern the promise of Scripture. These may be proportionally just as important to the dying patient as the reduction of pain by that extra edge.

In death the infinity of God confronts our finiteness. The eternity of God addresses our temporality. The holiness of God meets our moral inadequacies. These forms of immediate awareness are perhaps more sharp in the presence of death than any other time or place (Thomas Aquinas, *ST*, vol. 2, pp. 2102 ff.; Wesley, *WJW*, vol. 6, pp. 220 ff., 496; vol. 7, pp. 366 ff.).

Resurrection Faith

Nothing is needed more in ministry to the dying than the gospel: Christ died for sinners to take away the curse of guilt and death, to redeem death from its emptiness and terror by offering the faithful eternal life. The earnest believer who has for many years listened to sermons, studied Scripture, and shared in the prayers of the church has a right to hear in his or her final days or hours the Christian message stated in its simple power and applied to personal circumstances with clarity. The pastor is called to state the good news, as Wesley often said, "plain and home," that God was in Christ reconciling the world to himself, that he sent his Son to take the place of the sinner before the judgment of God, that when we trust in Christ we participate in both his death and resurrection, that we can trust that the same goodness of God revealed in Jesus will be present in the world to come, and that God will not give us a trial greater than we can endure. All of those statements are familiar to Christian preaching, but the Christian believer has a right to hear them appropriately stated within the context of impending death (Luther, *LCC*, vol. 18, pp. 26 ff.).

The Christian message is not only spoken to those who already believe it, but also may become an important word to those who had not previously heard it or believed it, but who under radical limitation now may be deeply grasped by it. That point should be made circumspectly, for we do not want to allow the deathbed to become an arena for manipulative coercion of superficial "faith." There has been far too much of that in pietistic Protestantism. But in correcting that distortion, we do not want to go to the opposite extreme and fail to share the good news with persons simply because they have not been to church or because we do not quite know how they might respond to it. It is better to risk on the side of clear, faithful, contextually sensitive witness, trusting the Holy Spirit to penetrate the heart in Her own way. In a deeper sense, it remains a pastoral duty to declare the word in due season, but always in a way that is fitting to the personally limited circumstances of the hearer (Calvin, *Inst.*, 2.16, 4.9).

This is why ministry is sought and valued. This is why the pastor is usually welcome in the hospital or home in the context of approaching death. If the pastor fails to declare this word, ministry may wilt into social trivia.

Elsewhere I have written on the meaning of resurrection and will not restate it here (Oden, 1969, 1976b, 1979). Minimally, however, it must be said that the Christian witness amid death is primarily a witness to the resurrection faith. Concisely stated, what the resurrection faith means is that in raising Jesus up from the dead, God affirmed his ministry as the decisive revelation of the divine will in history. When we participate by faith in the Christ event, we share his death and resurrec-

tion. In doing so we are offered freedom from the passing era of bondage to sin, death, guilt, and boredom, and awakened to a new life of
trust in God, love of the neighbor, and eternal life. Central to all Jewish
and Christian teaching concerning the future is the expectation of a
restored personal identity at the end time, not a disembodied existence,
but a resurrected body—a spiritual body, to be sure, but a restored
personal identity before God who rights all our historical wrongs (Irenaeus, *ANF,* vol. 1, pp. 542 ff.; Tertullian, *ANF,* vol. 3, pp. 447 ff.; Origen, *ANF,* vol. 4, pp. 260 ff., 293 ff.) That essentially is what the
resurrection means. Christians receive comfort from this hope in the
midst of death.

The Litany of Passing

In most Protestant books of worship there may be found special
prayers for the dying. This is the Protestant counterpart of the Catholic
Viaticum, or litany for the dying. Even if the pastor does not come from
a liturgical tradition, these resources may become significant models. In
order to gain a better grasp of these litanies and services, we will briefly
review the heart of two of them from which even the broadest free
church minister may make reasonable adaptations: The Anglican
Ministration at the Time of Death and the Roman Viaticum.

The Anglican Ministration at the Time of Death (*BCP* 1979) has
three principle acts. (1) A prayer for mercy is addressed to the triune
God asking that the sufferer be delivered from all evil, sin, and tribulation through participating in Christ's cross, death, burial, and resurrection. (2) The Lord's prayer is followed by a petition that the believer
may be set free from every bond and "rest with all your saints in the
eternal habitations." (3) The litany concludes with this simple-commen-
dation of the soul to God: "Depart, O Christian soul, out of this world,
in the name of God the Father Almighty who created you, in the name
of Jesus Christ who redeemed you, in the name of the Holy Ghost who
sanctifies you. May your rest be this day in peace, and your dwelling-
place in the Paradise of God" (*BCP,* 1979, p. 464).

In this brief service we have a centered ministry to the dying. It
focuses on *participatio Christi,* forgiveness of sin, and a prayer for grace
on the way. It stands as a concise summary of Christian teaching, of
God the Father, creator; Christ the Son, redeemer; and the Holy Spirit,
the sanctifier. The whole of Christian teaching is recollected and compacted in this brief moment of commending of the soul from this world
to God's eternity.

Prayers for the dying in other traditions are similar in tone. The
Eastern Orthodox tradition's prayer for the departing soul asks God to
loose this servant "from every bond and receive his soul in peace. Grant
him rest in thine eternal dwelling with all thy saints." The United Methodist Canticle of Conquest Over Death is a prayer for trust, taken from
Isaiah 25, addressed to the "everlasting rock," who keeps one in perfect

peace "whose mind is staid on God," who "swallows death up forever," and "wipes away tears from all faces" (*Book of Worship*, 1964, p. 310). The Lutheran prayer for the dying similarly invokes the triune God in a concise *summa* of faith addressed in the last moments: "Depart in peace thou ransomed soul, in the name of God the Father Almighty who created thee; in the name of Jesus Christ the Son of the living God, who redeemed thee; in the name of the Holy Ghost who sanctified thee. . . . The Lord preserve thy going out and thy coming in from this time and even forevermore. Amen."

Viaticum

There are three parts for the Roman Catholic service of care for the sick and dying: penance, anointing, and Viaticum. They are often enacted as three separate occasions: penance is an office of confession, anointing for healing of the sick, and Viaticum for the dying. The term *viaticum* simply means "with you on the way." It is a litany of the journey, given when hope of bodily restoration appears doubtful, when the person is "on the way" to life with God.

First the believer is symbolically reminded by water of her or his baptism, and thus of sharing in Christ's death and resurrection (Rom. 6). The underlying assumption is that Christ himself wishes to accompany the faithful on this final journey, and refresh him or her with hope of eternal life. This is followed by an act of penance, praying for the mercy of the Lord. Pardon for all sins is offered the true penitent in the name of the triune God. The faith professed in baptism is affirmed. It is essentially the Apostles' Creed in the form of three questions. Anointing of the sick person with oil and prayers of thanksgiving may follow. The oil is applied to the forehead (symbolizing the will, mind, and self-transcending capacities) and the hands (symbolizing the body and the active capacity), praying for the ease of suffering and the strengthening of hope.

After the Lord's Prayer and Agnus Dei, Holy Communion is received by all present, followed by an invocation for the dying, that the person may safely reach the kingdom of light, and concluding with a final blessing in the name of the triune God (*Rites of the Catholic Church*, 1976, p. 573 ff.).

All of these liturgical acts seek to bring together in a single moment of prayer and priestly activity the witness of the church to the dying person. Since the trinity is a summative doctrine, it plays a central role in Christian ministry to the dying. In medieval doctrine, the olive oil was consecrated by a bishop and the five senses were anointed with oil: eyes, ears, nose, lips, hands, and feet. Though extreme unction, considered as a sacrament, has been generally rejected by Protestants on the grounds that it was not instituted by Christ, nonetheless the basic idea of anointing with oil in critical illness has biblical warrant (Mark 6:13, James 5:14) and a long tradition.

The Service of Christian Burial

In order to ask how ministry serves through Christian burial, it is necessary to ask, "What is Christian burial?"

Early Christian burial practices followed the patterns of first-century Judaism with few exceptions. The Jews as well as most of the nations of antiquity buried their dead. Burial is distinguished from cremation in that it inters the deceased person in consecrated ground with religious rites. It was considered a duty of relatives to bury their dead (Gen. 23:3; 25:9). Deeply embedded in Jewish consciousness was the notion that death itself had an atoning power. It was thought that the process of decay was purgative and therefore itself a means of atonement. Burial should follow death reasonably soon. Embalming such as was known in Egypt was not known in Israel, but the use of spices to remove odors was common at funerals; they were burned or carried along with the procession. The bier was carried on the shoulders of friends.

All these Jewish practices were received into the Christian tradition, with one major shift in symbolism: a note of resurrection joy was clearly a part of early Christian services of burial. During the period of martyrdom, greater emphasis was given to the notion that one bears testimony (*marturion*) to Christ in faithful death. After the period of martyrdom and the Constantinian synthesis, Christian cemeteries became consecrated places where acts of devotion, meditation, and piety were considered appropriate ways of remembering the faithful.

The service of Christian burial consisted essentially of committal prayers, often preceded overnight by vespers, matins, or dirges and a requiem Eucharist the morning of the burial with special prayers for the passing faithful. The subsequent medieval practice was to say requiems the third, ninth, thirtieth, and three hundred and sixty-sixth day after death. The service of Christian burial was offered to all baptized communicants. Although cremation was not rejected, interment was the usual practice. Under canon law it was early decreed that no fee could be received for burial since burial is a spiritual and pastoral function, but indeed the custom of making modest gifts to the clergy or the poor in time became accepted in some areas.

The Rite of Burial

The rite of burial provides consolation to the bereaved through Scripture and prayer. It provides a community context of support amid loss. It offers a witness to the trustworthiness of God and to the hope of the resurrection (Augustine, *NPNF* 1st, vol. 3, pp. 539 ff.).

Prayers invoke the God who is the fount of life, our refuge and strength, from whom all things come and to whom all things return, to enable us to put our trust in him that we may attain comfort and find grace for this and every time of need, that we may lift up our eyes beyond this temporal loss and behold the light of eternity. The service poignantly recalls that God is our shepherd who leads us beside still waters and restores our soul, and even when we walk through the valley of the shadow of death we fear no evil, for God is with us (Ps. 23). "For we know that if the earthly tent we live in is destroyed, we have a building from God, a house not made with hands, eternal in the heavens" (2 Cor. 5:1, RSV). The key texts of Christian burial are psalms of consolation (Pss. 23, 27, 39, 90, 96, 121, and 130) and pivotal New Testament passages like Romans 8, 1 Corinthians 15, and John 14. The pastor's task is to hold up these scriptural affirmations meaningfully amid the crisis of loss.

The prayers of traditional burial services are saturated with these biblical images. The church prays "that out of the treasures of his glory he may grant you strength and power through his Spirit in your inner being, that through faith Christ may dwell in your hearts in love" (Eph. 3:16), thanking God that this person's trial and temptation are ended, that sickness and the dangers of this mortal life are past. God is asked to grant that the deceased may go on from strength to strength in the life of perfect service in the heavenly realm.

This is the service of Christian burial: thanksgiving, intercession, recollection, witness, committal. In all of this there is a deep sense of participation in a historical community of saints that far transcends this person or community. The prayers recall Christ who himself wept beside a grave, who was touched with feelings of grief and sorrow. They ask that God will awaken our hearts to hear the word of resurrection in true discernment, to fulfill his promises not to leave the people without comfort, and to enable them to abide in that living faith (Gregory Nazianzus, *NPNF* 2nd, vol. 7, pp. 234 ff., 254 ff.).

The funeral not only recollects the goodness of the individual, it wishes to put recollections of personal goodness in the larger context of God's unsurpassable goodness. The funeral is not fully grasped only sociologically—as an act of mutual community support—although it indeed is that. It is more a celebration of God's benevolence as understood by a transgenerational *communio sanctorum* into which the deceased faithful now enters. The funeral does not focus primarily on human companionship, vulnerable as it is to death and separation, but on our companionship with God, which does not end in death (Augustine, *NPNF* 1st, vol. 3, pp. 539 ff.).

Admittedly, the funeral has crucial social and psychological functions, bringing family and friends together in a supportive community. But it is more a Christian rite that places this event in a larger universal historical context (Chrysostom, *NPNF* 1st, vol. 13, p. 379). This is why the Christian funeral is more properly held in a church where the community gathers than in a funeral home.

Personal references in the service of burial need to be spare, well-

310

310 CRISIS MINISTRY

chosen, and gauged carefully to the situation. The funeral is not a time for fawning talk or sentimentalism. There may be a temptation subtly to exalt human merit so as to neglect the word of God's love for sinners amid their lack of merit (Calvin, *Inst.*, 3.25.8). Whatever is done in a funeral eulogy should be modest and richly scriptural and should balance a sense of genuine loss with a note of hope in resurrection that transcends all human losses (Irenaeus, *ANF*, vol. 1, pp. 531 ff.; Commodianus, *ANF*, vol. 4, p. 217).

The graveside ministry centers liturgically on an act of committal whose meaning is expressed in the committal prayer: "We commit his [her] body to its resting place, but his [her] spirit we commend to God." The living presence of Jesus is recollected as one who, himself facing death in his last breath said, "Father, into thy hands I commit my spirit" (Luke 23:46; cf. Thomas Aquinas, *ST*, vol. 2, pp. 2108 ff.). Jesus is recalled by John as having said, "Set your troubled hearts at rest. Trust in God always; trust also in me. There are many dwelling-places in my Father's house; if it were not so I should have told you; for I am going there on purpose to prepare a place for you" (John 14:1–3).

REFERENCES AND FURTHER READING

Among classical pastoral treatises on care for the dying and bereaved, see Irenaeus (*ANF*, vol. 1, pp. 542 ff.), Pastor of Hermas (*ANF*, vol. 2, pp. 32 ff.), Clement of Alexandria (*ANF*, vol. 2, pp. 253–257), Commodianus (*ANF*, vol. 4, pp. 217 ff.), Tertullian (*ANF*, vol. 3, pp. 447 ff.), Cyprian (*ANF*, vol. 5 pp. 469 ff.), Athanasius (*NPNF* 2nd, vol. 4), Eusebius (*NPNF* 2nd, vol. 1, pp. 342 ff.), Gregory Nazianzus (*NPNF* 2nd, vol. 7, pp. 255 ff.), Chrysostom (*NPNF* 1st, vol. 9, pp. 372 ff.; vol. 10, pp. 338–344), Augustine (*ACW*, vol. 9), John Cassian (*NPNF* 2nd, vol. 11), Leo the Great (*NPNF* 2nd, vol. 11, pp. 164 ff.), *Seven Ecumenical Councils* (*NPNF* 2nd, vol. 14), Boethius (524), John Climacus (d. 649, pp. 66 ff.), Thomas Aquinas (*ST*, vol. 2, pp. 2264 ff.), Gerson (d. 1429), Luther (*LCC*, vol. 8), Bucer (1523), More (1535), Bradford (d. 1555), Calvin (1559, 3.5, 3.25), Wermullerus (d. 1568), Donne (1623), Drelincourt (1651), Baxter (1656), Taylor (*TPW*), Doddridge (*Works*, vol. 3, pp. 404 ff.), Alberti (1735), Watts (d. 1748), Wesley (*WJW*, vol. 7, pp. 463 ff.), Ligouri (d. 1787), and Sailer (1788). Nineteenth-century writers on these themes include Bridges (1829), Harms (1820 ff.), Kierkegaard (1843b, 1849), Loehe (1851 ff.), Kidder, (1871), Fairbairn (1875), Hoppin (1884), and Gladden (1898).

Among twentieth-century writers on pastoral care of the dying we note particularly Worcester (1920), O'Connor (1942), Blackwood (1942), Irion (1954), E. Jackson (1957), Kazantzakis (1960), Lewis (1961), Rahner (1961a), Bachmann (1964), Oates and Lester (1969), Kübler-Ross (1969), Switzer (1970), and Gerkin (1979). Since I have dealt with the constellation of issues surrounding the moral quandaries of medical treatment of the dying in my book *Should Treatment Be Terminated?* (1976), I have not gone back over any of those issues, but the reader is referred to it in making up deficits of the above discussion.

Conclusion: The Trajectory of Pastoral Theology

Pastoral theology is that branch of Christian theology that deals with the office, gifts, and functions of the pastor. As theology, pastoral theology seeks to reflect upon that self-disclosure of God witnessed to by Scripture, mediated through tradition, reflected upon by critical reasoning, and embodied in personal and social experience. In the light of these resources, it seeks to give clear definition to the general ministry of the church, to the life and tasks of ordained ministry, and to the variety of major offices of ordered ministry, so as to provide an integral view of the pastoral office and its functions aimed at the improved practice of ministry.

The call to ministry requires both an inward conviction that one is called by God to ministry and the outward calling of the believing community that has assessed one's potential service to the body of Christ. Potential impediments are assessed by asking whether they constitute a probable encumbrance or burden on present or future congregations or the church body sufficient to outweigh other gifts, or whether other gifts outweigh the deficits so that grace will work through the individual all the more powerfully. Having conscientiously gone through the rigors of academic preparation and examination for orders, those candidates for whom the inward call has been confirmed by the outward call are prepared to be set apart for ministry in the sacred vow of ordination.

Essential to ordination is the reception of the gift of ministry and the rite through which that gift is received. Ordination combines an internal grace with an external act; the inner reality is the reception of the divine gift, and the external event is the laying on of hands with the church's intercessory prayer. The effective inner meaning of ordination is the earnest intercession of the church, invoking the Spirit to empower and bless this ministry. The intercession asks God for a continuing endowment of these gifts and for the abiding presence of the Holy Spirit.

Both men and women may be called to sacred ministry. If all the baptized are properly to be represented in a representative ministry, it is fitting that neither one sex nor the other be excluded from that representative ministry. For both males and females contribute inseparably to the wholeness of the human family. This view is deeply embedded in Christ's own intention for the church, even though it has had to await a slowly meandering stream of historical development to be, to some degree, actualized. But historical conditions make it now possible to fulfill the deeper intention of the Christian tradition.

The concept of "pastor," based on the shepherding analogy, is the unifying biblical image of ministry. The pastor (*poimen*, "shepherd") is a member of the body of Christ who is called by God and the church and set apart by ordination representatively to proclaim the word, administer the sacraments, and guide and nurture the Christian community toward full response to God's self-disclosure. Other important images of ministry such as teacher, overseer, liturgist, elder, or priest become infused with special significance by analogy to good shepherding. By both teaching and example, Jesus left the church a highly suggestive, if not explicitly developed, conception of pastoral ministry. He himself called individuals into discipleship and ministry, taught and nurtured them toward fuller responses to God's kingdom despite their resistances and misconceptions, and then sent them out with the promise of his continuing active presence.

The apostolic commissioning of Matthias (Acts 1:15–26) reflects the urgent concern of the newborn church to maintain intergenerational continuity with Christ's ministry after the resurrection. The main pattern of ministry remained Jesus himself who "came not to be ministered unto, but to minister." Three principle arenas and dimensions of ministry developed in order to carry on the same work of the ministry of Christ, yet with a meaningful division of labor: *diakonos* being relatively more focused on temporal needs and the serving role; *presbuteros* centering more specifically on the pastoral instruction, guidance, and leadership of the Christian congregation; and *episkopos* (or its corollary equivalents) relatively more concerned with the oversight and public defense of the flock, often on an area-wide basis. God the Spirit gives many gifts to the church to empower its mission. These gifts, which differ "according to the grace given to us," are intended for the benefit of the whole Christian community in its mission to the world. However diverse, taken together they express the complex unity of the body of Christ. Among the gifts given to ministry are the grace of the apostolate, prophecy, evangelism, shepherding, teaching, miracles, healing, administration, and ecstatic utterance—all given to equip God's people for work in his service, to the building up of the body of Christ (1 Cor. 12; Eph. 4).

It is the bold intention of Christ's ministry to combine the prophetic and priestly ministries into a single, unified ministry of word and sacrament in which one person serves both the priestly office of conducting public worship and the prophetic office of providing religious instruction, exegesis, and proclamation of the word of God. One of the most cohesive forces in pastoral identity is the public role of leader of the worshiping community. The community has the recurrent need to hear the word proclaimed authentically, not mistakenly; trustably, not half-informed; to receive the sacraments fittingly, not in idiosyncratic ways. That is why Christ gave order to ministry. The Christian minister intercedes on behalf of the faithful community before God in prayer as a timely, public, verbal, hearable act. The service has an implicitly triune structure and sequence. It proceeds from the Creator who gives us life, to the Redeemer who brings us back to the original purpose of life when fallen, to God the Spirit who sanctifies and completes what is offered and given in God the Son.

In the ministry of the sacraments, the believer is cleansed by the power of the Spirit through water and spiritually fed and refreshed through bread and wine. Life in Christ begins with a cleansing bath of pardon and continues with nurturing food and drink for the care of souls. Two pairs of analogous biblical rites rehearse the inner and outer aspects of covenant with the God of Israel: circumcision and Passover, baptism and Eucharist. All have a similar structure. They communicate God's promise by means of an outward and visible sign, divinely initiated, and received by the faithful covenant community. Just as baptism marks the beginning of participation in the body of Christ, so is the Lord's Supper the sacrament of continuing life in Christ to nurture further seasonal growth. Although the ministry of Holy Communion centers in the altar-table, its circumference is very broad, including many acts of confession, empathic listening, guidance of parishioners toward acts of reparation, and above all the representative offering of God's pardon. The four key acts of the ministry of the Supper are rehearsed in 1 Cor. 11:23–26: He took bread (Oblation), he gave thanks (Eucharist), he broke the bread (fraction), and he gave it to his disciples saying, "This is my body" (Communion).

Preaching (kerugma) means proclamation of the good news that Jesus Christ is Lord. Preaching is the continuous and public testimony that the church seeks to make to all who would hear it, and especially in the context of the worshiping community. Preaching consists in the clarification, exposition, interpretation, and re-appropriation of the written word that witnesses to the revealed word. It is a public expression of Christian truth, addressed to the here-and-now community of faith and to prospective believers.

Since the Christian community is a teaching community, its pastoral office is a teaching office. In each generation it faces the challenge of communicating the Christian message meaningfully in terms of the symbol systems and assumptions of the given historical period. The pastor is teaching elder in the community. The pastor teaches regularly and publicly through proclamation, worship, and Eucharist, and interpersonally through pastoral care, but more particularly through catechesis, confirmation, and Christian education and, above all, through exemplary behavior. The pastor's educational responsibility focuses first on the family as a primary learning context, yet it widens to include such diverse areas as the church school, summer youth camps, and lay theological academies. A high quality of lay teaching is best achieved by significant pastoral involvement in planning, organizing, recruiting, and actually teaching.

Pastoral theology seeks also to understand biblically, historically, and theologically the work of the pastor as steward of the church's temporal resources. It is precisely because the church has a ministry of word, sacrament, and order that it therefore has an administry ("towards ministry," that which is done in order to enable ministry). Its mission requires astute organizational skills, adept leadership, clear goals, careful planning, and wise administration of an efficient organization. In all three major areas of administry (general administration, educational administration, and financial administration), the pastor will be called upon to teach, inform, oversee, and motivate a complex organizational effort. The end in view is that of equipping the laity for their ministries in the world.

The duty to "visit from house to house" is widely recognized as intrinsic to the pastoral office. Its theological root: As Christ came to visit humanity with redemptive love, so we go to visit the neighbor in need. We can learn most of what we need to know about pastoral visitation simply by looking carefully at Jesus' ministry to people. Only by direct visitation does the pastor acquire the direct and immediate knowledge of the flock that is requisite to preaching. In each encounter the central task remains the same: embodying Christ to the world, mediating the love of God to humanity.

Although caring ministries are indeed a responsibility for the whole laity, the minister's care of souls (*cura animarum*) comes in the name of the whole church, offering word, sacrament, counsel, corrective guidance, and empathy, not on the basis of his or her own personal insight, but on the basis of being called, prepared, ordained, and authorized to representative ministry. Being a pastor precisely means undertaking the care of souls of the whole body of Christ in that place. Among personal competencies requisite to the care of souls are practical knowledge of how Scripture applies in various situations, mature self-knowledge, steady nondefensive compassion for people, accurate empathy, wise contextual discernment and judgment, adaptability, openness, courage, and humor. Good pastoral care sustains a holistic concern for the individual's physical, moral, and spiritual well-being, growth, and sanctification.

The pastoral guide owes the believer a corrective ministry of admonition when indicated, set always in the context of love. The only leverage for discipline is moral suasion, the inner claims of conscience, and the witness of Scripture. It should be free from compulsion or manipulation. *Nouthesia* (admonition) has as its purposes purification, reformation, reparation, and reconciliation.

Theodicy means to speak justly and well of God amid the awesome fact of suffering, to vindicate the divine attributes of justice, omnipotence, and love in relation to the existence of evil, to speak of God (*theos*) with justice (*dikē*) precisely at points where the divine purpose seems least plausible, namely, amid suffering. The classical pastoral theodicies seek to hold together the threefold affirmation of God's unsurpassably good will, God's incomparable power, and a realistic awareness of the awesome presence of evil and suffering in the world. Since this is among the most difficult and recurrent of theological problems for the pastor, the major classical pastoral theodicies are worthy of careful study. Among their key affirmations: that God does not directly will suffering, that creation would have been spared fallen freedom and sin only at the cost of giving the creature no free will, that God's power can draw good out of any evil, that evil does not finally limit God's power, that important lessons not easily discoverable otherwise may be learned precisely through the limits of suffering, that evil is a privation of the good, and that this world, being the creation of the infinitely good God, must be the best possible world simply because it is and remains God's world, even amid the fallenness of freedom. These pastoral consolations must be applied with great wisdom to specific situations in three arenas of special difficulty and challenge: care of the sick, care of the poor, and care of the dying and bereaved.

Although the laity has a general ministry to visit and care for the sick, the ordained ministry has a representative role in caring for the sick, interceding for them on behalf of the whole community, equipping and facilitating the laity in their ministry of care for the sick, and offering word, sacrament, and counsel in Christ's name to all who face bodily limitations and suffering. Unlike much religious wisdom, Christianity speaks of God's own participation in our suffering, God's own empathic intention to be with us fully as humans, even unto death. That word was uniquely clarified in Jesus' death and resurrection. Though sickness and suffering remain for Christians a reminder of finitude and challenge to patience, they are not absurd. Far from a masochistic fascination with pain, Christian ministry manifests a persistent and practical desire to transcend pain both by medical palliatives and cures and by beholding it from a reference point larger than its sheer physical discomfort.

In care for the poor, pastoral theology brings together many of its previous themes: ordained ministry equipping the laity, God's mercy and responsive human mercy, the relationship of faith, hope, and love. Care for the poor is a perennial concern of ministry because it is essential to the definition of the diaconate. The range of the church's caring acts for the poor has traditionally extended not only to widows and orphans, but also to travelers, those in need of employment or emergency food relief, political prisoners, and the disabled, and to the attempt to affect positive political change on behalf of the defenseless. Pastoral empathy for the poor is best informed by going to the places where the poor live and learning firsthand of actual needs. The Christian pastor at times is called upon to offer spiritual guidance both to the rich on behalf of the poor, and to the poor in their physical, moral, and spiritual struggles. Since Jesus and the apostles chose the way of voluntary poverty, Christian ministry also is well advised to live modestly on the voluntary gifts provided by the laity on behalf of the church's mission to the defenseless. The poor are by definition those who do not have needed resources in this world and cannot easily acquire them. They are in immediate need of our merciful care, just as we ourselves stand in radical need of the merciful care of God, before whom we possess nothing.

The mystery of death is illumined by analogy to birth. In both cases we learn that life is not easily comparable with other values, since all other values depend upon life to make them valuable. Christian ministry amid death is as much a matter of quiet presence as it is of empathic prayer and faithful proclamation. These heavily weighted moments of ministering to persons amid death may offer the most significant opportunities to mediate God's love to human brokenness, and to infuse the rest of ministry with profound but inconspicuous significance. The rite of Christian burial provides consolation to the bereaved through Scripture, prayer, a shared memory, and a supportive community amid loss. It offers a witness to the trustworthiness of God and to the hope of resurrection.

Abbreviations

ACW   *Ancient Christian Writers: The Works of the Fathers in Translation.* Edited by J. Quasten, J. C. Plumpe, and W. Burghardt. 40 vols. Westminster, Md.: Newman, 1946–.

AF   *The Apostolic Fathers.* Edited by J. N. Sparks. New York: Thomas Nelson, 1978.

ANF   *The Ante-Nicene Fathers.* Edited by A. Roberts and J. Donaldson. 10 vols. 1885–96. Reprint ed. Grand Rapids: Eerdmans, 1979.

Arndt   *A Greek-English Lexicon of the New Testament and Other Early Christian Literature.* By W. F. Arndt and F. W. Gingrich, Translation of W. Bauer, 1952). Chicago: University of Chicago Press, 1957.

ATP   *Anglicanism: The Thought and Practice of the Church of England, Illustrated from the Religious Literature of the Seventeenth Century.* Edited by P. W. More and F. L. Cross. London: S.P.C.K., 1935.

BC   *The Book of Concord.* 1580. Edited by T. G. Tappert. Philadelphia: Fortress, n.d.

BCP   *Book of Common Prayer.* 1662 unless otherwise noted. Royal Berviar's edition. London: S.P.C.K., n.d.

BD   *The Book of Discipline of the United Methodist Church.* Nashville: United Methodist Publishing House, 1980.

CC   *Creeds of the Churches.* Edited by J. Leith. Richmond: John Knox Press, 1979.

CCC   *Creeds, Councils, and Controversies,* Edited by J. Stevenson. London: S.P.C.K., 1966.

CE   *The Catholic Encyclopaedia.* 17 vols. New York: Encyclopedia Press, 1907–22.

CHSH   *The Church's Handbook for Spiritual Healing.* Edited by W. W. Dwyer. New York: Ascension Press, 1962.

CT   *The Church Teachers: Documents of the Church in English Translation.* Edited by J. F. Clarkson et al. St. Louis: Herder, 1955.

CWS   *Classic of Western Spirituality.* Edited by R. J. Payne. 30 vols. New York: Paulist Press, 1980–.

DAC   *Dictionary of the Apostolic Church.* Edited by J. Hastings. 2 vols. New York: Scribner's, 1915–18.

DACL   *Dictionnaire d'Archéologie Chretiénne et de Liturgie.* Edited by F. Cabrol and H. Leclerq. 13 vols. Paris: Letouzey et Ané, 1907–1953.

DCC   *Documents of the Christian Church.* Edited by H. Bettenson. New York: Oxford University Press, 1956.

DBT   *Dictionary of Biblical Theology.* Edited by Xavier Léon-Dufour. London: G. Chapman, 1969.

DNTT   *The New International Dictionary of New Testament Theology.* Edited by C. Brown. 3 vols. Grand Rapids: Zondervan, 1978.

DPT   *Baker's Dictionary of Practical Theology.* Edited by R. G. Turnbull. Grand Rapids: Baker, 1967.

DTC   *Dictionnaire de Théologie Catholique.* By A. Vacant and E. Mangenot. 15 vols. Paris: Letouzey et Ané, 1903–50.

EBT   *Encyclopedia of Biblical Theology.* Edited by J. B. Bauer. 3 vols. London: Sheed & Ward, 1970.

EKL   *Evangelisches Kirchenlexikon.* Edited by H. Brunotte and O. Weber. 3 vols. Göttingen: Vandenhoeck und Ruprecht, 1955–61.

ERE   *Encyclopedia of Religion and Ethics.* Edited by J. Hastings. 13 vols. 1908–26.

ExpT   *Expository Times.*

FC   *The Fathers of the Church, A New Translation.* Edited by R. J. Deferrari. 69 vols. to date. New York: Catholic University Press, 1948–.

HDB   *A Dictionary of the Bible.* Edited by J. Hastings. 5 vols. Edinburgh: T. & T. Clark, 1898–1904.

IDB   *The Interpreter's Dictionary of the Bible.* Edited by K. Crim. Nashville: Abingdon, 1962–76.

Inst.   *Institutes of the Christian Religions.* By John Calvin. LCC, vols. 21–22. Philadelphia: Westminster, 1960.

JAAR   *Journal of the American Academy of Religion.*

JE   *Jewish Encyclopedia.* Edited by I. Singer et al. 12 vols. New York: Funk & Wagnalls, 1901–06.

JPC   *Journal of Pastoral Care.*

LACT   *Library of Anglo-Catholic Theology.* 99 vols. Oxford: Oxford University Press, 1841–63.

LCC   *The Library of Christian Classics.* Edited by J. Baillie, J. T. McNeill, and H. P. Van Dusen. Philadelphia: Westminster, 1953–61.

LCF   *The Later Christian Fathers.* Edited by H. Bettenson. London: Oxford University Press, 1970.

LF   *A Library of Fathers of the Holy Catholic Church.* Edited by E. B. Pusey, J. Kebel, J. H. Newman, and C. Marriott. 43 vols. Oxford: Parker, 1838–75.

LLE   *Life and Literature in England.* Edited by D. Miles and R. Pooley. New York: Scott, Foresman and Co., 1943.

LP   *Lectures on Preaching.* By Philip Doddridge. London: W. Baynes and Son, n.d.

LPT   *Library of Protestant Thought.* Edited by John Dillenberger. 13 vols. New York: Oxford University Press, 1964–72.

LTK   *Lexikon für Theologie und Kirche.* Founded by M. Buchberger. Edited by J. Höfer and K. Rahner. 10 vols. Freiburg: Herder, 1957–65.

LW   *Luther's Works.* Edited by J. Pelikan. 54 vols. St. Louis: Concordia, 1953.

Moorman   *The Curate of Souls.* Edited by J. R. H. Moorman. London: S.P.C.K., 1958.

MPG   *Patrologia Graeca.* Edited by J. P. Migne. 162 vols. Paris: Migne, 1857–66.

MPL   *Patrologie Latina.* Edited by J. P. Migne. 221 vols. Paris: Migne, 1844–65.

NBD   *The New Bible Dictionary.* Edited by J. D. Douglas et al. London: Intervarsity, 1962.

NE   *A New Eusebius: Documents Illustrative of the History of the Church to A.D. 337.* Edited by J. Stevenson, (based on B. J. Kidd.) London: S.P.C.K., 1957.

NIDCC   *New International Dictionary of the Christian Church.* Edited by J. D. Douglas. Grand Rapids: Zondervan, 1974.

NPNF   *A Select Library of the Nicene and Post-Nicene Fathers of the Christian Church.* 1st Series, 14 vols.; 2nd series, 14 vols., Edited by H. Wace and P. Schaff. New York: Christian, 1887–92.

NWDB   *The New Westminster Dictionary of the Bible.* Edited by H. S. Gehman. Philadelphia: Westminster, 1970.

ODCC   *The Oxford Dictionary of the Christian Church.* Edited by F. L. Cross (1957). Revised by F. L. Cross and E. A. Livingstone. Oxford: Oxford University Press, 1974.

PA   *Patres Apostolici.* Edited by F. X. Funk. 2nd ed. 2 vols. Tübingen: Laupp, 1901.

PW   *Practical Works.* By Richard Baxter. 23 vols. London: James Duncan, 1830.

RA   *A Rabbinic Anthology.* Edited by C. G. Montefiore and H. Loewe. London: Macmillan, 1939.

RAC   *Reallexikon für die Antike und Christentum.* Edited by E. J. Doglen and H. Lietzmann. 9 vols. Stuttgart: Hiersemann, 1950–73.

RD   *Reformed Dogmatics.* Edited by J. W. Beardslee. Grand Rapids: Baker, 1965.

RE   *Realencyclopaedie für protestantische Theologie und Kirche.* Founded by J. J. Herzog. Edited by A. Hauck. 24 vols. Leipzig: J. C. Hinrichs, 1896–1913.

RGG3   *Die Religion in Geschichte und Gegenwart: Handwörterbuch für Theologie und Religionswissenschaft.* Edited by K. Galling et al. 3rd ed. 7 vols. Tübingen: J. C. B. Mohr, 1957–65.

SAOE   *St. Augustine on Education.* Edited by G. Howie. Chicago: Henry Regnery, 1969.

Schaff *The Creeds of Christendom.* By P. Schaff. 3rd ed. 3 vols. New York: Harper & Bros., 1919.

SCG   *On the Truth of the Catholic Faith, Summa Contra Gentiles.* By Thomas Aquinas. 4 vols. New York: Doubleday, 1955–57.

SJT   *Scottish Journal of Theology.*

SM   *Sacramentum Mundi: An Encyclopedia of Theology.* Edited by K. Rahner et al. 6 vols. New York: Herder, 1968–70.

ST   *Summa Theologica.* By Thomas Aquinas. 3 vols. New York: Benziger, 1947–48.

SWML   *Selected Writings of Martin Luther.* Edited by T. Tappert. 4 vols. Philadelphia: Fortress, 1967.

TCF   *Teachings of the Church Fathers.* Edited by J. Willis. New York: Herder, 1966.

TDOT   *Theological Dictionary of the Old Testament.* Edited by G. J. Botterweck and H. Ringgren. 4 vols. to date. Grand Rapids: Eerdmans, 1975.

TDNT   *Theological Dictionary of the New Testament.* Edited by G. Kittel. Translated by G. W. Bromiley. 9 vols. Grand Rapids: Eerdmans, 1964–74.

TGS   *Theology of God—Sources.* Edited by K. Kehoe. New York: Bruce, 1971.

TLZ   *Theologische Literaturzeitung.*

TPW   *Taylor's Practical Works.* By Jeremy Taylor. 2 vols. London: H. G. Bohn, 1854.

TWBB   *A Theological Word Book of the Bible.* Edited by A. Richardson. New York: Macmillan, 1957.

WJW   *Works of the Rev. John Wesley.* 14 vols. Jackson Edition. London: Wesleyan Conference, 1872.

WLS   *What Luther Says, An Anthology.* Edited by E. Plass. 3 vols. St. Louis: Concordia, 1959.

WML   *Works of Martin Luther.* Philadelphia Edition. 6 vols. Philadelphia: Muhlenberg Press, 1943.

ZNT   *Zeitschrift für die neutestamentlichen Wissenschaft und die Kunde der älteren Kirche.* Berlin: Walter de Gruyter, 1900–.

Bibliography

Abba, R. *Principles of Christian Worship.* New York: Oxford University Press, 1957.
_____. S.v. "Priests and Levites," *IDB.*
Abelard, Peter (1079–1142). *Ethics.* Edited by D.E. Luscombe. New York: Oxford University Press, 1971.
Achelis, Ernst Chr. *Lehrbuch der praktischen Theologie,* 2nd ed. Leipzig: J. C. Hinrichs, 1898.
_____. *Studien über das geistliche Amt.* Theologische Studien und Kritiken, 1889.
Adams, A. M. *Pastoral Administration.* Philadelphia: Westminster, 1964.
Adams, Jay E. *Competent to Counsel.* Grand Rapids: Baker, 1970.
_____. *Shepherding God's Flock.* Grand Rapids: Baker, 1979. (Originally published in three volumes: *The Pastoral Life,* 1974: *Pastoral Counseling,* 1975; and *Pastoral Leadership,* 1975.)
Adams, H. *The Pastoral Ministry.* Nashville: Abingdon-Cokesbury, 1932.
Advice to a Young Clergyman, How to Conduct Himself in the Common Offices of Life (1730). In Moorman, p. 171.
Ahern, M. B. *The Problem of Evil,* London: Routledge & Kegan Paul, 1971.
Aland, K. *Did the Early Church Baptize Infants?* London: SCM, 1963.
Alberti, Michael (1682–1752). *De therapia morborum morali.* Halle: J. C. Hendel, 1714a.
_____. *De medicinae et doctrinae moralis nexu.* Halle: J. C. Hendel, 1714b.
_____. *Specimen medicinae theologicae.* Halle: J. C. Hendel, 1726.
_____. *De dysthanasia et euthanasia medica.* Halle: J. C. Hendel, 1735.
Alexander, Archibald. *The Pastoral Office.* Philadelphia: Henry Perkins, 1834.
Allmen, Jean Jacques von. *Worship: Its Theology and Practice.* New York: Oxford University Press, 1965.
Altaner, B. *Patrology.* Translated by H. C. Gräf. New York: Herder, 1960.
Althaus, P. "Was ist die Taufe? Zur Antwort an Karl Barth." *Theologische Literaturzeitung,* 74 (1949), pp. 705 ff.
Allwohn, A. *Die Stellung der praktischen Theologie im System der Wissenschaften.* Giessen: Töpelmann, 1931.
Ambrose, (340–397). *Select Words and Letters. NPNF* 2nd, vol. 10, esp. "On the Duties of the Clergy," pp. 1–91, "Concerning Widows," pp. 391 ff., and various pastoral letters, pp. 411 ff.
_____. *Letters. FC,* vol. 26.
_____. *Theological and Dogmatic Works. FC,* vol. 44.
_____. *Seven Exegetical Works. FC,* vol. 65.

Ames, Wiliam (1571–1633). *Conscience with the Power and Cases Therof* (1639). English Experience Series. New York: Johnson Reprints, 1975.

Anderson, Ray S., ed. *Theological Foundations for Ministry*. Grand Rapids: Eerdmans, 1979.

Anderson, Stanley E. *Every Pastor a Counselor*. Wheaton, Ill.: VanKampen Press, 1949.

Andrewes, Lancelot (1555–1626). *Works*. 11 vols., LACT 1854. Cf. selections in *ATP*.

Anointing and Healing, Statement. Pamphlet. Adopted by the 1960 United Lutheran Church in America Convention. Detroit: 1962.

Anthony (251–356?). *Seven Letters of St. Anthony*. Translated by Derwas Chitty. London: S.L.G. Press, 1975.

Antonelli, Joseph. *Medicina pastoralis*. Rome: F. Pustet, 1904–05.

Aphrahat (Aphraates). "Of Pastors," in *Select Demonstrations* (337–345). *NPNF* 2nd, vol. 13, pp. 383–387.

Apostolic Constitutions (compiled 350–400). *ANF*, vol. 7.

Apostolic Fathers, The. Translated by Wm. Wake. Edinburgh: John Grant, 1909.

Aquinas. See Thomas Aquinas.

Ariés, Philippe. *Centuries of Childhood: A Social History of Family Life*. Translated by R. Baldick. New York: Knopf, 1962.

Aristotle (d. 322 B.C.) *Basic Works*. Edited by R. McKeon. New York: Random House, 1941.

———. *On the Soul and Parva Naturalia*. Translated by W. S. Hett. Cambridge: Harvard University Press (Loeb Library 8), 1935.

Arnold, F. X. *Grundsätzliches und Geschichtliches zur Theologie der Seelsorge*. Vol. 2 of *Untersuchungen, zur Theologie der Seelsorge*. Freiburg: Herder, 1949.

Arnold, F. X., and Rahner, K. *Handbuch der Pastoraltheologie*. Freiburg: Herder, 1964.

Ars moriendi, The (ca. 1450). Edited by W. H. Rylands. London: Wyman & Sons, 1881.

Asbury, Francis (1745–1816). *Journals and Letters*. Edited by E. T. Clark. 3 vols. Nashville: Abingdon, 1958.

Ashbrook, James B. *Responding to Human Pain*. Valley Forge, Pa.: Judson Press, 1975.

Asmussen, Hans. *Die Seelsorge: Ein praktisches Handbuch über Seelsorge und Seelenführung*, 4th ed. Munich: Chr. Kaiser Verlag, 1937.

Athanasius (296–373). *NPNF* 2nd, vol. 4, esp. *Letters*, pp. 495 ff.

———. *The Resurrection Letters*. Edited by J. N. Sparks. Nashville: Thomas Nelson, 1979.

Aubrey, M. E., ed. *A Minister's Manual*. London: Kingsgate Press, n.d.

Augustine, Aurelius (354–430), *NPNF* 1st, vols. 1–8.

———. *Commentary on the Lord's Sermon on the Mount* (394). Translated by J. Jepson. Westminster, Md.: Newman, 1948.

———. *On Lying* (395). [De mendacio.] *FC*, vol. 14, pp. 53 ff.

———. *The Christian Combat* (396a). [De agone christiano.] *FC*, vol. 2.

———. *Writings Against the Manicheans* (396b). *NPNF* 1st, vol. 4.

———. *On Christina Doctrine* (397–426). *NPNF* 1st, vol. 2.

———. *De catechizandis rudibus* (399–400). [On Catechizing the Uninstructed.] Oxford: Parker & Socios, 1885.

———. *Writings Against the Donatists* (400 ff.). *NPNF* 1st, vol. 4.

———. *On the Trinity* (399–419). In *Augustine: Later Writings*. *LCC*, Philadelphia: Westminster, 1954. (See also *NPNF* 1st, vol 3.)

———. *On the Spirit and the Letter* (412). *LCC*, vol. 8, pp. 182–251.

———. *Writings Against the Pelagians* (415 ff.). *NPNF* 1st, vol. 5.

———. *Patience* (417). *FCC*, vol. 16, pp. 237 ff.

———. *De civitate Dei* (417 ff). [The City of God.] *NPNF* 1st, vol. 2.

———. *Enchiridion* (423). In *Confessions and Enchiridion*. Translated by A. Outler. *LCC*, vol. 7.

———. *Admonition and Grace* (426–427). *FC*, vol 2.

———. *The Greatness of the Soul* [De Quantitate Animae]. Translated by W. Colleran, *ACW*, vol. 9.

———. *The Happy Life, Answer to Skeptics, Divine Providence and the Problem of Evil. FC*, vol. 5.

———. *Letters. FC*, vols. 12, 18, 20, 30.

Ayer, J. C. *A Source Book of Ancient Church History*. New York: n.p. 1913.

Bachmann, Charles C. "The Development of Lutheran Pastoral Care in America." Ph.D. dissertation, Boston University, 1949.

———. *Ministering to the Grief Sufferer*. Philadelphia: Fortress, 1964.

Bailey, Derrick S. *The Man-Woman Relation in Christian Thought*. London: Longmans, 1959.

Baillie, Donald M. *God Was in Christ*. New York: Scribner's, 1948.

Baker, Augustine (1571–1641). *Holy Wisdom*. Westminster, Md.: Christian Classics, 1973.

Baker's Dictionary of Practical Theology. Grand Rapids: Baker, 1957.

Balmforth, H.; Dewar, L.; Hudson, C.; and Sara, E. *An Introduction to Pastoral Theology*. New York: Macmillan, 1937.

Barclay, Robert. "Concerning the Ministry," from *An Apology for True Christian Divinity* (1678). Philadelphia: Friends' Bookshop, 1908, pp. 260–328.

Barnikol, E. *Das Diakonenamt*. Halle: Akademischer Verlag, 1941.

Barraclough, P. *Vocation for the Ministry*. London: Independent Press, 1955.

Barrett, Alfred. *Essay on the Pastoral Office*. London: John Mason, 1839.

Barrett, C. K. *The Signs of an Apostle*. Philadelphia: Fortress, 1972.

Barth, Karl. *Church Dogmatics*. Edited by G. W. Bromiley, T. F. Torrance, et al. 4 vols. Edinburgh: T. & T. Clark, 1936–1969.

———. *Epistle to the Romans*. Translated by E. C. Hoskyns. London: Oxford University Press, 1963.

———. *The Teaching of the Church Regarding Baptism*. London: SCM, 1948.

Basil (330–379). *Ascetical Works. FC*, vol. 9.

———. *Letters. FC*, vols. 13 and 28.

———. *Exegetic Homilies. FC*, vol. 46.

———. *Letters and Select Works. NPNF* 2nd, vol. 8.

Bauer, W. *Orthodoxy and Heresy in Earliest Christianity*. Philadelphia: Fortress, 1972.

Bauer, J. B. "Shepherd," *EBT*, vol. 3, pp. 844 ff.

Baumgarten, Siegmund (1706–1757). *Kurtzgefaste casuistische Pastoraltheologie*. Edited by J. F. Hesselberg. Halle: J. J. Gebauer, 1752.

Baur, F. C. "Über das Autoritätsprinzip des Apostels," *Theologisches Jahrbuch* (1852), pp. 32 ff.

Baxter, Richard (1615–1691). *Autobiography*. New York: E. P. Dutton, Everyman's Library, 1931.

———. *The Practical Works of the Rev. Richard Baxter*. 23 vols. London: James Duncan, 1830. Esp. on marriage counseling, vol. 4, pp. 1 ff., pp. 116 ff.; family counseling, vol. 4, pp. 90 ff.; care of children, pp. 105 ff., pp. 175 ff.; prayer, pp. 281 ff.; counsels for the poor, pp. 379 ff., the rich, pp. 389 ff.; the aged, pp. 396 ff.; worship, vol. 5, 1 ff.; pastoral duties, calling, office, vol. 5, pp. 107–33; duty of physicians, vol. 6, pp. 109–114; suicide, pp. 138–42; forgiveness, pp. 142–54; directions for holy conference, exhortation and reproof, pp. 246 –63; pastoral directions against sins of oppression, pp. 348 ff.; trusts and secrets, pp. 413–21; restitution, vol. 6, pp. 507–536; the right method for a settled peace of conscience and spiritual comfort, vol. 9, pp. 1 ff.; the reformed pastor, vol. 14, pp. 46 ff.; confirmation and restauration, vol. 9, pp. 403 ff.; the reformed liturgy, on catechizing, visitation, burial, admonition, vol. 15, pp. 492–517; the mischiefs of self-ignorance, vol. 16, pp. 33 ff.

———. *The Reformed Pastor* (1656). Edited by Wm. Brown. Carlisle, Pa.: Banner of Truth, 1979.

Bayly, Lewis. *The Practice of Piety: Directing a Christian How to Walk.* London: Philip Chetwinde, 1669.

Beck, J. T. *Pastoral Theology of the New Testament.* Translated by J. A. M'Clymont and T. Nicol. New York: Scribner and Welford, 1885.

Beckwith, R. T. "The Office of Women in the Church of the Present Day," *The Churchman* 83 (1969), pp. 170–83.

Becon, Thomas. *Prayers and Other Pieces by Thomas Becon.* Edited by John Ayre. Esp. "The Sick Man's Salve" (1561), pp. 87–192. Cambridge: At the University Press, 1844.

Bedell, G. T. *The Pastor—Pastoral Theology.* Philadelphia: Lippincott, 1880.

Beebe, James A. *The Pastoral Office.* New York: Abingdon, 1923.

Behm, J. "Noutheteo," *TDNT.*

Bellarmino, Robert. *De Laicis: Or, The Treatise on Civil Government.* Translated by K. E. Murphy. Westport, Conn.: Hyperion Press, 1979.

Benedict (480–550). *The Rule of St. Benedict in Latin and English.* London: Burns & Oates, 1932.

Bengel, Johann Albrecht (1687–1752). *Schatzkastlein zur Führung des geistlichen Amts, nach dessen Gnomon.* Edited by C. F. Werner. Ludwigsburg: Verlag F. Riehm, 1860.

Benoit, Jean. *Calvin, directeur d'âmes.* Strasbourg: Éditions Oberlin, 1947.

———. *Direction spirituelle et Protestantisme.* Paris: F. Alcan, 1940.

Berg, J. *The Moral Theology of Peter Dens.* Philadelphia: J. Harmstead, 1841.

Berger, P. and Neuhaus, R., eds. *Against the World for the World.* New York: Seabury, 1976.

Bergin, A. R. and Garfield, S. L., eds. *Handbook of Psychotherapy and Behavior Change.* New York: John Wiley, 1971.

Bergsten, G. *Pastoral Psychology.* New York: Macmillan, 1951.

Bernard of Clairvaux (1091–1153). *The Letters of St. Bernard of Clairvaux.* Translated by B. S. James. London: Burns & Oates, 1953.

———. *The Life and Works of St. Bernard.* Edited by Dom John Mabillon. Translated by S. J. Eales. 4 vols. London: J. Hodges, 1889–96.

———. *On Loving God. LCC,* vol. 13.

Bernard, T. A. *Homiletical and Pastoral Lectures.* New York: A. C. Armstrong, 1880.

Bertrangs, A. *The Bible on Suffering.* St. Norbert, Manitoba: Abbey of St. Norbert, 1966.

Best, E. "Spiritual Sacrifice: General Priesthood in the NT," *Interpretation* 14 (1960), pp. 280–90.

Betz, H. D. *Nachfolge und Nachahmung Jesu Christi im Neuen Testament,* Beiträge zur historischen Theologie, vol. 37 (1967).

Beyer, H. W. In *TDNT.* S.v. "Diakoneo," vol. 2, pp. 81–93; S.v. "Katecheo," vol. 3, pp. 638 ff. S.v.; "Therapeia," vol. 3, pp. 128 ff.

Bieler, Ludwig, ed. *The Irish Penitentials.* Dublin: Dublin Inst. for Advanced Studies, 1963.

Binsfeld, Pierre (1540–1598). *Enchiridion theologia pastoralis.* Brunntruti, Porentruy: Fabrum, 1599.

Birdsall, J. N. "John 10:29," *Journal of Theological Studies,* 11 (1960), pp. 342–44.

Blackwood, A. W. *The Funeral.* Philadelphia: Westminster, 1942a.

———. *Planning a Year's Pulpit Work.* Nashville: Abingdon, 1942b.

_____. *Pastoral Work*. Philadelphia: Westminster, 1945.

_____. *Pastoral Leadership*. Nashville: Abingdon, 1949.

_____. *The Preparation of Sermons*. London: Church Bookroom Press, 1951.

Blaikie, W. G. *For the Work of the Ministry: A Manual of Homiletic and Pastoral Theology*. London: Strahan, 1873.

Bliss, Kathleen. *The Service and Status of Women in the Churches*. Naperville, Ill.: Allenson, 1954.

Bloesch, Donald G. *The Evangelical Renaissance*. Grand Rapids: Eerdmans, 1973.

Bluff, M. J. *Pastoral-Medizin*. Cologne: J. P. Baclem, 1827.

Blumhardt, J. C. (1805–80). *Ausgewählte Schriften*, 4 vols. Vol. 2: *Verkündigung*. Zürich; Gotthelf, 1948.

Blunt, J. H. *Directorium Pastorale*. London: Murray, 1888 (1st ed. 1856).

Boethius (480?–524). *The Consolation of Philosophy* (524). Edited by H. F. Stewart. Loeb Classical Library. Cambridge: Harvard University Press, 1936.

Boisen, Anton T. *Out of the Depths*. New York: Harper & Bros., 1960.

Bonar, Andrew A. *The Visitor's Book of Texts*, 4th ed. New York: Robert Carter, 1867.

Bonaventure (1222–1274). *The Character of a Christian Leader*. Ann Arbor, Mich.: Servant, 1978.

_____. *The Works of St. Bonaventure*. 5 vols. Chicago: Franciscan Herald Press, 1972.

Bonhoeffer, Dietrich. *The Cost of Discipleship*. London: SCM, 1948.

_____. *Letters and Papers from Prison*. New York: Macmillan, 1953.

Bonhoeffer, Thomas. "Pastoralpsychiatrische Überlegungen zur Gotteslehre," in *Verifikationen*, edited by E. Jüngel et al. Tübingen: J. C. B. Mohr, 1982.

Bonnell, John S. *Pastoral Psychiatry*. New York: Harper & Bros., 1938.

Bonthius, Robert H. *Christian Paths to Self-Acceptance*. New York: King's Crown Press, 1948.

The Book of Common Order of the Church of Scotland. New York: Oxford University Press, 1940.

The Book of Common Prayer. (1662, 1928, and 1979 eds.) New York: Oxford University Press, various editions.

The Book of Common Worship. Philadelphia: Board of Christian Education, PCUSA, 1946.

The Book of Common Worship: The Church of South India. London: Oxford University Press, 1963.

The Book of Offices. London: Methodist Church of Great Britain, 1936.

The Book of Worship for Church and Home. New York: Methodist Publishing House, 1944, 1964.

Bornkamm, G. *Jesus of Nazareth*. New York: Harper & Bros. 1960.

Boroth, J. *Synopsis Theologie Pastoralis*, 1823.

Borromeo, Federigo (1564–1631). *Pastorum instructiones, monitiones ad clerum atque epistolae*. Louvain edition, 1701. Edited by E. W. Westhoff. Münster: n.p., 1860.

Boucher, M. "Some Unexplored Parallels to First Corinthians 11:11–12 and Galations 3:28," *Canadian Biblical Quarterly*, 31 (1969), pp. 50–58.

Bouyer, Louis. *A History of Christian Spirituality*. 3 vols. New York: Seabury. Vol. 1, *New Testament and the Fathers*, 1963; vol. 2, *Middle Ages*, 1968; vol. 3, *Orthodox Spirituality and Protestant and Anglican Spirituality*, 1974.

Bowles, Edward (1613–1662). *Good Counsell for Evil Times*. London: Samuel Gellibrand, 1648.

Bowles, Oliver (b. ca. 1571). *De pastore evangelico tractatus*. London: Samuel Gellibrand, 1649.

Bownas, Samuel. *A Description of the Qualifications Necessary to A Gospel Minister*. London: Bible in George-Yard, 1767.

Box, H. S., ed. *Priesthood*. London: S.P.C.K., 1937.

―――. *Spiritual Directions*. (Selections from Fr. Scaramelli, Augustine Baker, Faber, et al.) London: S.P.C.K., 1938.

Bradford, John (1510–1555). *The Writings of John Bradford*. 2 vols. Edited by A. Townsend. Cambridge: At the University Press, 1848–53.

Brandon, Owen. *Pastor and Ministry*. London: S.P.C.K., 1972.

Brattgard, Helge. *God's Stewards*. Minneapolis: Augsburg, 1963.

Brett, George Sidney. *A History of Psychology*. 3 vols. London: n.p. 1912–21; 2nd edition edited by R. S. Peters. Cambridge, Mass.: M.I.T. Press, 1965.

Brett, Thomas. "A Sermon of the Honour of the Christian Priesthood, and of the Necessity of a Divine Call to that Office" (1712). In Moorman, pp. 126 ff.

Bridges, Charles. *The Christian Ministry*. New York: Robert Carter, 1847 (1st ed. 1829).

Brightman, Frank E. *The English Rite, Being a Synopsis of the Sources and Revisions of the Book of Common Prayer*. 2 vols. London: Rivingtons, 1915.

Brilioth, Yngve. *A Brief History of Preaching*. Philadelphia: Fortress, 1965.

Brister, C. W. *Pastoral Care in the Church*. New York: Harper & Row, 1964.

―――. *The Promise of Counseling*. New York: Harper & Row, 1978.

Britzger, F. X. *Handbuch der Pastoral-medizin für Seelsorger auf dem Lande*. Regensburg and Ulm: Wichler, 1849.

Bromiley, G. W. *Baptism and the Anglican Reformers*. London: Lutterworth, 1953.

―――. *Christian Ministry*. Grand Rapids: Eerdmans, 1960.

Brooks, Phillips. *Lectures on Preaching*. New York: E. P. Dutton, 1877.

Brown, Charles Reynolds. *The Making of a Minister*. New York: Century, 1927.

Brown, Colin. "The Teaching Office of the Church," *The Churchman*, 83 (1969), pp. 184–96.

Brown, John, ed. (1784–1858). *The Christian Pastor's Manual*. Edinburgh: David Brown, 1826.

Brown, Peter. *Augustine of Hippo*. Berkeley: University of California Press, 1969.

Brown, Wm. A. *The Minister, His World and His Work*. Nashville: Abingdon-Cokesbury, 1937.

Browne, Thomas. *Religio Medici* (1635). Cambridge: At the University Press, 1963.

Browning, Don S. *Atonement and Psychotherapy*. Philadelphia: Westminster, 1966.

―――. *The Moral Context of Pastoral Care*. Philadelphia: Westminster, 1970.

Bruce, A. B. *The Training of the Twelve*. New York: Harper & Bros., 1871.

Bruce, Calvin E. "Nurturing the Souls of Black Folk," *Journal of Pastoral Care*, 30 (1976), pp. 259–63.

Bruce, F. F., and Rupp, E. G., eds. *Holy Book and Holy Tradition*. Grand Rapids: Eerdmans, 1968.

Bruce, Michael, and Duffield, G. E. *Why Not? Priesthood and the Ministry of Women*. Appleford, U. K.: The Marcham Manor Press, 1972.

Brunner, P. "The Ministry and the Ministry of Women," *Lutheran World* 6 (1959), pp. 247–74. (Cf. reply by A. Paulsen. *LW* 7, 1960, pp. 231 f.)

Bruns, J. E. "The Discourse on the Good Shepherd and the Rite of Ordination," *American Ecclesiastical Review* 149 (1963), pp. 389–91.

Buber, M. *I-Thou*. 2nd ed. New York: Scribner's, 1958.

Bucer, Martin (1491–1551). *Instruction in Christian Love* (1523). Translated by Paul T. Fuhrmann. Richmond: John Knox Press, 1952.

―――. *Pastorale, das ist von der waren Seelsorge und dem rechten Hirtendienst* (1538). In M. Bucer's *Deutsche Schriften*, vol. 7. Gütersloh: G. Mohn, 1960.

―――. *De Regno Christi, LCC*, vol. 19.

―――. *Common Places*. Translated by D. F. Wright. Appleford, U. K.: Sutton Courtenay Press, 1972. Esp. see ordination, pp. 253 ff.; and sick visitation, pp. 430 ff.

Bullinger, Heinrich (1504–1575). *Bericht der krancken: Wie man by den Krancken und sterbenden Menschen handeln.* Zürich: C. Froschoeur, 1538.

Bultmann, R. *Theology of the New Testament.* New York: Scribner's, 1952.

——. *Essays: Philosophical and Theological.* New York: Macmillan, 1955.

——. *Existence and Faith.* Translated by S. Ogden. New York: Meridian, 1960.

——. "The New Testament and Mythology" (1941). In *Kerygma and Myth.* Edited by H. Bartsch. New York: Harper & Row, 1969.

——. *The History of the Synoptic Tradition.* Translated by John Marsh. New York: Harper & Row, 1968.

Bunyan, John (1628–1688). *Grace Abounding* (1666). *The Pilgrim's Progress* (1678). In *Works of John Bunyan.* Philadelphia: Bradley, 1870.

——. *The Greatness of the Soul, and the Unspeakableness of the Loss Thereof.* New York: Wiley and Putnam, 1846.

Burgon, J. W. (1813–1888). *A Treatise on the Pastoral Office.* London: John Murray, 1883.

Burkle, Howard R. *God, Suffering and Belief.* Nashville: Abingdon, 1977.

Burnet, Gilbert. *A Discourse of the Pastoral Care* (1692). London: W. Baynes, 1818. (Cf. Moorman, pp. 81 ff.)

Bushnell, Horace. *The Moral Use of Dark Things.* New York: Scribner's, 1905.

——. *Christian Nurture* (1847). New York: Scribner's, 1916.

Butler, Joseph (1692–1752). *Five Sermons Preached at Rolls Chapel.* Edited by S. M. Brown (from 2nd edition, 1729). New York: Liberal Arts Press, 1950.

Cabot, Richard C. *Religion and Medicine.* New York: Moffat, Yard & Co., 1908.

Cabot, Richard C., and Dicks, Russell L. *The Art of Ministering to the Sick.* New York: Macmillan, 1936.

Cadbury, H. J., ed. *George Fox's "Book of Miracles."* Cambridge: At the University Press, 1948.

Caird, G. B. "Paul and Women's Liberty," *Bulletin of John Rylands Library,* 54, pp. 268–81.

Calkins, R. *How Jesus Dealt with Men.* New York: Abingdon, 1942.

Calkins, R. *The Romance of Ministry.* Boston: Pilgrim Press, 1941.

Calvin, John (1509–1564). *Letters of John Calvin.* Edited by J. Bonnet. 2 vols. Edinburgh: T. Constable & Co., 1855–57. (Philadelphia: Presbyterian Bd. of Publ., 1858, 4 vols.)

——. *Calvin: Theological Treatises. LCC,* vol. 22. Esp. "Articles Concerning the Organization of the Church and of Worship at Geneva" (1537), pp. 47–55; "Draft Ecclesiastical Ordinances" (1541a), pp. 56–72; "The Catechism" (1545), pp. 83–140; "Short Treatise on the Lord's Supper" (1541b), pp. 140–67; "The Ministry of the Word and the Sacraments," 170–78.

——. *Calvin: Institutes of the Christian Religion.* 2 vols. Edited by J. T. McNeill. Chiefly from 1559 edition. *LCC,* vols. 20–21. Standard references in Calvin are made by book, chapter, and section numbers, for all editions. Thus 4.1.3 means book 4, chapter 1, section 3.

——. *Commentaries.* 22 vols. Grand Rapids: Baker, 1979.

——. *John Calvin: Selections from His Writings.* Edited by J. Dillenberger. Missoula, Mont.: Scholars' Press, 1975.

Cameron, R. M. *The Rise of Methodism.* New York: Philosophical Library, 1954.

Cameron, W. A. *The Clinic of a Cleric.* New York: Ray Long and R. Smith, 1931.

Cannon, James Spencer. *Lectures on Pastoral Theology.* New York: Scribner's, 1853.

Capellmann, Carl F. N. (1841–98). *Pastoral Medicine.* Translated by Wm. Dassel. New York: F. Pustet, 1879.

Carey, K. M., ed. *The Historic Episcopate.* London: Dacre, 1954.

Carkhuff, R. R. *Helping and Human Relations.* 2 vols. New York: Holt, Rinehart & Winston, 1969.

Cassian, John (360–435). *Institutes and Conferences*. In *Western Asceticism*. Edited by Owen Chadwick. 1958. *LCC*, vol. 12.

———. *Writings of John Cassian. NPNF* 2nd, vol. 11.

Catherine of Siena (1347–1380). *St. Catherine of Siena as Seen in her Letters*. Edited by Vida Scudder. London: J. M. Dent, 1905.

Caussade, J. P. de (1675–1751). *Abandonment, or Absolute Abandonment to Divine Providence*. Edited by H. Ramiere. New York: Benziger, 1951.

Chadwick, Henry. *The Early Church*. Baltimore: Penguin, 1967.

Chadwick, Owen. *John Cassian*. Cambridge: At the University Press, 1950.

———. *Western Asceticism. LCC*, vol. 12.

Chaucer, Geoffrey. *The Canterbury Tales* (ca. 1386–90). Interlinear translation by V. Hopper. Brooklyn: Barron's, 1949.

Chemnitz, Martin. *Ministry, Word, and Sacrament: An Enchiridion* (1595). St. Louis: Concordia, 1981.

Childs, B. S. "Memory and Tradition in Israel," *Studies in Biblical Theology*, 37 (1962).

Chitty, Derwas J. *The Desert a City: Egyptian and Palestinian Monasticism under the Christian Empire*. Oxford: Blackwell, 1966.

Chrysostom, John (347–407). *NPNF* 1st, vols. 9–14. Esp. *On Priesthood* [de sacerdotio], (before 392), vol. 9, pp. 33–83; *Letters*, vol. 9; *Homilies on the Acts and Romans* (393), vol. 9; and *Corinthians*, vol. 12.

———. *Commentary on St. John the Apostle and Evangelist, Homilies* 1–47, *FC*, vol. 33; *Homilies* 48–88, *FC*, vol. 41.

———. *Baptismal Instructions*. Translated by P. W. Harkins. Westminster, Md.: Newman, 1963.

Cleary, Wm. H., ed. *Hyphenated Priests*. Washington: Corpus, 1969.

Clebsch, Wm. A. and Jaekle, C. R. *Pastoral Care in Historical Perspective*. Englewood Cliffs, N.J.: Prentice-Hall, 1964.

Clement of Alexandria (155–220). *ANF*, vol. 2; *LCC*, vol. 1.

Clementine Recognitions and Homilies (before 360). *ANF*, vol. 8, pp. 75–361.

The Clergyman's Instructor: Tracts on Ministerial Duties. Selections from Herbert (1632), Taylor, Sprat (1695), Wilson (1708), Gibson (1724, 1741, 1742), Hort (1742). Oxford: Oxford University Press, 1843.

Clinebell, Howard J. *Basic Types of Pastoral Counseling*. Nashville: Abingdon, 1966.

Cobb, John B., Jr. *Theology and Pastoral Care*. Philadelphia: Fortress, 1977.

Cocceius, Johannes (1603–1669). *Opera Omnia*. 8 vols. Amsterdam: J. van Someren, 1669.

Coggan, F. D. *The Ministry of the Word*. London: Canterbury Press, 1945.

Coleridge, S. T. (1722–1834). *Complete Works*. Edited by W. G. T. Shedd. 7 vols. New York: Harper & Bros., 1853.

Columbanus (543–615). *Columbanus in His Own Words*. Willits, Calif.: Eastern Orthodox Press, n.d.

Comenius, John Amos (1592–1670). *Analytical Didactic* (1657). Translated by Vladimir Jelinek. Chicago: University of Chicago Press, 1953. (Also in Great Issues in Education, vol. 1. Chicago: Great Books, pp. 133–76).

Common Service Book of the Lutheran Church. Philadelphia: United Lutheran Church in America, 1930.

Concerning the Ordination of Women. Geneva: World Council of Churches, 1964.

Cone, James. *The God of the Oppressed*. New York: Seabury, 1975.

Congar, Yves. *Lay People in the Church*. London: Geoffrey Chapman, 1959.

Conzelmann, H. *The Theology of St. Luke*. Translated by G. Buswell. New York: Harper & Bros., 1960.

———. *First Corinthians*. Translated by J. Leitch. Philadelphia: Fortress, 1975.

Cooke, Bernard. *Ministry to Word and Sacraments*. Philadelphia: Fortress, 1976.

Council of Trent (1545–1563). *Canons and Decrees*. Edited by H. J. Schroeder. St. Louis: Herder, 1941.

Crabb, Lawrence J. *Basic Principles of Biblical Counseling.* Grand Rapids: Zondervan, 1975.

Cranmer, Thomas (1489–1556). *The Works of Thomas Cranmer.* Edited by J. E. Cox. 2 vols. Cambridge: At the University Press, 1844–46.

Cremer, Hermann (1834–1903). *Die befähigung zum geistlichen Amte.* Berlin: Wiegandt und Grieben, 1878.

Cross, F. L. *The Early Christian Fathers.* London: Duckworth, 1960.

Cullmann, O. *Baptism in the New Testament.* London: SCM, 1950.

_____. *Peter: Apostle, Disciple, Martyr.* London: SCM, 1953.

_____. *Early Christian Worship.* London: SCM, 1953.

Cunningham, W. *The Cure of Souls: Lectures on Pastoral Theology.* Cambridge: At the University Press, 1908.

Cutten, George. *Three Thousand Years of Mental Healing.* New York: Scribner's, 1911.

Cyprian (d. 258). *ANF,* vol. 5. Esp. "On the Lapsed," pp. 437–47; "Prayer," pp. 447–57; and on alms, patience, jealousy, and envy, 476–95.

_____. *Letters* 1–81. *FC,* vol. 51.

_____. *Treatises. FC,* vol. 36.

Cyril of Alexandria (376–444). *Commentary on the Gospel According to St. John.* 2 vols. *LF,* vol. 43.

Cyril of Jerusalem (ca. 315–ca. 386). *Catechetical Lectures* (348). *NPNF* 2nd, vol. 7; see also *LCC,* vol. 4.

_____. *Works of St. Cyril of Jerusalem. FC,* vol. 61.

Dailey, Robert. *Introduction to Moral Theology.* New York: Bruce, 1970.

Dakin, A. *The Baptist View of the Church and Ministry.* London: Kingsgate, 1944.

Daly, Mary. *Beyond God the Father.* Boston: Beacon Press, 1973.

Danielou, Jean. *Origen.* Translated by W. Mitchell. New York: Sheed & Ward, 1955.

_____. *The Ministry of Women in the Early Church.* London: Faith Press, 1961.

_____. *Prayer as a Political Problem.* New York: Sheed & Ward, 1967.

Davies, J. G. *The Spirit, the Church, and the Sacraments.* London: Faith Press, 1954.

Davies, W. D. *Christian Origins and Judaism.* Philadelphia: Westminster, 1962.

Davis, Henry. *Moral and Pastoral Theology.* 4 vols. New York: Sheed & Ward, 1938.

Delahaye, K. "Überlegungen zur Neuorientierung der Pastoraltheologie heute." In *Gott in Welt.* Vol. 2 of *Festgabe für Karl Rahner.* Edited by J. B. Metz. Freiburg/Basel/Vienna, Herder, 1964.

Delling, G. "Zur Taufe von 'Haeusern' in Urchristentum," *Novum Testamentum* (1964 –65), pp. 285 ff.

Demerst, David D. *Pastoral Theology.* New Brunswick, N.J.: J. Heidingsfeld, n.d.

Denzinger, H. J. *The Sources of Catholic Dogma.* Translated by R. J. Deferrari. St. Louis: Herder, 1957.

Derrett, J. D. M. "The Good Shepherd: St. John's Use of Jewish Halakhah and Haggadah," *Studia Theologica,* 27 (1973), pp. 25–50.

Descartes, René (1596–1650). *Meditations on the First Philosophy* (1641) and *The Passions of the Soul* (1649). In *Philosophical Works.* 2 vols. Cambridge: At the University Press, 1967.

Desert Fathers, Sayings of the. Translated by B. Ward. London: A. R. Mowbray and Co., 1975.

Dewar, Lindsay and Hudson, Cyril. *A Manual of Pastoral Theology.* London: Philip Allen, 1932.

Deyling, Solomon (1677–1755). *Institutiones Prudentiae Pastoralis* (1734). Edited by C. W. Küstnerum. Leipzig: F. Lanckisii, 1768.

Dibelius, Martin. *From Tradition to Gospel.* Cambridge: J. Clarke, 1971.

Dicks, Russell. *And Ye Visited Me.* New York: Harper and Bros., 1939.

Dickson, David (1585–1665). *Therapeutica sacra.* London: T. Johnson, 1656.

Didache, The (2nd century). *ANF,* vol. 1; *LCC,* vol. 1.

Didascalia Apostolorum. Syriac version. Oxford: Clarendon, 1929.

Dionysius the Areopagite. *The Divine Names and Mystical Theology* (c. 500). Translated by C. E Rolt. London: S.P.C.K., 1975.

Dittes, James. *The Church in the Way.* New York: Scribner's, 1967.

———. *When the People Say No.* San Francisco: Harper & Row, 1979.

Dix, Gregory. *The Shape of the Liturgy.* London: A & C Black, 1945.

Dodd, C. H. *The Apostolic Preaching and Its Developments.* London: Hodder & Stoughton, 1936.

———. *Parables of the Kingdom.* London: Hodder & Stoughton, 1936.

Doddridge, Philip (1702–1751). *Works.* 10 vols. Leeds: Edward Baines, 1802–1805.

———. *Lectures on Preaching,* London: W. Baynes and Son, n.d.

Dodwell, Henry. *Two Letters of Advice, For the Susception of Holy Orders* (1672). In Moorman, pp. 27 ff.

Doniger, Simon, ed. *Healing: Human and Divine.* New York: Association Press, 1957.

Donne, John (1573–1631). *Essays in Divinity.* Edited by E. M. Simpson, Oxford: Oxford University Press, 1952.

———. *Devotions Upon Emergent Occasions* (1623). Ann Arbor: University of Michigan Press, 1959.

Dorotheus of Gaza (6th century). *Discourses and Sayings.* Kalamazoo, Mich.: Cistercian, 1977.

Drakeford, John W. *People to People Therapy.* San Fransisco: Harper & Row, 1978.

Drelincourt, Charles (1595–1669). *The Christian's Defense against the Fears of Death* (1651). Boston: Thomas Fleet, 1744.

Duchesne, Louis. *Christian Worship: Its Origins and Evolution.* 5th ed. London: S.P.C.K., 1919.

Dulles, Avery. *Models of the Church.* New York: Doubleday, 1974.

———. *The Resilient Church.* New York: Doubleday, 1977.

Dunbar, Helen Flanders. *Mind and Body: Psychosomatic Medicine.* New York: Random House, 1947.

Dunkerley, R., ed. *The Ministry and the Sacraments.* London: SCM, 1937.

Dunlop, J. B. ed. *Staretz Amvrosy,* (1812–1891). Belmont, Mass.: Nordland Publications, 1975.

Durnbaugh, D. F. *The Believers' Church: History and Character of Radical Protestantism.* New York: Macmillan, 1968.

Dwyer, Walter W. *The Churches' Handbook for Spiritual Healing.* New York: Ascension Press, 1960.

Dykes, J. Oswald. *The Christian Minister and His Duties.* Edinburgh: T. & T. Clark, 1909.

Easton, B. S. "Jewish and Early Christian Ordination," *Anglican Theol. Review,* 5 (1922–23), pp. 308–19; 6, (1923–24), pp. 285–95.

———. *The Pastoral Epistles.* New York: Scribner's, 1947.

Eastwood, C. *The Priesthood of All Believers.* London: Epworth, 1960.

Ebeling, G. *Word and Faith.* London: SCM, 1963.

Ebrard, J. H. A., ed., *Vorlesungen über praktische Theologie.* Königsberg: A. W. Unzer, 1854.

Eckhart, Meister. *Meister Eckhart: A Modern Translation.* By R. P. Blakney. New York: Harper and Bros., 1941.

Edwards, Jonathan (1703–1758). *Works.* Edited by Perry Miller. New Haven Conn., Yale University Press, 1957–.

Ehrenfeuchter, F. A. E. *Die praktische Theologie.* Göttingen: Dieterich, 1859.

Ehrhardt, A. *The Apostolic Succession in the First Two Centuries of the Church.* London: Lutterworth Press, 1953.

———. "Jewish and Christian Ordination," *Journal of Ecclesiastical History,* 5 (1954), pp. 125–38.

Eichrodt, W. *Theology of the Old Testament.* 2 vols. Translated by Baker. Philadelphia: Westminster, 1967.

Ellicott, C. J., ed. *Homiletical and Pastoral Lectures*. New York: A. C. Armstrong, 1880.

Eliade, M. *From Primitives to Zen*. New York: Harper & Row, 1977.

Elizabethan Puritanism. Edited by L. J. Trinterud. LPT.

Emerton, E. *Letters of St. Boniface*. New York: Columbia University Press, 1940.

English Recusant Devotional Prose, A Critical Anthology of. Edited by J. R. Roberts. Pittsburgh: Duquesne University Press, 1966.

Ephraim Syrus (ca. 306–ca. 373). *NPNF* 2nd, vol. 13; "On Admonition and Repentance," pp. 330–336.

Erasmus, D. and Luther, M. *Discourse on Free Will*. Translated by F. Ernst. New York: Ungar, 1960.

Erdman, Charles. *The Work of the Pastor*. Philadelphia: Westminster, 1924.

Erikson, Erik. *Identity and the Life Cycle*. New York: International Universities Press, 1959.

Eusebius (ca. 260–ca. 340). *Church History*. Translated by H. J. Lawlor and J. E. L. Oulton. 2 vols. London: S.P.C.K., 1927–28; also in *NPNF* 2nd, vol. 1.

Evagrius Ponticus (349–399). *Praktikos and Chapters on Prayer*. Translated by J. E. Bamberger. Kalamazoo, Mich.: Cistercian Press, 1970.

Faber, F. W. (1814–1863). *Spiritual Conferences*. Rockford, Ill.: TAN Books Publications, 1978.

Fairbairn, Patrick. *Pastoral Theology: A Treatise on the Offices and Duties of the Christian Pastor*. Edinburgh: T. & T. Clark, 1875.

Farrer, A. *Love Almighty and Ills Unlimited*. Garden City, N.Y.: Doubleday, 1961.

Fedotov, G. P. *A Treasury of Russian Spirituality*. New York: Sheed & Ward, 1948.

Feilding, Charles, et al. *Education for Ministry*. Dayton: American Association of Theological Schools, 1966.

Fendt, L. *Grundriss der Praktischen Theologie für Studenten und Kandidaten*. Tübingen: J. C. B. Mohr, 1938–39.

Fénelon, François (1651–1715). *Spiritual Letters*. Translated by M. W. Stillman. Cornwall-on-Hudson, N.Y.: Idlewild Press, 1945.

———. *Dialogue on Eloquence*. Translated by W. S. Howell. Princeton, N.J.: Princeton University Press, 1950.

———. *Christian Perfection*. Edited by C. F. Wilson. New York: Harper & Bros., 1947.

Fenn, D. F. *Parish Administration*. New York: Morehouse-Gorham, 1938.

Fensham, F. C. "Widow, Orphan and the Poor," *Journal of Near Eastern Studies*, 21 (1962), pp. 129–39.

Ferguson, Everett. "Laying on of Hands: Its Significance in Ordination," *Journal of Theological Studies*, New Series 26, nos. 1–12. 1975.

Feuillet, A. "La Dignité et le Role de la Femme d'aprés quelques Textes Pauliniens," *New Testament Studies*, 21 (1974–5), pp. 157–91.

Fichtner, Horst. *Systematik der Seelsorge, gegenwartspsychologische Grundlegung und Gestaltung des evangelischen Dienstes an der Seele*. Leipzig: U. Unger, 1931.

———. *Hauptfragen der praktischen theologie*. Schwerin: F. Bahn, 1939.

Fichter, J. *Religion as an Occupation*. Notre Dame, Ind.: University of Notre Dame Press, 1961.

Filson, F. V. "The Christian Teacher in the First Century," *Journal of Biblical Literature*, 60 (1941), pp. 317 ff.

Flemington, W. F. *The New Testament Doctrine of Baptism*. London: S.P.C.K., 1948.

Ford, Peter S. *The Healing Trinity*. New York: Harper & Row, 1971.

Forrell, George W. *Christian Social Teachings*. New York: Doubleday, 1966.

Forsyth, P. T. (1848–1921). *Positive Preaching and the Modern Mind*. London: Hodder & Stoughton, 1907.

———. *Socialism, the Church and the Poor*. London: Hodder & Stoughton, 1908.

———. *The Principle of Authority*. London: Hodder & Stoughton, 1912.

———. *Lectures on the Church and the Sacraments*. London: Longmans, Green, 1917.

Fox, George (1624–1691). *The Journal of George Fox.* Cambridge: At the University Press, 1911.

Francis of Assisi (1181–1226). *The Little Flowers, Life of St. Francis, Mirror of Perfection.* London: J. M. Dent, 1910.

Francis de Sales (1567–1622). *Introduction to the Devout Life* (1608). New York: E. P. Dutton, 1961.

————. *The Spiritual Conferences* (1628). Westminster, Md.: Newman, 1943.

————. *Spiritual Letters to Persons in Religion.* Translated by H. B. Mackey. Westminster, Md.: Newman, 1943.

Frankl, V. *The Doctor and the Soul.* New York: Knopf, 1955.

Freud, Sigmund (1856–1939). *The Standard Edition of the Complete Psychological Works of Sigmund Freud.* 24 vols. London: Hogarth Press, 1953–.

Fuller, Thomas (1608–1661). *The Holy State and the Profane State.* Boston: Little, Brown, 1864.

————. *The Cause and Cure of a Wounded Conscience* (1647). London: W. Tegg, 1867.

————. *Collected Sermons.* 2 vols. Edited by J. E. Bailey and W. E. A. Axon. London: Greshem Press, 1891.

Fulton, J. *Index Canonum: Containing the canons of undisputed general councils and some provincial councils in Greek and English, with a digest of canon law.* New York: Pott, Young, 1872.

Funk, Francis Xaver von (1840–1907). *A Manual of Church History.* Edited by W. H. Kent. New York: Benziger, 1910.

Galtier, J. "Imposition des mains," *DTC*, vol. 8, 1972, pp. 1302–1425.

Garfield, Sol L. "Basic Ingredients or Common Factors in Psychotherapy?" *Journal of Consulting and Clinical Psychology*, 41 (1973), pp. 10 ff.

Garvie, A. E. *The Holy Catholic Church from the Congregational Point of View.* London: Faith Press, 1920.

Garvie, A. E. *The Christian Preacher.* New York: Scribner's, 1921.

Gaume, Abbé Jean Joseph (1802–1879). *Manual for Confessors* (1854). Preface by E. B. Pusey. 2nd ed. Oxford: James Parker, 1878.

————. *Catéchisme de persévérance.* Brussels: Vanderborght, 1842.

Gee, H., and Hardy, W. J. *Documents Illustrative of English Church History.* New York: Macmillan, 1896.

Georgi, D. "Die Geschichte der Kollekte des Paulus für Jerusalem." *Theologische Forschung*, 38 (1965).

Gerard, Alexander. *The Pastoral Care.* Aberdeen: T. Cadell, Jr. and W. Davies, 1799.

Gerberding, G. H. *The Lutheran Pastor.* Philadelphia: Lutheran Publ. Soc., 1902.

Gerhard, J. *Loci Theologici* (1610). 2nd ed. Edited by J. F. Cotta. 20 vols. Tübingen: H. Mueller, 1772–1776.

Gerkin, Charles. *Crisis Experience in Modern Life.* Nashville: Abingdon, 1979.

Gerson, Jean de (1363–1429). *The Ad Deo Vadit of Jean Gerson.* Edited by D. H. Carnahan. Urbana, Ill.: The University of Illinois Press, 1917.

Gibbons, James Cardinal. *The Ambassador of Christ.* Baltimore: John Murphy Co., 1896.

Gibson, Edmund. "The Charge at his Primary Visitation Begun in the Year 1717," in Moorman, pp. 146 ff.

Gibson, M. D. "Phoebe," ExpT, 23 (1911–12), pp. 281 ff.

Gladden, Washington. *The Christian Pastor.* New York: Scribner's, 1898.

————. *The Church and Parish Problems.* New York: Thwing, 1911.

Glasse, James. *Profession: Minister.* Nashville: Abingdon, 1968.

Glasser, William. *Reality Therapy: A New Approach to Psychiatry.* New York: Harper & Row, 1965.

Glock, R. and B. *To Comfort and to Challenge: A Dilemma of the Contemporary Church.* Berkeley: University of California Press, 1967.

Godin, Andre. *The Pastor as Counselor.* New York: Holt, Rinehart and Winston, 1965.

Gollowitz, Domini Kus (1761–1809), *Anweisung zur Pastoraltheologie.* 2 vols. Land-shut: Phillip Krull, 1803.

Goppelt, L. *Apostolic and Post-Apostolic Times.* Translated by R. Guelich. Grand Rapids: Baker, 1977.

Gordon, A. J. *The Ministry of Healing.* 2nd ed. Harrisburg, Pa.: Christian Publications, 1961.

Gore, Charles. *The Church and the Ministry* (1888). London: Longmans, Green, 1900.

Gouge, Thomas (1609–1681). *Christian Directions, Shewing How to Walk with God All the Day Long* (1664). In *Works.* Glasgow: D. Hutchinson, 1790.

Gougel, G. *Theologie pastorale: Idées sur les ministère L'évangelique et principaux caractères du vrai pasteur.* Paris: n.p., 1834.

Goulooze, William. *Manual for Ministers, Elders and Deacons.* Grand Rapids: Eerdmans, 1937.

_____. *Pastoral Psychology: Applied Psychology in Pastoral Theology in America.* Grand Rapids: Baker, 1950.

Graeffe, J. F. C. (1764–1816). *Grundrisse der allgemeinen Katechetik.* Göttingen: Vandenhoeck und Ruprecht, 1796.

Graeffe, J. F. C. *Die Pastoraltheologie nach ihrem ganzen Umfange.* 2 vols. Göttingen: Vandenhoeck und Ruprecht, 1803.

Graham, R. W. "Women in the Pauline Churches: A Review Article," *Lexington Theological Quarterly,* 11 (1976), pp. 25–34.

Greeley, A. *Uncertain Trumpet: The Priest in Modern America.* New York: Sheed & Ward, 1967.

Gregory Nazianzus (330–389). *Orations and Letters. NPNF* 2nd, vol. 7.

_____. *Theological Orations. LCC,* vol. 3, pp. 128–215.

_____. *Funeral Orations. FC,* vol. 22.

Gregory of Nyssa (331–394). *Ascetical Works. FC,* vol. 58.

_____. *Dogmatic Treatises. NPNF,* vol. 5.

_____. *An Address on Religious Instruction. LCC,* vol. 3, pp. 268–327.

Gregory the Great (540–604). *The Book of Pastoral Rule, and Epistles. NPNF* 2nd, vol. 12, pp. 1–72. Annotated as "Gregory."

_____. *Pastoral Care* (591). Translated by Henry Davis. *ACW* vol. 11, Westminster, Md.: Newman, 1950.

_____. *Dialogues. FC,* vol. 39.

_____. *Morals on the Book of Job.* Translated by J. Bliss. 3 vols. *LF.* Oxford: Parker, 1844–50.

Green, Peter. *The Town Parson: His Life and Work.* New York: Longmans, Green, 1919.

Griffith-Thomas, W. H. *Ministerial Life and Work.* Grand Rapids: Baker, n.d.

Grimes, Howard. "What Is Practical Theology?" *Perkins Journal,* 30 (1977), pp. 31 ff.

Grou, Jean N. (1731–1803). *Manual for Interior Souls.* London: Burns & Oates, 1958.

Guffin, Gilbert L. *Called of God: The Work of the Ministry.* Westwood, N.J.: Fleming Revell, 1951.

Guibert, Joseph de. *The Theology of the Spiritual Life.* New York: Sheed & Ward, 1953.

Gury, Jean Pierre (1801–1866). *Compendium der Moraltheologie.* Regensburg: G. J. Manz, 1869.

Gusmer, C. W. "Anointing of the Sick in the Church of England," *Worship,* 45, (1971), pp. 262–72.

Haas, Nicolaus, *Wissenschaftliche Darstellung des geistlichen Berufs.* Bamberg: J. A. Göbhardt, 1812.

Haendler, Otto. *Grundriss der Praktichen Theologie.* Berlin: Evangelische Verlagsanstalt, 1957.

———. *Tiefenpsychologie, Theologie und Seelsorge, Aufsätze.* Göttingen: Vandenhoeck und Ruprecht, 1971.

Häring, Bernard. *Toward a Christian Moral Theology.* 2 vols. Notre Dame, Ind.: University of Notre Dame Press, 1966.

Hagenbach, K. R. *Encycklopaedie und Methodologie der Theologischen Wissenschaften.* Leipzig: S. Hirzel, 1889.

———. *Compendium of the History of Christian Doctrines.* Translated by Carl W. Buch, Edinburgh: T. & T. Clark, 1846–47.

Halmos, Paul. *The Faith of the Counsellors.* New York: Schocken, 1966.

Halsey, Luther, (1794–1880). *The Character of the Christian Ministry.* Pittsburgh: D. & M. MacLean, 1830.

Hamilton, Charles V. *The Black Preacher in America.* New York: Wm. Morrow, 1972.

Hamilton, James, ed. *Our Christian Classics.* 4 vols. London: J. Nisbet, 1859.

Hamilton, Neill G. *The Protestant Adventure.* New York: Seabury Press, 1981.

Hardeland, August. *Geschichte der speciellen Seelsorge in der vorreformatorischen Kirche und der Kirche der Reformation.* 2 vols. Berlin: Reuther & Reichard, 1897–1898.

Hardeland, August. *Pastoraltheologie: Gedanken und Erwägungen aus dem Amt für das Amt.* Leipzig: Bohme, 1907.

Harkness, Georgia. *The Dark Night of the Soul.* New York: Abingdon, 1945.

———. *Does God Care?* Waco, Tex.: Word Books, 1974.

Harms, Claus. *Pastoraltheologie* (1830). 3 vols. in 1. Gotha: F. A. Perthes, 1888.

Harnack, A. *A History of Dogma.* 7 vols. London: Williams and Norgate, 1896–1899.

Harnack, Theodosius (1817–1889). *Die Kirche, ihr Amt, ihr Regiment.* Nürnberg: U. C. Sebald, 1862: (Neuabdruck Gütersloh: C. Bertelsmenn, 1947).

———. *Praktische Theologie.* Erlangen: A. Deichert, vol. 1, 1877: vol. 2, 1878.

———. *Geschichte und Theorie der Predigt und der Seelsorge.* Erlangen: A Deichert, 1878.

Harsch, Helmut. *Das Schuldproblem in Theologie und Psychotherapie.* Heidelberg: Quelle und Meyer, 1965.

Hartley, David (1705–1757). *Observations on Man: His Frame, His Duty and His Expectations* (1749). 2 vols. Delmar, N.Y.: Scholars' Facsimilies, 1966.

Hartmann, Johann Ludwig (1640–1684). *Pastorale Evangelicum.* Nürnberg: W. M. Endteri, 1678.

Hazelton, R. *Providence.* London: SCM, 1958.

The Healing Church: The Tübingen Consultation 1964. World Council of Churches, 1965.

Hegel, G. W. F. *The Phenomenology of Mind* (1806). Translated by J. B. Baillie, New York: Macmillan, 1931.

Heidegger, Martin. *Being and Time.* Translated by J. Macquarrie and E. Robinson. New York: Macmillan, 1962.

Heinrici, Karl F. G. *Paul als Seelsorger. Zeit und Streitfragen.* vol. 6. Berlin: Wilhelm Hertz, 1910.

Heinroth, J. C. A. (1773–1843). *Die Psychologie als Selbsterkenntnislehre.* Leipzig: F. C. W. Vogel, 1827.

Hengel, M. *Nachfolge und Charisma: Eine exegetisch-religionsgeschichtliche Studie zu Mt. 8:21 ff und Jesu Ruf in die Nachfolge.* Berlin: Walter deGruyter, 1968.

———. *Property and Riches in the Early Church.* Translated by J. Bowden. Philadelphia: Fortress, 1975.

Henry, Matthew (1662–1714). *Aphorisms on the Ministry.* Selected by C. McIver. Princeton, N.J.: Thompson, 1847.

Henson, Herbert H. *Moral Discipline in the Christian Church.* London: Longmans, Green, and Co. 1905.

Heppe, H. *Reformed Dogmatics.* London: George Allen & Unwin, 1950.

Herberg, Will. *Faith Enacted as History*. Edited by B. Anderson. Philadelphia: West-
   minster, 1976.
Herbert, George (1593–1633). *The English Works of George Herbert*. Edited by G. H.
   Palmer. 3 vols. Boston: Houghton, Mifflin and Co., 1905.
_____. *The Country Parson* (1652). London: Henry Washbourne, 1832.
Hermas (fl. 140). The Pastor of Hermas. ANF, vol. 2. See Shepherd of Hermas.
Heuch, Johan Christian. *Pastoral Care of the Sick*. Translated by J. M. Moe. Min-
   neapolis: Augsburg, 1949.
Hewitt, Emily, and Hiatt, Suzanne. *Woman Priests: Yes or No*. New York: Seabury,
   1973.
Hick, John. *Evil and the God of Love*. New York: Macmillan, 1966.
Hielema, J. S. *Pastoral or Christian Counseling?* Leeuwarden, Netherlands: DeTille,
   1975.
Hilary of Poitiers (ca. 315–367) *NPNF* 2nd, vol. 9.
Hildegarde von Bingen (1098–1178). *Causae et curae* (ca. 1160). Edited by P. Kaiser,
   Leipzig: B. G. Teubneri, 1903.
Hilton, Walter (d. 1396). *Scale of Perfection*. Edited by I. Trethowan. London: Geof-
   frey Chapman, 1975.
Hiltner, S., ed. *Clinical Pastoral Training*. New York: Federal Council of Churches,
   1945.
Hiltner, S. *Pastoral Counseling*. Nashville: Abingdon, 1949.
_____. *Preface to Pastoral Theology*. Nashville: Abingdon, 1958.
_____. *The Christian Shepherd*. Nashville: Abingdon, 1959.
_____. *Ferment in the Ministry*. Nashville: Abingdon, 1969.
_____. *Theological Dynamics*. Nashville: Abingdon, 1972.
Hinkle, John E. "The 'Robin Hood' Policy: Ethical and Practical Issues Growing Out
   of the Use of Fee Scales in Pastoral Counseling Centers," *JPC*, 31 (1977), pp.
   119–24.
Hippocrates. *Works*. Translated by W. H. S. Jones. Cambridge: Harvard University
   Press, 1957.
Hippolytus (d. 236). *The Refutation of All Heresies. ANF*, vol. 5.
Hoch, W. *Evangelische Seelsorge*. Berlin: Furche, 1937.
Hodge, Charles (1797–1878). *The Church and Its Polity*. New York: Nelson, 1879.
Hodgson, L. *The Doctrine of the Trinity*. London: J. Nisbet, 1943.
_____. "Theological Objections to the Ordination of Women," *ExpT*, 77 (1966), pp.
   210–13.
Hoffmann, F. *Pastoral-Grundsätze*. Stuttgart: J. F. Steinkopf, 1829.
Hogue, Wilson. *Homiletics and Pastoral Theology* (1886). 10th ed. Winona Lake, Ind.:
   Free Methodist Publishing House, 1935.
Hollenweger, Walter J. *The Pentecostals*. Minneapolis: Augsburg, 1977.
Holman, Charles T. *The Cure of Souls*. Chicago: University of Chicago Press, 1932.
_____. *Getting Down to Cases*. New York: Macmillan, 1942.
Holmes, Urban T. *The Future Shape of Ministry*. New York: Seabury, 1971.
_____. *Spirituality for Ministry*. San Francisco: Harper & Row, 1982.
Holtz, G. "Seelsorge," RGG3 vol. 5, pp. 1640 ff.
Hooker, Richard (1554–1600). *On the Laws of Ecclesiastical Polity* (1594–1618). 2 vols.
   Esp. Book V: On Ministry and Ordination. Cambridge: Harvard University
   Press, 1977, 1980.
Hopko, Thomas. *All the Fulness of God*. Crestwood, N.Y.: St. Vladimir's Seminary
   Press, 1982.
Hoppin, James M. *The Office and Work of the Christian Ministry*. New York: Sheldon,
   1869.
_____. *Pastoral Theology*. New York: Funk & Wagnalls, 1884.
Hort, F. J. A. *The Christian Ecclesia*. London: Macmillan, 1897.

Hort, Josiah. *Instructions to the Clergy of the Diocese of Tuam* (1742). In *The Clergyman's Instructor*, pp. 349–72.

Hostie, R. *L'entretien Pastoral.* Brussels: Descleé de Brower, 1963.

How, W. Walsham. *Lectures on Pastoral Work.* London: Wells, Gardner, Darton, 1883.

Howe, Leroy T. *Prayer in a Secular World.* Nashville: Abingdon, 1974.

Hubbard, D. A. *NBD,* s.v. "Priests and Levites."

Hüffell, J. J. L. *Wesen und Beruf des evangelische Geistlichen.* 4th ed. Heidelberg: Giessen Heyer, 1843.

Hugh of St. Victor. *On the Sacraments of the Christian Faith* (1134). Edited by R. Deferrari. Cambridge. Mass.: Medieval Academy of America, 1951.

Hulme, William E. *Counseling and Theology.* Philadelphia: Muhlenberg, 1956.

——. *The Pastoral Care of Families.* Nashville: Abingdon, 1962.

——. *Pastoral Care Come of Age.* Nashville: Abingdon, 1970.

——. *Pastoral Care and Counseling: Using the Unique Resources of the Christian Tradition.* Minneapolis: Augsburg, 1981.

Hume, David (1711–1776). *A Treatise of Human Nature.* 2 vols. Oxford: Clarendon, 1888.

Iberian Fathers. *FC,* vols. 62, 63.

Ignatius of Antioch (ca. 35–ca. 107). *ANF,* vol. 1; *LCC,* vol. 1.

Ignatius Loyola (1491–1556). *The Spiritual Exercises of St. Ignatius.* Translated by L. J. Puhl. Westminster, Md.: Newman, 1953.

Inskip, James T. *The Pastoral Idea.* New York: Macmillan, 1905.

Irenaeus, (ca. 130–ca. 200). *ANF,* vol. 1.

Irion, Paul E. *The Funeral and the Mourners.* New York: Abingdon, 1954.

Jackson, Edgar N. *Understanding Grief: Its Roots, Dynamics, and Treatment.* Nashville: Abingdon, 1957.

——. *Coping with the Crises in Your Life.* New York: Hawthorn, 1974.

——. *Parish Counseling.* New York: Aronson, 1975.

Jackson, Paul R. *The Doctrine and Administration of the Church.* Des Plaines, Ill.: Regular Baptist Press, 1968.

Jacobi, Johann Friedric (1712–1791). *Beiträge zur Pastoral-Theologie oder Regeln und Muster für angehende Geistliche zu einer heilsamen Führung ihres Amtes.* 3rd ed. Hannover: Richter, vol. 1, 1774; vol. 2, 1782.

Jaeger, Werner. *Paideia: The Ideals of Greek Culture.* Translated by G. Highet. 2 vols. New York: Oxford University Press, 1943.

James, William. *The Will to Believe* (1897). Cambridge: Harvard University Press, 1979.

——. *The Varieties of Religious Experience* (1902). New York: Modern Library, 1936.

Jefferson, C. E. *The Minister as Prophet.* New York: Crowell, 1905.

——. *The Minister as Shepherd.* New York: Crowell, 1912.

Jenkins, Daniel T. *The Gift of Ministry.* London: Faber & Faber, 1947.

Jensen, Gustav. *Einführung in das geistliche Amt.* Leipzig: Weitere Literatur, vol. 2, no. 2, 1895.

Jeremias, J. *The Parables of Jesus.* New York: Scribner's, 1971a.

——. *New Testament Theology.* New York: Scribner's, 1971b.

——. "Poimen," *TDNT.*

Jerome (345–420). *NPNF* 2nd, vol. 6.

Jewel, John. *The Works of John Jewel.* Edited by J. Ayre. 4 vols. Cambridge. At the University Press, 1845–50.

Jewett, Paul K. *Man as Male and Female.* Grand Rapids: Eerdmans, 1975.

——. *The Ordination of Women.* Grand Rapids: Eerdmans, 1980.

John Climacus (d. 649). *The Ladder of Divine Ascent.* Edited by Moore and M. Feppell. Revised Edition. Boston: Holy Transfiguration Monastery, 1978.

John of Damascus (675–749). *The Orthodox Faith. NPNF* 2nd, vol. 9, pp. 30–44.

John of the Cross (1542–1591). Westminster, Md.: Christian Classics, 1973.
_____. *Dark Night of the Soul* (1577 ff.). Translated by E. A. Peers. New York: Doubleday, 1959.
_____. *Living Flame of Love* (1585). Translated by E. A. Peers. New York: Doubleday, 1962.
John of Kronstadt. *Spiritual Counsels of Father John of Kronstadt.* Edited by W. J. Gresbrooke. Greenwood, S.C.: Attic Press, 1967.
Johnson, Paul E. *Psychology of Pastoral Care.* Nashville: Abingdon, 1953.
Johnston, George. "Soul Care in the Ministry of Jesus," *Canadian Journal of Theology* 5–6, (1959–60).
Jones, Ilion T. *A Historical Approach to Evangelical Worship.* New York: Abingdon, 1954.
Jowett, John H. *The Preacher: His Life and Work.* New York: George Doran, 1912.
Jung, Carl G. *Collected Works.* 19 vols. Princeton, N.J.: Princeton University Press, 1959 ff.
Jungmann, Joseph A. *The Mass of the Roman Rite: Its Origins and Development.* New York: Benziger, 1959.
Justin Martyr (ca. 100–ca. 165). *ANF,* vol. 1.
Kadlovborsky, E. and Palmer, G. E. H. *Early Fathers from the Philokalia Writings.* Bridgeport, Conn.: Merrimack, 1954.
Kähler, Else. *Die Frau in den paulinischen Briefen,* Zürich: Gotthelf, 1960.
_____. *Das Amt der Frau in der Kirche.* Hannover: Colloquium, Ev-Luth. Kirche, 1962.
Kaiser, G. P. C. *Entwurf eines Systems der Pastoraltheologie.* Erlangen: Palm, 1816.
Kantonen, T. A. *A Theology for Christian Stewardship.* Philadelphia: Muhlenberg, 1956.
Käsemann, E. "Die Legitimität des Apostles," *ZNT,* 41 (1942), pp. 33 ff.
_____. *Essays in New Testament Themes.* London: SCM, 1964.
_____. *Jesus Means Freedom.* Philadelphia: Fortress, 1970.
_____. "Liturgie," *RGG3,* vol. 4, pp. 402 ff.
Kazantzakis, N. *Saviours of God: Spiritual Exercises.* New York: Simon & Schuster, 1960.
Keble, John (1792–1866). *Letters of Spiritual Counsel and Guidance.* Edited by R. F. Wilson. Oxford: Parker, 1881.
Keck, L. E. "The Poor Among the Saints in the New Testament," *ZNT,* 56 (1965), pp. 100–129.
Keedy, Edward E. *Moral Leadership and the Ministry.* Boston: Horace Worth, 1912.
Kelly, J. D. *Early Christian Doctrines.* New York: Harper & Bros., 1958.
Kelsey, Morton T. *Healing and Christianity.* New York: Harper & Row, 1963.
_____. *Tongue Speaking: An Experiment in Spiritual Experience.* Garden City, N.Y.: Doubleday, 1964.
Kemp, Charles F. *Physicians of the Soul: A History of Pastoral Counseling.* New York: Macmillan, 1947.
_____. *A Pastoral Triumph: The Story of Richard Baxter.* New York: Macmillan, 1948.
_____. *Pastoral Preaching.* St. Louis: Bethany, 1963.
_____. *A Pastoral Counseling Guidebook.* Nashville: Abingdon, 1971.
_____. *Pastoral Care with the Poor.* Nashville: Abingdon, 1972.
Kempf, T. *Christus der Hirte.* Rome: Libri Catholici, 1942.
Kidd. B. J. *Documents Illustrative of the Continental Reformation.* New York: Oxford University Press, 1911.
Kidder, Daniel P. *The Christian Pastorate: Its Character, Responsibilities, and Duties.* New York: Methodist Book Concern, 1871.
Kierkegaard, S. *Either/Or* (1843a). 2 vols. Princeton, N.J.: Princeton University Press, 1971.

———. *Fear and Trembling* (1843b) and *The Sickness Unto Death* (1849). Princeton, N.J.: Princeton University Press, 1968.

———. *Philosophical Fragments* (1844a). Princeton, N.J.: Princeton University Press, 1962.

———. *The Concept of Anxiety* (1844b). Princeton, N.J.: Princeton University Press, 1957.

———. *Stages on Life's Way* (1845). Princeton, N.J.: Princeton University Press, 1940.

———. *Concluding Unscientific Postscript* (1846a). Princeton, N.J.: Princeton University Press, 1941.

———. *The Present Age and Two Minor Ethical-Religious Essays.* (1846b). New York: Oxford University Press, 1940.

———. *Works of Love* (1847). New York: Harper & Row, 1962.

———. *Christian Discourses* (1849). New York: Oxford University Press, 1940.

———. *Training in Christianity* (1850). Princeton, N.J.: Princeton University Press, 1944.

———. *For Self-Examination and Judge for Yourselves!* (1851–52). Princeton, N.J.: Princeton University Press, 1940, 1944.

———. *Kierkegaard's Attack Upon "Christendom"* (1854–55). Princeton, N.J.: Princeton University Press, 1944.

———. *Søren Kierkegaard's Journals and Papers.* 7 vols. Bloomington, Ind.: Indiana University Press, 1967 ff.

Kirk, K. E. *The Vision of God: The Christian Doctrine of the Summum Bonum.* New York: Harper & Row, 1966.

Kirk, K. E., ed. *The Apostolic Ministry.* London: Hodder & Stoughton, 1946.

Kittel, Gerhaard. *Jesus als Seelsorger. Zeit und Streitfragen,* vol. 11, pp. 149–70. Berlin: Wilhelm Hertz, 1917.

Knodt, Emil, *Pastorallehren aus den paulinischen Briefen.* Gotha: G. Scholessmann, 1894.

Knox, John (1505–1572). *Writings.* London: Religious Tract Society, n.d. "A Fort for the Afflicted," pp. 39–71; "A Treatise on Prayer," pp. 71–92.

Knox, Ronald. *Enthusiasm.* Oxford: Clarendon, 1950.

———. *Pastoral Sermons.* New York: Sheed & Ward, 1960.

Köhler, G. *Praktische Anleitung für Seelsorger am Kranken- und Sterbebette.* Frankfurt: Andreäischen Buchhandlung, 1796.

Köster, F. B. *Lehrbuch der Pastor-Wissenschaft.* Kiel: Universitäts-Buchhandlung, 1827.

Köstlin, H. A. *Die Lehre von der Seelsorge nach evangelischen Grundsätzen.* Berlin: Reuther & Reichard, 1895.

Kortholt, Christian (1632–1694). *Pastor fidelis seu de officiis ministrorum ecclesiae opusculum.* Hamburg: Samuel Heylii and J. G. Leibezeiti, 1696.

Kraemer, Hendrik. *A Theology of the Laity.* Philadelphia: Westminster, 1958.

Krauss, A. *Lehrbuch der Praktischen Theologie.* 2 vols. Freiburg: J. C. B. Mohr, 1890–93.

———. *Pastoraltheorie.* Edited by F. Niebergall. Tübingen: J. C. B. Mohr. 1904.

Krimm, H. *Das diakonische Amt der Kirche.* Stuttgart: Evangelisches Verlagswerk, 1953.

Kübel, R. *Umriss der Pastoraltheologie.* 2nd ed. 2 vols. Stuttgart, J. F. Steindopf, 1874.

Kübler-Ross, E. *On Death and Dying.* New York: Macmillan, 1969.

Kuhn T. *The Structure of Scientific Revolutions.* 2nd ed. Chicago: University of Chicago Press, 1970.

Küng, Hans. *Structures of the Church.* New York: Nelson, 1964.

Küng, Hans. *The Church.* New York: Sheed & Ward, 1968.

Lactantius (240–320). *ANF,* vol. 7.

Lake, Frank. *Clinical Theology.* London: Darton, Longman & Todd, 1966.

————. "The Theology of Pastoral Counselling," *Contact,* vol. 68, no. 3. (1980), pp. 1–48.

————. *Studies in Constricted Confusion.* Nottingham: Clinical Theology Association, 1981a.

————. *Tight Corners in Pastoral Counselling.* London: Darton, Longman & Todd, 1981b.

Lampe, G. W. H. *The Church's Tradition and the Ordination of Women to the Historic Ministry.* London: Anglican Group for the Ordination of Women, 1967.

————. *The Seal of the Spirit.* Naperville: Allenson, 1967b.

LaPlace, Jean. *Preparing for Spiritual Direction.* Chicago: Franciscan Herald, 1975.

Lapsley, James N. *Salvation and Health.* Philadelphia: Westminster, 1972.

Latham, Henry. *Pastor Pastorum.* New York: James Pott, 1891.

Latimer, Hugh. *The Works of Hugh Latimer* (d. 1555). Edited by C. E. Corrie. 2 vols. New York: Johnson Reprints, 1844–46 ed.

Latourette, K. S. *A History of Christianity.* New York: Harper & Row, 1953.

Laud, William (1573–1645). *Works of Archbishop Laud.* Edited by W. Scott. 3 vols. New York: AMS Press, 1860, *LACT* ed.

Law, William. *A Serious Call to a Devout and Holy Life* (1728). Grand Rapids: Baker, 1977.

Lawson, J. *A Theological and Historical Introduction to the Apostolic Fathers.* New York: Macmillan, 1961.

Lea, Henry C. *A History of Auricular Confession and Indulgences.* 3 vols. Philadelphia: Lea Brothers & Co., 1896.

Leach, William H. *Handbook of Church Management.* Englewood Cliffs, N.J.: Prentice-Hall, 1958.

Lechleitner, Thomas. *Institutiones theologiae pastoralis.* Ulm: A. L. Stettinus, 1778.

————. *Katechismus der Gesundheit.* Augsburg: M. Riegers, 1795.

Lee, Bernard. *The Becoming of the Church.* New York: Paulist, 1974.

Leech, Kenneth. *Soul Friend.* San Francisco: Harper & Row, 1979.

Leeming, B. *Principles of Sacramental Theology.* London: Longmans, Green, 1956.

Leenhardt, F. J. *La Place de la Femme dans l'Église d'àpres le Nouveau Testament,* Neuchâtel: Delachaux, Niestle, 1948.

Lefroy, William. *The Christian Ministry.* New York: Funk & Wagnalls, 1981.

Leibniz, G. W. von. *Discourse on Metaphysics* (1686). Manchester: Manchester University Press, 1953.

Leipoldt, J. *Die Frau in der antiken Welt und im Urchristentum.* Gütersloh: Gerd Mohn, 1962.

Lell, J. "Pastoraltheologie," RGG3, vol. 5, pp. 149 f.

Leo the Great (390?–461). *NPNF* 2nd, vol. 12.

————. *Letters. FC,* vol. 34.

Letter to Barnabas. *ANF,* vol. 1.

Leuthner, J. N. A. *Praktische Pastoralarzneykunde für Seelsorger zu Hause, in der Kirche, bei Leichenbegräbnissen, bei Kranken und Sterbenden.* Nürnberg: W. Schwarzkopf, 1781.

————. *Diätetische Pastoralarzneykunde für Seelsorger.* Nürnberg: W. Schwarzkopf, 1782.

Levi-Strauss, Claude. *Structural Anthropology.* London: Penguin, 1968.

Lewis, C. S. *A Grief Observed.* New York: Bantam, 1961.

————. *God in the Dock: Essays on Theology and Ethics.* Edited by W. Hooper, Grand Rapids: Eerdmans, 1970.

————. *Undeceptions.* London: Bles, 1971.

————. *The Problem of Pain.* New York: Macmillan, 1943.

Lichliter, H. *The Healing of Souls.* New York: Abingdon, 1931.

Lietzmann, H. *The Beginnings of the Christian Church.* New York: Scribner's, 1937.

Liguori, Alphonsus (1696–1787). *St. Alphonsus Liguori, Extracts from Theologia Moralis.*
London: Reformation Society, 1852.
———. *The Religious State: On the Vocation to the Priesthood.* New York: Benziger,
1889.
———. *How to Face Death Without Fear.* Ligouri, Mo.: Ligouri Publications, 1976.
Lindsay, T. M. *The Church and the Ministry in the Early Centuries.* London: Hodder &
Stoughton, 1902.
Lloyd-Jones, D. M. *Preachers and Preaching.* Grand Rapids: Zondervan, 1972.
Löhe, Wilhelm (1808–1872). *Gesammelte Werke.* 4 vols. Edited by K. Ganzert. Neuen-
dettelsau: Freimund-Verlag, 1851 ff.
Lohse, E. *Die Ordination im Spätjudentum und im Neuen Testament.* Göttingen: Vanden-
hoeck and Ruprecht, 1951.
———. "Ursprung und Prägung des christlichen Apostolats," *TLZ,* 9 (1953), pp.
259–75.
———. "Katechismus im Urchristentum," RGG3, vol. 3, pp. 1179 ff.
Luethi, W. *Gott und das Böse,* Basel: Reinhardt, 1961.
Luther, Martin (1483–1546). *Works of Martin Luther.* 6 vols. Philadelphia: Muhlen-
berg, 1915–32.
———. *Luther: Letters of Spiritual Counsel.* Edited by T. Tappert, London: SCM, 1955.
LCC, vol. 18.
———. *Martin Luther: Selections from His Writings.* Edited by J. Dillenberger. New
York: Doubleday, 1961.
———. *Concerning the Ministry. LW,* vol. 40.
———. *Correspondence and Other Contemporary Letters.* Translated by P. Smith. 2 vols.
Philadelphia: Muhlenberg, 1913.
———. *Early Theological Works. LCC,* vol. 16.
Lutheran Confessional Theology in America. Edited by T. Tappert. *LPT.*
Lys, D. "L'Onctio dans la Bible," *Etudes Théologiques et Religieuses,* 29 (1954), pp.
3 ff.
Macarius of Egypt (ca. 300–390). *Fifty Homilies.* Translated by A. J. Mason. London:
S.P.C.K., 1921.
Macarius (1788–1860). *Russian Letters of Direction.* Tuckahoe, N.Y.: St. Vladimir's
Seminary Press, 1975.
Macher, M. *Pastoral-Heilkunde für Seelsorger.* Leipzig: A. G. Liebeskind 1838.
Maclaren, Ian. *The Cure of Souls.* New York: Dodd, Mead, 1896.
MacLennan, David. *Pastoral Preaching.* Philadelphia: Westminster, 1955.
Major, George (1502–1574). *Vitae patrum, in usum ministrorum verbi, quo ad eius fieri
potuit repurgatae.* Wittenberg: n.p., 1544.
Manson, T. W. *The Teaching of Jesus.* Cambridge: At the University Press, 1931.
———. *The Church's Ministry.* Naperville, Ill.: Allenson, 1956.
———. *Ministry and Priesthood: Christ's and Ours.* London: Epworth Press, 1958.
Marheineke, P. K. *Entwurf der praktischen Theologie.* Berlin: Duncker and Humbolt,
1837.
Martin of Braga (410?–580). *The Iberian Fathers, FC,* vol. 1.
Martin, Bernard. *The Healing Ministry in the Church.* Richmond: John Knox Press,
1960.
Martyrdom of St. Polycarp (c. 155). *ANF,* vol. 1.
Marx, K., and Engels, F. *Marx and Engels: Basic Writings on Politics and Philosophy.*
Edited by L. S. Feuer, New York: Doubleday, 1959.
Marxsen, Willi. *Der "Frühkatholizismus" in Neuen Testament.* Frankfurt: Neu-
kirchener Verlag, 1958.
Mascall, E. L. *Christ, the Christian, and the Church.* London: Longmans, Green, and
Co. 1946.
———. *Women Priests?* London: Church Literature Association, 1973.

Massillon, Jean Baptiste (1663–1742). *The Charges of Jean Baptiste Massillon, Bp. of Clermont, Addressed to his Clergy*. New York: D & G Bruce, 1806.

Mather, Cotton (1663–1728). *Student and Preacher, Manuductio ad Ministerium* (1728), London: John Ryland, 1781.

Mathews, Shailer. *The Atonement and the Social Process*. New York: Macmillan, 1930.

McClure, James. *The Growing Pastor*. Chicago: Winona, 1904.

McCoy, Charles S. "The Covenant Theology of Johannes Cocceius," Ph.D. dissertation, Yale University, 1957.

McDonnell, Kilian. "Ways of Validating Ministry," *Journal of Ecumenical Studies*, 7 (1970), pp. 221 ff.

McEwen, J. S. "The Ministry of Healing," *SJT*, 7 (1954), pp. 133–52.

McGiffert, A. C. *A History of Christian Thought*. 2 vols. New York: Scribner's, 1932–33.

McLemore, Clinton. *The Scandal of Psychotherapy*. Downers Grove, Ill.: Intervarsity Press, 1982.

McNeill, John T. *The Celtic Penitentials and Their Influence on Continental Christianity*. Paris: E. Campion, 1923.

_____. "Medicine for Sin as Prescribed in the Penitentials," *Church History*, 1 (1932), pp. 14–26.

_____. "Historical Types of Method in the Cure of Souls," *Crozer Quarterly*, 11 (1934), pp. 323–34.

_____. "Personal Counselling in Early Protestantism," *Christendom*, 6 (1941), pp. 364–75.

_____. *A History of the Cure of Souls*. New York: Harper & Bros., 1951.

McNeill, John T., and Gamer, Helena. *Medieval Handbooks of Penance: A translation of the Principal libri poenitentiales*. New York: Columbia University, Records of Civilization, no. 21, 1938. (Octagon ed. 1965).

Meade, William. *Lectures on the Pastoral Office*. New York: Stanford and Swords, 1849.

Medicina Clerica, or Hints to the clergy for the healthful and comfortable discharge of their ministerial duties, a series of letters. London: n.p., 1821.

Melanchthon, P. *The Loci Communes of Philip Melanchthon* (1st ed. 1521). Translated by C. L. Hill. Boston: Meador, 1944.

Melanchthon, P. and Bucer, M. *Melanchthon and Bucer*. LCC, vol. 19.

Menninger, Karl. *Whatever Became of Sin?* New York: Hawthorn, 1972.

Merton, T. *Contemplation in a World of Action*. New York: Doubleday, 1973.

Metz, Johannes. *Theology of the World*. New York: Seabury, 1969.

Meyendorff, John. *Byzantine Theology*. New York: Fordham, 1974.

Meyer, J. P. *Ministers of Christ*. Milwaukee: Northwestern, 1963.

Menno Simons (ca. 1496–1561). *The Complete Writings of Menno Simons*. Scottdale, Pa.: Herald Press, 1956.

Michalson, Carl. *The Rationality of Faith*. New York: Scribner's, 1963.

Mieg, Ludwig Christian. *Meletemata Sacra de Officio Pastoris Evangelici Publico et Privato*. Frankfurt: n.p. 1747.

Miller, Donald G. *The Way to Biblical Preaching*. New York: Abingdon, 1957.

Miller, R. C. *Biblical Theology and Christian Education*. New York: Scribner's, 1956.

Miller, Samuel. *An Essay on the Warrant, Nature, and Duties of the Ruling Elder in the Presbyterian Church*. 2nd ed. New York: Jonathan Levitt, 1832.

Minear, Paul. *Images of the Church in the New Testament*. Philadelphia: Westminster, 1960.

Minucius Felix (before 250). *The Octavius*. ANF, vol. 4., pp. 173–218.

Moberly, R. C. *Ministerial Priesthood*. London: Murray, 1899.

Moll, C. B. *Das System der praktische Theologie im Grundriss dargestellt*. Halle: Richard Muhlmann, 1853.

Moltmann, J. *Theology of Hope.* New York: Harper & Row, 1965.
———. *Hope and Planning.* New York: Harper & Row, 1971.
———. *The Experiment Hope.* London: SCM, 1975.
———. *The Church in the Power of the Spirit.* New York: Harper & Row, 1977.
Montaigne M. E. de. *The Complete Essays of Montaigne.* Translated by D. M. Frame. Stanford, Calif.: Stanford University Press, 1958.
Montefiori, C. G., and Loewe, H. *A Rabbinic Anthology.* London: Macmillan, 1938.
Montefiori, Hugh, ed. *Yes to Women Priests.* London: Mowbray, 1978.
Moorman, J. R. H. *The Curate of Souls, being a collection of writings on the nature and work of a priest* from the first century after the Reformation (1660–1760). London: S.P.C.K., 1958.
More, Thomas. *A Dialogue of Comfort Against Tribulation* (1535). London: Sheed & Ward, 1951.
Morgagni, Giovanni Battista. *Selections from De sedibus et causis morborum* (1761). Baltimore: William and Wilkins, 1940.
Morin, Jean. *Commentarius historicus de disciplina in administratione sacramenti poenitentiae tredecim primis seculis.* Paris: Antonius Vitray, 1651.
Moss, Thelma. *The Probability of The Impossible.* New York: New American Library, 1974.
Mosheim, Johann Lorenz von (1694–1755). *Pastoral-Theologie von den Pflichten und Lehramt eines Dieners des Evangelii.* 2nd ed. Leipzig: Weygand, 1763.
Mowrer, O. H. *The Crisis in Psychiatry and Religion.* Princeton, N.J.: van Nostrand, 1961.
Muirhead, J. A. *Education in the New Testament.* Monographs in Christian Education no. 2, 1965.
Muller, E. and Stroh, H. eds. *Seelsorge in der modernen Gesellschaft.* 2nd ed. Hamburg: n.p., 1964.
Munck, J. "Paul, the Apostles and the Twelve," *Studia Theologica,* 3 (1950), pp. 96–110.
Münter, W. O. *Begriff und Wirklichkeit des geistlichen Amts.* Munich: Beiträge zur evangelischen Theologie, vol. 21, 1955.
Murphy, Thomas. *Pastoral Theology: The Pastor in the Various Duties of His Office.* Philadelphia: Presbyterian Board of Publ., 1877.
Myers, C. Kilmer. "Should Women Be Ordained? No," *The Episcopalian,* 137, no. 2 (1972), pp. 8–9.
Myre, John. *Instructions for Parish Priests.* Edited by E. Peacock. Early English Text Society Publications. no. 31, 1868.
Narramore, Bruce, and Carter, John D. *The Integration of Theology and Psychololgy.* Grand Rapids: Zondervan, 1979.
Nebe, August. *Luther as Spiritual Adviser.* Philadelphia: Lutheran Publ. Soc. 1892.
Neill, Stephen, et al. *The Ministry of the Church.* London: Canterbury Press, 1947.
Nemesius of Emesa (late 4th cent.). *On the Nature of Man* (ca. 390). *LCC,* vol. 4.
Neuhaus, Richard J. *Freedom for Ministry.* San Francisco: Harper & Row, 1979.
Nevin, John W. (1803–1886). *Nevin's Works.* 6 vols. Mercersburg: P. A. Rice, 1844–50.
Newbigin, Lesslie. *The Household of God.* New York: Friendship Press, 1960.
———. *The Good Shepherd: Meditations on Christian Ministry in Today's World.* Grand Rapids: Eerdmans, 1977.
Newman, John Henry. *Arians of the Fourth Century* (1833). London: Basil, Montagu, Pickering, 1876.
———. *Parochial and Plain Sermons* (1834–43). 8 vols. London: Longmans, Green, 1891.
———. *Lectures on the Prophetical Office of the Church* (1837). London: Parker, 1838.
———. *Essay on the Development of Christian Doctrine.* Philadelphia: Appleton, 1845.
———. *Apologia pro Vita Sua* (1864). London: Everyman's Library, J. M. Dent, 1955.

_____. *An Essay in Aid of a Grammar of Assent.* London: Burns & Oates, 1870.

Niebergall, F. *Praktische Theologie.* 2 vols. Tübinger: Mohr, 1918–19.

Niebuhr, H. Richard. *The Meaning of Revelation.* New York: Macmillan, 1941.

_____. *Christ and Culture.* New York: Harper & Bros., 1951.

_____. *Radical Monotheism and Western Culture.* New York: Harper & Bros., 1960.

Niebuhr, H. Richard, and Williams D. D., eds. *The Ministry in Historical Perspective.* New York: Harper & Bros., 1956.

Niebuhr, H. Richard; Williams, D. D.; and Gustafson, J. M. *The Purpose of the Church and Its Ministry.* New York: Harper & Bros., 1956.

_____. *The Advancement of Theological Education.* New York: Harper & Bros., 1957.

Niebuhr, Reinhold. *Leaves from the Notebook of a Tamed Cynic.* New York: Willett, Clark, Colby, 1929.

_____. *The Contribution of Religion to Social Work.* New York: Columbia University Press, 1932a.

_____. *Moral Man and Immoral Society.* New York: Scribner's, 1932b.

_____. *The Nature and Destiny of Man.* New York: Scribner's; vol. 1, 1941; vol. 2, 1943.

_____. *The Self and The Dramas of History.* New York: Scribner's, 1958.

_____. *Essays in Applied Christianity.* Edited by D. B. Robertson. New York: Meridian, 1959.

_____. *Man's Nature and His Communities.* New York: Scribner's, 1965.

Niedermeyer, A. *Pastoralmedizinische Propädeutik.* Salzburg: A. Pustet, 1935.

_____. *Handbuch der speziellen Pastoralmedizin.* 6 vols. Vienna: Herder, 1949–52.

Nietzsche, F. *The Philosophy of Nietzsche.* New York: Modern Library, 1927.

Nitzsch, Karl Immanuel. *Praktische Theologie.* 3 vols. Bonn: Adolf Marcus, 1847–51.

Nolan, Richard, ed. *The Diaconate Now.* Washington: Corpus, 1968.

Nouwen, Henri. *The Wounded Healer: Ministry in Contemporary Society.* Garden City, N.Y.: Doubleday, 1972.

Nuttall, Geoffrey F. *Visible Saints: The Congregational Way, 1640–1660.* Oxford: Blackwell, 1957.

Nygren, Anders. *Christ and His Church.* Philadelphia: Westminster, 1956.

Oates, Wayne E. *The Bible in Pastoral Care.* Philadelphia: Westminster: 1953.

_____. *Christ and Selfhood.* New York: Association Press, 1961a.

Oates, Wayne E. ed. *The Minister's Own Mental Health.* Channel Press, 1961b.

Oates, Wayne E. *Protestant Pastoral Counseling.* Philadelphia: Westminster, 1962.

_____. *Pastoral Counseling.* Philadelphia: Westminster, 1974.

Oates, Wayne E. and Lester, A. D. eds. *Pastoral Care in Crucial Human Situations.* Valley Forge, Pa.: Judson Press, 1969.

Oberman, Heiko. *The Harvest of Medieval Theology: Gabriel Beil and Late Medieval Nominalism.* Grand Rapids: Eerdmans, 1967.

O'Connor, Mary Catherine. *The Art of Dying Well: The Development of the Ars Moriendi.* New York: Columbia University Press, 1942.

Oden, Thomas C. *The Community of Celebration.* Nashville: Methodist Student Movement, 1963.

_____. *Radical Obedience: The Ethics of Rudolf Bultmann.* With a reply by Rudolf Bultmann. Philadelphia: Westminster, 1964.

_____. *Expérience Thérapeutique et Révélation: un Symposium.* With A. Godin and A. Chappelle. Louvain: Nouvelle Revue Théologique, 1965.

_____. *Kerygma and Counseling.* Philadelphia: Westminster, 1966. (San Francisco: Harper & Row Ministers Paperback Library ed. 1978.)

_____. *Contemporary Theology and Psychotherapy.* Philadelphia: Westminster, 1967.

_____. *The Structure of Awareness.* Nashville: Abingdon, 1969.

_____. *Beyond Revolution.* Philadelphia: Westminster, 1970.

_____. *The Intensive Group Experience: The New Pietism.* Philadelphia: Westminster, 1972.

————. *Game Free: The Meaning of Intimacy.* New York: Harper & Row, 1974.

————. *After Therapy What?* With responses by N. Warren, K. Mulholland, C. Schoonhoven, C. Kraft, and W. Walker. Springfield, Ill.: Charles C. Thomas, 1974b.

————. *TAG: The Transactional Awareness Game.* New York: Harper & Row, 1976a.

————. *Should Treatment Be Terminated?* New York: Harper & Row, 1976b.

————. *Agenda for Theology: Recovering Christian Roots.* San Francisco: Harper & Row, 1979.

————. *Guilt Free.* Nashville: Abingdon, 1980.

Oepke, A. "Gyne," *TDNT*, vol. 1, pp. 776–89.

Offele, W. *Das Verständnis der Seelsorge in der Pastoral Theologischen Literatur der Gegenwart.* Mainz: Grünewald, 1966.

Oglesby, William B. ed. *The New Shape of Pastoral Theology: Essays in Honor of Seward Hiltner.* Nashville: Abingdon, 1969.

Oglesby, William B. *Biblical Themes for Pastoral Care.* Nashville: Abingdon, 1980.

Olearius, Gottfried (1604–1685). *Anleitung zur geistlichen Seelen-Cur.* Leipzig: Johannis Wittigan, 1718.

Olfers, E. W. M. von. *Pastoralmedizin: Ein Handbuch für den katholischen Klerus.* 3rd ed. Freiburg: 1911.

O'Malley, Austin. *Essays on Pastoral Medicine.* London: Longmans, 1906.

Oman, John. *Concerning the Ministry.* London: SCM, 1936.

Oosterzee, J. J. van. *Practical Theology.* Translated by M. J. Evans. New York: Scribner's, 1878.

Origen (185–254). *ANF*, vol. 4.

————. *Contra Celsum.* Translated by H. Chadwick. Cambridge: At the University Press, 1935.

————. Translated by R. P. Lawson. ACW, vol. 21.

Ostervald, Jean Frederic. *Lectures on the Exercise of the Sacred Ministry* (1781). Translated by T. Stevens. London: J. F. & O. Rivington, 1781.

Otto, Rudolf. *The Idea of the Holy.* Translated by J. W. Harvey. New York: Oxford, University Press, 1925.

Otto, Wilhelm. *Evangelische Praktische Theologie.* 2 vols. Dillenburg: C. Stell, 1866.

Outler, Albert C. *Psychotherapy and the Christian Message.* New York: Harper & Bros., 1954.

————. *The Christian Tradition and The Unity We Seek.* New York: Oxford University Press, 1957.

————. *Who Trusts in God.* New York: Oxford University Press, 1968.

Owen, John (1616–1683). *Works.* 28 vols. Edited by Tho. Russell. Oxford: J. Parker, 1826.

————. *The True Nature of a Gospel Church and its Government* (1689). London: J. Clarke, 1947.

Owens, John W. *The Pastor's Companion.* Dayton: Otterbein Press, 1935.

Oxendem, Ashton. *The Pastoral Office, Its Duties, Difficulties, Privileges, and Prospects.* New York: Protestant Episcopal Society for the Promotion of Evangelical Knowledge, 1857.

Paley, William (1743–1805). *Works.* 6 vols. Esp. *The Clergyman's Companion in Visiting the Sick,* vol. 4, pp. 243–347. Cambridge: Hilliard and Brown, 1830.

Palmer. Albert W. *The Minister's Job.* New York: Willett, Clark, 1937.

Palmer, C. D. F. *Evangelische Pastoraltheologie.* Stuttgart: J. F. Steinkopf, 1863.

Palmer, Phoebe. *The Way of Holiness.* New York: G. Lane & C. B. Tippett, 1846.

Paludan-Müller, Jens, the Elder. *Der Pfarrer Geistliche und sein Amt.* Translated by E. A. Struve. Kiel: n.p., 1874.

Pannenberg, W. *Jesus—God and Man.* Translated by L. Wilkins and D. Priebe. Philadelphia: Westminster, 1968.

———. *Basic Questions in Theology*. 3 vols. Translated by G. Kehm. Philadelphia: Fortress, 1970–73.

———. *Theology and the Kingdom of God*. Edited by R. J. Neuhaus. Philadelphia: Westminster, 1971a.

Pannenberg, W.; Dulles, A; and Braaten, C. *Spirit, Faith and Church*. Philadelphia: Westminster, 1971b.

Paracelsus (1493–1541). *Selected Writings*. Edited by J. Jacobi. Princeton: Princeton University Press, 1958.

Parratt, J. K. "The Laying on of Hands in the New Testament," *ExpT*, 80 (1968–69), pp. 210–14.

Park, E. A., ed. *The Preacher and the Pastor*. Andover, Mass.: Allen, Movull, Wardwell, 1845.

Pascal, Blaise. *The Provincial Letters of Blaise Pascal*. Translated by T. McCrie. Edinburgh: J. Johnstone, 1847.

Patrick, Simon. "The Work of the Ministry" (1692). In Moorman, pp. 49 ff.

Pattison, T. H. *For the Work of the Ministry*. Philadelphia: American Baptist Publication Society, 1907.

Patton, John. "Propositions and Pilgrimage," *JPC*, 30 (1976), pp. 219 ff.

Payne, E. D. *The Free Churches and Episcopacy*. London: Carey Kingsgate, 1952.

Pegis, Anton Charles (1905–). *St. Thomas and the Problem of the Soul*. Toronto: St. Michael's College, 1934.

Pelliccia, A. A. (1744–1822). *The Polity of the Christian Church of Early, Medieval and Modern Times*. Translated by J. C. Bellett. London: Masters, 1833.

Perkins, William (1558–1602). *The Whole Treatise of the Cases of Conscience*. London: Pickering, 1611.

Pfister, Oskar R. *Christianity and Fear*. Translated by W. Johnston. New York: Macmillan, 1949.

Pfliegler, Michael (1891–). *Pastoral Theology*. Translated by John Drury. Westminster, Md.: Newman Press, 1966.

Pin, E. "The Advantages and Disadvantages of the 'Professionalization of the Priesthood.'" Cuernavaca, Mexico: I.D.O.C., 1968.

Pittenger, W. N. *The Church, the Ministry and Reunion*. Greenwich, Conn.: Seabury, 1957.

Plato (d. 347 B.C.). *Works*. Edited by B. Jowett. 4 vols. New York: Random House, 1936.

Pleune, Peter H. *Some to Be Pastors*. New York: Abingdon-Cokesbury, 1943.

Plitt, J. J. (1727–1773). *Pastoral-Theologie*. Hamburg: W. Brandt, 1766.

Pompey, Heinrich. *Die Bedeutung der Medizin für die Kirchliche Seelsorge*. Freiburg: Herder, 1968.

Pond, Enoch. *The Young Pastor's Guide*. New York: Ezra Collier, 1844.

———. *Lectures on Pastoral Theology*. Boston: Draper & Halliday, 1847.

Porta, C. *Pastorale Lutheri* (1582). Edited by Nördlingen: C. H. Beck, 1842.

Powers, Joseph. *Spirit and Sacrament*. New York: Seabury, 1973.

Powondra, Thomas Joseph (1786–1832). *Systema theologiae pastoralis*. 6 vols. Vienna: Joseph Geistlinger, 1818–19.

Preston, John (1587–1628). *The Saint's Daily Exercise: A Treatise Unfolding the Whole Duty of Prayer*. 9th ed. London: E. Purslow, 1635.

Principles of Church Union. Cincinatti: Forward Movement Publications, 1966 (COCU).

Pruyser, Paul. *The Minister as Diagnostician*. Philadelphia: Westminster, 1976.

Pusey, Edward B. *Advice to Those who Exercise the Ministry of Reconciliation Through Confession and Absolution: Being the Abbé Gaumé's Manual for Confessors*. Abridged 2nd ed. Oxford: Oxford University Press, 1878.

————. *Spiritual Letters*. Edited by J. O. Johnston and W. C. E. Newbolt. London: Longmans, Green and Co., 1901.

Pym, T. W. *Spiritual Direction*. Milwaukee: Morehouse, 1928.

Quasten, J. "The Parable of the Good Shepherd: John 10:1–21," *Canadian Biblical Quarterly*, 10 (1948), pp. 1–12, 151–69.

————. *Patrology*. 4 vols. Westminster, Md.: Newman, 1950 ff.

Guayle, William A. *The Pastor-Preacher*. New York: Eaton and Mains, 1910.

Quenstedt, J. A. (1617–1688). *Ethica Pastorum et Instructio Cathedralis* (1678). 3rd ed. Wittenberg: Michael Wendt, 1708.

Rabanus Maurus (776–856). *De Institutione Clericorum* (840). Munich: Lentner, 1900.

Rahner, K. *Plan und Aufriss eines Handbuches der Pastoraltheologie*. Freiburg: Herder, 1960.

————. *On the Theology of Death*. New York: Herder, 1961a.

————. *Inspiration in the Bible*. New York: Herder, 1961b.

————. *The Church and the Sacraments*. New York: Herder, 1963a.

————. *Man in the Church*. Vol. 2 of *Theological Investigations*. Baltimore: Helicon, 1963b.

————. *The Dynamic Element in the Church*. New York: Herder, 1964a.

————. *On Heresy*. New York: Herder, 1964b.

————. *Later Writings*. Vol. 5 of *Theological Investigations*. Baltimore: Helicon, 1966.

————. *The Priesthood*. New York: Seabury, 1973.

————. *Encyclopedia of Theology: Sacramentum Mundi*. New York: Seabury, 1975.

————. *Penance in the Early Church*. Vol. 15 of *Theological Investigations*. New York: Seabury, 1979b.

————. *The Spirit in the Church*. New York: Seabury, 1979a.

Rahner, K. and Ratzinger, J. *Revelation and Tradition*. New York: Herder, 1964.

Rau, Gerhard. *Pastoraltheologie*. Munich: Chr. Kaiser Verlag, 1970.

Raymond of Penafort (ca. 1175–1275). *Summa de poenitentia*, and *Summa casuum* (1223–1238). Archiv für Litteratur und Kirchengeschichte des Mittelalter, 1889.

Recognitions of Clement (before 360). *ANF*, vol. 8, pp. 75 ff.

Reeves, Joan Wynn. *Body and Mind in Western Thought*. London: Pelican Books, 1958.

Reichenberger, Andre. *Pastoral-anweisung*. Vienna: Peter Rehm, 1805.

Relation of Christian Faith to Health. Adopted by 172nd General Assembly of United Presbyterian Church USA. Philadelphia: Presbyterian Board of Education, 1960.

Rengstorf, K. H. *Mann und Frau in Urchristentum*. Cologne: Westdeutscher Verlag, 1954.

————. *TDNT*, s.v. "Apostolos"; and s.v. "Didasko."

————. *Apostolate and Ministry: The New Testament Doctrine of the Office of Ministry*. Philadelphia: Fortress, 1969.

Renninger, Johann Baptist (1829–1892). *Pastoraltheologie*. Freiburg im Breisgav: Herder'sche Verlagshandlung, 1893.

Rensch, Adelheid. *Das seelsorgerliche Gespräch*. Göttingen: Vandenhoeck und Ruprecht, 1963.

Reuther, R. *Liberation Theology*. New York: Paulist, 1972.

Reuther, R. ed. *Religion and Sexism*. New York: Simon & Schuster, 1974.

Riecker, O. *Die seelsorgerliche Bewegnung*. Gütersloh: Bertelsmann, 1947.

Ridley, Edgar J. "Pastoral Care and the Black Community," *JPC*, 29 (1975), pp. 271–76.

Riemann-Magdeburg. "Evangelische Gedanken über evangelische Seelsorge," *Zeitschrift für praktische Theologie*. Frankfurt: 1890.

Rites of The Catholic Church, The. New York: Pueblo Publ. Co. Vol. 1, 1976; vol. 2., 1979.

River's Manuel: or Pastoral Instructions upon the Creed, Commandments, Sacraments ...
    Liverpool: Ferguson and Sadler, 1799.
Roberts, David E. *Psychotherapy and a Christian View of Man.* New York: Scribner's,
    1950.
Robertson, A. T. *The Glory of the Ministry.* New York: Fleming Revell, 1911.
Robinson, J. A. T. "The Parable of the Shepherd," *ZNT*, 46 (1955), pp. 133–40.
Rodenmayer, R. N. *We Have This Ministry.* New York: Harper & Bros., 1958.
Roessler, D. S.v. "Pastoralmedizin," *RGG3.*
_____. *Der "ganze" Mensch. Das Menschenbild der neueren Seelsorgelehre und des modern-
    en medizinischen Denkens im Zusammenhang der allgemeinen Anthropologie.* Göttin-
    gen: Vandenhoeck und Ruprecht, 1962.
Rogers, Carl R. *Client-centered Therapy.* Boston: Houghton, Mifflin and Co. 1951.
_____. *On Becoming a Person.* Boston: Houghton, Mifflin and Co. 1961.
Rogers, Clement F. *An Introduction to the Study of Pastoral Theology.* Oxford: Claren-
    don, 1912.
Rohde, E. *Psyche.* London: Kegan Paul, Trench, Trubner, 1925.
Roques, P. *Gestalt eines Evangelischen Lehrers.* German translation of *Le Pasteur Évan-
    gelique,* by F. E. Rambach. 3 vols. Halle: J.A. Bauer 1741–44.
Ross, R. J., et al. "In-kind Payment as Therapy in Pastoral Counseling," *JPC*, 31
    (1977) pp. 113–18.
Ross, M. G., and Hendry, C. F. *New Understandings of Leadership.* New York: Associa-
    tion Press, 1957.
Rowe, Kenneth. *Methodist Women: A Guide to the Literature.* Metuchen, N. J.: Scare-
    crow Press, 1980.
Rowley, H. H. *Worship in Ancient Israel.* Naperville, Ill.: Allenson, 1967.
Ryan, John. *Irish Monasticism: Origins and Early Development.* Dublin: Talbot, 1931.
Ryrie, Charles C. *The Place of Women in the Church.* New York: Macmillan, 1958.
Sarcerius, Erasmus (1501–1559). *Pastorale oder Hirtenbuch.* Frankfurt: n.p., 1565.
Sailer, J. M. *Vorlesungen aus der Pastoraltheologie.* Munich: J. J. Lentner, 1788.
_____. *Kurzgefasste Erinnerungen an junge Prediger.* Munich: J. J. Lentner, 1791.
_____. *Über Erziehung für Erzieher.* Munich: J. J. Lentner, 1807.
_____. *Handbuch der christlichen Moral zunächst für künftige katholische Seelsorger und
    dan für jeden gebildeten Christen.* 3 vols. Munich: J. J. Lentner, 1817.
Salvian (ca. 400–ca. 470). *The Writings of Salvian the Presbyter. FC,* vol. 3.
Sanford, Alexander. *Pastoral Medicine.* New York: J. F. Wagner, 1904.
Sartre, J. P. *Being and Nothingness.* New York: Philosophical Library, 1956.
Scandeus, Maximilian, S. J. *Theologia medica.* Cologne: 1635.
Scaramelli, Giovanni Battista. *The Directorium Asceticum, or Guide to the Spiritual Life.*
    Dublin: W. B. Kelly, 1870–71.
Schaff, P. *The Creeds of Christendom.* 6th ed. New York: 1931.
Schaller, John. *Pastorale Praxis.* Milwaukee: Northwestern, 1913.
Scharfenberg, Joachim. *Johann Christoph Blumhard und die kirchliche Seelsorge heute.*
    Göttingen: Vandenhoeck und Ruprecht, 1959.
_____. *Sigmund Freud und seiner Religionskritik.* Göttingen: Vandenhoeck und Ru-
    precht, 1968.
_____. *Seelsorge als Gespräch.* Göttingen: Vandenhoeck und Ruprecht, 1972.
Schempp, Johannes. *Seelsorge und Seelenführung bei John Wesley.* Stuttgart: Christ-
    liches Verlagshaus, 1949.
Schenck, F. S. *Modern Practical Theology.* New York: Funk & Wagnalls, 1903.
Schenkl, Maurus von. *Institutiones Theologiae pastoralis.* 2 vols. Ingolstadt: Aloysli At-
    tenkover, 1802.
Scherer, Paul E. *For We Have This Treasure.* New York: Harper & Bros., 1944.
Scherzer, C. J. *The Church and Healing.* Philadelphia: Westminster, 1950.

Schillebeeckx, E. *Christ the Sacrament of the Encounter with God.* New York: Sheed & Ward, 1963.
_____. "The Catholic Understanding of Office in the Church," *Texts and Studies,* 30 (1969), pp. 567–87.
_____. *The Mission of the Church.* New York: Seabury, 1973.
Schlegel, G. *Handbuch einer praktischen Pastoralwissenschaft.* Edited by J. E. Parow. Greifswald: n.p., 1811.
Schleiermacher, F. D. (1768–1834). *Sämmtliche Werke.* Esp. vol. 13: *Die praktische Theologie,* edited by J. Frerichs. Berlin: O. Reimer, 1850.
_____. *Brief Outline on the Study of Theology.* Richmond: John Knox Press, 1966.
Schlink, E. *Theology of the Lutheran Confessions.* Translated by P. F. Koehneke and H. Bouman. Philadelphia: LCA Board of Publications, 1961.
Schmid, Heinrich. *The Doctrinal Theology of the Evangelical Lutheran Church.* Minneapolis: Augsburg, 1961.
Schmidt, W. "Der gute Hirte. Biblische Besinnung über Lk. 15:1–7," *Evangelische Theologie,* 24 (1964), pp. 173 ff.
Schmithals, Walter. *The Office of the Apostle in the Early Church.* Translated by J. E. Stelly. Nashville: Abingdon, 1969.
Schanckenburg, R. "Episkopos und Hirtenamt," *Episcopus* (1949), pp. 66–88.
_____. *The Moral Teaching of the New Testament.* Translated by J. Holland-Smith and W. J. O'Hara. Freiburg: Herder, 1965.
Schöllgen, Werner. *Arzt, Seelsorger und Kurpfuscher. Eine moral pychologische Studie.* Würzburg: 1949.
_____. "Ontologie der Medizin." In *Gegenwartsfragen der Psychiatrie.* Freiburg: n.p., 1956, pp. 1–67.
Scholastic Miscellany, A. Anselm to Ockham. LCC, vol. 10.
Schreger, C. H. *Handbuch der Pastoral-Medizin für christliche Seelsorger.* Halle: n.p., 1823.
Schroeder, H. J. *Disciplinary Decrees of the General Councils.* St. Louis: Herder, 1937.
Canons and Decrees of the Council of Trent. St. Louis: Herder, 1941.
Schubert, F. *Grundzüge der Pastoraltheologie.* Gras and Leipzig: Ulrich Moser, 1922.
Schulz, M. *Der Begriff der Seelsorge bei Claus Harms and Wilhelm Loehe.* Gütersloh: n.p., 1934.
Schuster, H. "Geschichte der Pastoraltheologie." In *Handbuch der Pastoraltheologie.* Freiburg: Herder, 1964, pp. 40–92. (Also in same volume: "Wesen und Aufgabe der Pastoraltheologie als praktischer Theologie," pp. 93–115.)
Schuetze, A. W., and Habeck, I. J., *The Shepherd Under Christ.* Milwaukee: Northwestern Publication House, 1974.
Schweizer, A. *Pastoraltheorie oder die Lehre von der Seelsorge des evangelischen Pfarrers.* Leipzig: Weidmann, 1875.
Schweizer, E. *Lordship and Discipleship.* London: SCM, 1960.
_____. *Church Order in the New Testament.* London: SCM, 1961.
Schwermann, A. H. *The Pastor at Work.* Esp. "The Doctrine of the Call," pp. 85–124. St. Louis: Concordia, 1960.
Scott, C. A. *The Church, Its Worship and Sacraments.* London: SCM, 1927.
Scroggs, R. "Paul and the Eschatological Woman," *Journal of the American Academy of Religion,* 40 (1972), pp. 283–303.
_____. "Woman in the N.T." IDB Supplementary Volume, 1976, pp. 966 ff.
Seeberg. R. *Textbook of the History of Doctrines.* Translated by C. E. Hay. Grand Rapids: Baker, 1952.
Seidel, C. T. *Pastoral-theologie.* Helmstedt: C. F. Weygand, 1729.
Segler, Franklin M., *A Theology of the Church and Ministry.* Nashville: Broadman Press, 1960.

Segundo, Juan Luis. *A Theology for Artisans of a New Humanity.* 5 vols. Maryknoll: Orbis, 1975.

Seraphion, St. (d. after 360). *Bishop Seraphion's Prayer book.* Translated by J. Wordsworth. London: S.P.C.K., 1899.

Seven Ecumenical Councils, Decrees and Canons of the. NPNF 2nd, vol. 14.

Shedd, W. G. T. *Homiletics and Pastoral Theology.* New York: Scribner's, 1867.

The Shepherd of Hermas (fl. 140). *ANF,* vol. 2.

The Shepherd of Hermas. Translated by Edgar J. Goodspeed. *AF.*

Shepherd, M. H. *The Oxford American Prayer Book Commentary.* New York: Oxford University Press, 1950.

———. Articles in *IDB:* s.v. "Ministry," s.v. "Hands, Laying on of," s.v. "Prophet."

Sherrill, Henry Knox. *The Church's Ministry in Our Time.* New York: Scribner's, 1949.

Sherrill, Lewis J. *Guilt and Redemption.* Richmond: John Knox Press, 1945.

———. *The Struggle of the Soul.* New York: Macmillan, 1951.

Siirala, Aarne. *The Voice of Illness.* Philadelphia: Fortress, 1964.

Simeon, Charles (1759–1836). *Horae Homileticae.* 21 vols. London: Richard Watts, 1819–28.

Slater, Thomas. *A Manual of Moral Theology.* 2 vols. New York: Benziger Bros., 1908.

Smart, James D. *The Teaching Ministry of the Church.* Philadelphia: Westminster, 1954.

———. *The Rebirth of Ministry.* Philadelphia: Westminster, 1960.

Smith, H. P. "The Laying on of Hands," *American Journal of Theology,* 17 (1913), pp. 47–62.

Smith, H. Shelton. *Faith and Nurture.* New York: Scribner's, 1941.

Smith, Henry Wallis. *The Pastor as Preacher.* Edinburgh: Wm. Blackwood, 1882.

Smith, John. *Lectures on the Nature and End of the Sacred Office, and on the Dignity, Duty, Qualifications and Character of the Sacred Order* (1798). Baltimore: A. Neal, 1810.

Smith, Reuben. *The Pastoral Office.* Philadelphia: Presbyterian Board of Publication, 1859.

Smyth, Thomas. *Complete Works of the Rev. Thomas Smyth.* Edited by J. W. Flinn. 10 vols. Columbia, S.C.: R. L. Bryan, 1908–13.

Sommerlath, E. "Das Amt und die Ämter." In *Viva Vox Evangelii, Festschrift für Hans Meiser.* Munich: Verlag des Evangelischen Pressverbandes für Bayern, 1951, pp. 292 ff.

Southard, Samuel. *Counseling for Church Vocations.* Nashville: Broadman, 1957.

———. *Pastoral Authority in Personal Relationships.* Nashville: Abingdon, 1969.

Spangenberg, August Gottlieb (1704–1792). *Exposition of Christian Doctrine.* 2nd ed. London: S. Hazard, 1796.

Spann, J. Richard, ed. *The Ministry.* New York: Abingdon, 1949.

Spann, J. Richard, ed. *Pastoral Care.* New York: Abingdon, 1951.

Spencer, Ichabod S. *Pastor's Sketches, or Conversations with Anxious Inquirers.* 2 vols. New York: Dodd, Mead, 1851–53.

Spener, P. J. (1635–1705). "The Spiritual Priesthood" (1677). In Henry E. Jacobs, ed., *A Summary of The Christian Faith.* Philadelphia: General Council Board of Publication, 1905, pp. 581–595.

———. *Letzte Theologisches Bedencken.* Halle: Wäysenhauses, 1721.

Sprat, Thomas. "A Discourse to the Clergy of his Diocese, 1695." In *The Clergyman's Instructor,* pp. 235–68.

Spurgeon, C. H. *Autobiography.* Edited by D. O. Fuller. Grand Rapids: Zondervan, 1946.

Stagg, Frank; Huisin, E. G.; and Oates, Wayne E. *Glossolalia.* Nashville: Abingdon, 1967.

Stendahl, K. *The Bible and the Role of Women: A Case Study in Hermeneutics.* Philadelphia: Fortress, 1966.

Stewart, James S. *Heralds of God*. New York: Scribner's, 1946.

Stollberg, Dietrich. *Therapeutische Seelsorge*. München: Chr. Kaiser, 1969.

———. *Seelsorge praktisch*. Göttingen: Vandenhoeck und Ruprecht, 1970.

Stolz, Karl R. *Pastoral Psychology*. New York: Abingdon, 1940.

Stone, Howard W. *Crisis Counseling*. Philadelphia: Fortress, 1976.

Strathmann H. and Meyer, R. S.v. "Leitourgeo." *TDNT*.

Stumpff, A. P. J. "Spener über Theologie und Seelsorge als Gebiete kirchlicher Neugestaltung." Dissertation, University of Tübingen, 1934.

Sullivan, C. S., ed. *Readings in Sacramental Theology*. Englewood Cliffs, N.J.: Prentice-Hall, 1965.

Sullivan, H. S. *The Interpersonal Theory of Psychiatry*. New York: Norton, 1953.

Switzer, David K. *The Dynamics of Grief*. Nashville: Abingdon, 1970.

———. *The Minister as Crisis Counselor*. Nashville: Abingdon, 1974.

———. *Pastor, Preacher, Person: Developing a Pastoral Ministry in Depth*. Nashville: Abingdon, 1979.

Syriac Apophthegmata. Translated by Wallis Budge. *The Wit and Wisdom of the Christian Fathers of Egypt*. Oxford: n.p., 1934.

Szasz, Thomas S. *The Myth of Mental Illness*. New York: Harper & Bros., 1961.

Tarnow, Johann (1586–1629). *De Sacrosancto Ministerio*. 3 vols. Rostock: n.p., 1623.

Tatian (ca. 160). *ANF*, vol. 2.

Taylor, Jeremy (1613–1667). *The Whole Works of Rt. Rev. Jeremy Taylor*. Edited by R. Heber. Revised by C. P. Eden. 10 vols. London: Longman, 1851.

———. *The Practical Works of Jeremy Taylor*. 2 vols. London: H. G. Bohn, 1854.

———. *The Rule and Exercises of Holy Dying*. London: Bell and Daldy, 1857.

Taylor, Vincent. *The Formation of the Gospel Tradition*. London: Macmillan, 1933.

Teilhard de Chardin, P. *The Phenomenon of Man*. Translated by B. Wall. New York: Harper & Bros., 1961.

Teikmanis, Arthur L. *Preaching and Pastoral Care*. Englewood Cliffs, N.J.: Prentice-Hall, 1964.

Telfer, William. *The Office of Bishop*. London: Darton, Longman & Todd, 1962.

Temple, William. *Mens Creatrix*. London: Macmillan, 1917.

———. *Readings in St. John's Gospel*. 2 vols. London: Macmillan, 1939–40.

Teresa of Avila (1515–1582). *The Complete Works*. Translated by E. A. Peers. 3 vols. London: Sheed and Ward, 1946.

Teresa of Calcutta, Mother. *A Gift for God*. San Francisco: Harper and Row, 1979.

Tertullian (ca. 160–ca. 230). *ANF*, vol. 3: *On Idolatry* (196), *Apologia* (ca. 197); *Testimony of the Soul* (198), *Penitence* (200a), *Baptism* (ca. 200b), *Patience* (ca. 200), *Prescription Against Heretics* (203), *Against Marcion* (207), *On Flight in Persecution* (ca. 208).

———. *Moral Treatises*. Translated by W. P. LeSaint, *ACW*, vol. 12.

———. *Disciplinary, Moral and Ascetical Works*. *FC*, vol. 40.

Testaments of the Twelve Patriarchs (2nd cent.). *ANF*, vol. 8, pp. 9–38.

Theodoret of Cyrus (ca. 390–ca. 457). *NPNF* 2nd, vol. 3.

Theologica Germanica (14th cent.). Translated by S. Winkworth. Boston: J. P. Jewett & Co., 1856.

Theophilus of Antioch (late 2nd cent.). *ANF*, vol. 2.

Thilo, H. J. *Beratende Seelsorge*. Göttingen: Vandenhoeck und Ruprecht, 1971.

Thomas, W. D. "The Place of Women in the Church at Philippi," *ExpT*, 83 (1971–72), pp. 117–120.

Thomas a Kempis (ca. 1380–1471). *The Imitation of Christ*. New York: Doubleday, 1955.

Thomas Aquinas (1225–1274). *Summa Theologica*. 3 vols. New York: Benziger, 1947–48.

_____. *Summa Theologiae.* Edited by T. Gilby and T. C. O'Brien. 40 vols. New York: McGraw-Hill, 1963 ff.

_____. *Treatise on Happiness.* Engelwood Cliffs, N.J.: Prentice-Hall, 1964.

_____. *On The Truth of the Catholic Faith, Summa Contra Gentiles.* 4 vols. New York: Doubleday, 1957.

_____. *Commentaries on Ephesians* (1966), *Galatians* (1966), *Philippians and First Thessalonians* (1969), *and John* (1979); *Aquinas' Scriptural Commentaries,* 6 vols. Albany: Magi Books, 1976.

Thompson, Bard, ed. *Liturgies of the Western Church.* New York: World Publishing Co., 1961.

Thompson, Francis. *Health and Holiness.* St. Louis: Herder, 1905.

Thompson Henry. *Pastoralia: A Manual of Helps for the Pastoral Clergy.* London: n.p., 1830.

Thompson, J. G. S. "The Shepherd-Ruler Concept in the OT and its Application in the NT," *SJT,* 8 (1955), pp. 406–18.

Thornton, Edward E. *Theology and Pastoral Counseling.* Philadelphia: Fortress, 1964.

_____. *Professional Education for Ministry: A History of Clinical Pastoral Education.* Nashville: Abingdon, 1969.

Thornton, Lionel. *The Common Life in the Body of Christ.* London: Dacre, 1941.

Thornton, Martin. *Pastoral Theology: A Reorientation.* London: S.P.C.K., 1958.

_____. *Feed My Lambs: Essays in Pastoral Reconstruction.* Greenwich, Conn.: Seabury, 1961.

Thrall, M. E. "The Ordination of Women to the Priesthood," *Theology,* 57 (1954), pp. 330–35.

Thurneysen, E. *A Theology of Pastoral Care.* Translated by J. A. Worthington and T. Wieser. Richmond: John Knox Press, 1962.

Tilden, W. P. *The Work of the Ministry.* Boston: Geo. H. Ellis, 1899.

Tillich, Paul. "The Relation of Religion and Health," *Review of Religion,* 10 (1946),pp. 348–84.

_____. *Systematic Theology.* 3 vols. Chicago: University of Chicago Press, 1951 ff.

_____. *The Courage to Be.* New Haven, Conn.: Yale University Press, 1952.

_____. *Theology of Culture.* Edited by R. C. Kimball. New York: Oxford University Press, 1959.

Toellner, John Gottlieb (1724–1774). *Grundriss der Erwiessenen Pastoral-Theologie.* Leipzig: J. F. Hinz, 1767.

Tooley, W. "The Shepherd and Sheep Image in the Teaching of Jesus," *Novum Testamentum,* 7 (1964), pp. 15 ff.

Torrance, T. F. *Royal Priesthood.* Naperville, Ill.: Allenson, 1955.

_____. *Kingdom and Church: A Study in the Theology of the Reformation.* Edinburgh: Oliver & Boyd, 1956.

Torrance T. F., ed. *The School of Faith: The Catechisms of the Reformed Church.* New York: Harper & Bros., 1959.

Tournier, P. *The Meaning of Persons.* Translated by E. Hudson. New York: Harper & Bros. 1957.

Toynbee, A. *A Study of History.* Abridged ed. by D. C. Somervell. London: Oxford University Press, 1964.

Trent, Council of (1545–63). *Canons and Decrees of the Council of Trent.* Translated by J. Waterworth. In Schaff, P., *Creeds of Christendom.*

Trible, P. "Depatriarchalizing in Biblical Interpretation," *JAAR,* 41 (1973), pp. 30–48.

_____. "Woman in the OT." *IDB* Supplement, 1976, pp. 963–66.

Trillhaas, W. *Evangelische Predigtlehre.* München: Kaiser, 1964.

Troeltsch, E. *The Social Teachings of the Christian Churches.* Translated by O. Wyon. 2 vols. London: Allen & Unwin, 1931.

Truax, C. B., and Carkhuff, R. R. *Toward Effective Counseling and Psychotherapy*. Chicago: Aldine-Atherton, 1967.

Tucker, W. J. *The Making and the Unmaking of the Preacher*. Boston: Houghton, Mifflin, 1899.

Turretin, Francois (1623–1687). *Institutio theologicae elencticae*. 3 vols. Geneva: Samuel de Tournes, 1688–90. (English translation MS by George M. Giger in Princeton Theological Seminary Library, Princeton, N.J.).

Tying, Stephen H. *The Christian Pastor*. New York: Harper & Bros. 1874.

Tyndale, William (1494–1536). *The Works of the English Reformers William Tyndale and John Firth*. Edited by T. Russell. 3 vols. London: Ebenezer Palmer, 1831.

Uhsadel, W. *Evangelische Seelsorge*. Heidelberg: Quelle und Meyer, 1966.

Underhill, Francis, ed. *Feed My Sheep: Essays in Pastoral Theology*. Milwaukee: Morehouse, 1927.

Upham, S. F. *The Christian Pastorate*. Madison, N. J.: Drew University, 1898.

Upham, Thomas C. *Principles of the Interior Life*. Boston: Waite, Peirce & Co., 1845.

Valdés, Juan de (1500–1541). *The Christian Alphabet in Spiritual and Anabaptist Writers*. *LCC*, vol 25, pp. 353 ff.

Valenti, E. J. G. (1794–1871). *Medicina Clerica, oder Handbuch der Pastoral-Medizine für Seelsorger, Pädagogen und Ärzte*. 2 vols. Leipzig: F. K. Köhler, 1831.

Van der Leeuw, G. *Religion in Essence and Manifestation*. 2 vols. New York: Harper & Row, 1963.

Vatican II, Documents of. Edited by W. M. Abbott. New York: Guild Pres, 1966.

Vering, A. M. (1773–1829). *Versuch einer Pastoral-Medizin*. Leipzig: Barth, 1809.

––––––. *Über die Wechselwirkungen zwischen Seele und Körper im Menschen*. Leipzig: Barth, 1817.

Vieth, Paul H. *Worship in Christian Education*. Philadelphia: United Church Press, 1965.

Vilmar, A. F. C. (1800–1868). *Die Lehre vom geistlichen Amt*. Marburg/Leipzig: Elwert, 1870.

––––––. *Lehrbuch der pastoraltheologie*. Edited by K. W. Piderit. Gütersloh: Bertelsmann, 1872.

Vincent of Lerins (died before 450). *NPNF* 2nd, vol. 11.

Vinet, Alexandre. *Pastoral Theology; or the Theory of the Evangelical Ministry*. Translated by T. H. Skinner. New York: Harper & Bros., 1853.

Vinet, Alexandre. *Homiletics*. Translated by T. H. Skinner. New York: Ivison, Blakeman, Taylor, 1880.

Visitatio Informorum: Or, Offices for the Clergy in Praying with, Directing, and Comforting the Sick, Infirm, and Afflicted. 3rd ed. London: Joseph Masters, 1854.

Voetius, Gysbertus (1588–1676). *Concerning Practical Theology*. In *RD*, pp. 265 ff.

Vriezen, T. C. *An Outline of Old Testament Theology*. Oxford: Blackwell, 1958.

Wagner, C. U. *The Pastor: His Life and Work*. Schaumberg, Ill.: Regular Baptist Press, 1976.

Wagner, H. "Diakonie," *RGG3*, vol. 2, pp. 162 ff.

Wainwright, Geoffrey. *Doxology*. New York: Oxford University Press, 1980.

Walker, W. O. "I Cor. 11:2–16 and Paul's Views Regarding Women," *Journal of Biblical Literature*, 94 (1975), pp. 94–110.

Waltermann, Leo, ed. *Klerus zwischen Wissenschaft und Seelsorge: zur Reform der Priesterausbildung*. Essen: Verlag Herus Driewer, 1966.

Walther, C. F. W. *Amerikanisch-Lutherische Pastoraltheologie*. 4th ed. St. Louis: Concordia, 1890. (1st ed. 1869).

Ware, J. F. W. *The Silent Pastor, or Consolations for the Sick*. 3rd ed. Boston: Walker, Wise, 1864.

Waterhouse, Eric S. *Psychology and Pastoral Work*. Nashville: Abingdon-Cokesbury, 1940.

Watkins, O. D. *A History of Penance.* 2 vols. London: Longmans, Green, & Co., 1920.

Watson, J. B. *Behaviorism.* New York: W. W. Norton, 1925.

Watson, John. *The Cure of Souls.* New York: Dodd, Mead, 1896.

———. *The Clerical Life.* New York: Dodd, Mead, 1898.

Watts, Isaac (1674–1748). *Works.* 7 vols. Leeds: Edward Baines, 1800.

Watts, Isaac. *Rules for the Preacher's Conduct,* in *Young Minister's Companion.* Boston: S. T. Armstrong, 1813, pp. 642–90. Also in John Brown, ed. *Christian Pastor's Manual.* pp. 198–244.

Wayland, Francis. *Letters on the Ministry of the Gospel.* New York: Sheldon, 1863.

Weatherhead, Leslie D. *Psychology, Religion and Healing.* New York: Abingdon, 1951.

Webb, Robert L. *The Ministry as a Life Work.* New York: Macmillan, 1922.

Webb, William W. *The Cure of Souls: A Manual for the Clergy.* 2nd ed. Milwaukee: Morehouse, 1910. (1st ed. 1892).

Weber, Max. *From Max Weber.* Translated by H. Gerth and C. W. Mills. New York: Oxford University Press, 1958.

Weedner, R. F. *Practical Theology.* New York: Revell, 1891.

Weil, Simone. *Waiting for God,* New York: Harper & Bros., 1951.

Weiss, Johannes. *Earliest Christianity.* 2 vols. Boston: Peter Smith, 1979.

Weiss, K. "Paulus, Priester der christlichen Kultgemeinde," *TLZ,* 79 (1954), pp. 355–364.

Wegman, Hector. *Christliche und treuherzige Vermahnung an die katholischen Pfarer und Seelsorger.* Ingolstadt: Weissenhorn, 1577.

Welch, Claude. *The Reality of the Church.* New York: Scribner's, 1958.

Wermullerus, Otto (1488–1568). "Treatise on Death," pp. 37–135 of *The Remains of Miles Coverdale.* Cambridge: At the University Press, 1846.

Wescott, Roger. *The Divine Animal.* New York: Funk & Wagnalls, 1969.

Wesley, John (1703–1791). *The Works of the Rev. John Wesley.* edited by T. Jackson. 5th ed. 14 vols. London: Wesleyan Conference Office, 1877.

———. *Journal,* Edited by N. Curnock. 8 vols. London: Epworth, 1909 ff.

———. *Letters,* Edited by J. Telford. 8 vols. London: Epworth, 1931 ff.

———. *The Appeals to Men of Reason and Religion and Certain Related Open Letters* vol 11. Edited by G. R. Cragg. Oxford ed. Oxford: Clarendon, 1975.

———. *Letters.* Vol. 25, 1721–1739; vol. 26, 1740–1755. Edited by F. Baker. Oxford: Clarendon, 1975, 1982.

Westberg, Granger. *Minister and Doctor Meet.* New York: Harper & Bros., 1961.

Westerhoff, J. H. *Values for Tomorrow's Children.* Philadelphia: Pilgrim, 1970.

Westminster Confession of Faith (1643–47), *CC.*

Whitham, A. R. *Holy Orders.* London: Longmans, Green & Co. 1910.

Whyte, Lancelot Law. *The Unconscious Before Freud.* New York: Basic Books, 1960.

Wilkinson, J. "A Study of Healing in the Gospel According to John," *SJT,* 20 (1967), pp. 442–61.

Willard, Frances E. *Women in the Pulpit* (1889). Washington, D. C.: Zenger, 1978. 1978.

William of St. Thierry (1058–1148). *On Contemplating God.* Translated by Sister Penelope. Kalamazoo, Mich.: Cistercian Publications, 1970.

Williams, D. D. *The Minister and the Care of Souls.* New York: Harper & Bros., 1954.

Williams, G. H. *The Radical Reformation.* Philadelphia: Westminster, 1962.

Williams, J. Paul. "When the Clergy Abdicates," *The Christian Century,* 63 (1946), pp. 74–75.

Wilson, James M. *Six Lectures on Pastoral Theology.* New York: Macmillan, 1903.

Wilson, H. *Women Priests? Yes, Now!* Nutfield, Redhill, Surrey: Denholm House Press, 1975.

Wilson, Thomas. (1663–1755). *Parochalia* (1708). New York: T. & J. Swords, 1812.

Wingren, G. *The Christian's Calling.* Translated by C. C. Rasmussen. Edinburgh: Oliver & Boyd, 1958.

Wink, Walter. *The Bible and Human Transformation.* Philadelphia: Fortress, 1973.

Wise, Carroll A. *Pastoral Counseling.* New York: Harper & Bros., 1951.

Wolfson, H. *The Philosophy of the Early Church Fathers.* Cambridge: Harvard University Press, 1956.

Wollebius, Johannes (1586–1629). *The Abridgement of Christian Divinitie.* Translated by A. Ross (1622 ff). London: T. Longman, 1650, See also *RD*, pp. 19–163.

Wood, Thomas, ed. *Five Pastorals.* London: S.P.C.K., 1961.

Woolman, John. *Journal and Essays of John Woolman.* Edited by Amelia Mott Gummere. Philadelphia: Friends' Book Store, 1922.

Women and Holy Orders. Report of the Archbishops' Commission. London: Church Information Office, 1966.

Women and the Ordained Ministry. Joint Anglican-Methodist Commission Report London: Epworth and S.P.C.K., 1966.

Worcester, Alfred. "The Care of the Dying," In Emerson L. Eugene's *Physician and Patient: Personal Care.* Cambridge: Harvard University Press, 1920.

Workman, Herbert. *The Evolution of the Monastic Ideal.* Boston: Beacon Press 1962.

World Council of Churches. *Concerning the Ordination of Women.* Geneva: WCC, 1964.

World Council of Churches Studies No. 4. *The Deaconness.* Geneva: WCC, 1966.

Woywod, Stanislaw. *A Practical Commentary on Canon Law.* 2nd ed. New York: J. Wagner, 1926.

Wyclif, J. (1320–1384). *Tractatus de officio pastorali.* Edited by G. V. Lechler. Leipzig: A. Edelmannum, 1863.

Wyngaards, J. N. *Did Christ Rule Out Women Priests?* Greenwood, S. C.; Attic Press, 1977.

Wynn, J. C. *Pastoral Ministry to Families.* Philadelphia: Westminster, 1957.

Young Minister's Companion. Boston: Samuel T. Armstrong, 1813.

Young, Richard K. *The Pastor's Hospital Ministry.* Nashville: Broadman, 1954.

Young, Richard K., and Meiburg, A. L. *Spiritual Therapy: How the Physician, Psychiatrist and Minister Collaborate in Healing.* New York: Harper & Bros. 1960.

Zepper, Wilhelm (1550–1607). *De Politia Ecclesiastica.* Herborn: Christopher Corvini 1595.

Zezschwitz, Karl Adolf. von (1825–1886). *System der praktischen Theologie.* Translated by Matthiae and Petry. Leipzig: J. C. Hinrichs, 1876.

Zimmerman, L. M. *The Gospel Minister.* Baltimore: Meyer and Thalheimer, 1930.

Zinzendorf, N. L. von (1700–1760). *A Manual of Doctrine.* London: Jas. Hutton, 1742.

Zwingli, Huldreich (1484–1531). *Sämmtliche Werke.* Edited by E. Egli et al. 13 vols., Corpus Reformatorum, Berlin: C. A. Schwetschke, 1905.

――――. *Der Hirt.* Basel: C. Detloff, 1884.

――――. *Zwingli and Bullinger, LCC,* vol. 24.

Index of Names

Abba, R., 34, 103, 120 f.
Achelis, E., 17, 63
Adams, Jay E., 10, 165
Aland, K., 126
Alberti, M., 261
Alexander, A., 63
Ambrose, 19, 23, 25, 92,
 100 f., 108, 117 f., 127,
 138, 141, 144 f., 176,
 191 f., 194, 216, 269,
 272
Amos, 9, 76, 86
Anderson, R., 140
Anthony, 76
Aphrahat, 140
Aristotle, 204
Arnold, F. X., 16
Asbury, F., 175
Ashbrook, J., 266
Asmussen, H., 16
Athanasius, 7, 45 f.
Athenagoras, 232
Augustine, 7, 15, 19, 45 f.,
 50, 54, 58, 62, 76, 94,
 98, 100 f., 197 f., 109,
 111, 113, 115, 117, 133
 f., 137, 141 f., 144, 146,
 150, 155, 162, 186 ff.,
 189, 192, 194, 206, 216,
 225, 227 ff., 239 ff., 261,
 268, 275 ff., 293, 296,
 303, 308 f.

Baker, A., 205
Balmforth, H., 16, 118
Barclay, R., 16
Barnabas, 28, 115, 171
Barnikol, E., 81
Barrett, A., 63
Barth, K., 9, 128, 131, 177

Basil, 92, 117, 119, 125,
 146, 252
Baumgarten, S., 16
Baxter, R., xiv, 15, 25, 138,
 141, 143 f., 145, 147,
 170, 175, 180, 184, 188
 ff., 191, 216 f., 251 ff.,
 261, 275 ff., 282 ff., 289,
 294, 301 ff.
Beck, J., 324
Beckwith, R., 46
Bedell, G., 16
Beebe, J., 25, 182, 185
Beethoven, 245
Benedict, 190
Bengel, J., 63
Berger, P., 59
Bergin, A. R., 188
Bernard of Clairvaux, 204
Berne, E., 9, 175
Betz, H., 64
Binsfeld, P., 16
Binswanger, L., 15
Blackwood, A., 140
Blaikie, W., 16
Bliss, K., 46
Bloesch, D., 140
Blunt, J., 16
Boethius, 251, 261, 284
Boisen, A., 248
Bonaventure, 204
Bonhoeffer, D., 137
Bonhoeffer, T., 248
Borromeo, F., 16, 175
Bouyer, L., 16, 261
Bownas, S., 25
Brett, G., 16
Brett, T., 25
Bridges, C., xiv, 16, 127,
 134, 144, 190

Brister, C. W., xv
Bromiley, G. W., 63
Brown, J., 16
Browne, T., 266
Browning, D., xv, 16, 219
Bucer, M., 15, 188, 269 ff.,
 272, 287
Bultmann, R., 9, 15, 51,
 64, 177
Bunyan, J., 76
Burnet, G., 15, 63
Bushnell, H., 152

Cabot, R., 266
Calkins, R., 88
Calvin, J., 14, 23, 25, 33,
 38, 46, 50 f., 58, 65, 72,
 86 f., 92, 98, 105, 110,
 118, 124 f., 128, 131–
 133, 136, 142, 144 f.,
 147, 150, 153, 155 ff.,
 159–162, 180, 188, 231
 ff., 253, 272, 277, 281,
 303, 305, 310
Cannon, J., xv, 16, 33,
 185
Carkhuff, R., 188, 204
Carter, J., 16
Caruso, I., 15
Cassian, John, 206, 251
Chaucer, G., 175
Chemnitz, M., 31, 33, 51,
 106, 110, 134, 151
Chrysostom, John, 7, 13,
 15, 19, 25, 30 f., 33, 62,
 68, 87, 92, 122, 124 f.,
 127, 131 f., 143 f., 159,
 193, 250 ff., 262, 268 ff.,
 284 ff., 294 ff., 309
Clebsch, W., 16

Index of Subjects

Absurd, the, 251, 294
Accessibility, pastoral, 176 ff., 272 ff.
Accommodation to modernity, 3, 15, 55, 132, 195, 212 f. *See also* Modernity
Accountability, pastoral, 113 f., 149, 159 ff., 192 ff., 208, 213
Adiaphora, 217 f.
Administration, 4, 80, 153 ff., 212 f., 314
Administry, 153 ff.
Admonition, 138, 197, 206 ff., 315. *See also* Counsel; Correction
Adultery, clergy, 214, 219
Advice, 189 f., 200, 206 ff.
Adoration, 95, 99 ff.
Affliction, 232 ff., 247, 252 ff., 278. *See also* Suffering
Agape, 19 *See also* Love
Alienation, 52 ff., 275 ff.
Alms, 270. *See also* Poor, pastoral care of the
Ambassadorship, pastoral office as, 57, 61
Analogy, 36–38, 41, 49 ff., 57, 61, 70 ff., 105, 114, 131, 142, 147, 150, 161, 171 f., 202, 232, 237, 250, 268, 275, 293, 296 ff., *See also* Language; Method; Story
Angels, 198, 218
Anger, 45, 218
Anglican pastoral tradition, 11, 45, 121, 160, 258, 306 f.
Anointment, 139, 254 ff., 301
Anthropomorphism, 45
Antinomianism, 8, 14, 213 ff., 256. *See also* Law; Norm; Rule
Anxiety, 184, 291, 294 ff.
A priori, 239 ff., 243. *See also* Reason; Theodicy
Apostle, apostolicity, apostolic tradition, *apostolos*, 12, 20, 27, 31, 35, 60 ff., 74 ff., 118, 155, 174 f.

Apostles' Creed, 149, 151, 307
Apostolic Constitutions, 5, 24, 31 f., 46, 51, 62, 67 f., 81, 88, 98, 104, 121 f., 125, 152, 165, 269 ff., 291
Art, pastoral care as an, 192, 196 ff.
Ascension, 62
Atonement, 125, 305, 308. *See also* Christ; Sacrifice
Attorney, 13, 131, 169, 295
Augsburg Confession, 155, 165
Authenticity, 109, 180
Authoritarianism, 36, 133
Authority, 11, 21, 51 ff., 62, 88, 110, 137 ff., 161, 260
Autobiography, 14 ff.
Availability of the minister, 176, 179, 189, 210, 272 f.
Avoidance patterns, 218, 295 f., 301 ff.

Baptism, 26 f., 29, 38, 41–43, 62, 69, 85, 88, 101, 105 ff., 112 ff., 126, 147, 150 ff.; adult, 113 ff.; as bath, 106
Baptist tradition of ministry, 113 ff., 149
Baptized, ministry of the, 26 ff., 88 ff.
Behavior change, 184, 207 ff.
Behaviorist psychology, 15, 209 ff., 257, 303
Belief, believer, believing community, 37, 109, 142, 201, 209. *See also* Faith
Believer's baptism, 113 ff., 149
Benediction, 100, 102
Bereavement, 240, 293–310
Bible, in pastoral care, x, xiii, xv, 5, 11, 155, 164, 170 ff., 309. *See also* Scripture; *Index of Scripture References*
Bibliography and reference system, function of, x, 321
Birth, 293
Bishop, 30 f. *See also* Episcopal office
Blame, 206 ff.

Father, God as, 100 ff. *See also* Trinity
Fees for services, xiv, 4 f., 169, 286 ff., 308. *See also* Counsel; Profit; Psychotherapy; Support; Voluntary poverty
Felix culpa, 229
Fellowship, 66, 180, 233. *See also* Community
Femaleness in ministry, 7, 35 ff., 43, 46. *See also* Women
Fidelity, 52, 71, 296
Finitude, 227 ff., 234. *See also* Limit; Temporality
Finitude of the minister, 25, 71, 80
Flock, 30, 79, 161
Food, 41, 106, 119, 123, 272 ff., 284
Forgiveness, 89 f., 109, 147, 175, 198 f., 207, 213
Form, 134, 199
Formula of Concord, 134, 140, 142
Fraction of the bread, 123
Free church pastoral tradition, 27, 72, 75 f., 257
Freedom, 8, 14, 32, 133, 200, 213, 227 ff., 261, 303
Friendships in ministry, 55, 177, 192, 201 ff., 295
Functions, pastoral, 3 ff., 85 ff.
Funeral, 308 ff.

Garden, gardener analogy, 227, 246
General ministry, of the laity, 8, 20 f., 26 ff., 33, 38, 43, 53, 73, 153 ff., 189 f., 249 f., 268 f. *See also* Laity, Ordained ministry
Gentiles, 75, 160, 280 f.
Gestalt, 199
Gifts, 5 ff., 19, 22 f., 26 f., 28 ff., 44, 64–67, 72 ff., 109, 133, 159, 281 ff., 290 ff.
Glory, 42, 100
Glossolalia, 78. *See also* Charisma; Gifts; Language; Interpretation
Gluttony, 283
God, 13, 45, 80, 86, 94, 97, 99 ff., 128, 150, 161, 169, 182, 187, 223 ff., 249, 294; attributes of, 86, 97, 100, 150, 162, 223 ff., 304; purpose of, 13, 200; revelation of, xiii, 105 ff.
Godparents, 144
Good, 229 ff., 237 ff.
Gospel, 8, 15, 37, 41, 135, 213, 293, 305
Gossip, 202 f., 215. *See also* Confidentiality; Integrity
Governance, 154 ff; of God, 59 ff., 77, 172. *See also* Kingdom of God
Government, 37, 58, 275 ff., 279. *See also* Justice; Political ethics; Society
Grades of ministry, 31. *See also* Orders of ministry

Grace, x, 5, 8, 58, 73 ff., 106 ff., 113 ff., 143, 193, 232 f., 290
Grief, 293–310
Guardian, clergy as, 71 ff. *See also* Episcopal office, Shepherd
Guidance, pastoral, 21, 24, 30, 50, 59, 68, 148, 199 ff. *See also* Spirit
Guilt, 8, 89 ff., 213 f., 257, 291, 294, 303

Happiness, 13, 198 f., 262, 288
Harm, 199. *See also* Ethics; Outcome studies
Head, headship, 35 ff., 40, 53
Healing, 78, 173, 252 ff., 259 ff., 261 ff. *See also* Health; Sick; Therapy
Health, 22, 232
Hearing, 130, 133, 139, 202 ff., *See also* Empathy; Listening, ministry of
Heart, 130 f., 256, 262; hardened, 231
Hebraic tradition, 27, 86, 108, 251, 270
Hedonism, 177, 199, 212, 294, 303
Helper, 42
Heresy, 56 ff., 155, 214. *See also* Councils; Docetism; Ebionitism; Orthodoxy
Hierarchy, 171
History, 10 ff., 21, 28, 31, 37 f., 62, 81, 110, 119, 155, 162, 200 f., 237, 247, 268. *See also* Development; Interpretation; Tradition; Universal history
Historical theology, xiii, xiv
Holiness of heart and life, 40, 43, 56 f., 139, 202, 216–218, 262
Holiness of God, 8, 44, 52, 56, 108, 139, 216, 231, 304
Holism, 198 ff., 262, 294
Homiletics, xiv, 101, 127 ff., 180. *See also* Preaching, preacher; Proclamation
Hope, 43, 119, 263, 296 ff.
Hospitality, 71, 74
Human nature, 276, 303 ff. *See also* Body; Reason; Sin; Soul; Spirit
Human-relation training, 160
Humanity of ministry, 13, 43, 44, 57
Humility, 138, 143
Humor, 134, 257, 263
Hymns, 91, 96, 130, 141, 148
Hypocrisy, 211, 277

Ideology, 180
Idleness, 277, 283
Idolatry, 123, 133, 174, 232, 271
Illness, 249 ff.; acute, 262 ff.; social, 275 ff; terminal, 304 ff.
Image of God, 42
Impediments to ordination, 22
Imposition of hands, 27 ff.
Incarnation, 44, 52, 55 f., 61 ff., 90, 171, 202, 225 f., 251
Inclusiveness, sexual, 6, 36 ff., 41, 115, 201

Public: act, defense, witness, 50, 72, 130
f., 194, 203, 218; office, ministry as a,
72, 85, 91, 95, 130, 147
Punishment, 233, 251
Purgation, 232 f.
Purity, proximate purification, 209. *See
also* Admonition; Sanctification

Quadrilateral of sources, 11 ff. *See also*
Method
Qualifications for ministry, 18 ff., 68, 134
Qualities necessary for ministry of coun-
sel, 188 ff., 191 f., 256 ff., 298
Quantitative measurement in ministry,
163, 193

Realism, reality, 18, 195, 224, 245 ff., 301
Reason, 12, 22 ff., 128, 143, 239. *See also*
Method; System
Reception of church members, 112
Reconciliation, 218 f., 305. *See also* Christ
Records, church, 117, 281
Redemption, 45, 169, 209 f., 234
Reductionism, 11, 30, 54, 109, 236. *See
also* Naturalism
Reformed pastoral tradition, 9 f., 87, 93
Relief of the poor, 269 ff.
Religion, 57, 184, 251
Remedies, pastoral, 249 ff., 273 ff.
Reparation, 209 ff., 257, 303
Representative ministry, 26 ff., 37 ff., 87
ff., 131, 177, 191 f., 201, 208, 249, 295.
See also Ordained ministry; Set apart,
clergy as
Reproof, 138, 206 ff. *See also* Admonition
Resistance, 183
Response, responsiveness, responsibility,
5, 80, 187, 199, 209 ff., 263, 278 ff.
Restitution, 209 ff., 257, 303
Resurrection, 8, 41, 53, 62, 65, 75, 113,
119, 129, 247, 303–306
Reticence, 183
Revelation, xiii, 13, 24, 44, 58, 77, 105 ff.,
127, 137 f.
Revolution, 108, 162. *See also* Political eth-
ics
Right, civil, 37; of ordination, 23, 37 ff.
Right to know, patient's, 299 ff.
Risk-taking in ministry, ethic of, 254 ff.
Rites of the Catholic Church, 144, 151 ff.,
260, 266, 307
Ritual, rites, 23, 37, 51, 111, 120 ff., 125,
151, 308 f.
Roman Catholic pastoral tradition, 10 f.,
31, 86, 111, 174 ff., 258 f., 306 ff. *See
also* Councils, ecumenical; Medieval pastoral tradition; Patristic pastoral tradition; *Rites of the Catholic Church;* Sacrament

Rule, rules, rule-ethic in ministry, 181,
184, 198 ff., 208, 213, 256, 278, 302.
See also Command; Law; Norm

Sabbath, 94. *See also* Worship
Sacerdotal, 55. *See also* Priest
Sacrament, xiv, 8, 31, 49, 88 ff., 105 ff.,
313
Sacred ministry, 6, 88 ff., 128 ff. *See also*
Ordained ministry; Set apart, clergy as
Sacrifice, 36, 40, 51, 69 f., 88 f., 92 ff.,
110 f., 122–124
Salvation, 105, 120, 188. *See also* Order of
salvation
Sanctification, 50, 54, 100, 117, 136, 199,
207, 209 ff., 217. *See also* Holiness;
Spirit
Science, 59, 78, 98, 192, 276
Scripture, 11, 28, 36, 39, 128, 135, 159,
176, 256, 299. *See also* Bible; Exegesis;
Interpretation; Method
Seal, analogy of, 108, 151
Season, seasonable growth, 193 f., 200.
See also Development; Garden
Secular, secularization, 51, 54, 58, 93, 98,
184, 198
Sedation, 304 ff.
Self, 18, 22, 87 ff., 188; self-actualization,
8, 199, 212; self-assertion, 136, 211,
262; self-awareness, 22; self-deception,
97 ff., 133, 278, 282; self-examination,
18; self-initiative, 274 ff.; self-justifica-
tion, 43, 212; self-knowledge, 188; self-
righteousness, 20 f., 217, 277; self-suffi-
ciency, 161. *See also* Individual; Soul
Sell all, command to, 285 ff. *See also*
Property; Voluntary poverty
Sentiment, sentimentalism, 179, 202, 214,
262, 310
Sermon, 4, 128 ff. 178. *See also* Homily;
Preaching; Word
Servant, service, 30, 36, 53 ff., 57, 66 ff.,
157 *See also* Diaconate; Minister
Set apart, clergy as, 27, 50, 55, 60, 73, 88
ff., 105 f., 139, 191 f. *See also* Ordained
ministry; Sacred ministry
Seventy, the, 28, 60
Sexual inclusiveness, 6, 35 ff. *See also*
Equality; Female; Language; Male
Sexuality, 8, 35 ff., 42–44, 58, 68, 71, 74,
115
Shepherd and sheep analogy, 13, 46, 49
ff., 63, 69 f., 119, 161, 169 ff., 202,
294. *See also* Care; Pastor; Poimēn
Sick, pastoral care of the, 4, 78, 198, 240,
249 ff., 315
Sign, signature analogy, 106–111. *See also*
Sacrament
Silence, 257, 265, 301

Index of Scripture References